Exam Ref 70-768 Developing SQL Data Models

Stacia Varga

Exam Ref 70-768 Developing SQL Data Models

Published with the authorization of Microsoft Corporation by:
Pearson Education, Inc.

Copyright © 2017 by Pearson Education Inc.

ISBN-13: 978-1-5093-0515-5
ISBN-10: 1-5093-0515-7

Library of Congress Control Number: 2017938462

2 18

Trademarks

Microsoft and the trademarks listed at https://www.microsoft.com on the "Trademarks" webpage are trademarks of the Microsoft group of companies. All other marks are property of their respective owners.

Warning and Disclaimer

Special Sales

For information about buying this title in bulk quantities, or for special sales opportunities (which may include electronic versions; custom cover designs; and content particular to your business, training goals, marketing focus, or branding interests), please contact our corporate sales department at corpsales@pearsoned.com or (800) 382-3419.

For government sales inquiries, please contact governmentsales@pearsoned.com.

For questions about sales outside the U.S., please contact intlcs@pearson.com.

Editor-in-Chief	Greg Wiegand
Acquisitions Editor	Trina MacDonald
Development Editor	Troy Mott
Managing Editor	Sandra Schroeder
Senior Project Editor	Tracey Croom
Editorial Production	Backstop Media
Copy Editor	Christina Rudloff
Indexer	Julie Grady
Proofreader	Liv Bainbridge
Technical Editor	Ike Ellis
Cover Designer	Twist Creative, Seattle

Contents at a glance

Contents

What do you think of this book? We want to hear from you!

Microsoft is interested in hearing your feedback so we can continually improve our
books and learning resources for you. To participate in a brief online survey, please visit:

https://aka.ms/tellpress

Chapter 2   Design a tabular BI semantic model   97

What do you think of this book? We want to hear from you!

Microsoft is interested in hearing your feedback so we can continually improve our
books and learning resources for you. To participate in a brief online survey, please visit:

https://aka.ms/tellpress

Introduction

The 70-768 exam is designed for Business Intelligence (BI) developers and solution architects to test knowledge of a wide range of topics related to the design, querying, configuration, and administration of BI semantic models in Microsoft SQL Server 2016 Analysis Services (SSAS). Approximately half the exam covers multidimensional BI semantic models, while the remainder covers tabular BI semantic models. In addition, there are new development and query language features available for tabular models developed in SQL Server 2016, with which you should be familiar to successfully pass this exam.

For multidimensional models, the exam focuses not only on the steps required to design and develop the model in SQL Server Data Tools (SSDT), but also tests your understanding of the supported types of dimension models, the options for implanting measures, and the configuration of properties to enable specific behaviors, such as slowly changing dimensions and semi-additivity. It also covers the usage of Multidimensional Expressions (MDX), both to query the model and to embed business logic into the model in the form of calculated measures, named sets, Key Performance Indicators (KPIs), and additions to the MDX script.

The exam's coverage of tabular models requires you to understand how to import data into a model or use DirectQuery mode, and how the implementation of DirectQuery mode impacts the model development process. You must also know how to enhance the model by defining relationships between tables, adding measures and calculated columns by using Data Analysis Expressions (DAX), configuring partitions, and setting properties of model objects. Furthermore, you must know how to create KPIs from calculated measures and how to use DAX to write analytical queries.

Additionally, the exam focuses on considerations related to deploying and securing models and keeping them up-to-date by choosing the appropriate processing options for specific scenarios. It also requires you to understand how to use various tools to monitor and troubleshoot performance of BI semantic models and identify the necessary steps to take to resolve performance issues. Other areas of focus include the deployment and configuration of Analysis Services instances for memory management and scale-out scenarios.

To supplement your real-world experience with BI semantic models, this book reviews the concepts covered by the exam by using many different examples that you can follow yourself. To do this, you must install the SQL Server 2016 database engine and Analysis Services. For more information about SQL Server 2016 installation, see *https://msdn.microsoft.com/en-us/library/ms143219.aspx*. You must also download and install SQL Server Management Studio (SSMS) from and SQL Server Data Tools for Visual Studio 2015 (SSDT) from *https://docs.microsoft.com/en-us/sql/ssms/download-sql-server-management-studio-ssms* and *https://docs.microsoft.com/en-us/sql/ssdt/download-sql-server-data-tools-ssdt*, respectively.

This book covers every major topic area found on the exam, but it does not cover every exam question. Only the Microsoft exam team has access to the exam questions, and Microsoft regularly adds new questions to the exam, making it impossible to cover specific questions. You should consider this book a supplement to your relevant real-world experience and other study materials. If you encounter a topic in this book that you do not feel completely comfortable with, use the "Need more review?" links you'll find in the text to find more information and take the time to research and study the topic. Great information is available on MSDN, TechNet, and in blogs and forums.

Organization of this book

This book is organized by the "Skills measured" list published for the exam. The "Skills measured" list is available for each exam on the Microsoft Learning website: *https://aka.ms/examlist*. Each chapter in this book corresponds to a major topic area in the list, and the technical tasks in each topic area determine a chapter's organization. If an exam covers six major topic areas, for example, the book will contain six chapters.

Microsoft certifications

Microsoft certifications distinguish you by proving your command of a broad set of skills and experience with current Microsoft products and technologies. The exams and corresponding certifications are developed to validate your mastery of critical competencies as you design and develop, or implement and support, solutions with Microsoft products and technologies both on-premises and in the cloud. Certification brings a variety of benefits to the individual and to employers and organizations.

> **MORE INFO   ALL MICROSOFT CERTIFICATIONS**
>
> For information about Microsoft certifications, including a full list of available certifications, go to *https://www.microsoft.com/learning*.

Acknowledgments

Stacia Varga There are many people behind the scenes who make this book possible. Front and center on my mind are the people who ensure that my words make sense grammatically and are technically accurate. Thanks to Ike Ellis, Troy Mott, and Christina Rudloff for fulfilling that role. Also, I'd like to thank Trina MacDonald and her team at Pearson for ensuring the book production process runs smoothly. Throughout my career, there have been many individuals who have helped me fill in the gaps of knowledge about Analysis Services. While writing this book, so many memories came to mind reaching back to my start with SQL Server 2000 Analysis Services long ago with Mike Luckevitch, Scott Cameron, Hilary Feier, Liz Vitt, Scot Reagin, Dan Reh, and Denny Lee among others at the entity that began as EssPro, merged with Aspirity, and later was acquired by Hitachi Consulting. Most of all, my thoughts were with Reed Jacobson who was my mentor in many ways, but in particular he guided my deep learning of MDX and coached me during the writing of my first few books. He is gone now, but definitely not forgotten. Meanwhile, my wonderfully patient husband Dean Varga kept the coffee pot warm and my world relatively peaceful so I could write yet another book.

Microsoft Virtual Academy

Build your knowledge of Microsoft technologies with free expert-led online training from Microsoft Virtual Academy (MVA). MVA offers a comprehensive library of videos, live events, and more to help you learn the latest technologies and prepare for certification exams. You'll find what you need here:

https://www.microsoftvirtualacademy.com

Quick access to online references

Throughout this book are addresses to webpages that the author has recommended you visit for more information. Some of these addresses (also known as URLs) can be painstaking to type into a web browser, so we've compiled all of them into a single list that readers of the print edition can refer to while they read.

Download the list at *https://aka.ms/examref768/downloads*.

The URLs are organized by chapter and heading. Every time you come across a URL in the book, find the hyperlink in the list to go directly to the webpage.

Errata, updates, & book support

We've made every effort to ensure the accuracy of this book and its companion content. You can access updates to this book—in the form of a list of submitted errata and their related corrections—at:

https://aka.ms/examref768/errata

If you discover an error that is not already listed, please submit it to us at the same page.

If you need additional support, email Microsoft Press Book Support at *mspinput@microsoft.com.*

Please note that product support for Microsoft software and hardware is not offered through the previous addresses. For help with Microsoft software or hardware, go to *https://support.microsoft.com.*

Download the source code and sample database from the book's website

https://aka.ms/examref768/detail

We want to hear from you

At Microsoft Press, your satisfaction is our top priority, and your feedback our most valuable asset. Please tell us what you think of this book at:

https://aka.ms/tellpress

We know you're busy, so we've kept it short with just a few questions. Your answers go directly to the editors at Microsoft Press. (No personal information will be requested.) Thanks in advance for your input!

Stay in touch

Let's keep the conversation going! We're on Twitter: *http://twitter.com/MicrosoftPress.*

Important: How to use this book to study for the exam

Certification exams validate your on-the-job experience and product knowledge. To gauge your readiness to take an exam, use this Exam Ref to help you check your understanding of the skills tested by the exam. Determine the topics you know well and the areas in which you need more experience. To help you refresh your skills in specific areas, we have also provided "Need more review?" pointers, which direct you to more in-depth information outside the book.

The Exam Ref is not a substitute for hands-on experience. This book is not designed to teach you new skills.

We recommend that you round out your exam preparation by using a combination of available study materials and courses. Learn more about available classroom training at *https://www.microsoft.com/learning*. Microsoft Official Practice Tests are available for many exams at *https://aka.ms/practicetests*. You can also find free online courses and live events from Microsoft Virtual Academy at *https://www.microsoftvirtualacademy.com*.

This book is organized by the "Skills measured" list published for the exam. The "Skills measured" list for each exam is available on the Microsoft Learning website: *https://aka.ms/examlist*.

Note that this Exam Ref is based on publicly available information and the author's experience. To safeguard the integrity of the exam, authors do not have access to the exam questions.

CHAPTER 1

Design a multidimensional business intelligence (BI) semantic model

A business intelligence semantic model is a semantic layer that you create to represent and enhance data for use in reporting and analysis applications. Microsoft SQL Server Analysis Services (SSAS) supports two types of business intelligence semantic models: multidimensional and tabular. In this chapter, we review the skills you need to create a multidimensional database, whereas we explore the skills necessary for creating a tabular model in Chapter 2, "Design a tabular BI semantic model." We start with the steps required to physically instantiate a multidimensional database on an SSAS server. Then we work through the steps to perform, and the decisions to consider, for the two main objects in a multidimensional database, dimensions and measures.

> **IMPORTANT**
> ## Have you read page xiii?
> It contains valuable information regarding the skills you need to pass the exam.

Skills in this chapter:

- Create a multidimensional database by using Microsoft SQL Server Analysis Services (SSAS)
- Design and implement dimensions in a cube
- Implement measures and measure groups in a cube

Skill 1.1: Create a multidimensional database by using Microsoft SQL Server Analysis Services (SSAS)

Before you start the development process for a multidimensional database, you should spend some time thinking about its design and preparing your data for the new database. You are then ready to set up the database on the SSAS server and choose how you want SSAS to store data in the database.

> **This section covers how to:**
> - Design, develop, and create multidimensional databases
> - Select a storage model

Design, develop, and create multidimensional databases

The design process begins with an understanding of how people ask questions about their business. That is, you must decide how to translate your business requirements into a data model that is suitable as a source for a multidimensional database. Then after loading data into this data model, a process that is not covered in the exam, you proceed by creating a multidimensional database project in SQL Server Data Tools for Visual Studio 2015 (SSDT).

During the development process, you create supporting objects such as a data source and a data source view to define connectivity to your data model and to provide an abstraction layer for that data that you use for developing dimensions, measures, and cubes. As you work through each step, you deploy each newly created object to a multidimensional database on the SSAS server so you can test your work and ensure business requirements are met.

Source table design

An online transactional processing (OLTP) database is structured in third normal form with efficiency of storage and optimization of write operations, or low-volume read operations in mind. An SSAS multidimensional database is an online analytical processing (OLAP) database that is optimized for read operations of high-volume data. If you do not already have a data warehouse to use as a source for your multidimensional database, you should design a new data model in a relational database in which to store data that loads into SSAS.

Before you start the design of a new data model to use as a source for your multidimensional database, you should spend time understanding how the business users want to analyze data. You can interview them to find out the types of questions they want to answer with data analysis, and review the reports they use to find clues about important analytical elements. In particular, you want to discover the measures and dimensions that you need to create in the new data model. *Measures* are the numeric values to be analyzed, such as total sales, and *dimensions* are the people, places, things, and dates that provide context to these values. In this chapter, you learn how to develop a multidimensional database that can answer the following types of questions, also known as the business requirements, based on data for a fictional company, Wide World Importers:

- What is the quantity sold of items by date, customer, salesperson, or location?
- How many items are sold by color or by size?
- How many items that require chilling are sold as compared to stock items that do not require chilling (dry items)?
- How many sales occurred by date, customer, salesperson, or location?
- What are total sales (with and without tax included), taxes, and profit by date, salesperson, location, or item?
- When reviewing individual transactions, what is the tax rate and what is the unit price per item sold?
- For each customer billed for sales, how do those sales break down by the customers receiving the items?
- What reasons do customers give for making a purchase and how do sales dollars and sales counts break down by sales reason?
- How many distinct items are sold by date, customer, salesperson, or location?
- How many items are in inventory by date and what are the target stock levels and reorder points for each item?

When you evaluate questions, look for clues to measure, such as "how many," "total," "dollars," or "count." You should also note whether a value can be obtained directly from the OLTP system, or whether it must be calculated. If a value is calculated, decide whether it can be calculated on a scalar basis (row by row), and whether summing the calculated results can derive a grand total. Be on the alert for different terms that refer to the same measure, and then consult with your business users to determine which term to use in the multidimensional database. Using these criteria, the following measures emerge from the business requirements:

- Quantity
- Stock Item Distinct Count
- Chiller Items Count
- Dry Items Count
- Sale Count
- Sales Amount With Tax
- Sales Amount Without Tax
- Tax Amount
- Tax Rate

- Unit Price
- Quantity On Hand
- Reorder Level
- Target Stock Level

Your next step is to review the business requirements again to identify dimensions. A common clue for a dimension is the word "by" in front of a candidate dimension, although sometimes it is only implicitly included in the requirements. A second review of the business requirements for Wide World Importers yields the following dimensions:

- Date

  Sometimes there are multiple dates associated with a transaction. It is important to know how each user community within your organization associates data with dates. At Wide World Importers, the sales department is interested in analyzing sales by invoice date, whereas the warehouse department wants to review sales by delivery date.

- Customer
- Employee
- City
- Stock Item

  One of the Wide World Importers requirements is to analyze sales by color or size of an item. Although the word "by" is a clue, color and size are more accurately descriptors or characteristics of an item and therefore become part of a single dimension table for items. You do not normally create separate dimension tables for characteristics like this.

> **NEED MORE REVIEW?** **DIMENSIONAL MODELING TECHNIQUES**
>
> Ralph Kimball, the father of dimensional modeling, has several books and online resources that describe this topic in detail. A good place to start is "Dimensional Modeling Techniques" at *http://www.kimballgroup.com/data-warehouse-business-intelligence-resources/ kimball-techniques/dimensional-modeling-techniques/.*

In an ideal data model for a multidimensional database, data is denormalized to minimize the number of joins across multiple tables by using a *star schema*, which consists of dimension tables and at least one fact table in which measures are stored. If you create a diagram by placing the fact table in the center and surround it by related dimensions, the diagram resembles a star shape, as shown in Figure 1-1. This example of a star schema is a selection of six tables from the WideWorldImportersDW sample database for SQL Server 2016 that answer some of the questions established as the requirements for the multidimensional database that you build throughout this chapter.

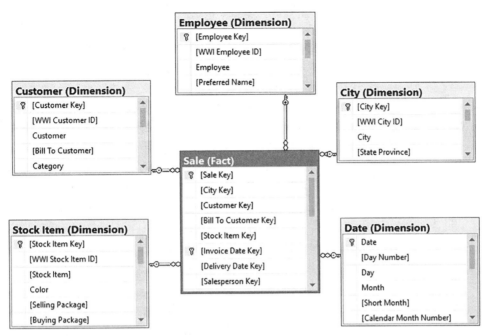

FIGURE 1-1 Star schema for a subset of tables in WideWorldImportersDW

NOTE **WIDEWORLDIMPORTERSDW SAMPLE DATABASE**

You can download the WideWorldImportersDW sample database from *https://github.com/ Microsoft/sql-server-samples/releases/tag/wide-world-importers-v1.0*. Installation instructions are at *https://msdn.microsoft.com/library/mt734217.aspx*.

Although a star schema is not required as a source for SSAS, it is a preferred structure for enterprise-scale multidimensional models for several reasons. First, the impact of accessing the OLTP system from SSAS adds resource contention to your environment that you can avoid by creating a separate data source. (The degree of impact on the OLTP depends on the storage model you select as explained in the "Select a storage model" section in this chapter.) Second, the amount of time to move data from the OLTP system into the multidimensional database is sometimes less optimal than it can be if you restructure the data first. Third, sometimes analysis requires access to historical information that is no longer preserved in the source system. Having a separate data model in which you store data as it changes becomes a necessity in that case. Other reasons for creating a separate data model include, but are not limited to, cleansing data that cannot be corrected in the OLTP system, having the results available not only to the multidimensional database, but other downstream reporting systems (often with better performance than querying the OLTP directly), and integrating data from multiple OLTP systems.

> **NOTE** **SNOWFLAKE DIMENSION DESIGN**
>
> Another type of design that you can implement for a dimension is a snowflake, in which you use multiple related tables for a single dimension. In traditional dimension modeling, the use of snowflake dimensions is not considered best practice because it adds joins back into the data model that a star schema design seeks to eliminate. For relational reporting scenarios, the additional joins can have an adverse impact on performance. However, when you use SSAS in its default storage mode, the snowflake structure has no impact on performance and can be a preferable design when you need to support analysis across fact tables having different levels of granularity, or to simplify the process that loads the dimension from the OLTP source. You can learn more about why you might use a snowflake dimension and how to design one properly in a series of blog posts by Jason Thomas that begins at *http://sqljason.com/2011/05/when-and-how-to-snowflake-dimension.html.*

To load the star schema with data on a periodic basis, you use an extract-transform-load (ETL) tool, such as SQL Server Integration Services (SSIS). The ETL tool is typically scheduled to run nightly to load new and changed rows into the star schema, although business requirements might dictate a different frequency, such as every five minutes when low latency is required, or once per week for source data that changes infrequently.

 EXAM TIP

Because the focus of the 70-768 exam is on the implementation of Analysis Services models, this exam reference does not explain how to convert data from an OLTP structure such as Wide World Importers to a star schema structure suitable for OLAP. The assumption for the exam is that the design of the dimension and fact tables is complete and an ETL process has loaded the tables with data from the source OLTP system. Nonetheless, you should be familiar with star schema concepts and terminology and understand how to implement Analysis Services features based on specific data characteristics and analysis requirements.

A *dimension table* contains data about the entities that a business user wants to analyze—typically a person, place, thing, or point in time. One consideration when designing a dimension table is whether to track history. A *slowly changing dimension* (SCD) is a dimension for which you implement specific types of columns and ETL techniques specifically to address how to manage table updates when data changes. You make this design decision for each dimension separately based on business requirements. The two more common approaches to managing history include the following SCD types:

- **Type 1** Only current data is tracked. The ETL process updates columns with changed values and loses the values previously stored in those columns. For example, you might not track history for employee name changes, as shown in Figure 1-2, because the effect on sales is not likely to be relevant.

Before

Employee Key	Employee
4	Amy Trefl

After

Employee Key	Employee
4	Amy Alberts

FIGURE 1-2 SCD Type 1 replaces existing values when source data changes

- **Type 2** Both current data and historical data is tracked. The ETL process expires the row containing the original data, thus identifying it as historical data, and creates a new active row containing the current data. When data in one of the columns changes in a row, the ETL process updates the Valid To date on the existing row to reflect the current date, and thus expires that record, and then adds a new record with the current values for each column and sets the Valid From date to the current date. Depending on the business rules, the Valid To date can be NULL or a future date such as 12/31/9999.

As an example, you might track history for changes to a stock item's data such as retail price, as show in Figure 1-3, because you might want to monitor whether sales change when the retail price changes.

Before

Stock Item Key	WWI Stock Item ID	Stock Item	Retail Price	Valid From	Valid To
15	205	Tape dispenser (Blue)	47.84	2013-01-01	

After

Stock Item Key	WWI Stock Item ID	Stock Item	Retail Price	Valid From	Valid To
15	205	Tape dispenser (Blue)	47.84	2013-01-01	2017-01-01
672	205	Tape dispenser (Blue)	35.00	2017-01-01	

FIGURE 1-3 SCD Type 2 expires original row and inserts new row when source data changes

NOTE   SLOWLY CHANGING DIMENSION TYPES

There are several different ways to model dimensions to accommodate changes besides Type 1 and Type 2, but these two are the most common. You can learn more about Type 1 from Ralph Kimball at *http://www.kimballgroup.com/2008/08/slowly-changing-dimensions/* and about Type 2 at *http://www.kimballgroup.com/2008/09/slowly-changing-dimensions-part-2/*.

Let's take a closer look at City, one of the dimension tables in the WideWorldImportersDW database, to understand the types of columns that it contains. Figure 1-2 shows the following types of columns commonly found in a dimension:

- **Surrogate key**   A primary key for the dimension table to uniquely identify each row. It normally has no business meaning and is often defined as an identity column. In the City table, the [City Key] column is the surrogate key. The purpose of a surrogate key is to prevent duplicate rows when combining data from multiple sources or capturing historical data for slowly changing dimensions. In addition, the source data for a dimension table might not use an integer value for its primary key whereas enforcing an integer-based key in a dimension table ensures optimal performance when processing the dimension to load its data in a multidimensional database.

NOTE   DATE DIMENSION

It is not uncommon to see a date dimension without a surrogate key defined. Instead, an integer value for the date in YYYYMMDD format is used to uniquely identify each date. By using this approach, uniqueness is guaranteed. Furthermore, the issues with combining data sources or managing slowly changing dimensions do not occur in a date dimension.

- **Natural or business key**   The primary key in the source table for the dimension, which is [WWI City ID] in the City table. This column is typically not displayed to business users for analytical purposes, but is used to match rows from the source system to existing rows in the dimension table as part of the ETL process.

- **Attributes**   Descriptive columns about a row in the dimension table. Attributes in the City table include City, State Province, Country, Continent, Sales Territory, Region, Subregion, Location, and Latest Recorded Population. Attributes can be used explicitly for analysis to aggregate numeric values from the fact table, much like you use a GROUP BY clause in a Transact-SQL (T-SQL) SELECT statement.

- **Slowly changing dimension history**   A pair of columns to show the date range for which a row is valid. Slowly changing dimension history columns specify the date range for which the set of attributes in the row is valid in a Type 2 SCD. In WideWorldImportersDW, Valid From and Valid To are the columns fulfilling this role. Another common naming convention is StartDate and EndDate.

Although the City table in WideWorldImportersDW is implemented as if it were a slowly changing dimension, because it includes history columns Valid From and Valid To, the data in the table does not reflect changed data across the historical records. Instead, you can observe an example of slowly changing dimension history in the Stock Item dimension table, which shows a change in Color that resulted in multiple rows for the WWI Stock Item ID 2, as shown in Figure 1-4.

	Stock Item Key	WWI Stock Item ...	Stock Item	Color	Valid From	Valid To
1	218	2	USB rocket launcher (Gray)	Gray	2013-01-01 00:00:00.0000000	2016-05-31 23:00:00.0000000
2	291	2	USB rocket launcher (Gray)	Steel Gray	2016-05-31 23:00:00.0000000	2016-05-31 23:11:00.0000000
3	604	2	USB rocket launcher (Gray)	Steel Gray	2016-05-31 23:11:00.0000000	9999-12-31 23:59:59.9999999

FIGURE 1-4 Multiple rows for a single stock item demonstrate Type 2 SCD handling

Notice there are three surrogate keys, Stock Item Key, for the same natural key, and WWI Stock Item ID. Each surrogate key is associated with a separate range of Valid From and Valid To dates.

- **Lineage or audit key**   An optional column in a dimension table that has a foreign key relationship to another table in which information about ETL processes is maintained. In WideWorldImportersDW, the City table, shown in Figure 1-5, has the Lineage Key column that relates to the Integration.Lineage table. This latter table includes the date and time when the ETL process started and ended, the table affected, and the success of the process.

City (Dimension)
- 🔑 [City Key]
- [WWI City ID]
- City
- [State Province]
- Country
- Continent
- [Sales Territory]
- Region
- Subregion
- Location
- [Latest Recorded Population]
- [Valid From]
- [Valid To]
- [Lineage Key]

FIGURE 1-5 City dimension table in WideWorldImportersDW database

A *fact table* contains many columns of numeric data. A business user analyzes the data in many of these columns in aggregate—typically by calculating sums, averages, or counts. Other numeric columns containing foreign keys are used to protect relational integrity with dimension tables through foreign key relationships. A fact table supports comparisons of these aggregate values over different time periods, such as this year's total sales versus last year's total sales, or across different groups, such as brands or colors of stock items. Figure 1-6 shows an example of Sale, a fact table in WideWorldImportersDW that contains the following types of columns:

- **Surrogate key**   A primary key for the fact table to uniquely identify each row. Like a surrogate key for a dimension table, it normally has no business meaning and is often defined as an identity column. Often, a fact table has no surrogate key because the collection of foreign key columns represents a unique composite key. The inclusion of a surrogate key for a fact table is a matter of preference by the data modeler.

> **NOTE**   **BENEFITS OF A SURROGATE KEY IN A FACT TABLE**
>
> Bob Becker, a member of the Kimball Group established by Ralph Kimball, recommends omitting a surrogate key in a fact table, but acknowledges it can be useful under special circumstances as he describes in his article on the topic at *http://www.kimballgroup. com/2006/07/design-tip-81-fact-table-surrogate-key/*.

- **Foreign keys**   One foreign key column for each dimension table that relates to the fact table. In the Sale table, the following columns are foreign key columns for dimensions: City Key, Customer Key, Bill To Customer Key, Stock Item Key, Invoice Date Key, Delivery Date Key, and Salesperson Key. The combination of foreign keys represents the *granularity*, or level of detail, of the fact table.

- **Degenerate dimension**   One or more optional columns in a fact table that represents a dimension value that is not stored in a separate table. Technically speaking, the column can be stored in a separate table because it represents a "thing," such as an invoice that could be the subject of analysis. Often the value in a degenerate dimension is unique in each row, such as an invoice identifier. However, due to the cardinality between the degenerate dimension and the fact table, the model is more efficient when the degenerate dimension is part of the fact table. In other words, no join is required to join two potentially large tables. An example of this type of degenerate dimension column in the Sale fact table is the WWI Invoice ID column.

  Another reason to create a degenerate dimension in a fact table is to optimize reporting for frequently requested data by avoiding a join between tables. In the Sale fact table, the Description and Package columns are examples of this other type of degenerate dimension.

- **Measure** One or more columns that contain numeric data that describes an event or business process. The Sale fact table presents individual sales, so each row contains the following measure columns: Quantity, Unit Price, Tax Rate, Total Excluding Tax, Tax Amount, Profit, Total Including Tax, Total Dry Items, and Total Chiller Items.

  Sometimes, a fact table contains no measure columns. In that case, it is known as a *factless fact table*. You might use a factless fact table when you need to count occurrences of an event and have no other measurements related to the event. Another type of factless fact table is a table that serves as a bridge table between a fact table and a dimension table, as described in the "Many-to-many dimension model" section in this chapter.

- **Lineage or audit key** An optional column in a fact table just like the same type of column in a dimension table. In the Sale table, Lineage Key is the lineage column.

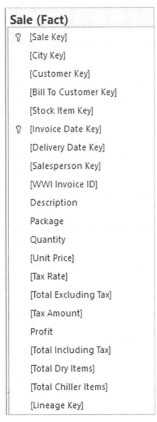

Sale (Fact)
- ⚷ [Sale Key]
- [City Key]
- [Customer Key]
- [Bill To Customer Key]
- [Stock Item Key]
- ⚷ [Invoice Date Key]
- [Delivery Date Key]
- [Salesperson Key]
- [WWI Invoice ID]
- Description
- Package
- Quantity
- [Unit Price]
- [Tax Rate]
- [Total Excluding Tax]
- [Tax Amount]
- Profit
- [Total Including Tax]
- [Total Dry Items]
- [Total Chiller Items]
- [Lineage Key]

FIGURE 1-6 Sales fact table in WideWorldImportersDW database

Project creation

Once you have a star schema implemented and loaded with data, you are ready to create a project in which you perform the development of your multidimensional database. To do this, you use SSDT for which there is a link to the current version at *https://msdn.microsoft.com/en-us/library/mt204009.aspx*.

> **NOTE LOCATION FOR SSDT DOWNLOAD IS SUBJECT TO CHANGE**
>
> From time to time, Microsoft revises SSDT to update and fix features. If the referenced link is no longer valid, you can search for SQL Server Data Tools for Visual Studio at *http://www.microsoft.com* to locate and download it.

To create a new project, perform the following steps:

1. In the File menu, point to New, and then select Project.

2. In the New Project dialog box, select Analysis Services in the Business Intelligence group of templates, and then select Analysis Services Multidimensional and Data Mining Project.

3. At the bottom of the dialog box, type a name for the project, select a location, and optionally type a new name for the project's solution. The project for the examples in this chapter is named 70-768-Ch1.

> **NOTE SOLUTION STRUCTURE IN SSDT**
>
> A solution is a container for one or more projects. For example, you can have a data project to define your table structures, an SSIS project to perform the ETL steps, an Analysis Services project to create your multidimensional database, and a Microsoft SQL Server Reporting Services (SSRS) project to develop reports to display data from your multidimensional database.

Data source development

Your next step is to define a relational data source for your multidimensional database. SSAS supports the following data sources:

- Microsoft Access 2010 or higher
- Microsoft SQL Server 2008 or higher
- Microsoft Azure SQL Database

- Microsoft Azure SQL Data Warehouse
- Microsoft Analytics Platform System
- Oracle 9i or higher
- Teradata V2R6 or V12
- Informix V11.10
- IBM DB2 8.1
- Sybase Adaptive Server Enterprise 15.0.2
- A data source accessible by using an OLE DB provider

> **NOTE** **DATA PROVIDER INSTALLATION**
>
> Depending on the data source that you are accessing, you might need to download and install the data source's data provider on your computer. SSDT installation does not install data providers.

To add a data source, perform the following steps:

1. Right-click the Data Sources folder in the Solution Explorer window, and select New Data Source.

2. Click Next in the Data Source Wizard, and then click New on the Select How To Define The Connection page of the wizard.

3. In the Connection Manager dialog box, select a data provider and provide connection details for your data source. To follow the examples in this chapter, use the default provider, Native OLE DB\SQL Server Native Client 11.0. Type your server name or type a period (.), **(local)**, or **localhost** if you are running SSDT on the same computer as your SQL Server database engine. If you have your database set up for SQL Server authentication, select SQL Server Authentication in the Authentication drop-down list, and then provide a user name and password in the respective text boxes. Last, select WideWorldImportersDW in the Select Or Enter A Database Name drop-down list, as shown in Figure 1-7.

FIGURE 1-7 Connection Manager dialog box for a data source

4. Click OK to close the Connection Manager dialog box, click Next in the Data Source Wizard, and then choose one of the following options for Impersonation Information, as shown in Figure 1-8, as authentication for the data source:

   ■ **Use Specific Windows User Name And Password** Use this option when you need to connect to your data source with a specific login. A security best practice is to establish a Windows login with low privileges that has read permission to the data source. When you deploy the data source to the server, SSAS encrypts the password to protect it. If you later need to script out the database, such as you might when you want to move from a development server to a production server, you must provide the password again.

   ■ **Use The Service Account** To follow the examples in this chapter, the selection of this option is recommended. With this option selected, the account running the SSAS service, which by default is NT Service\MSSQLServerOLAPService, is used to connect to the data source.

- **Use The Credentials Of The Current User**   Do not select this option when you are developing a multidimensional database. It is included to support authentication for data mining queries.
- **Inherit**   This option uses the impersonation information that is set for the DataSourceImpersonationInfo database property. Your options include Use A Specific Windows User Name And Password, Use The Service Account, Use The Credentials Of The Current User, or Default. If it is set to Default, the Inherit selection at the data source level uses the service account.

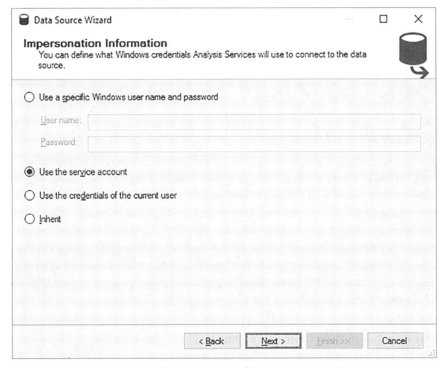

FIGURE 1-8 The Impersonation Information page of the Data Source Wizard

5. Click Next in the Data Source Wizard, change the value of the Data Source Name if you like, and then click Finish.

    A new file is added to your project, Wide World Importers DW.ds. This file, like all the other files that you add to your project during the development process, is an Extensible Markup Language for Analysis (XMLA) file that defines the object to create in the multidimensional database. You can view the contents of any XMLA file by right-clicking it in the Solution Explorer window, and then selecting View Code.

> **IMPORTANT** **READ PERMISSION FOR IMPERSONATION ACCOUNT**
>
> You should ensure that, whichever option you select for impersonation, the applicable login is granted the Read permission on the source database. Otherwise, when you later attempt to create the multidimensional database on the SSAS server, you receive an error message. If you configure writeback or ROLAP processing as described in Chapter 4, "Configure and maintain SQL Server Analysis Services (SSAS)," the account you use must also have write permission.
>
> To set up read permission for the service account, open SQL Server Management Studio (SSMS), connect to the Database Engine, expand the Security node in Object Explorer, right-click the Logins node, and select New Login. In the Login dialog box, type NT SERVICE\MSSQLServerOLAPService in the Login Name text box. Click the User Mapping page, select the WideWorldImportersDW check box in the Users Mapped To This Login section of the page, and then select the db_datareader check box in the Database Role Membership For: WideWorldImportersDW section of the page. Click OK to add the login.

Data source view design

The data source definition defines where the data is located and how to authenticate, but does not specify which data to use for loading into database objects, such as dimensions and cubes. A *data source view* (DSV) is the definition, which identifies the specific tables and columns within tables to use when populating the multidimensional database. It is also an abstraction layer that is useful when you have only read permission on the source database, or when you need a simplified view of its structures. You can make logical changes to the tables and views in the DSV to support specific requirements in SSAS without the need to change the physical data source. Generally speaking, you should attempt to change the physical data source as needed whenever possible because implementing logical changes in the DSV can introduce challenges into ongoing maintenance in addition to the troubleshooting process.

To create a DSV, perform the following steps:

1. Right-click the Data Source Views folder in Solution Explorer, and select New Data Source View.

2. In the Data Source View Wizard, click Next, select the data source that you created for the project in the previous section, and click Next.

3. Then, while pressing the CTRL key, select the following tables in the Available Objects list:

   - City (Dimension)
   - Customer (Dimension)
   - Date (Dimension)
   - Employee (Dimension)
   - Stock Item (Dimension)
   - Sale (Fact)

4. Then click the Right (>) arrow to add the selected tables to the Included Objects list.

5. Click Next, and then click Finish to complete the wizard. A new file, Wide World Importers DW.dsv, is added to the project, and Data Source View Designer is opened as a document window in SSDT, as shown in Figure 1-9.

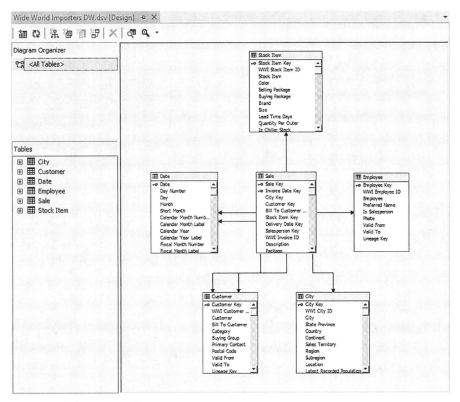

FIGURE 1-9 A data source view

When the source tables have primary keys and foreign key relationships defined, which is the ideal situation, the DSV includes them. If you are working with a well-defined star schema, the DSV probably does not require any modification.

If a primary key is not defined in a dimension table, either by design or because the source object is a view, you can add a logical key by right-clicking the column name in the table diagram or in the Tables pane, and then selecting Set Logical Primary Key. This command is not available when a key already exists for the table. If you press the CTRL key, and then select multiple columns, you can configure a composite key as the logical primary key.

To create a relationship between tables, such as between a fact table and a dimension table, click the foreign key column in the fact table and then drag it to the primary key column in the dimension table. The two columns must have the same data type before you can create the relationship. The definition of relationships is not required, but is useful because

SSDT can make recommendations or automatically configure certain objects based on the DSV relationships that it detects.

The structure of the DSV is important for the development of dimension and cube objects as you continue building out your multidimensional database. To satisfy specific structural requirements for subsequent development steps, or to simplify a star schema, you can make any of the following changes to the DSV:

- **Rename objects**   When you rename tables and columns in the DSV, the wizards that you use to create objects for the database reflect the new names, which should be a user-friendly name. Although you can later rename an object created by a wizard at any time, sometimes you might reference the same DSV object multiple times and can minimize the number of name changes required elsewhere in your project.

- **Create a named calculation**   The addition of a named calculation to a DSV is like adding an expression to a SELECT statement to add a derived column to a view. Ideally, when you need data structured in a particular way for SSAS, you design the source table to include that structure or create a view. A common reason to restructure data is to concatenate columns, such as you might need to do with First Name and Last Name columns to create one column for a person's name.

  If you are unable to make the change in the source, create a named calculation in the DSV by right-clicking the header of the table to update, and selecting New Named Calculation. In the Create Named Calculation dialog box, type a name in the Column Name box, optionally type a description for the calculation in the Description box, and then type a platform-specific Structured Query Language (SQL) expression for the new column in the Expression box. There is no validation of the expression when you click OK to close the dialog box, so be sure to test your expression in a query tool first. You use the syntax applicable to the version of SQL applicable to your data source, such as Transact-SQL when your data source is SQL Server.

- **Create a named query**   A named query in a DSV is the logical equivalent of a view in a relational database. Unlike a named calculation, which is limited to a SQL expression, a named query is a SELECT statement. You can use it to reduce the number of columns from a table to simplify the DSV, create new columns by using SQL expressions, or join tables together to simplify the data structures in the DSV and avoid a snowflake design. You can find examples of adding named queries to the DSV in Skill 1.2, "Design and implement dimensions in a cube," and Skill 1.3, "Implement measures and measure groups in a cube."

Develop a dimension

A dimension in a cube is based on one or more dimension tables in a star schema. Skill 1.2 details the various options you must consider when developing different types of dimension models in SSAS. Regardless of model type, the development process for all dimensions begins by performing the same steps explained in this section.

Let's review the basic dimension development process by adding the City dimension to the current database project. To this, perform the following steps:

1. Right-click the Dimensions folder in Solution Explorer, and click New Dimension.

2. In the Dimension Wizard, click Next on the first page, and then, on the Select Creation Method page, choose the Use An Existing Table option. Click Next.

> **NOTE OTHER DIMENSION CREATION METHODS**
>
> The Select Creation Method page of the Dimension Wizard also allows you to choose one of the following alternatives to the default option: Generate A Time Table In The Data Source, Generate A Time Table On The Server, or Generate A Non-time Table In The Data Source. These options are used more often when you develop a prototype multidimensional database and have not built the star schema source tables. If you are interested in learning more about these options, see "Select Creation Method (Dimension Wizard)" at *https://msdn.microsoft.com/en-us/library/ms178681.aspx*.

3. On the Specify Source Information page of the wizard, select the name of the table containing the most granular level of detail for a dimension in the Main Table drop-down list. For the current example, select City. When the DSV is designed correctly, the key column in the source table displays automatically in the Key Columns list. The selection of a Name Column, such as City, as shown in Figure 1-10, is optional, but recommended when the key column is a surrogate key.

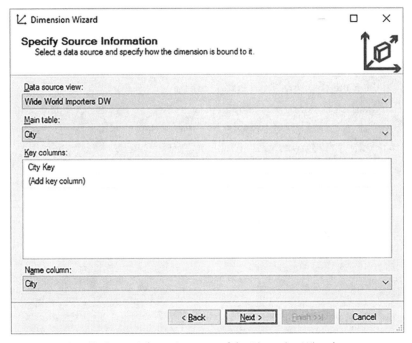

FIGURE 1-10 Specify Source Information page of the Dimension Wizard

If you follow proper dimensional modeling design principles as described in the "Source table design" section earlier in this chapter, your key column is an integer value. If you do not specify a name column during dimension development, business users will see the dimension's key column value when exploring a cube, which has no meaning to them. The Name Column should be set to a column in the dimension table that contains a meaningful value. Unlike the key column, which can be a composite key, the name column must reference a single column. If necessary, you can use a named calculation or named query to combine values from a multiple column into one column.

4. Click Next to continue. On the Select Dimension Attributes page of the Dimension Wizard, notice the existing selection of the City Key check box, and then select the check box for the following attribute columns, as shown in Figure 1-11:

    ■ State Province

    ■ Country

    ■ Continent

    ■ Sales Territory

    ■ Region

- Subregion
- Latest Recorded Population

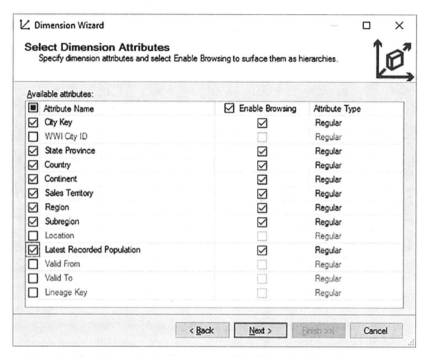

FIGURE 1-11 Select Dimension Attributes page of the Dimension Wizard

> **NOTE** **ADDITIONAL OPTIONS ON THE SELECT DIMENSION ATTRIBUTES PAGE OF THE DIMENSION WIZARD**
>
> For each attribute on the Select Dimension Attributes page of the Dimension Wizard, you can select the Enable Browsing check box, or change the value in the Attribute Type drop-down list. For the current example, you can accept the default settings. When you develop your own multidimensional database, you can decide whether to change the defaults here, or to set the corresponding properties in the dimension definition as described in Skill 1.2. Selecting the Enable Browsing check box changes the dimension's AttributeHierarchyEnabled property to False while changing the Attribute Type drop-down list selection updates the Type property for the attribute.

When business users analyze data by using a multidimensional model, they use attributes primarily for grouping aggregate values in a report, or to filter values, as shown in Figure 1-12. In this example, SSAS calculates the sum of the Sales Amount With Tax measure for each State Province attribute member appearing on rows. An *attribute member* is a distinct value from the source column that is bound to the attribute. Figure 1-12 shows attribute members for the State Province attribute such as Alaska, California, and so on. Above the set of State Province members, you can see a filter applied based on another attribute, Sales Territory. Specifically, the filter uses the Far West member of the Sales Territory attribute. SSAS ignores the values for any State Province attribute member that is not related to the Far West Sales Territory and eliminates those attribute members from the query results.

Sales Territory Far West	
Row Labels ⏷	**Sales Amount With Tax**
Alaska	$3,451,301.88
California	$10,153,238.90
Hawaii	$364,314.77
Nevada	$1,438,300.19
Oregon	$2,588,197.05
Washington	$4,859,724.86
Grand Total	**$22,855,077.65**

FIGURE 1-12 Attribute members used for aggregate grouping and filtering

As explained earlier in the "Source table design" section, a dimension table can include columns that are never used for analysis, such as the Valid From and Valid To columns in the City dimension table. These columns are used for managing historical data in the ETL process, but are not useful for business analysis and are therefore normally excluded from the dimension in the SSAS project.

5. To complete the wizard, click Next, and then click Finish. The City.dim file is added to the project, and the dimension designer window is displayed in SSDT, as shown in Figure 1-13. The attributes that you selected in the wizard now appear in the Attributes pane of the Dimension Structure page of the dimension designer. In addition, a diagram of the source table displays in the Data Source View pane. After you develop a cube for the multidimensional database, you can add this newly created dimension to that cube. However, there might be additional steps to perform as part of the dimension development process to satisfy specific analysis requirements, as described next, and later in Skill 1.2.

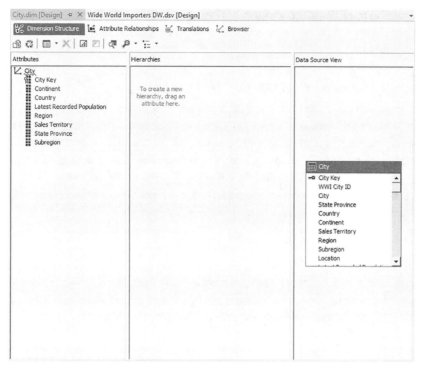

FIGURE 1-13 Dimension designer for City

When you create a dimension and then browse the members in the dimension, occasionally, a member named Unknown appears that does not exist in the source table. The addition of this member to a dimension is a feature in SSAS that gracefully accommodates data quality issues in a fact table. The Unknown member that SSAS creates does not correspond to a row in your dimension table, but serves as a bucket for values for which a key in the foreign key column in the fact table is missing or invalid. That way, when queries calculate totals for a measure, all rows in the fact table are included (after applying the applicable groupings and filters) even when they cannot be matched to existing dimension members.

The addition of the SSAS-generated member is determined by the value of the Unknown-Member property for a dimension, which you can access in the Properties window from the Dimension Structure page of the dimension designer after selecting the dimension object in the Attributes pane. The member is added if the UnknownMember property value is Visible or Hidden. Either way, the grand total values for a dimension show the correct aggregated value for a fact table. When this property is set to Visible and your query includes the dimension's members in the results, you can see the aggregated value for fact table rows with a missing or incorrect key for that dimension assigned to the Unknown member. When this property is set to Hidden, the Unknown member does not display in the query results, although the grand total correctly includes its values. However, hiding the Unknown member can be confusing to business users who might notice the aggregation of visible members does not equal the grand total. For this reason, it is not considered best practice to hide the Unknown member.

EXAM TIP

Be prepared to answer questions about working with the Unknown Member on the exam. For more review on this topic, see "Defining the Unknown Member and Null Processing Properties" at *https://msdn.microsoft.com/en-us/library/ms170707.aspx*.

In Skill 1.2, we review specific usage scenarios that require additional development steps. Meanwhile, as a general practice for all dimensions that you develop, you should evaluate which, if any, of the following tasks are necessary:

- **Rename objects**   For example, notice in the Attributes pane that there is a key icon next to City Key to designate it as the key attribute. In other words, this is the attribute that is referenced in the fact table. In the Dimension Wizard, you specified City Key as the key column and City as the name column. The attribute's name is inherited from the key column name. In this case, the name City Key is not user-friendly because many business users might not understand what Key means. More generally, consider avoiding technical terms and naming objects by using embedded spaces, capitalization, and business terms to create user-friendly objects. To rename a dimension or an attribute, select it in the Attributes pane. You can either right-click the object, select Rename, and type the new name, or replace the Name property in the Attributes pane. In this case, rename the City Key attribute to City.

- **Change the sort order**   Each attribute member has an OrderBy property that sets the default sort order that determines the arrangement of attribute members in a group, such as when you display many attribute members on rows in a pivot table. In most cases, the attribute members display in alphabetical order, but you can override this behavior if you have a column with values that define an alternate sort order. You can choose one of the following values for the OrderBy property.

  - **Key**   This value is the default for every attribute except the key attribute if you assigned it a name column in the Dimension Wizard because every attribute always has a key column, but optionally has a name column. The sort order is alphabetical if the key column is a string data type (Char or WChar), or numerical if the key column data type is not a string.

> **NOTE** **SORTING BY COMPOSITE KEY**
>
> Remember that an attribute can have a composite key based on multiple columns. This capability can be used to advantage for sorting purposes. In Skill 1.2, you learn how to use composite keys to not only manage uniqueness for attribute members in the Date dimension, but also to control the sort order of those members.

- **Name** The sort order is set to Name for the key attribute by default when you specify a name column in the Dimension Wizard. Any attribute in a dimension can have separate columns assigned as the key column or name column, so you can define the sort order based on the name column if that is the case.

- **AttributeKey** You can also define the sort order for an attribute based on the key column value of another attribute, but only if an attribute relationship (described in Skill 1.2) exists between the two attributes. As an example, in an Account dimension, you can have an Account Name attribute that you want to sort by the related Account Number attribute rather than alphabetically by the account's name.

- **AttributeName** This option is like the AttributeKey sort order, except that the ordering is based on the name column of the related attribute instead of the key column.

- **Convert an attribute into a member property** A *member property* is an attribute that is not used in a pivot table for placement on rows or columns, or as a pivot table filter, but is used instead for reporting purposes. For example, you can display sales by customer and include each customer's telephone number in a report, but would not typically show sales by telephone number. You can also use a member property as a filter in an ad hoc MDX query.

  In the City dimension, change the AttributeHierarchyEnabled property to False for the Latest Recorded Population attribute to convert it to a member property. When you do this, the attribute does not display with the other attributes in client applications, although you can still reference it in MDX queries. Its availability for use in reporting depends on the tool. As an example, you can display a member property as a tooltip when you hover your cursor over a related attribute in a Microsoft Excel pivot table.

- **Group attribute members into ranges** A less commonly used, but no less important, feature of SSAS is its ability to break down a large set of attribute members into discrete ranges. For example, if you have 100,000 customers, it is impractical for a user to add all customers at once to a pivot table. Instead, you can configure SSAS to create groups of customers by setting the DiscretizationBucketCount and DiscretizationMethod properties.

■ **Add translations** Global organizations can build a single multidimensional database and then add translations to display captions for dimensions and attributes that are specific to a user's locale. You can also optionally bind an attribute to columns containing translated attribute member names.

EXAM TIP

The WideWorldImportersDW database does not include translations, so you cannot explore this feature in the multidimensional database that you are building for this chapter. However, the exam is likely to test your knowledge on this topic. To learn more about adding translation definitions, see "Translations in Multidimensional Models (Analysis Services)" at *https://msdn.microsoft.com/en-us/library/hh230908.aspx* and "Defining and Browsing Translations" at *https://msdn.microsoft.com/en-us/library/ms166708.aspx.* Translations apply not only to dimensions, but also to cube captions as described in the Microsoft Developer Network (MSDN) article.

You can see examples of using translations if you explore the AdventureWorks Multidimensional Model for which you can find a download link and a ReadMe file that includes installation instructions at "Adventure Works 2014 Sample Databases" at *http://msftdb-prodsamples.codeplex.com/releases/view/125550.*

A best practice in programming is to build code once, and then to reference that code many times. You might think that a similar best practice exists in SSAS. Let's say that you have multiple SSAS servers set up in your company to support different departments, and host different multidimensional databases on each server. If you follow dimensional modeling best practices, you have *conformed dimensions* in your data mart. That is, you have dimension tables that you relate to different fact tables, such as a Date dimension that is common to all analysis. If you build a date dimension for use in one multidimensional database, why not use the same dimension object in the other multidimensional database? SSAS allows you to add a linked dimension to that other multidimensional database so that you only have one dimension to build and maintain. However, the use of linked dimensions is not considered to be best practice in SSAS development because it can introduce performance problems in large cubes.

Develop a cube

A *cube* is the object that business users explore when interacting with a multidimensional database. It combines measure data from fact tables with dimension data. At minimum, you associate a single fact table with a cube, although it is common to associate multiple fact tables with one cube.

Like dimension development, cube development begins by using a wizard. To add a cube to your project, perform the following steps:

1. Launch the Cube Wizard by right-clicking the Cubes folder in Solution Explorer, and selecting New Cube.

2. Click Next on the first page of the wizard, keep the default option, Use Existing Tables, and then click Next.

3. On the Select Measure Group Tables page of the wizard, select a fact table, such as Sale, and then click Next. In SSAS, a *measure group* table is synonymous with a fact table. The reason for a more generic term is due to the ability to create a measure group from any type of table as long as it contains rows that can be counted. Therefore, think about a measure group as a container of measures.

4. On the Select Measures page of the Cube Wizard, only columns with a numeric data type in the fact table are displayed. Clear each check box that you do not want to use for analysis, such as WWI Invoice ID and Lineage Key in this example, as shown in Figure

1-14. Notice the inclusion of Sale Count, which is not a column in the fact table. SSAS suggests this column because counting the number of rows in a fact table and grouping the result by dimension attributes is a common business requirement. You can clear the check box for this derived measure if it is not necessary in your own project.

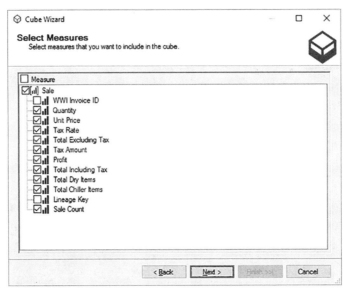

FIGURE 1-14 Select Measures page of the Cube Wizard

5. Click Next to continue to the Select Existing Dimensions page of the wizard. As shown in Figure 1-15, this page displays dimensions that currently exist in the project.

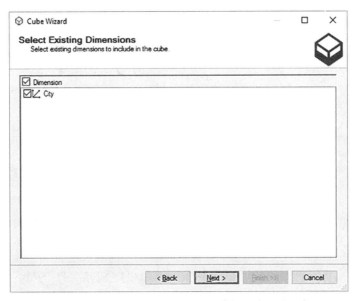

FIGURE 1-15 Select Existing Dimensions page of the Cube Wizard

A common development approach is to build one dimension, build a cube, deploy the project, and then review the results. (Troubleshooting any problems that arise is easier when you deploy one object at a time.) You then continue iteratively by defining another dimension, adding it to the cube, deploying the project, and then reviewing the changes.

However, you can decide to define multiple dimensions first. If you do, you see the available dimensions listed here and can include or exclude them as needed when using the Cube Wizard. On the other hand, when you create dimensions after you complete the Cube Wizard, you follow different steps to add them to the cube as explained in Skill 1.2.

6. Click Next, and then, on the Select New Dimensions page of the wizard, clear all of the check boxes, as shown in Figure 1-16, to continue the current example in which you are developing a simple cube with one dimension. You can do this in one step by clearing the Dimension check box at the top of the page.

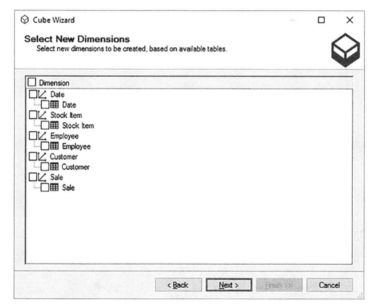

FIGURE 1-16 Select New Dimensions page of the Cube Wizard

The purpose of this page in the wizard is to identify dimension tables for which a relationship exists with the fact table or tables selected for the cube. If you keep a table selected on this page, the Cube Wizard creates a basic dimension for that table and adds it to the project as a new .dim file. You can then configure the dimension's properties as needed to meet your analysis requirements.

7. To finish the wizard, click Next, and then click Finish to add the Wide World Importers DW.cube file to the project and display the cube designer as an SSDT window.

8. Expand Sale in the Measures pane of the Cube Structure page of the cube designer to see all of the measures added to the cube, as shown in Figure 1-17.

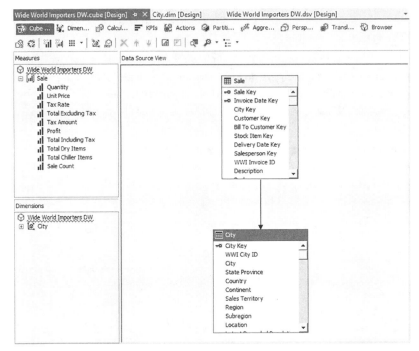

FIGURE 17 Cube designer

The cube designer also includes a Dimensions pane that displays the one dimension that is included in the cube, City. In addition, the Data Source View pane displays a diagram of the fact table, displayed with a yellow header, and the related dimension table, displayed with a blue header.

> **IMPORTANT DESIGN WARNINGS**
>
> Whenever you see a blue wavy underscore in a designer, you can hover your cursor over it to view the text of a design warning. In this case, the cube in both the Measures and Dimensions pane is associated with the same warning: Avoid cubes with a single dimension. Design warnings exist to alert you to potential problems that can affect performance or usability. Because it is a warning only, you can create your multidimensional database successfully if you ignore the warning. As you gain experience in developing multidimensional models, you can determine which warnings you should address, and which to ignore on a case-by-case basis. For more information about working with design warnings, see "Warnings (Database Designer) (Analysis Services-Multidimensional Data)" at *https://msdn.microsoft.com/en-us/library/bb677343.aspx*.

Create a multidimensional database

At this point, you have created the definitions of a data source, a data source view, a dimension, and a cube, which exist only in the context of a project, but the database does not yet exist on the server and no one can explore the cube until it does. To create the database on the server, you must deploy the project from SSDT. To ensure you deploy the project to the correct server, review, and if necessary, update the project's properties. To do this, right-click the project name in Solution Explorer and select Properties. In the 70-768-Ch1 Property Pages dialog box, select the Deployment page, as shown in Figure 1-18, and then update the Server text box with the name of your SSAS server if you need to deploy to a remote server rather than locally.

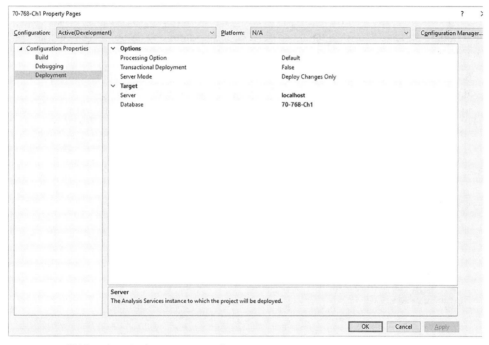

FIGURE 1-18 SSAS project deployment properties

The following additional deployment options are also available on this page:

- **Processing Option**   The default value is Default, which evaluates the processed state of each object in the solution and takes the necessary steps to put the object into a processed state when you deploy the project. You can change this value to Do Not Process if you want to manually instruct the server to process objects as a separate step, or Full if you want the database to process completely each time you deploy your project from SSDT. For now, the default value is sufficient for working through the examples in this chapter. In Chapter 4, these processing options are described in greater detail.

- **Transactional Deployment** The default value is False, which means that deployment is not transactional. In that case, deployment can succeed, but processing can fail. Choose True if you want to roll back deployment if processing fails.

- **Server Mode** The default value is Deploy Changes Only, which deploys only objects from your project that do not yet exist on the server, or are different from those on the server. This option is faster than the Deploy All option, which deploys all objects in your project to the server.

When you are ready to create the database on the server, right-click the project in Solution Explorer, and select Deploy. The first time you perform this step, the deployment process creates the database on the server and adds any objects that you have defined in the project. Each subsequent time that you deploy the project, as long as you have kept the default deployment options in the project properties, the deployment process preserves the existing database and adds any new database objects, and updates any database objects that you have modified in the project.

You can confirm the creation of the multidimensional database by opening SSMS and connecting to Analysis Services. In Object Explorer, expand the Databases folder to view the existing databases, and then expand the subfolders to see the objects currently in the database, as shown in Figure 1-19.

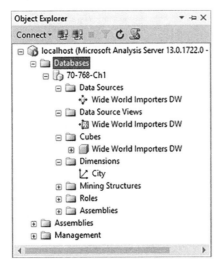

FIGURE 1-19 Multidimensional database objects visible in the SQL Server Management Studio Object Explorer

Now the cube is ready to explore using any tool that is compatible with SSAS, such as Excel, Microsoft Power BI Desktop, or SSRS, but it is not yet set up as well as it can be. There are more dimensions and fact tables to add, as well as many configuration changes to the dimension and cube to consider and implement that you learn about in Skills 1.2 and 1.3.

Select a storage model

The storage model you select for your multidimensional model determines the type of data that SSAS stores and how it physically stores that data on disk. SSAS supports the following storage models:

- **Multidimensional OLAP (MOLAP)**
- **Relational OLAP (ROLAP)**
- **Hybrid OLAP (HOLAP)**

Regardless of which storage model you select, cube data is always stored separately from dimension data. Furthermore, you can specify a different storage model for cube data than you do for dimension data. You can even separate cube data into multiple partitions, each using a different storage model. For now, consider which storage mode is most appropriate for your requirements in general. In Chapter 4, you learn the reasons why you might configure different storage models for partitions and how to implement storage models by partition.

EXAM TIP

Be prepared to answer questions on the exam related to the selection of an appropriate storage model for a specific scenario. In addition, review the information in Chapter 4 to understand how proactive caching affects data latency.

MOLAP

MOLAP is the default storage mode. Generally speaking, it is also the preferred storage mode unless you have specific requirements that only one of the other two storage modes can meet because it performs fastest. On the other hand, it requires the most storage space.

MOLAP storage compresses data and distributes it more efficiently on disk than the other storage models, but it also requires the most time to process data. When SSAS processes data for MOLAP storage, it uses the DSV to generate the necessary SQL statements that retrieve data from the relational source, restructures the results for storage on disk in a proprietary format, and then calculates and stores aggregations for measures, as shown in Figure 1-20. Aggregations are calculated only if you have defined aggregation rules as described in Chapter 4. When SSAS receives a request for data from a Multidimensional Expression (MDX) query, it gets the aggregated data or detail data in MOLAP storage to prepare the results.

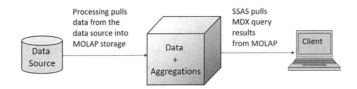

FIGURE 1-20 MOLAP storage

> **NOTE   DATA RETRIEVAL FOR MDX QUERIES**
>
> More precisely, SSAS retrieves data from MOLAP storage if the data is not currently in memory. SSAS uses both disk and cache storage for managing multidimensional data. For the purposes of contrasting storage models, assume that the data for a query is not available in memory and must be retrieved from the applicable storage model. Chapter 4, delves deeper into the mechanics of query processing by explaining the relationship between disk and cache storage.

ROLAP

With ROLAP storage, SSAS does not retrieve data from the relational source during processing. Instead, processing involves only checking the consistency of the data and therefore runs much faster than MOLAP processing. If you configure aggregations in addition to ROLAP storage, the aggregated values are stored in the data source, as shown in Figure 1-21. When SSAS receives an MDX request for data, it uses the DSV to translate the request into an SQL statement and sends that statement to the data source. For example, if the data source is SQL Server, the MDX is translated into T-SQL.

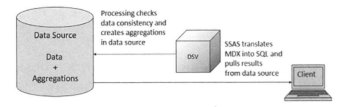

FIGURE 1-21 ROLAP storage

ROLAP storage is the best choice when your business users require near real-time access to data or when a dimension table has hundreds of millions of rows. A potential trade-off is slower query performance due to the translation of the query from MDX to SQL. However, there are techniques you can apply to mitigate the performance degradation as explained in Chapter 4.

HOLAP

HOLAP storage is a combination of MOLAP and ROLAP. Detail data is kept in the relational data source, but aggregate data and indexes are loaded into MOLAP storage during processing, as shown in Figure 1-22. When SSAS processes an MDX query, it determines where the data necessary to resolve the query resides. If it needs detail data, it translates the query to SQL and sends the translated statement to the data source. Otherwise, it retrieves aggregated data from MOLAP storage.

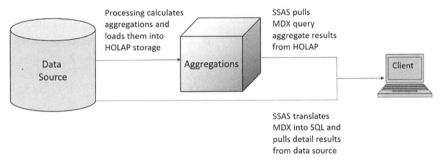

FIGURE 1-22 ROLAP storage

HOLAP queries are potentially slower to resolve. Furthermore, storage requirements on the SSAS server are not truly lower because SSAS must read all the data from the data source to build the aggregations and indexes and requires enough space to do this. SSAS disposes of the data afterwards, thus reducing storage requirements. Because you must factor in enough storage overhead for processing, HOLAP is not a good choice if your goal is to minimize storage.

Skill 1.2: Design and implement dimensions in a cube

After using the Dimension Wizard to add a dimension object to your multidimensional database, you must then add it to one or more cubes to make it available to client applications. Additionally, there are some configuration steps to perform when you need to improve the user experience for browsing the cube, enable specific SSAS features, or optimize performance.

> **This section covers how to:**
> - Select an appropriate dimension model, such as fact, parent-child, roleplaying, reference, data mining, many-to-many, and slowly changing dimension
> - Implement a dimension type
> - Define attribute relationships

Select an appropriate dimension model, such as fact, parent-child, roleplaying, reference, data mining, many-to-many, and slowly changing dimension

There are several different types of dimension models that you can define for your multidimensional database. For some of the dimensional models, you define the type by configuring its dimension usage relationship type on the Dimension Usage page of the cube designer. For the other dimensional models, you configure dimension or cube properties. In this section, we review each type of dimension model and the steps required to configure it.

Regular dimension model

When a dimension does not meet the criteria for any of the other dimensional models described in this section, it is considered to be a regular dimension. When you add it to a cube, the existence of a foreign key relationship between its corresponding dimension table and a measure group's fact table usually results in the addition of a regular relationship type. Sometimes, for various reasons, you might need to add this relationship type manually.

You can confirm the existence of a regular relationship by reviewing dimension usage. To do this, perform the following steps:

1. In Solution Explorer, double-click Wide World Importers DW.cube to open the cube designer, and then click the Dimension Usage tab. When you see text displayed without an icon in the cell intersection between a dimension and a measure group, as shown in Figure 1-23, the relationship type is Regular.

FIGURE 1-23 Cube dimension usage defining a relationship between a dimension and a measure group

2. Click the ellipsis button in the cell intersection to open the Define Relationship dialog box, shown in Figure 1-24.

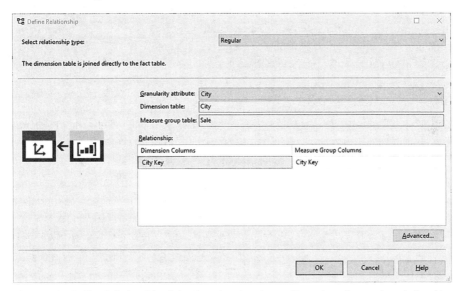

FIGURE 1-24 Define Relationship dialog box showing the configuration of a regular relationship

When Regular is selected in the Select Relationship Type drop-down list, you must identify the granularity attribute in the dimension, and the corresponding column in the measure group table.

In the Granularity Attribute drop-down list, you can select any attribute that exists in the dimension object in your project. This list does not include attributes from the dimension table appearing in the DSV if those attributes are not added to the dimension object.

When you select a granularity attribute, the attribute's corresponding key columns in the dimension table, as defined in the dimension object, display in the Dimension Columns list at the bottom of the dialog box. You then match each key column to a foreign key column in the fact table associated with the measure group.

Think of dimension usage for a regular relationship as the SSAS definition of a foreign key relationship. The existence of that relationship in the DSV is not sufficient because that is used whenever SSAS needs to generate SQL statements during processing, or when translating MDX to SQL. The DSV represents the physical modeling of the data source, even if it includes derived elements. The purpose of dimension usage is to define the logical relationships between dimension and measure groups objects. It represents the logical modeling of your multidimensional database.

Fact dimension model

A fact dimension model allows you to define a relationship between a measure group and dimension object that you create from a degenerate dimension. Remember from Skill 1.1 that a degenerate dimension is a type of column found in a fact table. Because both the measure group and the dimension come from the same table, there is no additional configuration required after you specify the Fact relationship type.

Let's set up a new dimension, configure a fact dimension model, and check the results by following these steps:

1. In Solution Explorer, right-click the Dimensions folder, select New Dimension, and click Next twice to proceed to the Specify Source Information page of the wizard.

2. In the Main Table drop-down list, select Sale.

   The two primary keys in the Sale table display in the Key Columns list, which requires you to select an item in the Name Column list. However, there is no column that adequately represents a value for each row in this table and the invoice date is not required to uniquely identify each row in the table. Therefore, you can clear this value.

3. Open the drop-down list containing Invoice Date Key, scroll to the top of the list, and then select the blank row at the top of the list to remove Invoice Date Key. Now you no longer need to provide a Name Column value, so click Next to continue.

4. On the Select Related Tables page, clear each check box, and click Next.

5. On the Select Dimension Attributes page, select the check box to the left of WWI Invoice ID, scroll down, and clear the check boxes for Delivery Date Key, Stock Item Key, Invoice Date Key, Salesperson Key, Customer Key, City Key, and Bill To Customer Key, and then click Next.

6. Type **Invoice** in the Name box, and click Finish to complete the wizard.

7. In the Attributes pane, click Sale Key to highlight it. Then, in the Properties window, select False in the AttributeHierarchyVisible drop-down list.

   By setting this property to False, you render the Sale Key attribute inaccessible to business users when they browse the cube. As a surrogate key, it has no meaning for business analysis, but is required in the dimension to uniquely identify each row and to establish the fact relationship in dimension usage.

8. Rename the WWI Invoice ID attribute by right-clicking it in the Attributes pane, selecting Rename, and then typing **Invoice**.

9. Double-click the Wide World Importers DW.cube file in Solution Explorer, go to the Cube Structure page, right-click the white space in the Dimensions pane, select Add Cube Dimension, select Invoice, and click OK. Now the dimension in the project is included in the cube.

10. Click the Dimension Usage tab of the cube designer, click the cell labeled Sale Key, and click the ellipsis button in the cell.

11. In the Define Relationship dialog box, select Fact in the Select Relationship Type drop-down list, as shown in Figure 1-25. There is nothing else to configure because the column for the granularity attribute for the dimension is also a column in the fact table for the measure group.

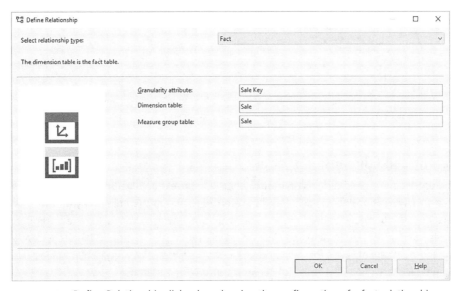

FIGURE 1-25   Define Relationship dialog box showing the configuration of a fact relationship

12. Click OK to close the dialog box. An icon displays in the Sale Key cell to indicate the fact relationship between the Invoice dimension and the Sale measure group.

13. Right-click the project in Solution Explorer, and select Deploy.

14. After the Deployment Completed Successfully message displays, click the Browser tab in the cube designer, expand the Measures node in the cube metadata tree, expand the Sale folder, and drag Sale Count to the query window labeled Drag Levels Or Measures Here To Add To The Query.

15. Expand the Invoice node, and drag Invoice (next to the rectangular collection of blue squares) to the area next to Sale Count. The browser generates an MDX query behind the scenes and displays the results, as shown in Figure 1-26. Here you can see some

invoices have only one item sold, while others have multiple items sold. As you add dimensions to the cube, you can create a query to see the specific stock items sold, the salesperson selling the item, and more.

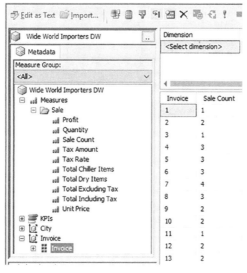

FIGURE 1-26 Browser in the cube designer showing Sale Count by Invoice

Parent-child dimension model

You use a parent-child dimension model when you have a dimension table that includes a foreign-key relationship to itself. It is also referred to as a ragged hierarchy or self-referencing relationship. Unlike a standard hierarchical structure in which there are a fixed number of levels, such as Month, Quarter, and Year in a Date dimension, a ragged hierarchy can have varying numbers of levels for each node. Common examples of ragged hierarchies are organizational charts, financial charts of accounts, or bills of materials.

EXAM TIP

A ragged hierarchy can be a standard or a parent-child dimension structure. For the exam, you should know how to use the HideMemberIf property to manage navigation across levels of a ragged hierarchy as described in "Ragged Hierarchies" at *https://msdn.microsoft. com/en-us/library/ms365406.aspx*. Xian Wang has a blog post entitled "Ragged Hierarchies and HideMemberIf: an in-depth look" that illustrates your options for modeling ragged hierarchies at *https://xzwang.wordpress.com/2013/07/10/ragged-hierarchy-and-hidemem- berif/.* You should also review Chris Webb's commentary on ragged hierarchy behavior in his blog post "Ragged Hierarchies, HideMemberIf and MDX Compatibility" at *https://blog. crossjoin.co.uk/2009/11/11/ragged-hierarchies-hidememberif-and-mdx-compatibility/.*

The WideWorldImportersDW database does not include a parent-child dimension, but you can artificially create one by converting the Employee table in the DSV to a named query in which you arbitrarily assign employees to managers. To do this, double-click Wide World Importers DW.dsv in Solution Explorer to open the DSV designer. In the Tables pane, right-click the Employee table, point to Replace Table, and select With New Named Query. In the Create Named Query dialog box, replace the SELECT statement with the statement shown in Listing 1-1, as shown in Figure 1-27, and then click OK.

LISTING 1-1 Named query statement to arbitrarily assign managers to employees

```
SELECT
    [Employee Key],
    CASE
        WHEN [WWI Employee ID] >= 3 AND [WWI Employee ID] <= 11 THEN 194
        WHEN [WWI Employee ID] >= 12 AND [WWI Employee ID] <= 15 THEN 203
        WHEN [WWI Employee ID] >= 16 AND [WWI Employee ID] <= 19 THEN 208
        WHEN [WWI Employee ID] = 20 THEN 210
        ELSE NULL
    END AS [Manager Key],
    [WWI Employee ID],
    [Employee],
    [Preferred Name],
    [Is Salesperson]
FROM [Dimension].[Employee];
```

FIGURE 1-27 Create Named Query dialog box showing a SELECT statement to generate a DSV table

Next, create the Employee dimension in the project by first following the steps described in the "Develop dimension" section earlier in this chapter and then performing these steps:

1. In the Specify Source Information page of the Dimension Wizard, use Employee as the Main Table and set Employee Key as the Key Column, and Employee as the Name Column. Click Next.

2. In the Select Dimension Attributes page of the wizard, select the Manager Key check box. Then click Next, and click Finish.

3. In the Attributes pane of the dimension designer, rename Employee Key as Employee, and Manager Key as Employees.

4. With Employees selected, locate the Usage property in the Properties window, and then select Parent in the Usage drop-down list. After you set this property, an icon displays next to the Employees attribute to designate its status as a parent-child hierarchy.

5. To observe the effect of this change, right-click the project in Solution Explorer, and select Deploy to update the multidimensional database on the server with the new dimension.

6. When you see the message the deployment is complete, click the Browser page of the dimension designer, and select Employees in the Hierarchy drop-down list.

7. Expand the All member in the browser, and then expand each member with a plus symbol next to it to view the parent-child hierarchical structure, as shown in Figure 1-28. In the Employees table in the WideWorldImportersDW table, there are multiple rows for many employees due to its slowly changing dimension design, which results in the appearance of duplicates in the dimension browser. You can safely ignore these duplicates for the purposes of this example.

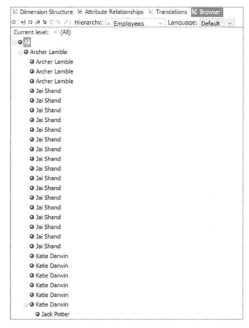

FIGURE 1-28 Browser in the dimension designer showing the Employees parent-child hierarchy

When you create a parent-child dimensional model and set an attribute's Usage property to Parent, you can also optionally configure the following additional properties for that attribute:

- **MembersWithData** The default setting for this property is NonLeafDataVisible. The assumption with this setting is that the fact table's key column associated with this dimension contains values for both parent and child members. In the case of the WideWorldImportersDW data (after creating a contrived relationship for managers and employees in the named query), that means managers and employees are associated with rows in the fact table, such as Archer Lamble and Jack Potter. When you browse the cube, when you drill down to break out the total sales for Archer Lamble, you see it includes Archer's sales reported as a separate value from Jack's sales (which you can see if you drill down from Jack's manager Katie Darwin).

  If you change this property to NonLeafDataHidden, the totals for each manager are calculated correctly. However, you do not see the manager's data in the query results when you drill down to view the employees' sales for that manager. This behavior can be confusing to business users and is not recommended as a best practice.

> **IMPORTANT** **TESTING THE EFFECT OF THE MEMBERSWITHDATA ATTRIBUTE PROPERTY**
>
> Although you can view the relationship between parent and child attribute members by using the Browse page of the dimension designer, you cannot view the effect of modifying the MembersWithData attribute property until you add the dimension to the cube, ensure the relationships on the Dimension Usage page of the cube designer is correct, and process the cube. Then you can browse the cube and use the parent attribute of the dimension in your query to see its behavior.

- **MembersWithDataCaption** If you use the NonLeafDataVisible setting for the MembersWithData property, you can set the caption for the attribute member that displays when you drill from the parent to the child attribute members. If you leave this property blank, the caption for both parent and child is identical. To more clearly differentiate the parent member as an aggregate value and its corresponding child member, you can use an asterisk as a wildcard and a string value to combine the actual member name with a static string.

  As an example, you can type *** (Manager)** in the MembersWithData Caption. For the WideWorldImportersDW named query in this chapter's sample project, Archer's sales as a parent member is the aggregate value of sales made by Archer and Jack and displays as Archer Lamble. If you drill down, you see Archer's sales as a child member displayed as Archer Lamble (Manager).

- **NamingTemplate** You use this property when you want to assign level names to each level in a parent-child hierarchy, which is important when your users browse the cube by using Excel or Power BI. If you leave this property blank, SSAS assigns a level names like Level 01, Level 02, and so on.

In a standard hierarchy, you define the level names when you create the hierarchy, as explained later in this chapter in the "Define attribute relationships" section. If you want to provide a name for levels in a parent-child hierarchy, your only option is to use the naming template.

A parent-child hierarchy does not have a fixed number of levels, and each branch of the hierarchy tree can have zero to many different levels. The second level down one branch does not necessarily have the same context as the second level down another branch. For example, in the Employee dimension, Archer Lamble is a manager on the first level below the All member, and the second level below Archer includes Jai Shand, Katie Darwin, and Piper Koch. Let's say hypothetically that each of these employees is a customer service representative. However, another member on the first level is Kayla Woodcock and the child members on the second level of this branch of the hierarchy are all sales staff. Therefore, it does not make sense to use a naming template in this scenario where the second level varies by branch.

When you have a parent-child hierarchy with a more consistent structure, you can use the NamingTemplate property to define a unique string for each level of the hierarchy. On the bottom level in the template, append an asterisk to the name to instruct SSAS to add a number that increments by 1 for each subsequent level when there are more levels in the hierarchy than named levels in the template.

- **RootMemberIf**   You use this property to help SSAS distinguish parent members from child members. You can choose from one of the following values in the property's drop-down list.

  - **ParentIsBlankSelfOrMissing**   This is the default setting, which covers any possible scenario to define a parent member. SSAS looks in the column defined as the parent key column, which is the attribute with the Usage property set to Parent, and if that column is blank, contains the same value as the dimension's key attribute column, or is not also found in the dimension's key attribute column on another row, the member is flagged as a parent member at the top level of the hierarchy. In other words, the member displays as the first level of members below the All member.

  - **ParentIsBlank**   You use this setting when you want SSAS to consider a member as a parent only when the parent attribute column is blank.

  - **ParentIsSelf**   You use this setting when you want SSAS to define a parent only when the parent attribute column matches the value in the key attribute column.

- **ParentIsMissing**   You use this setting when SSAS should identify a parent based on a parent attribute column value is not found anywhere in the table in the key attribute column.

- **UnaryOperatorColumn**   This property is used only for special design scenarios, such as a financial account dimension in which you need to change the default rollup behavior. Although many data warehouse developers opt to use positive and negative values in a financial fact table to manage rollup behavior for account balances, another less commonly used option is to include a column in the financial account dimension to contain operators that define this behavior. For example, when you want to compute a parent account member's aggregate value, such as Income (Loss), you typically want to subtract one of its children, Expenses, from another of its children, Revenue. That is, Income (Loss) equals Revenue minus Expenses. You must include a value, such as a plus or minus symbol, in a column in your dimension table, and then map that column to the UnaryOperatorColumn property to define the rollup behavior.

NOTE **EXAMPLES OF USING PROPERTIES SPECIFIC TO PARENT ATTRIBUTES**

"Defining Parent Attribute Properties in a Parent-Child Hierarchy" at *https://msdn.microsoft. com/en-us/library/ms167115.aspx* explains how to set some of these properties and demonstrates the effect of making changes to these attribute properties.

You can see a description of the unary operators in the article "Unary Operators in Parent-Child Dimensions" at *https://msdn.microsoft.com/en-us/library/ms175417.aspx*. Jose Chinchilla provides a good example of using this property in his blog post "Using Unary Operators to control Analysis Services hierarchy aggregations" at *https://sqljoe. wordpress.com/2011/09/23/using-unary-operators-to-control-analysis-services-hierarchy-aggregations/*.

Roleplaying dimension model

A roleplaying dimension is one for which you define one dimension in the project, but use that dimension multiple times with the same fact table. In the WideWorldImportersDW database, you can see two examples of a roleplaying dimension—Customer and Date. Specifically, the Sale fact table has two foreign key relationships to the Customer table and two foreign key relationships to the Date table, as shown in Figure 1-29.

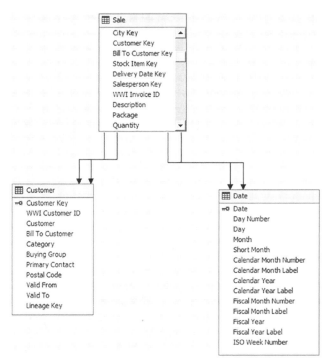

FIGURE 1-29 Roleplaying dimensions in the WideWorldImportersDW database

When multiple foreign key relationships exist between a fact table and a dimension table, each relationship has a different business meaning or role. For the Customer dimension, the CustomerKey column in the Sale table represents the customer to whom the sale was made, whereas the BillToCustomerKey column represents the customer who is responsible for paying the invoice. For the Date dimension, the InvoiceDateKey column in the Sale table reflects the date of the sale while the DeliveryDateKey is the date the stock item was delivered to the customer.

First, add the Customer and Date dimensions to the project by following the steps described in the "Develop dimension" section earlier in this chapter and then perform the following steps:

1. Configure each dimension and its attributes by using the settings shown in Table 1-1.

> **NOTE** **COMPOSITE KEY ASSIGNMENT IN THE DIMENSION DESIGNER**
>
> To configure two columns for the KeyColumn property of the Calendar Month Label attribute in the dimension designer, select Calendar Month Label in the Attributes pane, click the KeyColumns box in the Properties window, and then click the ellipsis button. In the Key Columns dialog box, click Calendar Month Label in the Key Columns list, click the < button. Next, click Calendar Year in the Available Columns List, click the > button, select Calendar Month Number in the Available Columns list, click the > button, and click OK.

TABLE 1-1 New dimensions for roleplaying

Dimension	Attribute to add	Attribute property	Attribute Property Value
Customer	Customer Key	Name	Customer
		KeyColumn	Customer Key
		NameColumn	Customer
	Category	KeyColumn	Category
	Buying Group	KeyColumn	Buying Group
Date	Date	KeyColumn	Date
	Calendar Month Label	Name	Calendar Month
		KeyColumn	Calendar Year Calendar Month Number
		NameColumn	Calendar Month Label
	Calendar Year Label	Name	Calendar Year
		KeyColumn	Calendar Year Label
	ISO Week Number	KeyColumn	ISO Week Number

2. Next, add the Customer and Date dimensions to the cube. Double-click the Wide World Importers DW.cube, and then, on the Cube Structure page, right-click the white space in the Dimensions pane, and select Add Cube Dimension. While pressing the CTRL key, select Customer and Date, and then click OK.

    Notice that although you selected two new dimensions to add to the cube, there are four new dimensions: Customer, Bill To Customer, Delivery Date, and Invoice Date. The cube designer detected the roleplaying characteristics of the Customer and Date dimensions based on the relationships defined in the DSV. If you check the relationship definitions on the Dimension Usage tab, you can see that the granularity attributes for each new dimension is correctly matched to a separate column in the measure group table.

> **NOTE DATABASE DIMENSIONS VERSUS CUBE DIMENSIONS**
>
> When you have a roleplaying dimension, there is only one .dim file in the project, known as a *database dimension*, but you have multiple dimensions in the cube, which are known as *cube dimensions*.

3. After you deploy the project to update the server with the changes (and click Yes to confirm overwriting the database if necessary), open the Browser tab in the cube designer.

4. Click Reconnect, the third button from the left on the cube designer toolbar, to restore the connection to the SSAS server after deployment.

NOTE **RECONNECTING TO SSAS SERVER**

Whenever you process the database, whether by initiating the operation from SSDT or by launching the operation in SSMS or SSIS, all client connections are disconnected. It does no harm to click the Reconnect button if you are already connected, but it is a required step after processing. Therefore, you should develop the habit of using the Reconnect button when you open the Browser tab of the cube designer to ensure your connection is active.

5. Expand the Measures node and Sale folder, and then drag Sale Count to the query window.
6. Then expand Customer and drag Customer.Customer to the query window to view sale counts by individual customers, as shown in Figure 1-30.

Customer	Sale Count
Tailspin Toys (Absecon, NJ)	319
Tailspin Toys (Aceitunas, PR)	344
Tailspin Toys (Airport Drive, MO)	404
Tailspin Toys (Alstead, NH)	315
Tailspin Toys (Amanda Park, WA)	349
Tailspin Toys (Andrix, CO)	356
Tailspin Toys (Annamoriah, WV)	365
Tailspin Toys (Antares, AZ)	369
Tailspin Toys (Antonito, CO)	357
Tailspin Toys (Arbor Vitae, WI)	344
Tailspin Toys (Arietta, NY)	390
Tailspin Toys (Armstrong Creek, WI)	380
Tailspin Toys (Arrow Rock, MO)	377
Tailspin Toys (Ashtabula, OH)	387
Tailspin Toys (Aspen Park, CO)	335
Tailspin Toys (Astor Park, FL)	356
Tailspin Toys (Avenal, CA)	380
Tailspin Toys (Baraboo, WI)	303
Tailspin Toys (Batson, TX)	386

FIGURE 1-30 Query results showing sales counts by customer on the Browser page of the cube designer

7. You can then change the query to test the Bill To Customer roleplaying dimension. Drag the Customer column from the query window to the left side of the screen.

8. Then expand Bill To Customer and drag Bill To Customer.Customer to the query window to view sale counts by Bill To Customer, as shown in Figure 1-31. Notice that each roleplaying cube dimension based on the Customer dimension has the same set of attributes: Buying Group, Category, and Customer. The difference in queries is a result of the join to a different column in the measure group table.

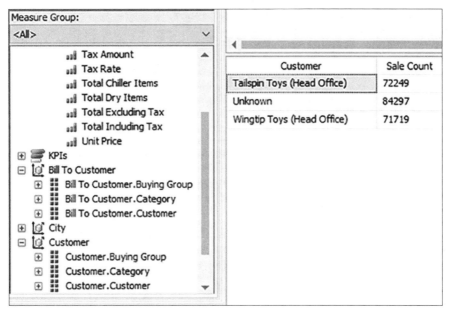

FIGURE 1-31 Metadata pane and query window on the Browser page of the cube designer showing sale counts by Bill To Customer

Reference dimension model

A reference dimension model is useful when you want to analyze measures by a dimension for which a relationship does not exist directly in the fact table. Instead, the fact table has a relationship with another dimension, which also has a relationship with the reference dimension. As an example, we need to consider how to model the multidimensional database if the WideWorldImportersDW database were missing the roleplaying dimension for Bill To Customer, and instead were to have a separate dimension table to reference it. Figure 1-32 shows a hypothetical structure in the sample database if it were designed to use a reference dimension for the Bill To Customer rather than include its relationship directly.

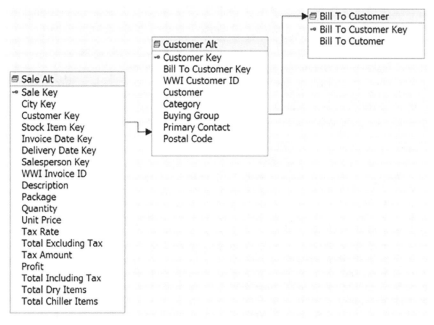

FIGURE 1-32 Source tables for a reference dimension model

You can simulate this structure in the project by creating a second DSV and then creating a cube based on the new DSV by following these steps:

1. Right-click the Data Source Views folder, select New Data Source View, click Next, select the Wide World Importers DW data source, click Next twice, type **WWI DW Alt** in the Name box, and click Finish.

2. Right-click the DSV window, select New Named Query, type **Sale Alt** in the Name box, and then replace the SELECT statement with the statement in Listing 1-2.

LISTING 1-2 Named query statement to remove Bill To Customer Key from the Sale table

```
SELECT
    [Sale Key],
    [City Key],
    [Customer Key],
    [Stock Item Key],
    [Invoice Date Key],
    [Delivery Date Key],
    [Salesperson Key],
    [WWI Invoice ID],
    [Description],
    [Package],
    [Quantity],
    [Unit Price],
    [Tax Rate],
    [Total Excluding Tax],
    [Tax Amount],
```

```
        [Profit],
        [Total Including Tax],
        [Total Dry Items],
        [Total Chiller Items]
FROM [Fact].[Sale];
```

3. Right-click again in the DSV, select New Named Query, type **Customer Alt** in the Name box, and then replace the SELECT statement with the statement in Listing 1-3.

LISTING 1-3 Named query statement to add Bill To Customer Key to the Customer table

```
SELECT
    c1.[Customer Key],
    c2.[Customer Key] as [Bill To Customer Key],
    c1.[WWI Customer ID],
    c1.Customer,
    c1.Category,
    c1.[Buying Group]
FROM [WideWorldImportersDW].[Dimension].[Customer] c1
LEFT OUTER JOIN [WideWorldImportersDW].[Dimension].[Customer] c2
    ON c1.[Bill To Customer] = c2.[Customer];
```

4. Right-click once more in the DSV, select New Named Query, type **Bill To Customer** in the Name box, and then replace the SELECT statement with the statement in Listing 1-4.

LISTING 1-4 Named query statement to create Bill To Customer

```
SELECT
    [Customer Key] AS [Bill To Customer Key],
    [Customer] AS [Bill To Customer]
FROM [Dimension].[Customer]
WHERE
    [Customer Key] in (1, 202);
```

5. Next, define logical primary keys for each named query. To this, right-click Sale Key in the Sale Alt named query and select Set Logical Primary Key. Repeat this step for the Customer Key in the Customer Alt named query and the Bill To Customer Key in the Bill To Customer named query.

6. Then create a relationship between Sale Alt and Customer Alt by selecting Customer Key in Sale Alt and dragging it to Customer Key in Customer Alt. Repeat this process to create relationship between Bill To Customer Key in the Customer Alt named query and Bill To Customer Key in the Bill To Customer named query.

7. Add the two dimensions to the project by following the steps described in the "Develop dimension" section earlier in this chapter using the settings shown in Table 1-2. Be sure to change the DSV in the Dimension Wizard to WWI DW Alt. When you create the Customer Alt dimension, do not clear the Bill To Customer check box on the Select Related Tables page, and do not clear the Bill To Customer Key check box on the Select Dimension Attributes page of the wizard.

TABLE 1-2 New dimensions for a reference dimensional mode

Dimension	Attribute to add	Attribute property	Attribute Property Value
Customer Alt	Customer Key	Name	Customer
		KeyColumn	Customer Key
		NameColumn	Customer
	Category	KeyColumn	Category
	Buying Group	KeyColumn	Buying Group
	Bill To Customer Key	AttributeHierarchyVisible	False
Bill To Customer	Customer Key	Name	Bill To Customer
		KeyColumn	Bill To Customer Key
		NameColumn	Bill To Customer

8. Next create a cube based on the new DSV. Right-click the Cubes folder, select New
   Cube, click Next twice, select WWI DW Alt in the Data Source View drop-down list,
   select the Sale Alt check box, click Next, clear the Measure check box, select Sale Alt
   Count, click Next twice, clear the Sale Alt check box on the Select New Dimensions
   page, click Next, type **Reference Dimension Cube** in the Cube Name box, and click
   Finish.

   Although the Bill To Customer dimension was listed on the Select Existing Dimensions,
   because it is in the same DSV as the Sale Alt measure group, it is not added as a cube
   dimension automatically. No direct relationship exists between the Sale Alt and Bill To
   Customer named queries in the DSV. Nonetheless, you can add the dimension to the
   cube manually as a reference dimension.

9. Right-click inside the Dimensions pane on the Cube Structure page of the cube designer, select Add Cube Dimensions, select Bill To Customer, and click OK.

10. Click the Dimension Usage tab, click the cell intersection between the Bill To Customer
    dimension and the Sale Alt measure group, click the ellipsis button that appears, select
    Referenced in the Select Relationship Type drop-down list, select Customer Alt in the
    Intermediate Dimension drop-down list, select Bill To Customer in the Reference Di-
    mension Attribute drop-down list, and select Bill To Customer Key in the Intermediate
    Dimension Attribute drop-down list, as shown in Figure 1-33. Click OK.

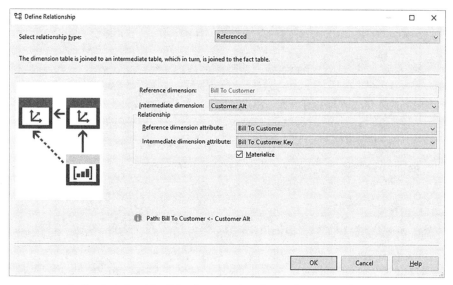

FIGURE 1-33 Define Relationship dialog box showing the configuration of a referenced relationship

---

NOTE **REFERENCE DIMENSION MATERIALIZATION**

When you use a reference dimension model, you can experience performance issues during processing or querying, depending on whether you materialize the dimension. If you select the Materialize check box in the Define Relationship dialog box, processing time of the measure group increases, but the query performance is better. If you clear the Materialize check box, the processing time is lower, but there is a performance penalty at query time.

---

11. Deploy the project by right-clicking the project in Solution Explorer, and selecting Deploy.

12. Click the Browser tab in the cube designer, expand Measures, expand the Sale Alt folder, and drag Sale Alt Count to the query window. Then expand Bill To Customer, and drag Bill To Customer to the query window, as shown in Figure 1-34.

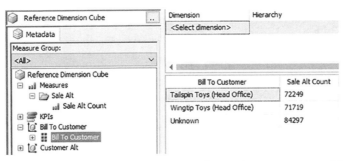

FIGURE 1-34 Metadata pane and query window on the Browser page of the cube designer showing sale counts by Bill To Customer

NOTE   **REFERENCE MODEL CONSIDERATIONS**

Ideally, when you are in control of the dimensional modeling of the source tables, you include a foreign key column for each dimension and do not rely on an intermediate table as you do with the reference dimension model. An alternate approach is to consolidate the data into a single denormalized table. Because of the potential for performance degradation during processing or querying, a reference dimension model implementation is not recommended as a best practice.

For some additional background information about whether to materialize a reference dimension, see "SSAS: Reference materialized dimension might produce incorrect results" by Alberto Ferrari at *http://sqlblog.com/blogs/alberto_ferrari/archive/2009/02/25/ssas-reference-materialized-dimension-might-produce-incorrect-results.aspx*.

Data mining dimension model

You can take advantage of the data mining engine built into SSAS to build a new dimension by which you can analyze data. A common implementation approach is to use the clustering algorithm to use demographic and other data to group customers into clusters and then add the clusters as a dimension to your cube where you can slice and dice your data by clusters.

The source data in WideWorldImportersDW does not lend itself well to clustering or any other data mining algorithm available in SSAS. Nonetheless, you can perform the following steps to understand the mechanics of implementing a data mining model in a multidimensional database:

1.   Your first step is to set up a data mining model in your project by right-clicking the Mining Structures folder in Solution Explorer and selecting New Mining Structure.

2.   Click Next in the Data Mining Wizard, select From Existing Cube, and click Next. Select Microsoft Clustering in the Which Data Mining Technique Do You Want To Use drop-down list, and then click Next.

3. On the Select The Source Cube Dimension page, select Customer, and then click Next.

4. On the Select The Case Key page, select Customer. Click Next.

5. On the Select Case Level Columns page, select Profit, Quantity, and Sale Count. Click Next.

   The case level identifies the granularity of the data mining structure. In other words, it identifies the level of detail to data mine. In this example, a case is a unique customer.

6. On the Specify Mining Model Column Usage page, select the check box for Profit in the Predictable column, as shown in Figure 1-35.

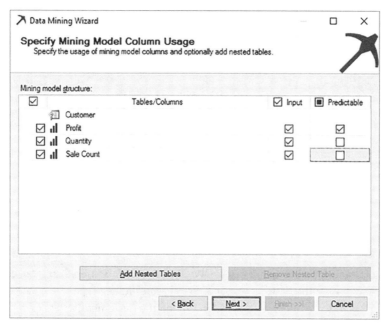

FIGURE 1-35 Specify Mining Model Column Usage page of the Data Mining Wizard

7. Click Next four times to complete the wizard.

> **NOTE DATA MINING WIZARD**
>
> You can find a starting point for learning more about this wizard in "Data Mining Wizard (Analysis Services – Data Mining) at *https://msdn.microsoft.com/en-us/library/ms175645.aspx.*

8. On the Completing The Wizard page, keep the Create Mining Model Dimension check box selected, type **Customer Clusters** in the text box to the right of this check box, select the Create Cube Using Mining Model Dimension, as shown in Figure 1-36, and then click Finish.

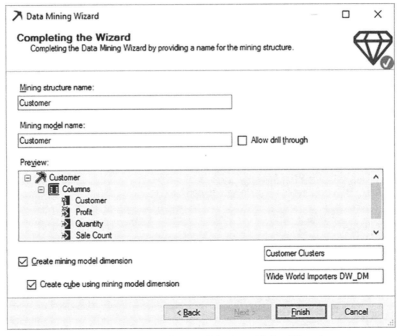

FIGURE 1-36 Completing The Wizard page of the Data Mining Wizard

9. Right-click the project in Solution Explorer, and select Deploy to deploy the updates to the SSAS server and process.

10. Double-click the Wide World Importers DW_DM.cube file in Solution Explorer, click the Browser tab in the cube designer, expand the Measures folder, expand the Sale folder, and drag Profit to the query window. Then expand the Customer Clusters folder and then drag MiningDimensionContentNodes to the query window to view the break-down of sales by cluster. When you use more realistic data than WideWorldImport-ersDW, more clusters are likely to be available for analysis.

> **NOTE DATA MINING MODEL VIEWER**
>
> To view the characteristics of each cluster, double-click the Customer.dmm file in Solu-tion Explorer and click the Mining Model Viewer tab. Here you can switch between the Cluster Diagram, Cluster Profiles, Cluster Characteristics, and Cluster Discrimination tabs to explore visualizations, statistics, and other information about the clusters created by the data mining algorithm. You are not tested on the use of the data mining model viewer on the exam, but you can learn more about using it in "Browse a Model Using the Microsoft Cluster Viewer" at *https://msdn.microsoft.com/en-us/library/ms174801.aspx*.

Many-to-many dimension model

The use of a many-to-many dimensional model is necessary when you need to support a more complex type of analysis than we have explored to this point. Traditional analysis is a one-to-many model in which one dimension member can be associated with many fact rows. Put another way, a single fact row is associated with one member in a related dimension. In a many-to-many relationship, a single fact row can be associated with many dimension members.

This type of modeling is common in banking analysis in which a single bank account can be associated with multiple account holders, and therefore a transaction in a fact table has a many-to-many relationship with account holders. The medical industry also often requires many-to-many modeling. As an example, a patient can have multiple diagnoses, so an event such as a hospital stay can be associated with multiple members in a diagnosis dimension.

As a result of implementing this type of model, you can roll up aggregated values within a dimension by different members without overcounting values. Let's say in a simple cube you have a bank account with two account holders and the account has a $100 balance. If you query balances for all account holders, SSAS lists each account holder separately with the $100 balance, but the aggregate value for all account holders is $100. SSAS knows how to associate the fact rows individually to each dimension member, but also correctly computes the aggregate values for the dimension.

Before you can implement a many-to-many dimension model in SSAS, you need to structure your source tables or DSV appropriately. Nothing in the WideWorldImportersDW source tables lends itself to this type of modeling, so let's set up a simple scenario in which a new dimension contains sales reasons. Sales reasons describe why a customer made a purchase and are captured in a survey conducted at the time of the purchase. Any sale transaction can be associated with zero to many sales reasons. To model this scenario, you need to add a new Sales Reason dimension and a Sales Reason Bridge to associate sales transactions from the Sale table to the sales reasons in the new dimension, as shown in Figure 1-37.

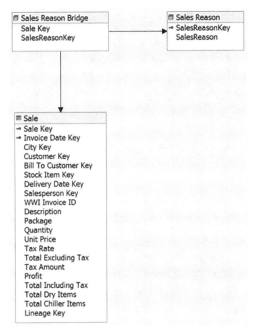

FIGURE 1-37 Source tables for a many-to-many dimension model

To set up this scenario in the current project, perform the following steps:

1. Create a named query as a source for the Sales Reason dimension. To do this, double-click Wide World Importers DW.dsv in Solution Explorer to open the DSV designer.

2. In the diagram pane, right-click anywhere in the diagram pane, and select New Named Query.

3. In the Create Named Query dialog box, type **Sales Reason** in the Name box, replace the SELECT statement with the statement shown in Listing 1-5, and then click OK.

LISTING 1-5 Named query statement to create Sales Reason dimension

```
SELECT
    1 AS SalesReasonKey, 'Value' AS SalesReason
UNION
SELECT
    2 AS SalesReasonKey, 'Manufacturer' AS SalesReason
UNION
SELECT
    3 AS SalesReasonKey, 'Sales Person' AS SalesReason;
```

4. Right-click SalesReasonKey in the diagram, and select Select Logical Primary Key.

5. Now create a bridge table to define the relationship between the fact table and the new dimension. In the diagram pane of the DSV, right-click anywhere, and select New Named Query.

6. In the Create Named Query dialog box, type **Sales Reason Bridge** in the Name box, replace the SELECT statement with the statement shown in Listing 1-6, and then click OK.

LISTING 1-6 Named query statement to create Sales Reason fact bridge

```
SELECT
    CAST(1 AS bigint) AS [Sale Key],
    1 AS SalesReasonKey
UNION
SELECT
    CAST(1 AS bigint) AS [Sale Key],
    2 AS SalesReasonKey
UNION
SELECT
    CAST(1 AS bigint) AS [Sale Key],
    3 AS SalesReasonKey
UNION
SELECT
    CAST(2 AS bigint) AS [Sale Key],
    1 AS SalesReasonKey;
```

7. Select the Sale Key column in the Sales Reason Bridge table and drag it to the Sale key column in the Sale table to define a new relationship.

8. Repeat the previous step to create a relationship between SalesReasonKey in the Sales Reason Bridge table and the SalesReasonKey column in the Sales Reason table.

9. Create the Sales Reason dimension in the project by following the steps described in the "Develop dimension" section earlier in this chapter, using Sales Reason as the Main Table and setting Sales Reason Key as the Key Column and Sales Reason as the Name Column. Click Next twice, and click Finish.

10. Rename the Sales Reason Key attribute to Sales Reason.

11. Double-click Wide World Importers DW.cube in Solution Explorer to open the cube designer.

12. Right-click in the Dimension pane on the Cube Structure page, select Add Cube Dimension, select Sales Reason, and click OK.

13. Right-click the Measures pane, select New Measure Group, and select Sales Reason Bridge to add the bridge table to the cube.

14. Expand the Sales Reason Bridge folder in the Measures pane, select Sales Reason Bridge Count, and then, in Properties window, select False in the Visible drop-down list.

15. Open the Dimension Usage page of the cube designer. Notice the Invoice and Sales Reason dimensions have a regular relationship with the Sales Reason Bridge measure group.

16. To set up the many-to-many relationship, click the intersection between Sales Reason and Sale, click the ellipsis button, select Many-To-Many in the Select Relationship Type drop-down list, select Sales Reason Bridge in the Intermediate Measure Group drop-down list, as shown in Figure 1-38, and click OK.

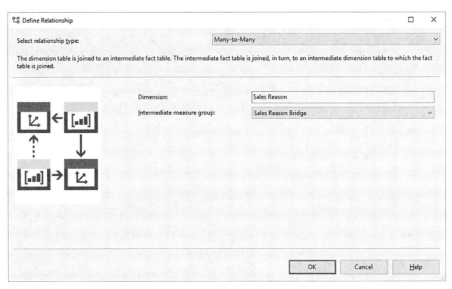

FIGURE 1-38 Define Relationship dialog box showing the configuration of a many-to-many relationship

17. Deploy the project, and then open the Browser page of the cube designer, click Reconnect in the toolbar.

18. On the Cube menu, select Analyze In Excel. Click Enable in the Microsoft Security Notice message box.

19. In the PivotTable Fields list, drag the Invoices check box to the Filters pane below the list.

20. In the pivot table, open the drop-down list, select the Select Multiple Items check box, clear the All check box, expand All, and select the 1 and 2 check boxes.

21. In the PivotTable Fields list, select the Sale Count check box, and notice the pivot table displays a total of 3.

22. In the PivotTable Fields list, select the Invoice check box and notice there are two invoices, 1 and 2. Invoice 1 has a sale count of 1 and Invoice 2 has a sale count of 2.

23. Now select Sales Reason in the PivotTable Fields list. A second level is added to the pivot table in which there are three sales reasons for Invoice 1, each with a sale count of 1: Value, Manufacturer, and Sales Person. Invoice 2 has one sales reason, Value, with a sale count of 1. Notice the total remains 3 in spite of the four instances of sales reasons in the pivot table having a sale count of 1. The sale counts are not overcounted even when a many-to-many relationship is present in the query's dimensions.

Slowly changing dimension model

As explained in the "Source table design" section in Skill 1.1, "Create a multidimensional database by using Microsoft SQL Server Analysis Services (SSAS)," there are two types of SCD tables that you can design and then add to your DSV—Type 1 for which you do not track historical changes, and Type 2 for which you track historical changes. When you use the Type 1 SCD design, you do not need to perform any additional tasks in the DSV or dimension design, although you should be aware of the effect of data changes during processing as explained in Chapter 4, which in turn can influence how you configure attribute relationships as described later in this skill. On the other hand, when you use the Type 2 SCD design, there are some specific tasks you should perform in the dimension design to support the ability to browse both the current version and the historical version of dimension attributes.

The first task is to ensure your Type 2 SCD table design includes columns to support slowly changing dimensions as described in Skill 1.1. That is, you must have a surrogate key, a business key, SCD history columns, and at least one attribute for which values change over time for which you want to preserve history.

The Stock Item table in the Wide World Importers DW DSV meets these criteria; so let's add it to the project as a slowly changing dimension by following the steps described in the "Develop dimension" section earlier in this chapter and then performing these steps:

1. In the Dimension Wizard, use Stock Item as the Main Table, set Stock Item Key as the Key Column, and set Stock Item as the Name Column.

2. In the Select Dimension Attributes page of the wizard, keep the Stock Item Key check box selected, and then select the WWI Stock Item ID check box to add the business key, the Color check box to add the SCD attribute, and the Size check box to add an unchanging attribute. Then click Next, and click Finish.

3. Your next set of tasks is to change properties for the surrogate key and business key attributes. First, rename the Stock Item Key as Stock Item History, and WWI Stock Item ID as Stock Item.

4. Next, set the NameColumn property for the business key. The NameColumn property is set automatically for the surrogate key by the wizard. In this case, you use the same column to define the Name Column property for the business key. To do this, select Stock Item (the renamed business key attribute) in the Attributes pane of the dimension designer, scroll down to locate the NameColumn property, click the box to the right of the property name, click the ellipsis button that displays, select Stock Item in the Name Column dialog box, and then click OK.

5. Last, add the dimension to a cube. In Solution Explorer, double-click Wide World Importers DW.cube, right-click inside the Dimensions pane on the Cube Structure page of the cube designer, select Add Cube Dimension, select Stock Item, and click OK. The dimension usage is set correctly by default with a regular relationship due to the relationship defined between the Sale fact table and the Stock Item dimension table, so no additional configuration is required.

6. There is no data in the World Wide Importers DW sales to properly illustrate the effect of SCD changes, so execute the statement shown in Listing 1-7 to add a new sale using the surrogate key for a current stock item.

LISTING 1-7 Insert a row into the sales fact table for a current stock item

```
INSERT INTO [Fact].[Sale]
  ([City Key],
   [Customer Key],
   [Bill To Customer Key],
   [Stock Item Key],
   [Invoice Date Key],
   [Delivery Date Key],
   [Salesperson Key],
   [WWI Invoice ID],
   [Description],
   [Package],
   [Quantity],
   [Unit Price],
   [Tax Rate],
   [Total Excluding Tax],
   [Tax Amount],
   [Profit],
   [Total Including Tax],
   [Total Dry Items],
   [Total Chiller Items],
   [Lineage Key])
VALUES
  (0,
   0,
   0,
   604,
   '2016-05-31',
   '2016-05-31',
   0,
   70511,
   'USB rocket launcher (Gray)',
   'Each',
   1000,
   25,
   15,
   25000,
   3750,
```

```
15500,
28750,
1000,
0,
11);
GO
```

7. Deploy the project to see how the SCD design affects query results. Right-click the project in Solution Explorer, select Deploy, and click Yes to overwrite the database on the server.

8. After deployment is complete, click the Browser page of the cube designer, and click the Reconnect button in the toolbar.

9. Now set up the query. Expand the Measures folder in the metadata pane, expand the Sale folder, and then drag Sale Count to the query window.

10. Next, expand Stock Item in the metadata tree. This top-level Stock Item node represents the dimension as indicated by the icon containing a cube and arrows pointing in three directions. Below this is another Stock Item node, which is an attribute as indicated by the set of blue squares arranged in a rectangular shape.

11. Drag the Stock Item attribute to the query window, and then drag the right edge of the column header to the right to widen the column for better visibility of each stock item's name, as shown in Figure 1-39. Notice that the current count for USB Rocket Launcher (Gray) is 1079.

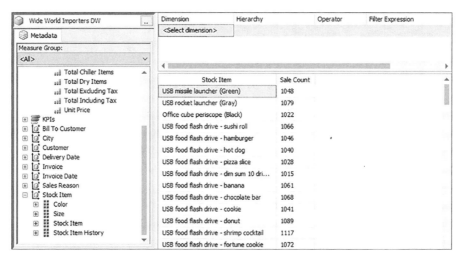

FIGURE 1-39 Metadata pane and query window on the Browser page of the cube designer showing sale counts by stock item

12. If you drag the Color attribute into the query window, you see the Sale Count is 1078 for the historical color Gray and 1 for the current color Steel Gray. The Stock Item attribute is an aggregate of all historical information, but you can also view the historical information for the changing attribute Color when you add it to the query.

13. Now drag the Stock Item column header from the query window to the left to remove it from the query, and then drag Stock Item History from the metadata pane to the query window. Drop it to the left of the Color column.

14. Next, filter the query to more easily locate the stock item in the previous query. To do this, select Stock Item in the Dimension drop-down list above the query window, and select Stock Item History in the Hierarchy drop-down list.

15. In the Operator drop-down list, select Begins With. In the Filter Expression box, type **USB rocket launcher** and press Enter. Then remove the Color column. Now you see two stock items with the same name, as shown in Figure 1-40, because these two dimension members have separate surrogate keys, and each surrogate key appears in one or more rows in the fact table.

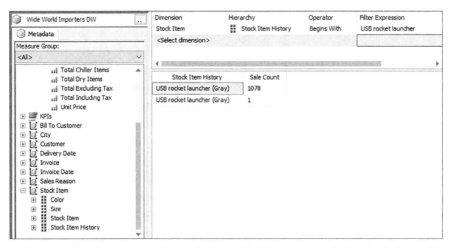

FIGURE 1-40 Metadata pane and query window on the Browser page of the cube designer showing sale counts by stock item history

When you include the Color attribute in the query, you can see that each Stock Item History member corresponds to a different color. However, when Color is not included in the query, the appearance of two separate rows in the query results is potentially confusing to business users. For this reason, a common design approach for modeling SCDs is to hide the attribute associated with the surrogate key so that business users cannot accidentally use it in a query when exploring the cube.

16. In this case, you can hide the Stock Item History attribute by returning to the Stock Item dimension designer, selecting Stock Item History in the Attributes pane, and changing the AttributeHierarchyVisible property in the Properties window to False.

17. After you deploy the project, you can reconnect to the cube on the Browser page of the cube designer and confirm that the Stock Item History attribute no longer appears in the metadata pane, as shown in Figure 1-41.

FIGURE 1-41 Metadata pane in the Browser page of the cube designer showing the Stock Item dimension's attributes after hiding the key attribute

Implement a dimension type

Each dimension has a Type property that is set by default to Regular. In general, when the property is not set to Regular, the Type setting instructs either the SSAS server, the client application, or both the server and client application how to perform certain types of calculations to alleviate the need to create complex calculated members, custom rollup formulas, or MDX scripts. Typically, you must also define a Type property for one or more attributes in the dimension to configure the desired behavior.

You can choose from the following Type values to define the applicable calculation behavior for a dimension:

- **Accounts** Sets specific server-side behaviors for aggregating financial accounts. When you use this dimension type, you must also configure an attribute's Type property as AccountType for the attribute containing members such as Assets, Liabilities, Revenue, and so on. SSAS uses the account type to determine whether to aggregate values for dates within a calendar or fiscal year for income statement accounts (such as revenue and expenses), or to compute point-in-time values for balance sheet accounts (such as assets and liabilities).

> **NOTE FINANCIAL ACCOUNT DIMENSION TYPE**
>
> There is no financial account data available in the WideWorldImportersDW database to help you explore working with the Accounts type, but you should be familiar with the concepts for the exam. You can learn more about working with this type of dimension by reading "Create a Finance account of parent-child type Dimension" at *https://technet.microsoft.com/en-us/library/ms174609(v=sql.130).aspx*.

- **BillOfMaterials (BOM)** Organizes a dimension by attributes that define how parts comprise a unit and requires you to define attributes such as organizational unit, BOM resource, and quantitative. A client application controls how this information drives dimension behavior.
- **Channel** Represents channel information and requires a client application to determine how this information is used.
- **Currency** Defines the currency conversion behavior for a dimension.

- **Customers** Organizes attributes for information about customers, such as name, address, demographic details, and more. You must use a client application that supports this dimension type to see behavior change.

- **Geography** Requires a client application to define dimension behavior, such as displaying aggregated data projected onto a geographic visualization. This dimension type contains attributes for geographical areas, such as postal code, city, or country.

- **Time** Sets the behavior for calculations that are dependent on time. By setting the Type property appropriately for each attribute, you identify the attributes containing years, quarters, months, days, and so on.

- **Organization** Defines a dimension containing attributes about subsidiary organizations, ownership percentages, and voting rights percentages. A client application controls how this information affects calculations or dimension behavior in an application.

- **Products** Organizes a dimension by attributes describing characteristics of parts, such as color, size, category, and so on. This dimension type requires a client application to use this information.

- **Promotion** Describes a dimension containing information about marketing promotions. This information is used only within a client application that supports this dimension type.

- **Quantitative** Requires a client application that can use attributes containing quantitative values.

- **Rates** Defines the dimension containing currency rate information that the SSAS server uses for currency conversions in conjunction with the Currency dimension type.

Refer to the additional resource recommended for the Currency dimension type to learn how to use this dimension type properly.

- **Scenario** Identifies a dimension containing attributes to define a scenario, such as budgeting or forecasting, and a version.

- **Utility** Flags a dimension for a purpose to be defined by a client application.

The most common implementation of a dimension type other than the default of Regular is to set a Date dimension as a Time dimension type. Let's add some additional attributes to this dimension and then explore the additional configuration required in the dimension to achieve the desired results.

To set the Type property of the Date dimension, double-click the Date.dim file in Solution Explorer, click the dimension name (the top level node) in the Attributes pane of the dimension designer, and then select Time in the Type drop-down list in the Properties window. You must also configure each attribute with the applicable type by selecting the attribute in the Attributes pane, and selecting the correct value, shown in Table 1-3, in the Type drop-down list. When you navigate through the list of values in the Type drop-down list, you must expand nodes within a type category to find the type you want. For example, you can expand Date, and then Calendar to find Months (shown in the table as Date/Calendar/Months), or expand ISO to find Iso8601WeekOfYear. In addition, change the Name property of each attribute if it is included in Table 1-3.

TABLE 1-3 Attribute configuration in the Date dimension

Attribute	Attribute property	Attribute Property Value
Calendar Month	Type	Date/Calendar/Months
Calendar Year	Type	Date/Calendar/Years
Date	Type	Date/Calendar/Date
ISO Week Number	Type	Date/ISO/Iso8601WeekOfYear

EXAM TIP

Each specific property setting requires different additional configuration settings and results in different behaviors. If the dimension type is used only by client applications, you must refer the application documentation to learn how to configure the dimension and its attributes properly. For this reason, the exam does not test your knowledge about those dimension types. However, you should know how to work with the Time, Account, Currency, and Rate dimension types.

Define attribute relationships

A best practice in multidimensional database development is the addition of user-defined hierarchies. A *user-defined hierarchy* (in which the user is you, as the developer, and not the business user who queries the cube) is a pre-defined navigation path for moving from summary to detail information. For example, you use a hierarchy to make it easier to view sales by year, then by month, and then by day, as shown in Figure 1-42.

1	Row Labels	▾	Sale Count
2	⊟CY2013		60968
3	⊟CY2013-Jan		5246
4	2013-01-01		89
5	2013-01-02		207
6	2013-01-03		215
7	2013-01-04		146
8	2013-01-05		114

FIGURE 1-42 Pivot table displaying sale counts by day, month, and year

Each level of a hierarchy corresponds to a separate attribute in the dimension. For example, in the hierarchy shown in Figure 1-42, the top level of the hierarchy is the Calendar Year attribute, the middle level is the Calendar Month attribute, and the bottom level is the Date attribute.

After creating a hierarchy, you might also need to define *attribute relationships* between each level in the hierarchy. Attribute relationships determine how SSAS calculates aggregate values within a cube and how it stores data on disk. For this reason, the presence or absence of attribute relationships potentially affects query performance.

Before you can work with attribute relationships, you must first create a hierarchy. To do this for the Date dimension, perform the following steps:

1. Open the dimension designer for Date, drag the Calendar Year attribute from the Attributes pane to the Hierarchies pane of the designer. When you drop it, a new hierarchy is created.

2. You can then add levels to the new hierarchy by dragging the Calendar Month attribute into the hierarchy object below the Calendar Year attribute, and then repeating this process with the Date attribute.

3. Right-click the Hierarchy caption for the new hierarchy in the Hierarchies pane, select Rename, and type **Calendar** to rename it.

   You can create as many hierarchies as you like. Technically speaking, you can create only 2,147,483,647 user-defined hierarchies, but you probably do not need that many!

4. For now, create another hierarchy renamed as ISO Calendar by using the Calendar Year, ISO Week Number, and Date attributes, as shown in Figure 1-43.

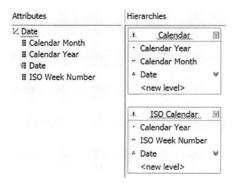

FIGURE 1-43 User-defined hierarchies in the Date dimension

Notice the warning icon and best practice warning indicated by the wavy underscore below each hierarchy name to indicate a potential problem. If you hover the cursor over each warning, the following message displays: "Attribute relationships do not exist between one or more levels of this hierarchy. This may result in decreased query performance." This is a very common warning.

Behind the scenes, SSAS sets up attribute relationships between the hierarchy levels and the key attribute where possible. To review the current definition for attribute relationships, click the Attribute Relationships tab in the dimension designer. As shown in Figure 1-44, the relationships between the key attribute, Date, and the attributes on the levels of each hierarchy are visible as arrows connecting Date to ISO Week Number, Calendar Year, and Calendar Month.

FIGURE 1-44 Attribute Relationships page of the dimension designer for the Date dimension

The hierarchy warnings on the Dimension Structure page displays because Calendar Year is part of both hierarchies, but does not connect directly to the attribute in the child level in either hierarchy. The dimension can process successfully in this state, but the warning message alerts you that there could be an adverse impact on query performance. With this database, the volume of data is too small for you to notice slow query performance. However, once you start working with fact tables having millions or billions of rows, the performance problem becomes more noticeable.

Before you decide whether you need to fix this particular warning, you must know what type of hierarchy you have created. A *natural hierarchy* is a hierarchy for which each attribute has a one-to-many relationship between dimension members on a parent level and dimension members on a child level, as shown in Figure 1-45. In the Date dimension, the Calendar hierarchy is a natural hierarchy because each Calendar Month member corresponds to one, and only one, member on the Calendar Year level.

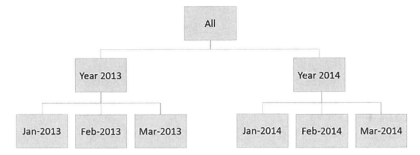

FIGURE 1-45 Natural hierarchy

NOTE **NATURAL HIERARCHY ATTRIBUTE RELATIONSHIPS BENEFIT QUERY PERFORMANCE**

The primary reason that natural hierarchy attribute relationships improve query performance is the materialization of hierarchical data on disk for faster retrieval. At query time, SSAS can navigate specific structures built for hierarchical data storage to find specific combinations, such as ISO Week Number 1 for CY2013, quickly rather than starting with a key attribute such as 2013-01-01 and working through the attribute structures to locate the related ISO Week Number and Calendar Year. Also, SSAS maintains indexes to know which combinations exist or not and thereby retrieve data more efficiently. For example, by scanning the index, SSAS knows that 2013-01-07 is not associated with ISO Week Number 1, and can eliminate the combination when constructing query results that require a cross join of Date and ISO Week Number values.

Admittedly, in a relatively small dimension such as Date, the difference in query performance with or without a natural hierarchy is negligible. However, in large dimensions, the existence of accurate attribute relationships has a measurable impact on performance.

Furthermore, when attribute relationships exist, SSAS can design and store aggregations that also contribute to faster queries. You learn how to work with aggregations to improve query performance in Chapter 4.

By contrast, an *unnatural hierarchy* is one for which there is the potential to have a many-to-many relationship between members on a parent and child levels. To create an unnatural hierarchy, open the Stock Item dimension designer and create a hierarchy named Color-Size with Color as the top level, and Size as the bottom level. Figure 1-46 illustrates the partial results of these attribute combinations in a hierarchy.

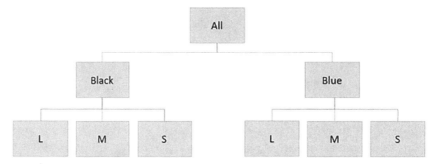

FIGURE 1-46 Unnatural hierarchy

You use an unnatural hierarchy to enable users to report on combinations of dimension members that are not hierarchical. That way, you can build into your multidimensional database the ability to produce the same result as a relational query that aggregates the quantity sold and group the aggregate value by two different, non-hierarchical columns, as shown in Listing 1-8.

LISTING 1-8 Retrieve aggregate results from a relational database by using a GROUP BY clause

```
USE WideWorldImportersDW;
GO
SELECT
    Color,
    Size,
    SUM(Quantity) AS QuantitySold
FROM Fact.Sale s
INNER JOIN Dimension.[Stock Item] si
    ON s.[Stock Item Key] = si.[Stock Item Key]
GROUP BY
    Color,
    Size;
```

If you review the attribute relationships of an unnatural hierarchy, as shown in Figure 1-47, you can see there is no arrow connecting the attributes of the hierarchy's level. Instead, each level's attribute relates back to the key attribute, Stock Item History. In the case of an unnatural hierarchy, this lack of attribute relationships between the hierarchy's attributes is appropriate.

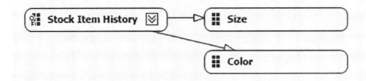

FIGURE 1-47 Attribute relationships for the Stock Item dimension

Whenever you see the warning about non-existent attribute relationships between hierarchy levels, you should evaluate whether the hierarchy is natural or unnatural. If it is natural, you must fix the attribute relationships, but you can ignore the warning if the hierarchy is unnatural. However, you should test whether the performance of queries using the unnatural hierarchy is acceptable. If it is not, consider modify the dimension structure to transform the unnatural hierarchy into a natural hierarchy.

Let's say that you want to optimize the natural hierarchies, Calendar and ISO Calendar, by fixing the attribute relationships. To do this, perform the following steps:

1. Open the Attribute Relationships page of the Date dimension designer. Then drag the ISO Week Number object in the diagram to the Calendar Year object and drag the Calendar Month object to the Calendar Year object to create the relationships shown in Figure 1-48.

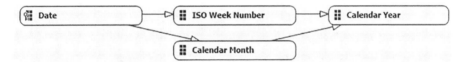

FIGURE 1-48 Corrected attribute relationships for the Date dimension

These adjustments clear the warnings from the Dimension Structure page of the dimension designer. However, a new problem is introduced because the data is not currently structured to support a natural hierarchy for ISO Calendar.

2. To see the results caused by this problem, deploy the project. Deployment fails due to the following warning that displays in the Output window: "Errors in the OLAP storage engine: A duplicate attribute key has been found when processing: Table: 'Dimension_Date', Column: 'ISO_x0020_Week_x0020_Number', Value: '15'. The attribute is 'ISO Week Number'."

3. The best way to see the problem with the duplicate attribute key is to process the Date dimension manually so that you can extract the SQL query that SSAS generates, and review the query results in SSMS. First, right-click Date.dim in Solution Explorer, select Process, select Process Full in the Process Options drop-down list if it is not already selected, and click Run.

4. In the Process Progress dialog box, expand Processing Dimension 'Date' Completed, expand Processing Dimension Attribute 'ISO Week Number' Completed, expand SQL Queries 1, click the SELECT statement, and click View Details to see the full query, as shown in Figure 1-49.

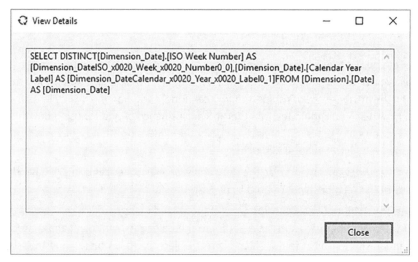

FIGURE 1-49 Processing query in the View Details dialog box

5. Highlight the entire SELECT statement, and press CTRL+C to copy the statement to the clipboard. Click Close three times to close all open dialog boxes.

6. Next, open SSMS, connect to the database engine hosting the WideWorldImporters-DW database, click the New Query button in the toolbar, select WideWorldImporters-DW in the Available Databases drop-down list in the toolbar, paste the statement into the Query window. Modify the query to add an ORDER BY clause as shown in Listing 1-9, and click Execute.

LISTING 1-9 Review results of query generated by SSAS for populating the ISO Week Number attribute

```
SELECT
DISTINCT
[Dimension_Date].[ISO Week Number] AS
    [Dimension_DateISO_x0020_Week_x0020_Number0_0],
[Dimension_Date].[Calendar Year Label] AS
    [Dimension_DateCalendar_x0020_Year_x0020_Label0_1]
FROM [Dimension].[Date] AS [Dimension_Date]
ORDER BY [Dimension_Date].[ISO Week Number];
```

As you can see by the partial results shown in Figure 1-50, each ISO Week Number value in the first column corresponds to four different Calendar Year values in the second column. Because of the attribute relationship that exists between ISO Week Number and Calendar

Year, there can be only one Calendar Year parent member for each ISO Week Number child member. Otherwise, dimension processing fails.

	Dimension_DateISO_x0020_Week_x0020_Number0_0	Dimension_DateCalendar_x0020_Year_x0020_Label0_1
1	1	CY2013
2	1	CY2014
3	1	CY2015
4	1	CY2016
5	2	CY2013
6	2	CY2014
7	2	CY2015
8	2	CY2016

FIGURE 1-50 Results of query that populates the ISO Week Number attribute

An easy way to fix this problem is to modify the key column for the ISO Week Number attribute to create a unique value for each ISO Week Number-Calendar Year combination. To do this, perform the following steps:

1. Open the Dimension Structure tab of the dimension designer, select ISO Week Number in the Attributes pane, click the KeyColumns box in the Properties window, and then click the ellipsis button.

2. In the Key Columns dialog box, click Calendar Year in the Available Columns List, click the > button, select Calendar Year in the Key Columns list, click the Up button to place Calendar Year ahead of ISO Week Number in the list, and click OK.

3. Next, click the NameColumn box in the Properties window, click the ellipsis button, select ISO Week Number, and click OK.

4. Last, deploy the project to update the multidimensional database on the server with your changes.

> **IMPORTANT   CHANGING A DIMENSION IMPACTS MINING STRUCTURES**
>
> If you created the Customer mining structure in the "Data mining dimension model" section earlier in this chapter, the change to the ISO Week Number key columns invalidates the Customer mining structure. Because you no longer use this mining structure and the related dimension and cube in the project used in this chapter, you can safely delete these three files. Right-click Wide World Importers DW_DM.cube in Solution Explorer, select Delete, and click OK to confirm. Repeat these steps to remove Customer Clusters.dim and Customer.dmm from the project. You can then successfully deploy the project to update the Date dimension on the server.

Like attributes, attribute relationships have properties. You can select an arrow in the diagram or select a relationship in the Attribute Relationships pane to view the following properties in the Properties window.

- **RelationshipType** Determines how SSAS manages changes to the key column for a related attribute. The default value is Flexible, which allows changes to occur without requiring you to perform a full process of the dimension. (The implications of relationship types on dimension processing is described more fully in Chapter 4.) For example, if you expect Color to change frequently for a stock item, you can set the relationship between Stock Item History and Color to Flexible.

  Your other option is to set this property to Rigid. In that case, any change in the relationship between an attribute and a related attribute requires you to fully process the dimension. You use this option when you expect the relationships between attributes rarely or never to change, such as the assignment of a date to a month, or when you expect values to rarely change. The date 2013-01-01 always remains a child of CY2013-Jan and never gets reassigned to CY2013.

- **Attribute** Specifies the attribute on which the attribute relationship is based. In other words, this property defines the parent attribute in the relationship.

- **Cardinality** Describes the relationship has a many-to-one or one-to-one relationship between the child attribute and the parent attribute. The default is Many to indicate a many-to-one relationship, such as exists between Date and Calendar Month in which there are many dates related to a single month. This is the most common scenario that you find in attribute relationships.

  You change the value to One when you want to specify a one-to-one relationship. For example, if you had an attribute for telephone number in the Customer dimension, you would define the relationship between that attribute and the Customer attribute by setting the Cardinality property to one.

- **Name** Provides a unique name for the relationship. This value defaults to the name of the parent attribute.

- **Visible** Determines whether a client application can access the parent attribute as a member property in an MDX query. Working with member properties is described in more detail in Chapter 3.

> **NEED MORE REVIEW?** **ATTRIBUTE RELATIONSHIPS AND PERFORMANCE TUNING**
>
> Although written for SQL Server 2012 and 2014, you can find performance tuning recommendations related to attribute relationships in "Analysis Services MOLAP Performance Guide for SQL Server 2012 and 2014" by Karan Gulati and John Burchel. This whitepaper is available for download at *https://msdn.microsoft.com/en-us/library/dn749781.aspx*. The architectural changes to the multidimensional database engine in SQL Server 2016 do not change the recommendations in this whitepaper for attribute relationships.

Skill 1.3: Implement measures and measure groups in a cube

Often you continue adding measures and measure groups to a cube after using the Cube Wizard because it is easier to develop and test a cube incrementally rather than trying to add everything at once in the wizard. Another post-wizard task is to configure various properties for measures and measure groups in your cube to control behavior. Among other reasons, you can use properties to control how values aggregate from detail to summary levels or to apply a format string for better legibility.

> **This section covers how to:**
> - Design and implement measures, measure groups, granularity, calculated measures, and aggregate functions.
> - Define semi-additive behavior.

Design and implement measures, measure groups, granularity, calculated measures, and aggregate functions

The cube designer provides a lot of functionality for developing your cube beyond the basic configuration defined by using the Cube Wizard. You can use it to add new measures and configure properties for those measures in addition to bringing in multiple measures in a bulk for a new measure group. You can also use it to adjust the granularity of relationships between measure groups and dimensions. Not only can you define measures from which values are retrieved from a source fact table, but you can also define *calculated measures*, which are measures derived by defining expressions that operate on fact-sourced measures. Last, an important step in cube development is ensuring that SSAS applies the appropriate aggregate function to each measure, which you also configure in the cube designer.

Measures

The "Develop a cube" section of Skill 1.1 described how to add measures to a cube in bulk by using the Cube Wizard. You can also add measures manually to an existing cube or change properties for measures by using the cube designer.

To add a new measure to an existing cube, perform the following steps:

1. Double-click the Wide World Importers DW.cube file in Solution Explorer, right-click the Sale measure group in the Measures pane on the Cube Structure page of the cube designer, and select New Measure.

    In the current cube, all numeric columns that represent measures already exist in the cube, but if you had omitted a measure based on one of these columns when using the Cube Wizard, you could select it in the Source Columns list in the New Measure dialog box, and add it to your cube.

2. Another option is to create a distinct count measure based on a key column in the fact table. For example, let's say that you want to include the ability to show the distinct count of stock items sold to each customer or sold on a given day. To do this, select the Show All Columns check box in the New Measure dialog box, select Distinct Count in the Usage drop-down list, select Stock Item Key in the Source Column list, as shown in Figure 1-51, and click OK.

FIGURE 1-51 Selection of a measure in the New Measure dialog box

Rather than appearing in the Sales measure group, Stock Item Key Distinct Count appears in a newly added measure group named Sale 1 because distinct count measures are managed differently from other measures by SSAS. Because the calculation of a distinct count value at query time is expensive for SSAS to perform, SSAS places each distinct count measure into its own measure group. You can rename the measure group by right-clicking it and typing a new name.

After you create a measure, or after adding several measures by using the Cube Wizard, you should review measure properties to ensure that each measure behaves as expected when business users browse the cube. You can review a measure's properties by selecting the measure in the Measures pane of the cube designer, and then scrolling through the Properties window. Each measure has the following set of properties that you can configure:

- **AggregateFunction** Determines how SSAS aggregates detail rows from the fact table to summary values. The most commonly used AggregateFunction property is Sum. The other AggregateFunction values are explained later in this section.

- **DataType** Inherits from the data type for the measure column in the source fact table.

- **DisplayFolder** Specifies the folder in which to display the measure in the client application. You type in the name of a new folder or select the name of an existing folder in the property's drop-down list. Using a display folder is helpful for logically organizing measures when the measure group contains a lot of measures.

- **MeasureExpression** Defines an MDX expression that resolves the value for a measure at the leaf level before aggregation. A common reason to implement a measure expression is to multiply a sales value by an exchange rate prior to summing up the sales values.

- **Visible** Determines whether the client application displays the measure. If you change this property to False, you can still reference the measure in MDX expressions, which is useful when the base measure is not required for analysis.

- **Description** Allows you to provide additional information about a measure for display in a client application.

- **FormatString** You can select a format string from a list of possible formats, such as Percent or Currency, or type in a user-defined format, such as #,# to display an integer value with a thousands separator. You can use any valid Microsoft Visual Basic custom format for numeric values as a format string.

- **Name** Provides a name for display in client applications or for reference in MDX expressions.

- **Source** Binds the measure to a specific table and column in the DSV.

Currently, when you browse the cube, the default properties for each measure are in effect. If you browse the cube in the cube designer, you cannot see formatting. Although no formatting is set yet, you can set up a baseline query by using Excel to browse the cube. To do this, perform the following steps:

1. Open the Browser tab of the cube designer, and then select Analyze In Excel on the Cube menu.

2. Click Enable in the Microsoft Security Notice message box.

3. Next, in the PivotTable Fields list, select the following measures: Profit, Quantity, Sale Count, Tax Rate, Total Excluding Tax, and Unit Price. Scroll down in the PivotTable Fields List to locate and select the Buying Group check box in the Customer dimension.

   The results of these selections display in a pivot table, as shown in Figure 1-52. Notice none of these values are formatted for better legibility and currently you can sum the values in each row of a column to produce the Grand Total value in the bottom row.

FIGURE 1-52 A pivot table that displays unformatted measures

The three most common changes that are necessary to produce desired results in a cube are to change the AggregateFunction, FormatString, and Name properties of a measure. The AggregateFunction property affects the totals that appear for dimension members in the query as well as the grand total. The FormatString property makes it easier to view the individual values in the query results, whereas the Name property should be a user-friendly name that clearly communicates what the value represents using terms that business users recognize.

To observe the effect of changing the properties of these measures, return to the Cube Structure page of the cube designer, and update the property values as shown for each measure listed in Table 1-4.

TABLE 1-4 New property values for selected measures

Measure	Property Name	Property Value
Quantity	FormatString	#,#
Unit Price	AggregateFunction	None
	FormatString	Currency
Tax Rate	AggregateFunction	None
Total Excluding Tax	FormatString	Currency
	Name	Sales Amount Without Tax
Tax Amount	FormatString	Currency
Profit	FormatString	Currency
Total Including Tax	FormatString	Currency
	Name	Sales Amount With Tax
Total Dry Items	FormatString	#,#
	Name	Dry Item Count
Total Chiller Items	FormatString	#,#
	Name	Chiller Item Count
Sale Count	FormatString	#,#
Stock Item Key Distinct Count	FormatString	#,#
	Name	Stock Item Distinct Count

Deploy the project, and then switch to Excel. On the PivotTable Analyze tab of the ribbon, click Refresh to update the pivot table with the cube changes. Notice the new formatting of some measures, the missing values for other measures, and missing measures, as shown in Figure 1-53.

	A	B	C	D	E	F
1	Row Labels ▼	Profit	Quantity	Sale Count	Tax Rate	Unit Price
2	N/A	$31,676,352.75	3,284,017	84,298		
3	Tailspin Toys	$27,125,589.10	2,847,550	72,249		
4	Wingtip Toys	$26,942,739.05	2,820,061	71,719		
5	Grand Total	$85,744,680.90	8,951,628	228,266		

FIGURE 1-53 A pivot table that displays formatted measures

Each measure that you renamed no longer appears in the pivot table and must be added back again manually. Add Sales Amount With Tax and Sales Amount Without Tax to the pivot table, and then add Tax Amount so that you can validate the Sales Amount With Tax value in a row by highlighting the Sales Amount Without Tax and Tax Amount columns in the same row, and checking the Sum in the status bar at the bottom of the window, as shown in Figure 1-54.

	A	B	C	D	E	F	G	H	I	J
1	Row Labels ▼	Profit	Quantity	Sale Count	Tax Rate	Unit Price	Sales Amount With Tax	Sales Amount Without Tax	Tax Amount	
2	N/A	$31,676,352.75	3,284,017	84,298			$73,065,793.78	$63,553,695.70	$9,512,098.08	
3	Tailspin Toys	$27,125,589.10	2,847,550	72,249			$62,654,262.56	$54,497,209.60	$8,157,052.96	
4	Wingtip Toys	$26,942,739.05	2,820,061	71,719			$62,352,133.11	$54,235,435.90	$8,116,697.21	
5	Grand Total	$85,744,680.90	8,951,628	228,266			$198,072,189.45	$172,286,341.20	$25,785,848.25	
6										

tmpF0F4 ⊕

Ready | Average: $36,532,896.89 | Count: 2 | Sum: $73,065,793.78 | 100%

FIGURE 1-54 Validation of Sales Amount With Tax values by summing Sales Amount Without Tax and Tax Amount

All measures that display with values in the pivot table have the AggregateFunction value set to Sum. These values reflect the sum of all rows in the fact table for the column associated with the respective measure with a grouping by Buying Group. After the AggregateFunction property for Tax Rate and Unit Price is changed to None, the values in the pivot table for those measures no longer display for those measures because SSAS skips the aggregation step when retrieving results for the query. Those values at the row level are still accessible to SSAS for MDX calculations when requested, but summing the tax rate or the unit price for a sale is meaningless for analyzing sales. You can view the values for these two measures at the detail level by double-clicking a cell, such as E2, to open a new Excel sheet that displays the row-level detail in the fact table for the selected cell, as shown in Figure 1-55 in which some columns and rows have been hidden to focus on the columns of interest.

	A	B	H	I	J	K	
1	Data returned for Tax Rate, N/A (First 1000 rows).							
2								
3	[Sale].[$City.City Key] ▼	[Sale].[$Invoice.Sale Key] ▼	[Sale].[Quantity] ▼	[Sale].[Unit Price] ▼	[Sale].[Tax Rate] ▼	[Sale].[Sales Amount Without Tax] ▼	
4	West Elkton	198840	5	13	15	65	
5	Toughkenamon	199028	5	13	15	65	
6	Lorentz	199046	5	13	15	65	
7	Oakshade	199166	5	13	15	65	
8	Sea Island	199227	5	13	15	65	
9	Hanaford	199641	5	13	15	65	
10	Lunds	199675	5	13	15	65	
11	Gallipolis Ferry	199908	5	13	15	65	
12	Makoti	200057	5	13	15	65	
13	Liberty Plain	200136	5	13	15	65	

FIGURE 1-55 Transaction detail for the N/A buying group in a new Excel sheet

If you switch back to the original sheet containing the pivot table, remove all measures except Sale Count by dragging each measure individually out of the Values pane at the bottom of the PivotTables Fields List. In addition, remove Buying Group from the Rows pane. Then select the Stock Item Distinct Count measure and State Province (from the City dimension) to add them to the pivot table, a portion of which is shown in Figure 1-56.

	A	B	C
1	Row Labels ▼	Sale Count	Stock Item Distinct Count
2	Alabama	5,279	226
3	Alaska	4,079	227
4	Arizona	3,641	226
5	Arkansas	2,846	227
6	California	11,871	227
7	Colorado	6,054	227
8	Connecticut	1,206	225
9	Florida	7,593	227
10	Georgia	4,091	227
11	Hawaii	416	186
12	Idaho	2,347	223

FIGURE 1-56 A pivot table showing a standard measure, Sale Count, and a distinct count measure, Stock Item Distinct Count

Here you can see the number of sales transactions as the Sale Count value, which counts each row in the fact table and sums it by State Province. However, the Stock Item Distinct Count reflects the distinct count of stock items sold to customers in a specific State Province. If you scroll to the bottom of the pivot table to locate the Grand Total, you find the Sale Count Grand Total is 228,266 and the Stock Item Distinct Count Grand Total is 228. That means there are a total of 228.266 rows in the fact table, but 228 distinct stock item keys in the same table.

Most of the time, measures are *additive*. That is, regardless of which dimension you include in the query with the measure, the aggregation of the measure by any of the dimension's attributes is a value that accurately adds up. AggregateFunction property values like Sum or Count are additive measures. You can also define nonadditive measures semiadditive measures as described in more detail in the "Aggregate functions" and "Define semi-additive behavior" sections of this chapter.

Measure groups

Remember from Skill 1.1 that a measure group is a collection of measures that come from the same fact table. A cube can contain multiple measure groups. Ideally, these measure groups share one or more dimensions in common to facilitate analysis and reduce the potential of confusing users. If there are no overlapping dimension, consider creating separate cubes for each measure group.

Before you can add a measure group to a cube, a corresponding table must exist in the DSV. To review how to add a measure group (and later how to work with semi-additive measures), let's add another fact table to the DSV by performing the following steps:

1. Double-click Wide World Importers DW.dsv in Solution Explorer.

2. Right-click anywhere in the diagram pane of the DSV designer, select Add/Remove Tables, select Stock Holding (Fact) in the Available Objects list, click the > button, and then click OK. The table is added to the DSV with a primary key defined as Stock Holding Key and a relationship added between the Stock Holding table, and the Stock Item table based on the Stock Item Key column.

The Stock Holding table is similar to an inventory table that shows a quantity for each stock item among other information. However, a typical inventory table also includes a date column to show the quantity of each stock item on different dates. Inventory can be tracked yearly, quarterly, monthly, or even daily, depending on business requirements. To better explore semi-additive behavior later in this chapter, you can replace the Stock Holding table with a named query that simulates changes in inventory over time by performing the following steps:

1. Right-click the Stock Holding table in the diagram, point to Replace Table, and select With New Named Query.

2. Replace the SELECT statement in the Create Named Query dialog box with the statement shown in Listing 1-10.

LISTING 1-10 Named query to simulate changes in stock item inventory over time

```
SELECT
    CONVERT(date, '2013-01-01') as DateKey,
    [Stock Item Key],
    [Quantity On Hand],
    [Bin Location],
    [Reorder Level],
    [Target Stock Level]
FROM
    Fact.[Stock Holding]
UNION ALL
SELECT
    CONVERT(date, '2013-06-01') as DateKey,
    [Stock Item Key],
    [Quantity On Hand] - [Stock Item Key] AS [Quantity On Hand],
    [Bin Location],
    [Reorder Level],
[Target Stock Level]
FROM
    Fact.[Stock Holding] AS t;
```

A surrogate key column is not necessary in a fact table, so the named query eliminates that column along with other extraneous columns so that the results of the named query are simplified as much as possible. In addition, an arbitrary date column is added and a new value is computed for the quantity on hand for the second time period to force a difference in inventory between time periods.

3. Before clicking OK, be sure to type **Stock Holding** in the Name box at the top of the dialog box if it is not currently correctly named.

4. Press CTRL+S to save the DSV with the new named query.

5. Create a relationship between the Stock Holding and Date tables. Select DateKey in the Stock Holding named query diagram and drag it to the Date column in the Date table.

6. Now you are ready to use the new named query as a new measure group. Double-click the Wide World Importers DW.cube file in Solution Explorer, right-click in the Measures pane of the cube designer, and select New Measure Group. In the New Measure Group dialog box, select Stock Holding, and click OK.

7. In the Measures pane, expand the Stock Holding measure group to review the added measures: Quantity On Hand, Reorder Level, Target Stock Level, and Stock Holding Count.

   All numeric columns that are not used in relationships in the DSV are assumed to be measures and added as a group when you create the new measure group. If you do not want to include a measure, such as Stock Holding Count, right-click the measure in the Measures pane, select Delete, and then click OK to confirm the deletion.

8. Set the FormatString property for each of the remaining three measures to #,#.

   Each measure group has many different properties available to configure. For the most part, you can keep the default values. Chapter 4 explains more about the properties that affect aggregation design, file placement, and partition processing. For now, let's consider only the following properties:

   ■ **IgnoreUnrelatedDimension** Determines whether SSAS displays a top-level aggregation value for all members in an unrelated dimension, as shown in Figure 1-57. The default is True.

Buying Group	Quantity On Hand
N/A	60563697
Tailspin Toys	60563697
Wingtip Toys	60563697

FIGURE 1-57 Query results showing quantity on hand by buying group

- **Name** Provides a name for display in client applications or for reference in MDX expressions. You can rename a measure group at any time. For example, consider changing the Sale 1 measure group name to Stock Item Sales Distinct Count.

9. On the Dimension Usage page, select the Stock Holding measure group, and then, in the Properties window, change the IgnoreUnrelatedDimension property's value to False.

10. Deploy the project, open the Browser page of the cube designer, click Reconnect, and set up a query to view Quantity On Hand by Buying Group.

    The following message displays: No Rows Found. Click To Execute The Query. Because no relationship exists between the measure and the dimension, and the IgnoreUnrelatedDimension property is False, SSAS has no results to display in the query.

> **IMPORTANT REMOTE LINKED MEASURE GROUPS DEPRECATED IN SQL SERVER 2016**
>
> A linked measure group is a measure group that is created in one database and referenced in one or more separate databases as a method of reusing a common design. For performance reasons, Microsoft recommends that both databases reside on the same server. Linking to a measure group on a remote server is deprecated in SQL Server 2016 and will not be possible in a future release. In general, the usage of linked measure groups even when both databases are on the same server is not considered best practice. Therefore, the exam does not test your knowledge of this topic. However, if you would like to know more about the limitations of this feature, see "Linked Measure Groups" at *https://msdn.microsoft.com/en-us/library/ms174899.aspx*.

Granularity

Normally, the granularity attribute is the one that is set as the key in the dimension, but there can be modeling scenarios in which it is a different attribute. To further clarify granularity, consider a situation in which you have a Date dimension that has Day, Month, and Year attributes, and you have a Sale fact table that includes a DayKey column that you associate with the Day attribute as a regular relationship. In the Date dimension, the Month attribute has two key columns, Month and Year. Let's say you also have a Forecast fact table in which forecasted sales by month and year is stored, as shown in Figure 1-58.

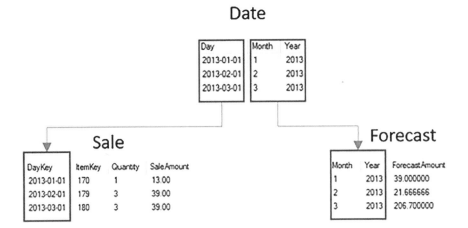

FIGURE 1-58 Fact tables with different granularity sharing a common dimension

To configure the dimension usage properly for the hypothetical Forecast measure group and the Date dimension, create a regular relationship between them and set the granularity attribute to Month. When you define this granularity attribute, the Dimension Columns list in the Define Relationships dialog box displays the two key columns, Month and Year, for the selected granularity attribute and then you can map those two columns to the Month and Year measure group columns.

Calculated measures

An important feature of SSAS is the ability to define calculated measures. Whereas reporting against a relational database requires you to define business logic for calculations such as profit margins in a report, you can add this business logic to a cube and thereby ensure that every query that returns profit margin performs the calculation consistently. SSAS stores only the calculated measure definition and performs the calculation at query time. However, SSAS does cache the query results to improve performance for subsequent queries requesting the same calculation, which Chapter 4 explains in more detail.

To review the steps necessary to add a calculated measure, let's add a simple calculated measure to the Wide World Importers DW cube to compute profit margin:

1. Open the cube designer, and then click the Calculations tab.

2. Click the Form View button in the cube designer toolbar, and then click the New Calculated Member button in the cube designer toolbar.

A *calculated measure* is a member of the Measures dimension that is calculated by using an MDX expression. You can also create calculated members for other dimensions in the cube, as explained in Chapter 3.

3. Type **[Profit Margin Percent]** in the Name box.

4. In the Expression box, type the following MDX expression:

```
[Measures].[Profit]/[Measures].[Sales Amount Without Tax]
```

Chapter 3 explains the principles of MDX expressions and its syntax rules in more detail. This expression is a simple example of computing the profit margin percentage by dividing the total profit by the total sales amount. SSAS automatically aggregates the numerator separately from the aggregation of the denominator and then performs the division. If you add a filter to a query, SSAS applies the filter to the numerator and denominator aggregations separately and then performs the division.

5. In the Format String drop-down list, select "Percent" to apply a format string.

6. Deploy the project to update your multidimensional database.

7. Check the calculation by opening the Browser tab of the cube designer, clicking Reconnect, and dragging Profit Margin Percent from the Measures folder in the metadata pane to the query window. The result is 0.497687049958665. (The cube browser in SSDT does not apply the format string.)

This calculation is functionally equivalent to executing the following T-SQL statement in SSMS, which yields 0.497687:

```
SELECT
    SUM(Profit) / SUM([Total Excluding Tax]) AS ProfitMarginPercent
FROM Fact.Sale;
```

Aggregate functions

By default, each new measure you create is assigned Sum as the AggregateFunction property value. By far, this is the most common type of aggregation that you use when developing a cube. However, SSAS supports the use of other aggregate functions, some of which are additive like the Sum function while others are semiadditive and nonadditive. A *semiadditive* function performs an aggregation across some dimension, but not necessarily all dimension, which is described in more detail in the next section. A *nonadditive* function does not aggregate at all, but performs a specific type of calculation. Table 1-5 lists all aggregate functions supported by SSAS.

TABLE 1-5 Aggregate functions

Aggregate Function	additivity	Description
Sum	Additive	Sums the values for each child member.
Count	Additive	Counts the number of child members.
Min	Semiadditive	Returns the lowest value for child members.
Max	Semiadditive	Returns the highest value for child members.
DistinctCount	Nonadditive	Performs a count of unique child members.
None	Nonadditive	Ignores aggregation and returns a value only for child members requested in the query
ByAccount	Semiadditive	Applies the aggregate function applicable to the current member of a dimension with its type set to Accounts.
AverageOfChildren	Semiadditive	Sums the total of the child members and then divides the result by the count of non-empty child members.
FirstChild	Semiadditive	Returns the value of the first child member.
LastChild	Semiadditive	Returns the value of the last child member.
FirstNonEmpty	Semiadditive	Returns the value of the first child member that is not empty.
LastNonEmpty	Semiadditive	Returns the value of the last child member that is not empty.

> **NOTE ADDITIONAL CONFIGURATION REQUIRED BY THE BYACCOUNT AGGREGATE FUNCTION**
>
> To use the ByAccount aggregate function, there are many other steps that you must perform to configure the dimension and cube behavior properly. First, the account dimension must include an attribute with its type set to Account Type. You then define the mapping of account types to aggregate functions on the database designer, which is accessible from the Database menu by selecting Edit Database. To review the full set of requirements, see "Create a Finance account of parent-child type Dimension" at *https://msdn.microsoft.com/en-us/library/ms174609.aspx*.

Define semi-additive behavior

Semi-additive aggregation is important when you need to analyze values from point-in-time fact tables, such as inventory. In this case, you add together at the values across one dimension, but choose a point-in-time value or average value when aggregating across the Date dimension. For example, if you have inventory counts for July and December, but you want to return the inventory count for the year, you typically want the last value of the year, which is associated with December. Another common scenario for semi-additivity is financial reporting. You add together revenue and expenses from month to month when viewing quarterly or yearly data, but you use the last value for assets or liabilities.

Let's explore an example of semi-additive behavior by using the Stock Holding measure group added in the previous section. Before we make any changes, open the Browser tab in the cube designer to review the behavior of the measures when keeping the default values for the AggregateFunction property. Expand the Measures folder, expand Stock Holding, and then add Quantity On Hand, Reorder Level, and Target Stock Level to the query window. Next expand Date and add Date.Calendar to the query window to add all three levels of the hierarchy—Calendar Year, Calendar Month, and Date, as shown in Figure 1-59.

Calendar Year	Calendar Month	Date	Quantity On Hand	Reorder Level	Target Stock Level
CY2013	CY2013-Jan	2013-01-01	30343296	5098	15511
CY2013	CY2013-Jun	2013-06-01	30220401	5098	15511

FIGURE 1-59 Query results showing selected measures by attributes of the Date dimension on the Browser page of the cube designer

Currently, the aggregate function applied to each of these measures is the Sum function. Therefore, the resulting values represent a total for all stock items, which is not the desired result. Let's change the query to focus on a single stock item to help see measure behavior more clearly. Add a filter by selecting Stock Item in the Dimension drop-down list above the query window and Stock Item in the Hierarchy drop-down list. In the Filter Expression drop-down list, expand All, select the USB missile launcher (Green) check box, and click OK. Now you can see two separate inventory counts for January and June, as shown in Figure 1-60.

Calendar Year	Calendar Month	Date	Quantity On Hand	Reorder Level	Target Stock Level
CY2013	CY2013-Jan	2013-01-01	175609	20	100
CY2013	CY2013-Jun	2013-06-01	175006	20	100

FIGURE 1-60 Query results for a single stock item

If you remove the Calendar Month and Date attributes from the query, the query returns a single row, as shown in Figure 1-61. The measure values reflect the sum of CY2013-Jan and CY2013-Jun aggregated values for each measure.

Calendar Year	Quantity On Hand	Reorder Level	Target Stock Level
CY2013	350615	40	200

FIGURE 1-61 Query results for a single stock item for Calendar Year CY2013

This aggregation behavior is incorrect because the measures should reflect the value as of the last inventory date instead of the sum. To change this behavior, perform the following steps:

1. Open the Cube Structure page of the cube designer and set the AggregateFunction property for each of these measures to LastNonEmpty.

2. Deploy the project and then return to the Browser in the cube designer.

3. Click Reconnect in the toolbar, and then add the same three measures to the query window, add Calendar Year from the Date dimension, and set the filter for Stock Item to USB missile launcher (Green) to produce the results shown in Figure 1-62.

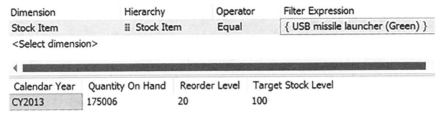

FIGURE 1-62 Corrected query results for a single stock item for Calendar Year CY2013

Chapter summary

- Before you start building a multidimensional database, you should spend time designing a star schema to support business requirements in an OLAP environment. The star schema consists of one or more fact tables and multiple dimension tables that you populate from OLTP systems by using ETL processes. In a multidimensional project that you create in SSDT, you connect to this star schema by creating a data source, and then reference tables in the star schema by creating a data source view. Then you can add dimension objects to your project by using the Dimension Wizard and add a cube by using the Cube Wizard. You can then fine-tune the dimension and cube objects by configuring properties in the dimension and cube designers, respectively. You must deploy your SSDT to create the multidimensional database and its objects on the SSAS server.

- The storage model you choose determines not only how SSAS stores data, but also what type of data it stores. MOLAP is the default storage model that stores both detail and aggregate data for the optimal data retrieval. SSAS stores only metadata when you use the ROLAP storage model, creates aggregations in the relational data source, and retrieves requests for data from the data source by translating MDX queries into platform-specific SQL statements. ROLAP is beneficial when you need near real-time access to data. SSAS stores aggregate data for the HOLAP storage model and determines at query time whether to retrieve aggregate data from SSAS or from the relational source after converting the MDX query into a SQL statement. HOLAP is useful when most queries require aggregate data.

- SSAS supports many different types of dimensional models. The exam tests your knowledge regarding the selection and configuration of the following types:

  - **Fact** Use this dimensional model when you want to include a degenerate dimension in your database. On the Dimension Usage page of the cube designer, you must relate the dimension a measure group by using the Fact relationship type.

  - **Parent-child** Use this dimensional model when a dimension table includes a foreign-key relationship to itself. Add the column containing the foreign key as an attribute in the dimension and set its Usage property to Parent. Optionally, you can configure properties applicable only to a parent attribute.

- **Roleplaying** Use this dimensional model when you have a dimension represented multiple times in a fact table in different contexts. For example, you might have Invoice Date and Delivery Date based on the same Date dimension. You create one dimension object in your project, but add the dimension as many times as applicable to the cube. On the Dimension Usage page of the cube designer, you relate each cube dimension to the same measure group by using the Regular relationship type, but define different granularity attributes, which relate to different measure group columns.

- **Reference** Use this dimensional model when you need to support slice and dice by a dimension for which no foreign key exists in the fact table although it is related to an intermediate dimension having a foreign key in the fact table. The key attribute for the reference dimension must exist as a non-key attribute in the intermediate dimension. On the Dimension Usage page of the cube designer, you define a Referenced relationship between the reference dimension and the measure group, and specify the intermediate dimension.

- **Data mining** Use this dimensional model when you want to use a data mining algorithm to create a dimension useful for slicing and dicing, such as clusters of customers. You must first create a data mining model to define the data mining technique and columns to which the data mining algorithm is applied. The Data Mining Wizard allows you to create a dimension in which to store the results and optionally a cube.

- **Many-to-many** Use this dimensional model when you need to rollup measures by different dimension attributes without overcounting the results in aggregations. Typically, you must add a bridge table as a measure group to the cube to support this structure and hide the measure group from the cube. On the Dimension Usage page of the cube designer, define a Regular relationship between the dimension and the bridge table and a Many-To-Many relationship between the dimension and the original measure group. You specify the bridge table as the Intermediate Measure group for the many-to-many relationship.

- **Slowly changing dimension** Use this dimensional model when you need to track changes to an attribute over time for a Type 2 SCD design. In the dimension design, you must include the key attribute as well as the attribute containing the business key in the source table, and then hide the key attribute by setting its AttributeHierarchyVisible property to False.

- Use the Type property for dimension and attribute objects when you need SSAS or client applications to invoke a specific behavior when that object is queried. The most common dimension type to implement is Time, although you should also be familiar with the concepts for implementing the Accounts and Currency dimension types.

- After you add a user-defined hierarchy to a dimension, you should review and correct attribute relationships as necessary. A user-defined hierarchy provides a pre-defined navigation path that simplifies cube exploration in a client application. SSAS uses corresponding attribute relationships to optimize both data storage and data retrieval for natural hierarchies.

- Use the cube designer to add and configure measures and measure groups after initially creating a cube by using the Cube Wizard. Importantly, configure the AggregateFunction and FormatString properties correctly for each measure to ensure values are aggregated appropriately and display legibly in client applications. You can also add calculated measures to include business logic for non-scalar values that are important to business analysis.

- SSAS includes the following aggregate functions to support semiadditivity: Min, Max, ByAccount, AverageOfChildren, FirstChild, LastChild, FirstNonEmpty, and LastNonEmpty. A semiadditive aggregation adds values together across one dimension, but not across others. Common use cases for semiadditive behavior are financial account reporting and inventory analysis.

Thought experiment

In this thought experiment, demonstrate your skills and knowledge of the topics covered in this chapter. You can find the answers to this thought experiment in the next section.

Humongous Insurance is a company that sells insurance policies to individual consumers and companies in a single country and has offices in four different regions in this country. The amount for which each insurance policy is sold is called a premium. Each year, the sales manager projects monthly quotas for insurance premiums by region. You have been hired as a BI developer at Humongous Insurance to create an SSAS multidimensional database that enables users to analyze sales and quotas.

The current database environment includes one OLTP system called Sales, and another OLTP system called Quotas. Both databases currently run on SQL Server 2016.

Before you can create the multidimensional database, you must design and populate a data warehouse that can answer the following types of questions:

- How many policies have been sold by line of insurance (Personal or Commercial), customer, sales territory, and date?

- What is the revenue, cost, profit, and profit percent of policies sold by line of insurance, customer, sales territory, and date?

- What is the quota for insurance policies by sales territory and month?

To satisfy the business requirements, the multidimensional database must have the following characteristics:

- A customer can have multiple policies, but each policy is limited to one customer.

- The customer dimension must include the customer name and the customer's phone number. The phone number must be available for reporting, but not for slicing and dicing operations.

- The sales territory dimension must support drilling from region to state/province to city.

- The date dimension must support drilling from year to month to date.

Based on this background information and business requirements, answer the following questions:

1. Sketch the fact tables, dimension tables, and relationships in the star schema that meets the business requirements.

2. Describe the steps necessary to support the drilldown functionality in the sales territory dimension with optimal query performance.

3. What property do you set to hide the phone number attribute in the customer dimension from slicing and dicing operations, but allows it to be included in the dimension as a member property?

    A. AttributeHierarchyOrdered

    B. AttributeHierarchyVisible

    C. AttributeHierarchyEnabled

    D. IsAggregatable

4. What property do you set for each measure to improve the legibility of values in a client application?

    A. DataType

    B. MeasureExpression

    C. AggregateFunction

    D. FormatString

5. When you browse the date dimension, you notice the members of the Month attribute sort in alphabetical order. How do you correct this problem?

6. What is the granularity attribute to configure when defining the relationship between the quota measure group and the date dimension?

7. How do you support the profit percentage in your solution design?

    A. Add a fact table column and set the FormatString for the new measure to Percent.

    B. Create a calculated measure to divide profit by revenue.

    C. Add a new measure group to the cube to isolate the measure.

    D. Define the MeasureExpression property on a new measure to divide profit by revenue.

8. When you process and then query the cube to view quota by customer, you see the same quota value repeating on each row. What step can you take to prevent the display of these values?

Thought experiment answers

This section contains the solution to the thought experiment.

1. The design for the star schema includes two fact tables—Policy Sales and Policy Quotas—and four dimension tables: Date, Customer, InsuranceLine, and SalesTerritory. The table columns and relationships between the fact tables and dimension tables are shown in Figure 1-63.

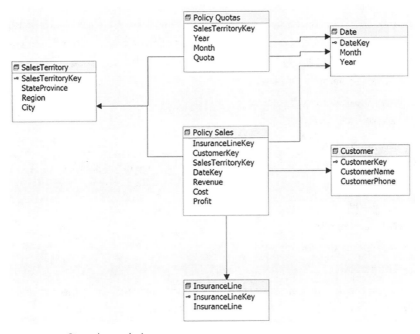

FIGURE 1-63 Star schema design

2. On the Dimension Structure page of the dimension designer for the sales territory dimension, drag the Year to the Hierarchies pane to create a new user-defined hierarchy, drag the Month attribute to the new hierarchy and drop it below Year, and then drag the Date attribute to the hierarchy and drop it below Month. Right-click the Hierarchy name and type a new name, such as Calendar. On the Attribute Relationships page of the dimension designer, drag the Month attribute and drop it on the Year attribute to arrange the attributes from left to right in the following sequence: Date, Month, and Year. You can set the RelationshipType property for each attribute relationship to Rigid because members do not change in this dimension.

3. The answer is **C**. AttributeHierarchyEnabled. This attribute property prevents SSAS from storing data for this attribute's members and hides it from client applications for use in queries on rows, or columns, or as a filter.

   Answer A, AttributeHierarchyOrdered, is incorrect because this property only specifies whether the attribute members are ordered. Answer B, AttributeHierarchyVisible, is incorrect because, although it hides the attribute from the client application for slicing and dicing, it does not enable the attribute as a member property. Answer D, IsAggregatable, is incorrect because this property removes the All member from the attribute hierarchy.

4. The answer is **D**. The FormatString property adds a thousands separator, sets the number of decimal places, or adds symbols such as a currency symbol or percent sign, which makes the values easier to read in client applications.

   Answer A, DataType, is incorrect because the data type does not improve the legibility of measure values. Answer B, MeasureExpression, is incorrect because it affects the calculation of a measure, but does not change its appearance. Answer C, Aggregate-Function, is also incorrect because it changes how SSAS returns a value for parent members, by summing or counting for example, but does not change the appearance of the measure.

5. For the Month attribute, bind the KeyColumn property to both the Year and Month columns in the source. Also, ensure the OrderBy property is set to Key.

6. Set Month as the granularity attribute. You then map this attribute to the Year and Month columns in the measure group in the Define Relationship dialog box.

7. The answer is **B**. Add profit as a calculated measure by defining an MDX expression like this:

   ```
   [Measures].[Profit] / [Measures].[Revenue]
   ```

8. Answer A is incorrect because profit percentage is nonadditive and must be calculated at query time, and therefore it cannot be stored in the fact table. Answer C is incorrect for a similar reason. A measure group requires a measure based on a fact table column, and profit percentage cannot be stored in the fact table. Answer D is incorrect because the MeasureExpression calculation is performed at the detail level and then aggregated, which produces an incorrect result. The profit percentage calculation must be based on the aggregated value for profit and divide that value by the aggregated value for revenue.

9. Set the IgnoreUnrelatedDimension on the measure group containing the quota measure to False.

CHAPTER 2

Design a tabular BI semantic model

The skills necessary to develop a tabular model for SQL Server Analysis Services (SSAS) are much different than the skills required to develop a multidimensional model. In some ways, the tabular modeling process is much simpler and more flexible than the multi-dimensional modeling process. Although it is not required to transform the source data for a tabular model into a star schema, the development steps are in general easier if you work from a star schema and the processing necessary to load a tabular model with data can often run faster. For this reason, in this chapter we use the same data source introduced in the previous chapter to walk through key development and administrative tasks for a tabular model. In addition, we explore your options for keeping the data in your tabular model up-to-date, either by importing the data into the model on a periodic basis or by configuring the model for real-time data access.

Skills in this chapter:

- Design and publish a tabular data model
- Configure, manage, and secure a tabular model
- Develop a tabular model to access data in near real time

Skill 2.1: Design and publish a tabular data model

By comparison to multidimensional model development, the steps to design and publish a tabular data model are simpler. The first difference you notice is the ability to add data from a variety of data sources and to filter the data prior to loading it into the data model. Rather than focus on dimensions, attributes, and dimension usage as you do in a multidimensional model, you focus on tables, columns, and relationships.

EXAM TIP

In many cases, the decision to use a tabular or multidimensional model is a result of existing skill levels in an organization. Both model types support similar types of analysis, but there can be special business requirements that favor one type of model over the other. You should be familiar with the strengths and limitations of each type of model as described in "Comparing Tabular and Multidimensional Solutions (SSAS)" at *https://msdn. microsoft.com/en-us/library/hh212940.aspx*.

This section covers how to:

- Design measures, relationships, hierarchies, partitions, perspectives, and calculated columns
- Create a time table
- Publish from Microsoft Visual Studio
- Import from Microsoft PowerPivot
- Select a deployment option, including Processing Option, Transactional Deployment, and Query Mode

Design measures, relationships, hierarchies, partitions, perspectives, and calculated columns

The examples in this chapter are based on the same business requirements and the WideWorldImportersDW data source as described in the "Source table design" section of Chapter 1, "Design a multidimensional business intelligence semantic model." To build a similar business intelligence semantic model using SSAS in tabular mode, perform the following steps:

1. Open Microsoft SQL Server Data Tools for Visual Studio 2015 (SSDT). If you have trouble connecting to the tabular instance in a later step, you should right-click SSDT in the Start Menu or in the All Apps list, and then click Run As Administrator to elevate permissions while developing the tabular model.

2. In the File menu, point to New, and then click Project.

3. In the New Project dialog box, click Analysis Services in the Business Intelligence group of templates, and then click Analysis Services Tabular Project. At the bottom of the dialog box, type a name for the project, select a location, and optionally type a new name for the project's solution. The project for the examples in this chapter is named 70-768-Ch2.

4. When you create a new tabular project, the Tabular Model Designer dialog box prompts you for the workspace server name and compatibility level. If necessary, type the SSAS tabular server name (or server and instance name, such as localhost\TABULAR). Performance during model development is generally better if you work with a

local tabular server. Keep the default compatibility level, SQL Server 2016 RTM (1200) to enable features specific to the SQL Server 2016 version of SSAS tabular on which the exam tests your knowledge. The other compatibility levels are included for backward compatibility. Click OK to create the project and add the Model.bim file to your project in the Solution Explorer window.

> **NOTE CHANGING COMPATIBILITY LEVEL AFTER MODEL CREATION**
>
> If you set a compatibility level lower than 1200 when you create the tabular project, you can always upgrade the compatibility level later. To do this, select the Model.bim file in Solution Explorer. In the Properties window, select SQL Server 2016 RTM (1200) in the Compatibility Level drop-down list. Once a tabular model is set to the 1200 compatibility level, you cannot change it to a lower level.

When you add the Model.bim file to your project, SSDT creates a workspace database on the SSAS server. Each model has its own workspace database that you can recognize in SSMS by its name that is a concatenation of the database name specified in the project's properties (described in the "Select a deployment option, including Processing Option, Transactional Deployment, and Query Mode" section of this chapter) and a globally unique identifier (GUID). You should not use SSMS to make changes to the workspace database while the model is open in SSDT to avoid damaging the model.

Your next step is to add data to your project. Whereas a multidimensional database requires your data to be in a relational data source, a tabular database can import data from the following data sources:

- Microsoft SQL Server 2008 and later
- Microsoft Azure SQL Database
- Microsoft Azure SQL Data Warehouse
- Microsoft Analytics Platform System
- Microsoft Access 2010 and later
- Oracle 9i and later
- Teradata V2R6 and later
- Sybase 15.0.2
- Informix
- IBM DB2 8.1
- OLE DB or ODBC
- Microsoft SQL Server 2008 and later Analysis Services
- Microsoft Reporting Services
- Microsoft Azure Marketplace

- Data feed in Atom 1.0 format or exposed as Windows Communication Foundation (WCF) Data Service

- Microsoft Excel 2010 and later

- Text file

- Office Database Connection (.odc) file

Let's add a few tables from the WideWorldImportersDW database to the tabular model. To do this, perform the following steps:

1. Click Import From Data Source on the Model menu, click Microsoft SQL Server on the Connect To A Data Source page of the Table Import Wizard, and click Next.

2. On the Connect To A Microsoft SQL Server Database page of the wizard, type the name of your SQL Server in the Server Name box, set the authentication if not using Windows authentication, select WideWorldImportersDW in the Database Name drop-down list, and click Next.

3. On the Impersonation Information page of the wizard, you can choose one of the following options:

   - **Specific Windows User Name And Password**   Use this option when you need to connect to your data source with a specific login, such as a Windows login with low privileges that has read permission to the data source. This information is kept in memory only and not persisted on disk. If the model is not in memory when you attempt to deploy it from SSDT, you are prompted to provide the credentials.

   - **Service Account**   Use this option to connect to the data source by using the account running the SSAS service. If you use this option, be sure that it has read permission on the database.

   - **Unattended Account**   Ignore this option because it is not supported.

> *NOTE* **SERVER-SIDE VERSUS CLIENT-SIDE IMPERSONATION**
>
> Import and process operations in SSDT are server-side operations that are executed by SSDT. Server-side operations use the credentials you specify for impersonation to connect to each data source and load data into the workspace database, which is hosted on the SSAS server, regardless of whether this server is your local computer or a remote computer on your network. On the other hand, client-side operations use your credentials and occur when you preview data in the Preview And Filter feature of the Table Import Wizard, in the Edit Table Properties dialog box, or in the Partition Manager. If your credentials have different permissions in the data source than the specified impersonation account's permissions, you can observe a difference between the preview data and the data loaded into the model.

4. Click Next to continue to the Choose How To Import The Data page of the wizard. This page displays only when you are connecting to a relational data source. Here you can choose one of the following options:

- **Select From A List Of Tables And Views To Choose The Data To Import** Use this option to choose one or more tables or views from the data source.

- **Write A Query That Will Specify The Data To Import** Use this option when you want to create a single table in the model based on a Structured Query Language (SQL) query. Your query can be as simple or complex as you need to return the required results from the data source. However, you cannot call a stored procedure by using this option.

To follow the examples in this chapter, click the Select From A List Of Tables And Views To Choose The Data To Import option, and click Next to see the list of available tables and views.

5. Select the check box to the left of each of the following tables: City, Customer, Date, Employee, Stock Item, and Sale.

6. You can apply a filter to an individual table to eliminate specific columns or remove rows based on criteria that you supply. For example, let's remove the Sale Key and Lineage Key columns from the Sale table. Select the Sale table in the list of tables and views, and then click Preview And Filter button. A dialog box displays a preview of the rows in the table. Here you can clear the check box for the Sale Key column, as shown in Figure 2-1.

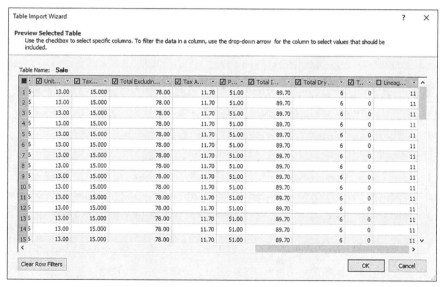

FIGURE 2-1 Preview and filter a data source

7. You can apply a row filter by clicking the arrow in the column header to open the AutoFilter menu, the contents of which depend on the data type of the column. Figure 2-2 shows the AutoFilter menu for a date column. You can point to Date Filters to display a list of filtering options, such as Before, After, and Last Year, among others. If the column is numeric, the filtering options include Equals, Greater Than, and Between, to name a few. Text filtering options include Begins With, Contains, and several others. As an alternative approach, you can individually clear or select check boxes in the list of items that display in the Autofilter menu. However, it's possible that the item list is not complete, as indicated by the Not All Items Showing message. Click OK to close the Autofilter menu, and then click OK to close the Preview Selected Table dialog box.

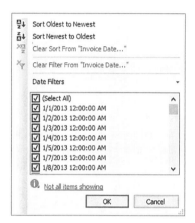

FIGURE 2-2 Autofilter menu for a date column

IMPORTANT **ROW AND COLUMN FILTERS**

Rather than load all rows and all columns from a table, consider carefully whether you need all of the data. Data that never gets used consumes memory resources. One optimization technique recommended by Microsoft is to filter the data as much as you can prior to loading it into the tabular model.

Furthermore, consider adding row filters during the development cycle when the source data contains millions of rows to speed up model development. As you add more calculations to the model, you can experience latency in the SSDT interface as it performs these calculations and communicates with the server. After you complete development, you can remove the filters by changing the partition definitions prior to deploying the final model. Partition management is described in more detail later in this chapter.

8. After adding and optionally filtering the tables you need for the models, click Finish on the Select Tables And Views page of the Table Import Wizard. SSDT then executes

the queries against your relational data source and copies the data into memory on the SSAS server. This version of the model is not deployed yet, but exists on the server nonetheless as a result of creating the project as described at the beginning of this section. Tabular models on the SSAS server are managed by the tabular engine, also known as the xVelocity engine.

> **NOTE XVELOCITY**
>
> xVelocity is the technology behind the in-memory data management feature in SSAS as well as the memory-optimized tables and columnstore indexing capabilities in SQL Server.

9. Click Close to close the Table Import Wizard after the data is successfully copied. After the tables are loaded, the model designer displays in SSDT with one tab per table, as shown in Figure 2-3. Notice the status bar at the bottom of the page in which you can see the number of rows imported for the current table.

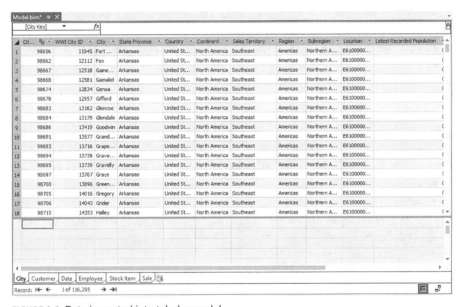

FIGURE 2-3 Data imported into tabular model

You can continue to load data from other data sources by repeating this process. There is no requirement for all data to be combined into a single source before you load it into the tabular model or that all data comes from a single type of data source, such as a relational database. Your primary consideration should be whether the data from different sources are related, and how much transformation of the data is necessary for it to be useful in the model. If you need to perform complex or many transformations, you should consider using an extract-transform-load (ETL) tool to prepare the data in advance of loading it into a tabular model, or even consider building a data mart or data warehouse to transform and conform the data as needed.

> **NOTE** **INCREMENTAL DEVELOPMENT**
>
> In a real-world development cycle, a common approach is to import one table at a time and then configure and test new objects for that table before adding another table. By taking an incremental approach, you can more easily identify the root cause of any problems that occur in the model. At this point, you can query the tabular model to test the results. However, there are a few more steps to perform to improve the model, such as adding measures, fixing relationships, and so on, as explained in the remainder of this section. In addition, you should review which columns should be visible to users exploring the model. Every column in every table that you imported is visible right now, but some of these columns are not useful for analysis or meaningful to users. Although these columns can be necessary for modeling relationships, as one example, you can hide them from users to create a user-friendlier model. As an example, you can right-click a column header, such as City Key in the City table, and click Hide From Client Tools. SSDT dims the values in the column as a visual indicator that these values are unavailable to client tools.

Measures

A measure in a tabular model is an aggregated value that calculates in the context of a query. In other words, SSAS considers the rows, columns, and filters specified in a query and returns the applicable result. In a multidimensional database, there is a distinction between a measure definition in a cube, and a calculated measure. By contrast, all measures in a tabular model are calculations. At minimum, a measure's calculation specifies an aggregate function to apply to a numeric column in a table. However, you can create complex expressions to apply time intelligence, such as a year-to-date calculation, or to compute percentage of totals, as two examples of possible measures. To define a measure, you use the Data Analysis Expression (DAX) language.

Let's add a simple measure to the Sale table to compute the total sales by summing the Total Excluding Tax column. To do this, perform the following steps:

1. Click the Sale tab, and then click a cell in the measure grid. The measure grid is the section of the model designer that displays below the data grid. You can click any cell, but a good habit to develop is to place measures in the cells in the first few columns of the grid to make it easier to find them later if you need to make changes.

2. After you click a cell in the measure grid, use the formula bar above the data grid to type a measure name followed by a colon, an equal sign, and a DAX expression (shown in Listing 2-1), as shown in Figure 2-4. In this measure expression, the SUM aggregate function is applied to the [Total Excluding Tax] column in the Sale table. After you press

Enter, SSDT computes the result and displays it next to the measure name in the calculation grid below the data grid in the model designer.

LISTING 2-1 Total Sales measure expression

```
Total Sales := SUM(Sale[Total Excluding Tax])
```

> **NOTE DAX**
>
> **DAX functions and syntax are explained in more detail in Chapter 3, "Developing queries using Multidimensional Expressions (MDX) and Data Analysis Expressions (DAX)."**

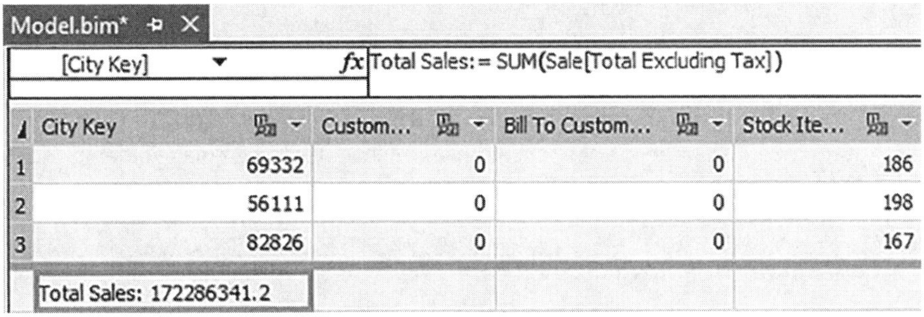

Model.bim*					
[City Key] ▼		*fx* Total Sales: = SUM(Sale[Total Excluding Tax])			
ⓘ City Key	🔢 ▼ Custom...	🔢 ▼ Bill To Custom...	🔢 ▼ Stock Ite...	🔢 ▼	
1	69332	0	0	186
2	56111	0	0	198
3	82826	0	0	167
Total Sales: 172286341.2				

FIGURE 2-4 Formula bar containing a measure expression

The formula bar in the model designer has several features that help you write and review DAX formulas easier:

- **Syntax coloring**   You can identify formula elements by the color of the font: functions display in a blue font, variables in a cyan font, and string constants in a red font. All other elements display in a black font.

- **IntelliSense**   IntelliSense helps you find functions, tables, or columns by displaying potential matches after you type a few characters. In addition, it displays a wavy red underscore below an error in your expression.

- **Formatting**   You can improve legibility of complex or long expressions by pressing ALT+Enter to break the expression into multiple lines. You can also type // as a prefix to a comment.

- **Formula fixup**   As long as your tabular model is set to compatibility level 1200, the model designer automatically updates all expressions that reference a renamed column or table.

- **Incomplete formula preservation**   If you cannot resolve an error in an expression, you can save and close the model, if it is set to compatibility level 1200, and then return to your work at a later time.

Next, create additional measures in the specified tables as shown in Table 2-1. Unlike a multidimensional model in which you create measures only as part of a measure group associated with a fact table, you can add a measure to any table in a tabular model.

TABLE 2-1 New measures to add to tabular model

Table	Expression
Sale	Sale Count := COUNTROWS('Sale')
City	City Count := COUNTROWS('City')

Each measure has the following set of editable properties that control the appearance and behavior of the measure in client applications:

- **Display Folder** You can type a name to use as a container for one or more measures when you want to provide a logical grouping for several measures and thereby help users more easily locate measures within a list of many measures. The use of this feature depends on the client application. Excel includes the Display Folder in the Pivot-Table Field List, but the Power View Field List does not.

> *NOTE* **PIVOTTABLE AND POWER VIEW**
>
> Excel provides two features to support the exploration of tabular models, PivotTables and Power View. The Analyze In Excel feature in SSDT creates a PivotTable. Simple examples of using a PivotTable are provided throughout this chapter. If you are new to PivotTables, you can review its key capabilities in "Create a PivotTable to analyze worksheet data" at *https://support.office.com/en-us/article/Create-a-PivotTable-to-analyze-worksheet-data-a9a84538-bfe9-40a9-a8e9-f99134456576*. Power View is a product that Microsoft initially released in SQL Server 2012 as part of Reporting Services (SSRS). It has since been added to Excel 2013 and Excel 2016, and similar capabilities are available in Microsoft Power BI. You can review more about working with Power View in Excel in "Power View: Explore, visualize, and present your data" in *https://support.office.com/en-us/article/Power-View-Explore-visualize-and-present-your-data-98268d31-97e2-42aa-a52b-a68cf460472e*. If you are using Excel 2016, you must enable Power View explicitly as described in "Turn on Power View in Excel 2016 for Windows" at *https://support.office.com/en-us/article/Turn-on-Power-View-in-Excel-2016-for-Windows-f8fc21a6-08fc-407a-8a91-643fa848729a*.

- **Description** You can type a description to provide users with additional information about a measure. This feature requires the client application to support the display of a description. Excel does not display the measure's description, but Power View includes the description in a tooltip when you hover the cursor over the measure in the Power View Field List.

- **Format** You can apply an appropriate format to your measure by choosing one of the following values in the Format drop-down list: General, Decimal Number, Whole Number, Percentage, Scientific, Currency, Date, TRUE/FALSE, or Custom. If the selected format supports decimal places, the Decimal Places property is added to the Properties window, which you can configure to define the measure's precision. Some format types allow you to specify whether to show thousand separators. If you select the Currency format, you can also configure the Currency Symbol property. Selection of the Custom format adds the Format String property, which you can configure to use a Visual Basic format string.

- **Measure Name** If you need to rename the measure, you can type a new name for this property. A measure name must be unique within your tabular model and cannot duplicate the name of any column in any table. Consider assigning user-friendly names that are meaningful to users and use embedded spaces, capitalization, and business terms.

- **Table Detail Position** This property defines behavior for specific client tools, such as Power View in SharePoint. When you set this property, a user can double-click the table to add a default set of fields to a table.

Let's set the format for each of the measures, as shown in Table 2-2.

TABLE 2-2 Measure properties

Table	Measure	Property	Value
Sale	Total Sales	Format	Decimal Number
		Show Thousand Separator	True
	Sale Count	Format	Whole Number
		Show Thousand Separator	True
City	City Count	Format	Whole Number
		Show Thousand Separator	True

Relationships

Relationships are required in a tabular model to produce correct results when the model contains multiple tables. If you design your model based on multiple tables for which foreign key relationships are defined, the tabular model inherits those relationships as long as you add all of the tables at the same time. Otherwise, you can manually define relationships.

Because the WideWorldImportersDW database tables have foreign key relationships defined in the Sale table, the addition of the dimension tables associated with that fact table also adds corresponding relationships in the model. Click the Diagram icon in the bottom right corner of the model designer (or point to Model View in the Model menu, and then select Diagram View) to see a diagram of the model's tables and relationships, as shown in Figure 2-5.

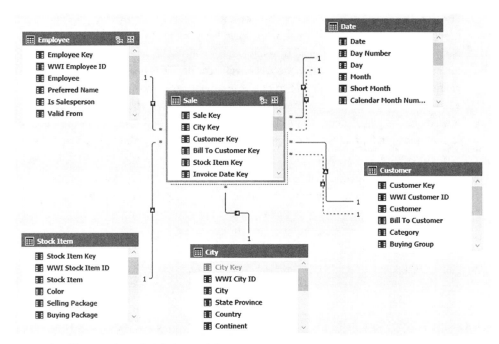

FIGURE 2-5 Diagram view of a tabular model

You can review the Properties window to understand an individual relationship by clicking its line in the diagram. For example, if you click the line between Employee and Sale, you can review the following three properties:

- **Active** Most of the time, this value is set to True and the relationship line is solid. When this value is set to False, the relationship line is dashed. This property is the only one that you can change in the Properties window.

NOTE **INACTIVE RELATIONSHIP USAGE**

Notice the dashed lines between Sale and Date, and between Sale and Customer. Only one relationship can be active when multiple relationships exist between two tables. This situation occurs when your tabular model includes roleplaying dimensions, as described in Chapter 1. You can reference an inactive relationship in a DAX expression by using the USERELATIONSHIP function. Marco Russo explains how to do this in his blog post, "USERELATIONSHIP in Calculated Columns" at *https://www.sqlbi.com/articles/userelationship-in-calculated-columns/.*

- **Foreign Key Column** This column contains the foreign key value that must be resolved by performing a lookup to the primary key column. For the relationship between Employee and Sale, the foreign key column is set to Sale[Salesperson Key].

- **Primary Key Column** This column contains the primary key column holding unique values for a lookup. For the relationship between Employee and Sale, the primary key column is set to Employee[Employee Key].

A relationship is not always automatically created when you add tables. As one example, if your tables come from a relational data source and no foreign key relationship exists between tables, you must define the relationship manually. As another example, if you add the tables in separate steps, the relationship is not inherited by the tabular model. Last, if your tables come from different data sources, such as when one table comes from a Microsoft Excel workbook and another table comes from a text file, there is no predefined relationship to inherit and therefore you must add any needed relationships.

To manually add a relationship, you can use one of the following techniques:

- **Drag and drop (Diagram View)** In the Diagram view, you can drag the foreign key column from one table and drop it on the corresponding primary key column in another table to create a relationship.

- **Column relationship (Grid View)** To access the Grid view, click the tab for the table that has the foreign key column, right-click the foreign key column, and click Create Relationship. In the Table 2 drop-down list, select the table containing the primary key column, and then click the primary key column in the list that displays. You can then specify the cardinality and filter direction as described later in this section.

> *NOTE* **SWITCH TO GRID VIEW**
>
> **To access the Grid view, click the Grid icon in the bottom right corner of the model designer, or point to Model View in the Model menu, and then select Grid View.**

- **Manage Relationships dialog box** On the Table menu, select Manage Relationships to open the Manage Relationships dialog box, as shown in Figure 2-6. In this dialog box, you have a comprehensive view of all relationships defined in the tabular model. The dialog box includes buttons to create a new relationship, edit an existing relationship, or delete a relationship.

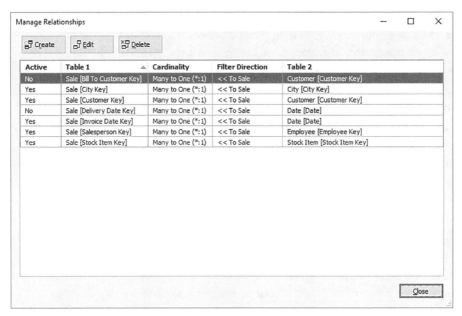

FIGURE 2-6 Manage Relationships dialog box

In the Manage Relationships dialog box, you can tell at a glance the cardinality of each relationship and the filter direction. These settings directly influence the behavior of queries that involve these tables.

CARDINALITY

Cardinality describes the type of relationship between two tables. You can assign one of the following cardinality types:

- **Many To One** Many-to-one cardinality describes a relationship in which Table 1 can have many rows that reference a single row in Table 2. For example, the Sale table can have many rows that refer to a single stock item, or a single customer.

- **One To One** One-to-one cardinality describes a relationship in which only one row in Table 1 refers to a single row in Table 2. None of the tables in the tabular model have one-to-one cardinality.

Regardless of the cardinality type that you define for a relationship, the lookup column in Table 2 must contain unique values in each row. Although a null or blank value is valid, you cannot have multiple rows that are null or blank in the lookup column.

Furthermore, the lookup column must be a single column. You cannot use composite keys in a table. You must combine multiple columns into a single column prior to loading the data into your model, or by creating a calculated column. (Calculated columns are described later in this section.)

FILTER DIRECTION

The filter direction defined for a relationship determines how SSAS applies filters when evaluating results for a query. When you set the filter direction of a relationship to a single table, the filter type is one-directional and Table 2 filters Table 1. Your other option is to select To Both Tables in the Filter Direction drop-down list to set a bidirectional filter. This latter option is new to SQL Server 2016 Analysis Services, so you must set the compatibility level of your model to 1200 to enable this capability.

Let's look at an example of each type of filter direction to understand the ramifications of each option by performing the following steps:

1. First, consider the relationship between the Sale and City table for which the filter direction is set To Sale, a one-directional filter. On the Model menu, click Analyze In Excel, and click OK in the Analyze In Excel dialog box to open a new Excel workbook connected to your model.

2. In the PivotTable Fields list, select the following check boxes: Sale Count, City Count, and Sales Territory (in the City table).

   In the resulting PivotTable, shown in Figure 2-7, the row labels are values in the Sales Territory column from the City table. Because of the one-directional filter between Sale and City, SSAS uses each sales territory to filter the Sale table and compute the Sales Count value. In other words, SSAS starts by filtering the Sale table to include only rows for cities that have the value External in the Sales Territory column and counts the rows remaining in the filtered Sale table. Then it repeats the process to filter the Sale table for the Far West sales territory and counts the rows in the Sale table, and so on. Each measure value in the Sales Count column is the result of a separate filter based on a value in the City table applied to the Sale table. The City Count value counts rows in the City table, and uses the Sales Territory filter from the same table and computes correctly.

	A	B	C
1	Row Labels	Sale Count	City Count
2	External	2,894	731
3	Far West	26,397	13,028
4	Great Lakes	26,599	18,145
5	Mideast	33,763	13,531
6	N/A	1	1
7	New England	10,519	5,358
8	Plains	31,039	16,435
9	Rocky Mountain	14,778	8,500
10	Southeast	50,520	27,402
11	Southwest	31,756	13,164
12	Grand Total	228,266	116,295

FIGURE 2-7 One-directional filter with one field on rows and measures from separate tables

3. Now let's add another row label to the PivotTable to summarize the results by both Sales Territory and Calendar Year. In the PivotTable Fields List, expand the More Fields

folder for the Date table, and drag Calendar Year below the Sales Territory field in the Rows pane to produce the PivotTable for which a few rows are shown in Figure 2-8.

◢	A	B	C
1	Row Labels ▾	Sale Count	City Count
2	⊟External	2,894	731
3	2013	783	731
4	2014	782	731
5	2015	921	731
6	2016	408	731
7			731
8	⊟Far West	26,397	13,028
9	2013	7,136	13,028
10	2014	7,720	13,028
11	2015	8,281	13,028
12	2016	3,260	13,028
13			13,028

FIGURE 2-8 One-directional filter repeating values for a measure in an unrelated table

Now the Sale Count values are computed correctly because the Sale table is filtered by Sales Territory on rows 2 and 8, and by both Sales Territory and Calendar Year on rows 3 through 7, and rows 9 through 13 because both the City and Date tables have a one-directional filter for the Sale table. However, values in the City Count column compute correctly only on rows 2 and 8 because they are filtered by Sales Territory, which is in the same table as the City Count column. For the other rows, SSAS is unable to apply an additional filter by Calendar Year because the Date table has no relationship with the City table, nor should it. Consequently, the City Count for a specific sales territory repeats across all years for that sales territory.

4. To change this behavior, you can set up a bidirectional relationship between City and Sale by leaving Excel open, switching back to SSDT, and clicking Manage Relationships on the Table menu.

5. In the Manage Relationships dialog box, select the row with Sale [City Key] in the Table 1 column, and City [City Key] in the Table 2 column, and click Edit.

6. In the Filter Direction drop-down list, select To Both Tables. Click OK to close the Edit Relationship dialog box, and then click Close to close the Manage Relationships dialog box. Press CTRL+S to save the model.

7. Switch back to Excel and click Refresh in the Analyze tab of the ribbon to update the PivotTable, shown in Figure 2-9. Now the City Count values change for each year. For each row containing a Calendar Year, SSAS filters the Sale table by sales territory and by calendar year, and then filters the City table by using the City Key values in the filtered Sale Table. To compute City Count, it counts the rows in the filtered City table.

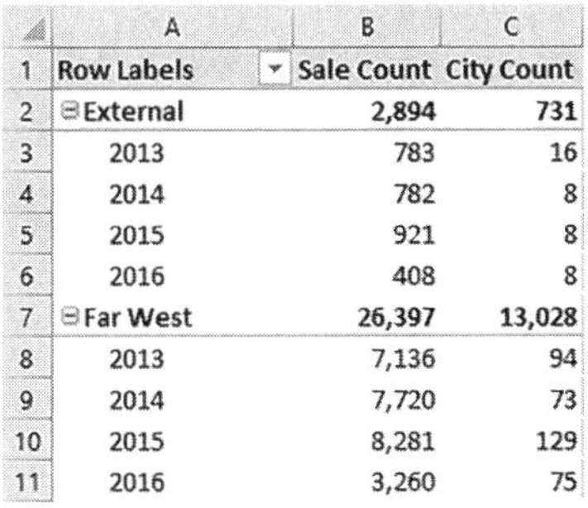

FIGURE 2-9 Bidirectional filter updates City Count value

The ability to use a bidirectional filter in a relationship means you can now model a many-to-many relationship in a tabular model rather than create complex DAX expressions, which was the only way to handle a many-to-many scenario in previous versions of SSAS. You can simulate a many-to-many relationship in the tabular model like the one described in Chapter 1 by adding a new table to the model based on a query. To do this, perform the following steps:

1. Switch back to SSDT, and then, on the Model menu, click Import From Data Source, click Next in the wizard, type the server name for your SQL Server, and select Wide-WorldImportersDW in the Database Name drop-down list.

2. Click Next, select the Service Account option for impersonation, click Next, select the Write A Query That Will Specify The Data To Import option, click Next, and then type the query shown in Listing 2-2.

LISTING 2-2 Query statement to create Sales Reason dimension

```
SELECT
    1 AS SalesReasonKey, 'Value' AS SalesReason
UNION
SELECT
    2 AS SalesReasonKey, 'Manufacturer' AS SalesReason
UNION
SELECT
    3 AS SalesReasonKey, 'Sales Person' AS SalesReason;
```

3. Click Finish, and then click Close. In the model designer, right-click the tab labeled Query, click Rename, and type Sales Reason.

4. Next, repeat these steps to add the bridge table by using the query shown in Listing 2-3.

LISTING 2-3 Named query statement to create Sales Reason Bridge

```
SELECT
    CAST(1 AS bigint) AS [Sale Key],
    1 AS SalesReasonKey
UNION
SELECT
    CAST(1 AS bigint) AS [Sale Key],
    2 AS SalesReasonKey
UNION
SELECT
    CAST(1 AS bigint) AS [Sale Key],
    3 AS SalesReasonKey
UNION
SELECT
    CAST(2 AS bigint) AS [Sale Key],
    1 AS SalesReasonKey;
```

5. Rename the query as Sales Reason Bridge. You can do this by replacing the Friendly Name when you add the query to the Table Import Wizard, or after the table is added to the model. Because this table is used only for modeling purposes, you can hide it by right-clicking its tab, and clicking Hide From Client Tools, just as you can hide a column.

6. Now you need to define relationships between Sale and Sales Reason Bridge. Switch to the Sale table, right-click the Sale Key column header, and click Create Relationship. In the Create Relationship dialog box, select Sales Reason Bridge in the Table 2 drop-down list table, and select To Both Tables in the Filter Direction drop-down list. Notice the One To Many relationship between the tables is automatically set for you. Click OK.

7. You also need a relationship between Sales Reason Bridge and Sales Reason. Switch to the Sales Reason Bridge table, right-click the Sales Reason Key column header, and click Create Relationship. In the Table 2 drop-down list, select Sales Reason. Keep the cardinality and filter direction settings, and click OK. Click CTRL+S to save the model.

8. You can check the results of modeling this many-to-many relationship by creating a PivotTable to show sales counts by sales reason. Click Analyze In Excel in the Model menu, click OK, and then set up the PivotTable by selecting the Total Sales, Sales Count, WWI Invoice ID (from the Sale table) and SalesReason (from the Sales Reason table) check boxes. Partial results are shown in Figure 2-10. No direct relationship exists between Sales Reason and Sale, but the subtotal for each invoice reflects the correct count of sales, which does not match the sum of the individual rows.

	A	B	C
1	Row Labels	Total Sales	Sale Count
2	⊟1	2,300.00	1
3	Manufacturer	2,300.00	1
4	Sales Person	2,300.00	1
5	Value	2,300.00	1
6	⊟2	405.00	2
7	Value	117.00	1

FIGURE 2-10 Many-to-many relationship with bidirectional filtering

> ***NOTE*** **USE BIDIRECTIONAL FILTERING SPARINGLY**
>
> **Bidirectional filtering can produce unexpected results and introduce performance problems if you configure it for all relationships. You should test the behavior of each filter direction whenever you use bidirectional filtering to ensure that you get the correct results.**

When you create a new relationship between two tables, the filter direction is one-directional by default. However, you can change this behavior for the current model by clicking the Model.bim file in Solution Explorer, and then, in the Properties window, choosing Both Directions in the Default Filter Direction drop-down list. If you want to change the default for all new tabular projects, click Options on the Tools menu, expand Analysis Services Tabular Designers in the navigation pane on the left, click New Project Settings, and then select Both Directions in the Default Filter Direction drop-down list.

> ***NEED MORE REVIEW?*** **BIDIRECTIONAL FILTERING WHITEPAPER**
>
> **Download "Bidirectional cross-filtering in SQL Server Analysis Services 2016 and Power BI Desktop" to review bidirectional filtering and scenarios that it can solve from *https://blogs.msdn.microsoft.com/analysisservices/2016/06/24/bidirectional-cross-filtering-whitepaper/*.**

Hierarchies

Hierarchies in a tabular model provide a predefined navigation path for a set of columns in the same table. Tabular models support both natural and unnatural hierarchies. Unlike a multidimensional model in which natural hierarchies are also useful for optimizing query performance, hierarchies in tabular models provide no performance benefits.

To create a hierarchy in a tabular model, perform the following steps:

1. Switch to the Diagram view in SSDT.
2. Let's create a hierarchy in the Date dimension to support drill down from year to month to date. To do this, right-click Calendar Year Label, click Create Hierarchy, and type Calendar as the new hierarchy name. You can then either drag the next column, Calendar Month Label, below Calendar Year Label in the hierarchy, or right-click the column, point to Add To Hierarchy, and then click Calendar.

3. Repeat this step to add Date to the hierarchy. You can see the resulting hierarchy and its columns in the Diagram view, as shown in Figure 2-11.

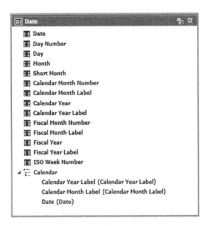

FIGURE 2-11 Natural hierarchy

4. You can now test the hierarchy. If Excel remains open from a previous step, you can click Refresh on the PowerPivot Tools Analyze tab of the ribbon. Otherwise, click Analyze In Excel on the Model menu, and click OK in the Analyze In Excel dialog box. In Excel, select the following check boxes in the PivotTable Fields List: Total Sales and Calendar.

5. In the PivotTable, you can expand CY2013 and CY2013-Apr to view each level of the hierarchy related to April 2013, as shown in Figure 2-12.

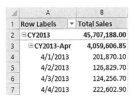

FIGURE 2-12 Hierarchy navigation in Excel PivotTable

The behavior of the hierarchy is normal, but its sort order is not because the default sort order of values in a column with a Text data type is alphabetical. However, the sort order for months should be chronological by month number. In a tabular model, you can fix this by configuring a Sort By Column to manage the sort order. If you have control over the design over the data source, you can add a column to define a sort order for another column. Otherwise, you need to modify the table structure in your model, as described in the "Calculated columns" section later in this chapter.

6. To fix the sort order for Calendar Month Label, switch back to SSDT from Excel, toggle to the Grid view, and select the Date tab at the bottom of the model designer.

7. Select the Calendar Month Label column to view its properties in the Properties window.

8. In the Sort By Column property's drop-down list, select Calendar Month Number.

9. Press CTRL+S to save the model, and then switch back to Excel. In the Analyze tab of the ribbon, click Refresh. The months for CY2013 now sort in the correct sequence from CY2013-Jan to CY2013-Dec.

> **NOTE** **MODELING A HIERARCHY FOR A SNOWFLAKE DIMENSION OR PARENT-CHILD HIERARCHY**
>
> When your table structure includes a snowflake dimension (described in Chapter 1), you must consolidate the columns that you want to use in a hierarchy into a single table. To do this, create a calculated column as described later in this section by using the RELATED() function. The WideWorldImporters database does not have a data structure suitable for illustrating this technique, but you can see an example in "Using the SSAS Tabular Model, Week 5 – Hierarchies 2" at *https://sharepointmike.wordpress.com/2012/11/03/using-the-ssas-tabular-model-week-5-hierarchies-2/*.
>
> There is no option for defining a ragged or parent-child hierarchy in a tabular model as there is in a multidimensional model. Instead, you use DAX functions to evaluate results within a table structured as a parent-child hierarchy. Marco Russo describes how to use DAX to flatten, or naturalizing, a parent-child hierarchy as a set of calculated columns in his article "Parent-Child Hierarchies" at *http://www.daxpatterns.com/parent-child-hierarchies/*. Although this article was written primarily for Excel's Power Pivot models, the principles also apply to tabular models in SQL Server 2016.

EXAM TIP

Be prepared for questions that define an analysis scenario and a table structure and then ask you how to construct a hierarchy. The hierarchy can require columns from a single table or from multiple tables. Also, be sure you understand the difference between hierarchies supported in tabular models as compared to multidimensional models as well as the performance differences.

Partitions

When you add a table to the tabular model, the data that is currently in the source is loaded into memory, unless you are using DirectQuery mode as described in Skill 2.3, "Develop a tabular model to access data in near real-time." When the source data changes, you must refresh the table in the tabular model to bring it up-to-date. When a table is large and only a subset of the data in it has changed, one way that you can speed up the refresh process is to partition the table and then refresh only the partitions in which data has changed. For example, you can set up a sales table with monthly partitions. Typically, sales data for prior months do not change, so you need to refresh only the partition for the current month.

Another scenario for which you can consider partitioning is a rolling window strategy. In this case, your business requirements can be to support analysis of sales over the last 24 months. If you partition by month, you can add a new partition as sales data comes in for a new month and remove the oldest partition so that you always have 24 partitions at a time. The addition of a new partition and removal of an existing partition is much faster than re-loading the entire 24 months of data into the tabular model.

By default, each table in your tabular model is contained in one partition. You can define more partitions in the Partition Manager, which you open by selecting Partitions on the Table menu. Figure 2-13 shows the Partition Manager for the Sale table. Here you can see the name and last processed date of the single partition that currently exists in the tabular model as well as a preview of the rows in the selected partition.

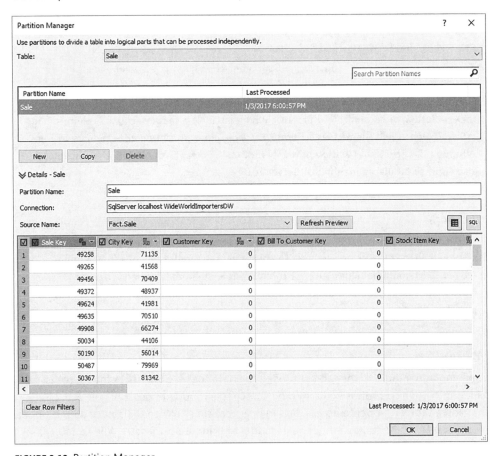

FIGURE 2-13 Partition Manager

You use the Partition Manager to manually define a specific number of partitions. If each partition is based on the same source, you define a filter for each partition. As an example, let's say that data for each Bill To Customer comes into the source system at different times and you want to refresh the tabular model for each Bill To Customer separately. To change the filter for the existing partition, perform the following steps:

1. Click the drop-down arrow in the Bill To Customer Key column, clear the (Select All) check box, select the 0 check box, and click OK.

2. Change the partition name by typing Bill To Customer 0 after the existing name, Sale, in the Partition Name text box.

3. Next, click Copy to create another partition and then change the filter for the new partition to the Bill To Customer key value of 1, and change its name to Sale Bill To Customer 1.

4. Create a final partition by copying either partition, setting the Bill To Customer key to 202, and changing its name to Bill To Customer 202.

5. Click OK to save your changes, and then, on the Model menu, point to Process, and then select Process Table to replace the single partition for Sale in your tabular model with the three new partitions.

> **NOTE** **QUERY EDITOR TO DEFINE PARTITION FILTERS FOR RELATIONAL DATA SOURCES**
>
> Rather than use the filter interface in the Partition Manager, you can click the Query Editor button on the right side of the dialog box to open the query editor and view the SQL statement associated with the table, if the data source is a table or view from a relational database. You can append a WHERE clause to a previously unfiltered SQL statement or modify an existing WHERE clause to define a new filter for the selected partition. If you modify the WHERE clause in the Query Editor, you cannot toggle back to the Table Preview mode without losing your changes.

> **IMPORTANT** **AVOID DUPLICATE ROWS ACROSS PARTITIONS**
>
> When you define multiple partitions for a table, you must take care that each filter produces unique results so that a row cannot appear in more than one partition. SSAS does not validate your data and does not warn you if the same row exists in multiple partitions.

When your partitioning strategy is more dynamic, usually because it is based on dates, you can use a script to define partitions instead of Partition Manager. You can then create a SQL Server Integration Services (SSIS) package to execute the script by using an Analysis Services DDL Task, and then schedule the SSIS package to run on a periodic basis.

To generate a script template, perform the following steps:

1. Right-click the project in Solution Explorer, and select Deploy. SSDT deploys your project to the server you identified when you created the project using the name of your project as the database name, but you can change these settings in the project's properties.

2. Next, open SQL Server Management Studio (SSMS), connect to the tabular instance of Analysis Services, expand the Databases folder, expand the 70-768-Ch2 database, expand the Tables folder, right-click the Sale table, and select Partitions to open the Partitions dialog box, as shown in Figure 2-14.

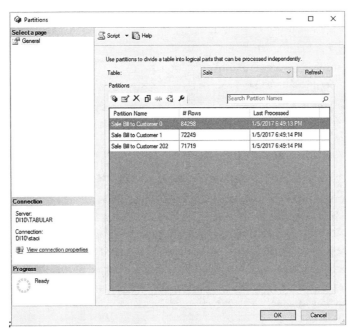

FIGURE 2-14 Partitions dialog box in SSMS

3. Click the Script drop-down arrow, select Script Action To New Query Window, and click Cancel to close the Partitions dialog box. You can then update the script that displays in the query window by replacing the sections of the script with a new name for the partition and a revised query, as shown by the bold text in Listing 2-4. Although this listing does not include the annotations, you can keep the annotations in the script if you like.

LISTING 2-4 Create a new partition

```
{
  "createOrReplace": {
    "object": {
      "database": "70-768-Ch2",
      "table": "Sale",
      "partition": "Sale Bill To Customer 100"
```

```
      },
    "partition": {
      "name": "Sale Bill To Customer 100",
      "source": {
        "query": "SELECT [Fact].[Sale].* FROM [Fact].[Sale]
                  WHERE ([Bill To Customer Key] = 100)",
        "dataSource": "SqlServer localhost WideWorldImportersDW"
      }
    }
  }
}
```

> **NOTE** **SCRIPTING PARTITIONS NOT RECOMMENDED DURING DEVELOPMENT CYCLE**
>
> During the development cycle of a tabular model, you should not script partitions
> because the deployed tabular model no longer matches the tabular model in your SSDT
> project. Scripting partitions is a task that is better to perform after deploying a tabular
> model into production. If additional development work is required later, you should
> create a new project by using the Import From Server template in SSDT.

4. Be sure to select 70-768-Ch2 in the Available Databases drop-down list, and then click
    Execute, or press F5 to execute the script.

5. Right-click the Sale table in the Object Explorer window, and select Process Table.

6. In the Process Table(s) dialog box, click OK to perform a Process Default operation on
    the Sale table. (We explain processing operations in more detail in Skill 2.2.)

7. Click Close in the Data Processing dialog box when processing is complete.

8. Check to confirm the addition of the new partition by right-clicking the Sale table in
    the Object Explorer window, and selecting Partitions to open the Partitions dialog box.
    Because there is no Bill To Customer key value of 100 in the table, the new partition
    appears in the dialog box with a last processed date but zero rows.

> **NOTE** **COMPARISON WITH PARTITIONS IN MULTIDIMENSIONAL MODELS**
>
> Partitions in tabular models differ from partitions in multidimensional models in two
> important ways. First, you can partition any table in a tabular model whereas you can parti-
> tion only measure groups in a multidimensional model. Second, the addition of a partition
> in a tabular model has no effect on query performance, whereas partitioning in a multidi-
> mensional model can improve the performance of queries in some cases, as described in
> Chapter 4, "Configure and maintain SQL Server Analysis Services."

EXAM TIP

You should be able to identify scenarios for which partitioning is best suited and understand how partitions in tabular models differ from partitions in multidimensional models.

Perspectives

When a client application displays the list of available fields from a tabular model, the default behavior is to display columns from all tables and all measures collectively as fields. However, some users can be interested in using only a subset of the model. To accommodate these users, you can add one or more perspectives to display selected columns and measures.

To create a new perspective, perform the following steps:

1. Point to Perspectives on the Model menu, and select Create And Manage.

2. In the Perspectives dialog box, click New Perspective, and type a name for the perspective, such as Stock Items By Date.

3. Scroll down, expand Date, and select the check box for each of the following fields: Calendar Month Label, Calendar Year Label, Date, and Calendar.

4. Expand Sale, and select the check box for Sales Count and Total Sales.

5. Next, expand Stock Item, and select the check box for the following fields: Brand, Color, Size, and Stock Item.

6. Click OK to save the perspective.

7. You can test the perspective by selecting Analyze In Excel on the Model menu, and then, in the Analyze In Excel dialog box, select Stock Items By Date in the Perspective drop-down list. Click OK to open Excel. The PivotTable Fields list now shows a subset of the available fields as defined by the perspective, as shown in Figure 2-15. Close the workbook when your review is finished.

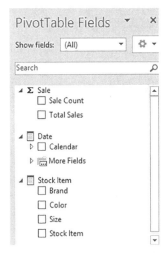

FIGURE 2-15 Fields available in the Stock Item By Date perspective

When a user connects to a tabular model directly from Excel, the Data Connection Wizard displays the option to connect to the tabular model (called a Cube in the user interface) or to the perspective. In other client applications, you must specify replace the model name with the perspective name in the Cube property of the connection string.

Calculated columns

Sometimes the data that you import into a tabular model is not structured in a way that is suitable for analysis and you do not have the ability to make changes in the source to structure it in the way that you need. Consider the following scenarios:

- A table contains columns for FirstName and LastName, but you need to display a single column with the values concatenated like "LastName, FirstName."
- A table contains null values and you want to display a default value, such as "NA."
- You need to perform a mathematical operation on values in two separate columns to derive a new scalar value.
- You need unique values in a column to use as a lookup.

To resolve any of these situations, you can create a *calculated column* to define a new column in the table and populate it by using a DAX expression. There is no limitation on the data type that you assign to a calculated column, nor is there any limitation on the number of calculated columns that you can add to a table. That said, bear in mind that the data in a calculated column is stored in memory just like data imported from a data source, unlike a measure which is computed at query time.

In general, to add a calculated column, click the cell in the first row of the column labeled Add Column, and then type the expression for the calculated column in the formula bar. You do not provide a name for the calculated column in the expression as you do for a measure. Instead, after adding the expression, select the column, and then type the name in the Column Name property in the Properties window.

Enhance the 70-768-Ch2 model in SSDT by adding the calculated columns shown in Table 2-3. Refer to Chapter 3 to review these types of DAX expressions.

TABLE 2-3 New calculated columns to add to the tabular model

Table	Column Name	Expression
City	City State	=[City] & ", " & [State Province]
Sale	Discount Amount	=RELATED('Stock Item'[Recommended Retail Price])-[Unit Price]

At this point, the tabular model is ready to explore using any tool that is compatible with SSAS, such as Excel or SSRS, but it is not yet set up as well as it can be. There are more dimensions and fact tables to add as well as many configuration changes to the dimension and cube to consider and implement that you explore in Skills 1.2 and 1.3.

> **IMPORTANT** **EXAMPLE DATABASE FOCUSES ON EXAM TOPICS**
>
> The remainder of this chapter describes additional development tasks for a tabular model that you must know how to perform. At the end of the chapter, the 70-768-Ch2 tabular model is functionally correct, but is not as user-friendly or as complete as it could be because to do so is out of scope for this book.
>
> To complete your own tabular modeling projects, be sure to test the model thoroughly in client applications and enlist the help of business users for testing. Be sure to review the naming conventions of tables, columns, hierarchies, measures, and KPIs. Then check the sort order of values in columns for which an alphabetical sort is not appropriate. Review the aggregate values with and without filters and especially test filter behavior for related tables configured for bidirectional filtering. Last, hide any columns or tables that are not necessary for analysis.

Create a time table

When you use a data warehouse as a data source, it often includes a time table, also known as a date table, as a dimension in the star schema design. However, a tabular model is less strict about the use of a star schema as a data source. If you create a simple tabular model from a variety of sources, or are building a simple prototype before starting a complex project, you probably do not have a date table available even though it can be useful to include one in the tabular model to better support analysis of data over time.

A new feature in SQL Server 2016 Analysis Services, which requires your model to be set to a compatibility level of 1200, is the ability to create a *calculated table*. A calculated table is built solely by using a DAX expression. You can select a few columns from another table in the model, combine columns from separate tables, or transform and filter data to restructure it as a separate table. Use this feature sparingly because the addition of a calculated table to your model requires more memory on the SSAS server to store its data and increases the model's processing time.

One use case for the addition of a date table is to support a roleplaying Date dimension. In the Sale table, there are two date columns—Invoice Date Key and Delivery Date Key. Rather than use DAX to change a query's context from Invoice Date to Delivery Date, you can set up a calculated table for Delivery Date, and then define a relationship between the new date table and the Delivery Date Key column in the Sale table.

To create the date table, perform the following steps:

1. Click New Calculated Table on the Table menu, or click the Create A New Table Calculated From A DAX Formula tab at the bottom of the model designer.

2. In the formula bar above the new empty table grid, type a DAX expression or query that returns a table. For example, you can use a simple expression, such as ='Date' to copy an existing roleplaying dimension table, Date.

A simpler method to create a date table is to use one of the following DAX functions:

- CALENDAR   Use this function to create a table with a single date column. You define the date range by providing a start and end date.

- CALENDARAUTO   Use this function to create a table with a single date column. The date range is determined by the model designer, which uses the earliest and latest dates found in any column in any table in the model.

Regardless of the method you use, you can then work with the table just like any other table for which data was imported in to the model. That means you can rename it, define relationships, add calculated columns, and configure properties.

> **NOTE   DATE TABLE AS A DATA FEED IN AZURE MARKETPLACE**
>
> Boyan Penev has created a data feed for a date table that you can access by connecting to Azure Marketplace. You can find information about the data feed and a link to its location in Azure Marketplace by visiting "DateStream" at *https://datestream.codeplex.com/*.

Publish from Microsoft Visual Studio

To publish a tabular model from SQL Server Data Tools for Visual Studio 2015 (SSDT), you use the Deploy command for the project. You can right-click the project in Solution Explorer, and click Deploy, or click Deploy on the Build menu. The Deploy dialog box displays the status of deploying metadata and each table. If deployment takes too long, you can click Stop Deployment to end the process. Click Close if deployment completes successfully.

Before deployment, SSAS stored your model in memory as a workspace database, which you can also access in SSMS. This workspace database stores the data that you added to the model by using the Table Import Wizard. When you view data in the model designer, or use the Analyze In Excel feature, SSAS retrieves the data from the workspace database. There are properties associated with the model that manage the behavior of the workspace database. Click the Model.bim file in Solution Explorer to view the following properties in the Properties window:

- **Data Backup**   You can change the setting from the default, Do Not Backup To Disk, to Backup To Disk to create a backup of the workspace database as an ABF file each time you save the Model.bim file. However, you cannot use the Back To Disk option if you are using a remote SSAS instance to host the workspace database.

- **Workspace Database**   This property cannot be changed. It displays the name that SSAS assigns to the workspace database.

- **Workspace Retention**   This setting determines whether SSAS keeps the workspace database in memory when you close the project in SSDT. The default option, Unload From Memory, keeps the database on disk, but removes it from memory. SSDT loads the model faster when you next open the project when you can choose the Keep In Memory option. The third option, Delete Workspace, deletes the workspace database from both memory and disk, which takes the longest time to reload because SSAS requires additional time to import data into the new workspace database. You can change the default for this setting if you open the Tools menu, select Options, and open the Data Modeling page in the Analysis Server settings.

- **Workspace Server**   This property specifies the server you use to host the workspace database. For best performance, you should use a local instance of SSAS.

Import from Microsoft PowerPivot

If you have an Excel workbook containing a PowerPivot model, you can import it into a new project in SSDT and jumpstart your development efforts for a tabular model. In the SSDT File menu, point to New, and then click Project. In the New Project dialog box, select Analysis Services in the Business Intelligence group of templates, and then select Import From Power-Pivot. At the bottom of the dialog box that opens, type a name for the project, select a location, and optionally type a new name for the project's solution. The metadata in the model as well as the data it contains are imported into your model. Afterwards, you can continue to develop the tabular model in SSDT.

> ***NOTE* LINKED TABLES ROW LIMIT**
>
> When a PowerPivot workbook contains a linked table, the linked table is stored like a pasted table. However, pasted tables have limitations, which you can find at "Copy and Paste Data (SSAS Tabular)," *https://msdn.microsoft.com/en-us/library/hh230895.aspx*. For this reason, there is a 10,000-row limit on the linked table data. If the number of rows in the table exceeds this limit, the import process truncates the data and displays an error. To work around this limit, you should move the data into another supported data source, such as SQL Server. Then replace the linked table with the new data source in the PowerPivot model and import the revised model into a tabular model project.

Select a deployment option, including Processing Option, Transactional Deployment, and Query Mode

To ensure you deploy the project to the correct server, review, and if necessary, update the project's properties. To do this, perform the following steps:

1. Right-click the project name in Solution Explorer and select Properties.

2. In the 70-768-Ch2 Property Pages dialog box, select the Deployment page, as shown in Figure 2-16, and then update the Server text box with the name of your SSAS server if you need to deploy to a remote server rather than locally.

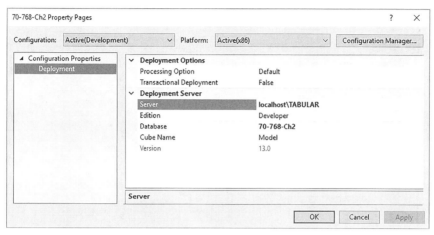

FIGURE 2-16 SSAS project deployment properties

The following additional deployment options are also available on this page:

- **Processing Option**   Just as you can with multidimensional databases, you can specify whether to process the tabular model after deployment, and what type of processing to perform. When this option is set to Default, which is the default setting, SSAS processes only the objects that are not currently in a processed state. You can change this setting to Do Not Process if you want to perform processing later, or to Full if you want the database to process all objects whenever you deploy your project from SSDT. In Skill 2.2, "Configure, manage, and secure a tabular model," we explain these and other processing options in greater detail.

- **Transactional Deployment**   When the value in this option is False, the deployment does not participate in a transaction with processing. Consequently, if processing fails, the model is deployed to the server, but remains in an unprocessed state. If you change this option's value to True, deployment rolls back if processing fails.

3. When you are ready to create the database on the server, right-click the project in Solution Explorer, and click Deploy.

The first time you perform this step, the deployment process creates the database on the server and adds any objects that you have defined in the project. Each subsequent time that you deploy the project, as long as you have kept the default deployment options in the project properties, the deployment process preserves the existing database and adds any new database objects, and updates any database objects that you have modified in the project.

4. You can check the tabular model on the server by opening SSMS and connecting to the tabular instance of Analysis Services. In Object Explorer, expand the Databases folder, expand the 70-768-Ch2 folder, and then expand the Connection and Tables folders to review the objects in each folder, as shown in Figure 2-17.

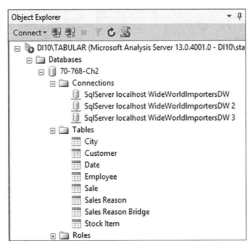

FIGURE 2-17 Tabular database objects visible in Object Explorer

If your tabular model is set to a lower compatibility level (1100 or 1103), you have the following two additional options available in the project's properties:

- **Query Mode**   You use this option to determine the type of storage that SSAS uses for the tabular model. You can choose one of the following options:

  - **DirectQuery**   This mode stores metadata on the SSAS server and keeps the data in the relational storage as described in Skill 2.3.

  - **DirectQuery With In-Memory**   This option is a hybrid mode. SSAS resolves queries by using DirectQuery by default. It retrieves data from cache only if the client connection string requests a change in mode as described in Skill 2.3.

  - **In-Memory**   This mode stores both metadata and data imported from data sources on the SSAS server.

  - **In-Memory With DirectQuery**   This is another type of hybrid mode. With this option, queries are resolved from the data stored in cache on the SSAS server unless the client connection string switches the query to DirectQuery mode as described in Skill 2.3.

- **Impersonation Settings**   This option is applicable only if you set the Query Mode option to DirectQuery. If you keep the default value of Default, user connections to the tabular model use the credentials set in the Table Import Wizard to connect to the backend database. You can change this to ImpersonateCurrentUser if you want SSAS to pass the user's credentials to the backend database.

You can also change data source impersonation after deploying the model to the server. In SSMS, connect to the Analysis Services server, and then, in Object Explorer, expand the Databases folder, the folder for your database, and the Connections folder. Right-click the data source object, and click Properties. In the Impersonation Info box, click the ellipsis button, and then select Use The Credentials Of The Current User in the Impersonation Information dialog box. When you click OK, the Impersonation Info property changes to ImpersonateCurrentUser.

When using the ImpersonateCurrentUser option, your authorized users must have Read permission on the data source. In addition, you must configure constrained delegation so that SSAS can pass Windows credentials to the backend database.

> **NOTE CONSTRAINED DELEGATION CONFIGURATION**
>
> The specific steps to configure trusted delegation for your SSAS server are described in "Configure Analysis Services for Kerberos constrained delegation" at *https://msdn. microsoft.com/en-us/library/dn194199.aspx.*

Skill 2.2: Configure, manage, and secure a tabular model

In addition to knowing how to design and publish a tabular model, you must also understand your options for configuring storage for the model, know how to choose an appropriate processing operation to refresh the data in your model, and demonstrate the ability to secure the model appropriately.

> **This section covers how to:**
>
> - Configure tabular model storage and data refresh
> - Configure refresh interval settings
> - Configure user security and permissions
> - Configure row-level security

Configure tabular model storage and data refresh

You have two options for defining tabular model storage, in-memory and DirectQuery. The considerations for DirectQuery storage are discussed in Skill 2.3. A single SSAS server can host databases using either storage mode.

To configure storage for a tabular model, click the Model.bim file in Solution Explorer in SSDT. In the Properties window, confirm the DirectQuery Mode option is set to Off, the default value, to configure in-memory storage for the tabular model.

For in-memory storage, the data imported from the tabular model's data sources is stored on disk when the SSAS service is not running. When the service starts, SSAS reads the metadata of the deployed databases. When a user query requests on object from a database, the entire database is then loaded into memory from disk. On the other hand, all databases are loaded when you connect to the SSAS server by using SSMS. The time required to load a database into memory can be a few seconds or several minutes depending on the size of the database and the speed of the disk. The database then stays in memory until the SSAS service is stopped.

> **NOTE HARDWARE GUIDANCE FOR TABULAR MODELS**
>
> The most important factors to consider when setting up a tabular instance on a server are memory and CPU. You can download "Hardware Sizing a Tabular Solution (SQL Server Analysis Services)" from *https://msdn.microsoft.com/en-us/library/jj874401.aspx* to review this topic. Although the whitepaper was written for SQL Server 2012, the guidance is still applicable to SQL Server 2016 tabular models. Another good resource is an article by Jason Thomas, "5 Tips to Ensure Super Fast SSAS Tabular Models," at *https://www.blue-granite. com/blog/5-tips-fast-ssas-tabular-models*.

When you use the in-memory storage mode, you must plan to periodically refresh the data. Changes to the underlying data source are not automatically reflected in the tabular model. If you need that capability, configure the tabular model to use DirectQuery as described in Skill 2.3. You can choose to refresh the entire model, or you can refresh data in specific partitions, as explained in Skill 2.1.

Columnar storage

The goal of processing is to load a copy of the data from your data sources into server memory. Specifically, the data is transformed from its original state into in-memory columnar storage. Unlike a row-oriented relational database that organizes information about a single entity as one row with multiple columns, a columnar database organizes information into columns. Each column can store data in a different way. SSAS analyzes the data in a column to determine which storage technique to apply.

Let's take a closer look at data storage by considering some simple examples. When a relational database engine resolves a query, it must read entire rows of data from a row-oriented table, such as the simple version of the Employee table shown in Table 2-4. It must read columns from the entire row and then ignore the columns that the query does not request. Row-oriented storage is efficient for inserting a new row or retrieving a single record, but is less efficient when aggregating data across multiple rows.

TABLE 2-4 Employee table in relational storage

Employee Key	WWI Employee ID	Employee	Preferred Name	Is Sales person
1	14	Lily Code	Lily	TRUE
2	4	Isabella Rupp	Isabella	FALSE
3	11	Ethan Onslow	Ethan	FALSE
4	7	Amy Trefl	Amy	TRUE
5	19	Jai Shand	Jai	FALSE

By contrast, when the tabular engine resolves a query from a column-oriented table, as shown in Table 2-5, it reads only the columns necessary to resolve the query. If the query is filtered, such as when you need only the names of employees who are also a salesperson, the engine reads through the Is Salesperson column to find the rows having a TRUE value, and then finds the corresponding rows in the Employee column.

TABLE 2-5 Employee table in columnar storage

Employee Key	WWI Employee ID	Employee	Preferred Name	Is Sales person
1	14	Lily Code	Lily	TRUE
2	4	Isabella Rupp	Isabella	FALSE
3	11	Ethan Onslow	Ethan	FALSE
4	7	Amy Trefl	Amy	TRUE
5	19	Jai Shand	Jai	FALSE

More precisely, SSAS creates a dictionary of the distinct values in each column and a bitmap index for the dictionary, compresses these objects, and stores them both in random access memory (RAM) and disk. When the SSAS service starts, it reads the disk version of the dictionary and bitmap indexes to avoid the need to read data from the original data sources.

To compress the data, SSAS uses one of the following techniques:

- Dictionary encoding
- Value encoding
- Run Length encoding

Let's look at an example of each of these compression techniques in the context of the Employee table. Table 2-6 shows how SSAS applies dictionary encoding to the Is Salesperson column.

TABLE 2-6 Dictionary encoding of Is Salesperson column

Is Sales person ID
0
1
1
0
1

ID	Is Sales Person
0	TRUE
1	FALSE

Sometimes a more efficient compression method is to use value encoding. In this case, SSAS looks for a way to use mathematical relationships to reduce the number of bytes required to store the data. For example, let's say each employee key has a prefix of 100, as shown in Table 2-7. As SSAS evaluates the column, it determines that it can subtract 1000 from each employee key value and store the result, which uses fewer bytes overall. The number of distinct values is the same before and after encoding, but overall storage is reduced. When a query requests values from a value-encoded column, SSAS reverses the mathematical operation and adds 1000 to the stored value return the original value of each employee key.

TABLE 2-7 Value encoding of Employee Key column

Employee key
1001
1002
1003
1004
1005

Employee key
1
2
3
4
5

To understand run length encoding, let's start with a simplified version of the row-oriented Sale table as shown in Table 2-8. The goal of run length encoding is to avoid the repetition of values. Notice the repetition of the same customer key in the Sale table, although this repetition is not always in a consecutive row. On the other hand, the Invoice Date Key column contains the same value for all rows shown in the example while the Total Excluding Tax column has no repeated values.

TABLE 2-8 Simplified Sale table using row-oriented storage

customer Key	invoice date key	total excluding tax
0	2013-01-01	2300.00
0	2013-01-01	288.00
0	2013-01-01	117.00
105	2013-01-01	90.00
57	2013-01-01	259.20
0	2013-01-01	480.00

Table 2-9 shows the result of run length encoding on the Sale table. The structure that SSAS creates to store the data reduces the size of the column by storing a value once for each set of contiguous rows in which it exists in row-oriented storage in addition to storing an index to the row in which the value appears, and the number of subsequent rows containing the value. When a column such as Total Excluding Tax has high cardinality, encoding cannot compress the column's data.

TABLE 2-9 Run length encoding of the simplified Sale table

Customer Key	Start	Count
0	1	3
105	4	1
57	5	1
0	6	1

Invoice Date Key	Start	Count
2013-01-01	1	6

Total Excluding Tax
2300.00
288.00
117.00
90.00
259.20
480.00

Whenever a model is deployed the first time, or when data changes in a partition, SSAS must also process the following types of dependent objects:

- **Calculated columns** A dependent calculated column can exist in a table other than the one that is being processed. For example, let's say you use the RELATED() function in a calculated column in Table A to use a value from related Table B, and then Table B is reprocessed. In that case, even though Table A is not reprocessed, the calculated column is updated based on Table B's new values. Calculated columns are stored in the same way as table columns.

- **Indexes** Because an index is dependent on the column dictionary, which could have changed for a processed table, SSAS rebuilds dependent indexes for the processed table.

- **Relationships** When a relationship exists between two tables, SSAS creates a file storing the unique values from the foreign key column and mapping those values to the corresponding row numbers in the lookup table. For example, the relationship between the Sale and Stock Item tables stores the Stock Item Key values from the Sale table, and the row number in which those keys are found in the Stock Item table, as shown in Table 2-10. When either of these tables are processed, the relationship table must also be rebuilt.

TABLE 2-10 Relationship storage

SAle [Stock Item Key]	Stock Item[Row num]
168	169
173	174
194	195
202	203
204	205

Hierarchies   SSAS creates a separate storage structure for hierarchies defined in a table. Reprocessing a table containing hierarchies also requires reprocessing each hierarchy to make it consistent with the updated table.

> **NEED MORE REVIEW?**   **XVELOCITY (VERTIPAQ) STORAGE**
>
> For more background, see "The VertiPaq Engine in DAX" by Alberto Ferrari and Marco Russo at *https://www.microsoftpressstore.com/articles/article.aspx?p=2449192&seqNum=3.*

Processing options

You have many choices for performing processing operations. The simplest option is to execute Process Full to process every object in the database. However, this option can require the most time and consume the most resources on the server. When some data in a model remains static over a period of time while other data changes more frequently, you can selectively process objects to minimize the processing time and resource consumption requirements. Table 2-11 lists the available processing options and the objects to which each processing option is applicable.

TABLE 2-11 Processing options by object

Processing option	database	table	partition
Process Add	No	No	Yes
Process Clear	Yes	Yes	Yes
Process Data	No	Yes	Yes
Process Default	Yes	Yes	Yes
Process Defrag	Yes	Yes	No
Process Full	Yes	Yes	Yes
Process Recalc	Yes	No	No

EXAM TIP

There are many different choices that you have for refreshing data in a model, including which objects to process, which order to process them in, and what type of processing to perform. The exam is likely to describe a situation, including possible error conditions, and then ask you to identify the steps to perform to best satisfy the stated requirements.

PROCESS ADD

You use the Process Add operation to load new rows into a partition. In this case, you must be able to identify the new rows because SSAS does not automatically identify new rows for you. Because there is no interface to use this option, you must use Tabular Model Scripting Language (TMSL) instead. The table's dictionary is updated to add the new rows, and dependent objects are automatically recalculated.

> ***NOTE*** **RESOURCES FOR TMSL AND TOM**
>
> For the exam, you do not need to know how to perform a Process Add operation by using TMSL, or the Analysis Services Management Object (AMO) client library. However, you can learn more at "Refresh command (TMSL)" at *https://msdn.microsoft.com/en-us/library/mt697588.aspx* or at "Introduction to the Tabular Object Model (TOM) in Analysis Services AMO" at *https://msdn.microsoft.com/en-us/library/mt706505.aspx*.

PROCESS CLEAR

You use the Process Clear operations when you want to remove all data from the selected object—a database, table, or partition. After this operation executes, the cleared objects are no longer accessible by user queries.

One way to conserve memory during processing is to use the Process Clear operation before using Process Full. That way, SSAS does not keep two copies of the data as described later in the "Process Full" section. On the other hand, when you take this approach, users cannot query the object until the Process Full operation is complete.

PROCESS DATA

This operation reads the data for a partition or a table, and updates the dictionary, but makes no changes to the dependent objects. Because this operation leaves the dependent objects in an invalid state, you must perform a Process Recalc operation afterward. Furthermore, the target object of the operation cannot be queried until the dependent objects are rebuilt.

This is your best option when you want to minimize the time required for processing when data has not changed in all tables. Run the Process Recalc only after processing all tables so that dependent objects are not unnecessarily refreshed more than once.

PROCESS DEFAULT

When you choose this processing operation, SSAS determines the current state of each object. If an object is unprocessed or partially processed, SSAS brings it to a processed state by loading data. SSAS performs a Process Data operation if an object is empty because it has been recently deployed, or a Process Clear operation was executed. It also performs a Process Recalc only on dependent objects invalidated by a Process Data operation performed in a previous step, or as a result of performing the Process Default operation. The best practice for using the Process Default operation depends on which of the following objects is the target of the operation:

- **Database** All objects in the database can be queried without performing any additional operation.

- **Table** Ideally, if processing multiple tables using Process Default, use one transaction for processing. If you choose to process the tables in separate transactions, you should choose the sequence of process operations carefully to ensure a table with a calculated column dependent on another table is processed after that other table. Either way, perform a Process Recalc operation at the database level after processing the tables to ensure all dependent objects are rebuilt correctly.

- **Partition** The partition is loaded with data only if it was empty prior to the Process Default operation, but the dependent objects are not refreshed. Therefore, you must still perform a Process Recalc at the database level afterward.

PROCESS DEFRAG

When you process partitions independently or remove partitions from a table, the dictionary is not rebuilt. Instead, new data is added to the dictionary, but values that no longer exist in any partition are not removed. Consequently, the dictionary can become fragmented. The Process Defrag operation rebuilds table data and optimizes the dictionary for all partitions, but does not require read operations on the data source.

Although a fragmented dictionary does not yield incorrect query results, it does cause queries to consume more memory and thereby adversely impacts performance. Therefore, you should perform a Process Defrag operation periodically if you run refresh operations on partitions only.

> **NOTE DICTIONARIES REBUILT BY PROCESS FULL OR PROCESS DATA OPERATIONS ON A TABLE**
>
> Dictionary fragmentation does not occur when you perform the Process Full or Process Data operations on a table. Both of these processing operations rebuild the dictionary.

Process Defrag at the database level (which you can run only by using TMSL) also causes data for unprocessed tables to be loaded. However, these tables are ignored when you run Process Defrag at the table level.

PROCESS FULL

When you choose to fully process a database, every partition in every table is refreshed from its corresponding data source and calculated columns are recalculated. If a table is new, SSAS creates a dictionary and at least one data file for each column in the table. Multiple data files are created if the table is partitioned. If a data file already exists, SSAS empties the file and reloads it with data from the data source. Behind the scenes, SSAS preserves the existing copy until the process operation is complete for all tables at which point the previous version of each object in the database is removed and replaced with its rebuilt version.

You can perform the Process Full operation at the database level to rebuild all tables. If you perform this on a table or partition, SSAS performs a Process Data operation on the target object, and a Process Recalc operation is performed only for the table's or partition's dependent objects. If your Process Full operation is performed for multiple objects in a single transaction, the Process Recalc executes only once. If you use separate transactions, the Process Recalc executes once per transaction.

It is important to note that if a calculated column has a dependency on another table that is in an unprocessed state, the calculation is performed as if that other table were empty. When that other table is processed with a Process Data operation, you must perform a Process Recalc to correct the calculated column. However, if you run Process Full on that table, the refresh of the calculated column occurs automatically, but more memory is required to complete the operation.

PROCESS RECALC

You should always include a Process Recalc operation after a Process Data operation. However, you can perform this operation only at the database level. If you need to refresh only specific structures, you use Process Full or Process Default instead because they invoke the Process Recalc only for objects invalidated by other processing operations.

Configure refresh interval settings

You can manually set up process operations in SSMS as needed. However, a more practical approach is to script the processing operations, which you can then use to automate the refresh of your tabular model in a number of ways.

First, let's review how to create a processing operation. In SSMS, connect to the tabular instance. In Object Explorer, expand the Databases folder. To perform a process operation at the database level, right-click the database, and select Process Database. In the Process Database dialog box, select the desired processing operation in the Mode drop-down list, as shown in Figure 2-18.

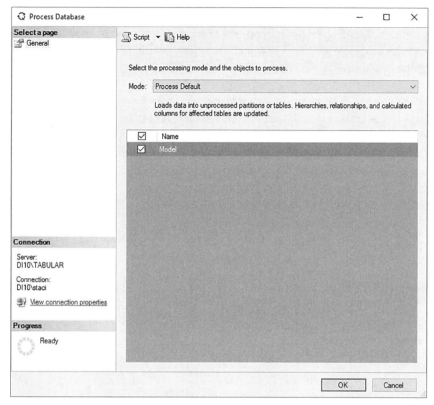

FIGURE 2-18 Process Database processing mode selection

Rather than click OK, you can generate a script by clicking Script, and then clicking Script Action To New Query Window, and clicking Cancel. In a query window, you see the TMSL for the selected operation, as shown in Listing 2-5. In this example, Process Default is reflected as the automatic type.

LISTING 2-5 TMSL script to refresh database by using the Process Default mode

```
{
  "refresh": {
    "type": "automatic",
    "objects": [
      {
        "database": "70-768-Ch2"
      }
    ]
  }
}
```

You can use this same technique to generate a processing script for one or more tables by right-clicking one of the tables in the database, and selecting Process Table. In the Process Table(s) dialog box, select the process operation in the Mode drop-down list, and select the check box for each table to process. Last, click Script, and then Script Action To New Query Window. Listing 2-6 shows an example of processing three tables in a single transaction.

LISTING 2-6 TMSL script to refresh tables by using the Process Default mode

```
{
  "refresh": {
    "type": "automatic",
    "objects": [
      {
        "database": "70-768-Ch2",
        "table": "Customer"
      },
      {
        "database": "70-768-Ch2",
        "table": "Stock Item"
      },
      {
        "database": "70-768-Ch2",
        "table": "Sale"
      }
    ]
  }
}
```

Similarly, you can create a processing script for partitions by right-clicking a table in Object Explorer, and selecting Partitions. In the Partitions dialog box, select a partition, and click the Partitions button in the dialog box's toolbar. In the Process Partition(s) dialog box, select a processing operation in the Mode drop-down list, and select the check box for one or more partitions. You can then click Script, and Script Action To New Query Window to generate the TMSL script for partitions, such as the one shown in Listing 2-7.

LISTING 2-7 TMSL script to refresh partitions using the Process Default mode

```
{
  "refresh": {
    "type": "automatic",
    "objects": [
      {
        "database": "70-768-Ch2",
        "table": "Sale",
        "partition": "Sale Bill To Customer 202"
      },
```

```
    {
      "database": "70-768-Ch2",
      "table": "Sale",
      "partition": "Sale Bill To Customer 100"
    }
    ]
  }
}
```

You can execute the scripts that you generate from the dialog boxes in the SSMS query window as needed. However, to automate the execution of the scripts, the most common approach is to use a SQL Server Agent job. To do this, perform the following steps:

1. Connect to the database engine in Object Explorer, and start SQL Server Agent if necessary. SQL Server Agent should be running continuously to run refresh operations at scheduled intervals.

2. Expand SQL Server Agent, right-click the Jobs folder, and select New Job.

3. In the New Job dialog box, type a name for the job in the Name box, such as Process Tabular Database, and then click the Steps tab.

4. Click New, type a name in the Name box, select SQL Server Analysis Services Command in the Type drop-down list, type the server name (with the instance name if necessary) in the Server text box, and paste in the TMSL command in the Command box, as shown in Figure 2-19.

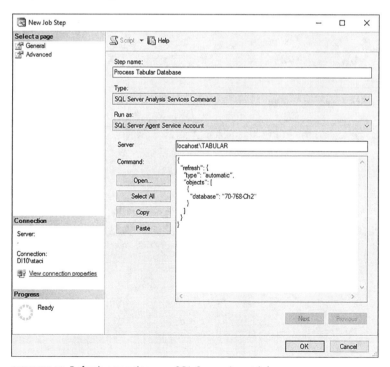

FIGURE 2-19 Refresh operation as a SQL Server Agent job

5. Click OK to close the New Job Step dialog box.

6. In the New Job dialog box, select the Schedules tab, click New, type a name for the schedule, and configure the frequency. For example, you can execute processing each day at midnight, as shown in Figure 2-20.

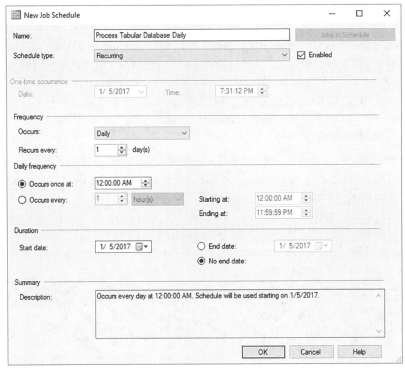

FIGURE 2-20 SQL Server Agent job schedule

7. Click OK twice to add the job to SQL Server Agent.

> **NOTE** **ADDITIONAL AUTOMATION OPTIONS FOR REFRESH OPERATIONS**
>
> You can use TMSL in an Analysis Services DDL Task in SQL Server 2016 Integration Services (SSIS) if you prefer to manage refresh operations as part of workflow. You can also create a client application by using AMO. A third alternative is using PowerShell cmdlets as described in "Analysis Services PowerShell Reference" at *https://msdn.microsoft.com/en-us/library/hh758425.aspx*.

Configure user security and permissions

SSAS uses a role-based security model to control who can perform which

tasks. Unlike the SQL Server database engine, which allows you to choose between Windows integrated security or SQL Server authentication, you are required to use Windows integrated security for tabular models. You can assign a tabular model role to a Windows group, or to individual Windows logins.

When you assign a group or individual to a role, you can use one of the following types of roles:

- **Server administrator** This role grants administrative permissions at the server level. In addition to reading data from any database on the server, a user that is a member of this role can also create or delete any object on the server, perform process operations on any object, and configure security.

- **Database role** This role grants selected administrative or read permissions at the database level.

> **IMPORTANT ROLES ARE ADDITIVE**
>
> A characteristic of SSAS security is the effect of assigning a user to multiple roles. If one role grants permissions and another permission removes a permission, the user continues to have the permissions granted by the first role. This behavior is the opposite of security in SQL Server in which the removal of permissions supersedes the addition of permissions. As an example, if you assign a user to the server administrator role, but also assign that user to a database role that has only read permission, the user continues to have full permissions on the database.

Server administrator

During installation, you must add at least one user or group to the server administrator role. By default, local administrators and the service account running SSAS are also assigned to the SSAS administrator role.

To manage members of the server administrator role, open SSMS, connect to the SSAS instance, and then, in Object Explorer, right-click the server node, select Properties, and then click Security in the Analysis Server Properties dialog box, as shown in Figure 2-21. Click Add, provide a user login or Windows group in the Select Users Or Groups dialog box to add a new member to the server administrator role, and then click OK.

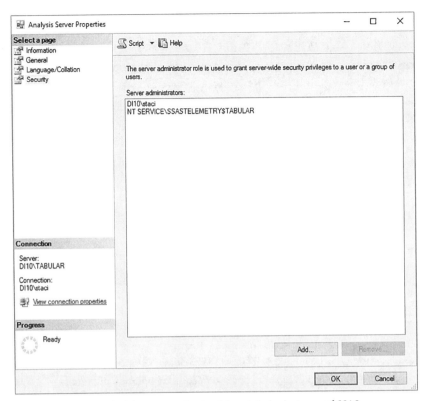

FIGURE 2-21 Server administrators authorized for a tabular instance of SSAS

You can remove local administrators or the SSAS service account from the SSAS server administrator role in one of two ways. You can either change the properties using the graphical interface in SSMS, or manually reset properties in the Msmdsrv.ini file located in C:\Program Files\Microsoft SQL Server\MSAS13.<tabular instance>\OLAP\Config folder, replacing <tabular instance> with the name of the instance running SSAS in tabular mode.

To use the SSMS interface, open the Analysis Server Properties dialog box as described earlier in this section, select General, and then select the Show Advanced (All) Properties check box. Scroll to locate the Security properties, select False in the drop-down list for the following two properties, as shown in Figure 2-22, and click OK when finished:

- Security \ BuiltinAdminsAreServerAdmins
- Security \ ServiceAccountIsServerAdmin

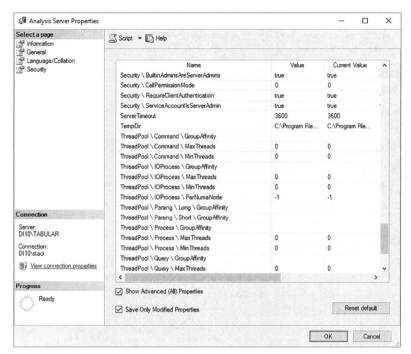

FIGURE 2-22 Advanced security properties for a tabular instance of SSAS

> **NOTE CHANGING SERVER ADMINISTRATOR ROLE DEFAULTS IN THE MSMDSRV.INI FILE**
>
> If you choose to edit the Msmdsrv.ini file instead of using SSMS to change the server administrator defaults, you must run the editor application, such as Notepad, as an administrator to have the necessary permissions to open the file. After opening it, locate the Security node near the top of the file, and then change the BuiltinAdminsAreServerAdmins or ServiceAccountIsServerAdmin property from 1 to 0. In case you inadvertently make other changes to the Msmdsrv.ini file that adversely affects your SSAS server, be sure to make a backup of this file before making changes.

Database role

No one has permissions to a newly deployed database except members of the server administrator role. The person who deployed the database must be a member of this role to have the necessary permissions to create objects on the server. To grant access to other users, you can assign them to database roles in either SSDT or SSMS.

To define a database role in SSDT, click Roles on the Model menu. In the Role Manager, click New. Type a name for the role in the Name box, and then select one of the following options in the Permissions drop-down list, as shown in Figure 2-23:

- **None** You can explicitly define members who have no access to the database. Remember that no one has access unless it is granted or until that user is added as a member to another role that does have access.

- **Read** A user assigned to this role only can read the database by using a client application to query the tabular model. You can further restrict the user to read only a subset of the tabular model by configuring row-level security as described in the next section of this chapter.

- **Read And Process** This role allows a user to read a database and to perform any processing operation.

- **Process** A user assigned to this role only can perform processing operations. Furthermore, these operations can be performed only by using a tool like SQL Server Integration Services (SSIS) because the user has insufficient permissions to connect to the database in SSMS.

- **Administrator** With this role, a user can read any data in the database, process any object, and configure security by creating roles and assigning members to roles. Administrator permissions also allows a user to create or delete objects in the database.

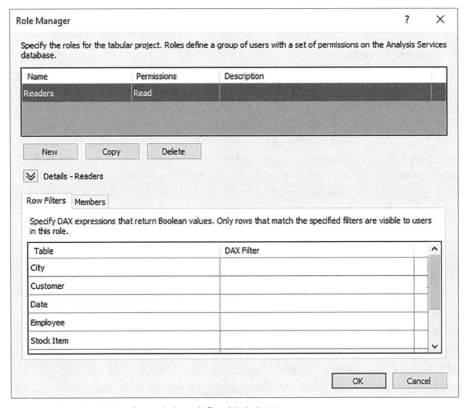

FIGURE 2-23 Role with Read permissions defined in Role Manager

Your next step is to assign members to the role. Click the Members tab, and then click Add. You can then specify the users or groups to add to this role, and click OK twice to save the role and its members.

To define a database role in SSMS, connect to the tabular instance, expand the Databases folder, expand the folder for your database, right-click the Roles folder, and click New Role. In the Create Role dialog box, shown in Figure 2-24, type a name for the role in the Role Name box, optionally type a description, and then select one or more of the following database permissions:

- **Full Control (Administrator)**   A user assigned to this role has full permissions on the database just like the Administrator permission that you can specify in SSDT.

- **Process Database**   This role is like the Process role in SSDT and allows the user only to perform processing operations by using SSIS.

- **Read**   Use this role to grant permissions to query the tabular model. Use row-level security as described in the next section of this chapter if you need to restrict the user to a subset of the model.

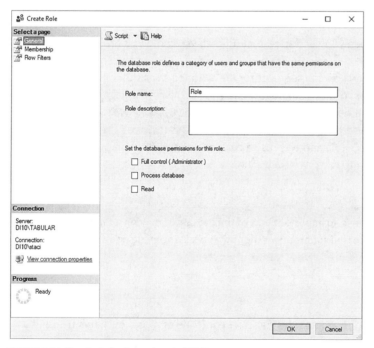

FIGURE 2-24 Create Role dialog box in SSMS

Unlike SSDT in which you specify a single type of permission, you can select multiple options in SSMS. After selecting Full Control (Administrator), the selection of either of the other two options is superfluous because the role already has full administrative permissions, which permit processing and reading the database. On the other hand, if you need a user to be able to both read a database and process it, which is the equivalent of Read And Process in SSDT's Role Manager, then select both the Process Database and Read check boxes in the Create Role dialog box in SSMS.

After you select the permissions, select the Membership page of the Create Role dialog box. Then click Add to open the Select Users Or Groups dialog box in which you can add one or more users or groups. Click OK twice to complete the addition of the role and role assignments.

> **NOTE** **DEFINING ROLES IN SSMS NOT RECOMMENDED DURING DEVELOPMENT CYCLE**
>
> For the same reason described earlier regarding the scripting of partitions in SSMS, you should avoid defining roles in SSMS until you are ready to deploy the tabular model into production to avoid a mismatch between the server version of the tabular model, and the version in your SSDT project.

Configure row-level security

Use row-level security when you need to restrict users to viewing only portions of a model. For example, you can have security requirements in which a salesperson can see his or her sales only and that the manager can see sales for the assigned sales staff only, whereas executives can see all sales. You can define row filters for a role by using DAX expressions to designate which rows members of that role can read. When you have a lot of users for which you need to define separate roles for row-level security, you can instead use dynamic security in which you define a single role and then use a custom client application or a permissions table to determine what the user can view at query time.

> **EXAM TIP**
>
> Security implementation is an important part of the process of moving a tabular model into production. Be prepared for exam questions that pose a scenario and ask you to identify the best way to configure security for the given scenario.

Row filter security

For each role that you add to a database, you can define one or more row filters by using a DAX expression that evaluates as true or false. When it evaluates as true, the user can see the data. As the name of this security model implies, you can filter only rows in a table. You cannot define security to restrict access to perspectives, measures, or columns.

You define row filter security in the Row Filters section of the Role Manager dialog box in SSDT, or on the Row Filters tab of the Create Role dialog box in SSMS. Figure 2-25 shows how you can use the Role Manager in SSDT to add a filter on the Stock Item table to restrict role members to viewing data for the Northwind brand in the Stock Item table by using an expression like this:

```
='Stock Item'[Brand] = "Northwind"
```

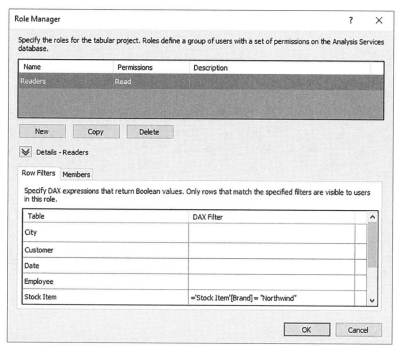

FIGURE 2-25 Row filter expression to restrict access to a single brand in the Stock Item table

You can create more complex expressions when you need to reference multiple columns and apply AND or OR logic using the && or || operators, respectively. To restrict users to cities in the Far West and External sales territories having populations greater than 100,000, create an expression like this:

```
=('City'[Sales Territory] = "Far West" || 'City'[Sales Territory] = "External") &&
'City'[Latest Recorded Population] > 100000
```

If you need to allow users access to all rows in a table except the rows containing a single value, set up an inequality expression. For example, you can prevent users from seeing any row in the Stock Item table with color N/A by using this expression:

```
='Stock Item'[Color] <> "N/A"
```

To block access to any row in a table, use an expression like this:

```
=FALSE()
```

One way to test row-level security is to click Analyze In Excel in the Model menu. In the Analyze In Excel dialog box, you can impersonate another user by specifying a user in the Other Windows User text box, or by selecting a role, as shown in Figure 2-26. If you select the Role option, you can select multiple roles at once to test the security for users who are members of multiple roles.

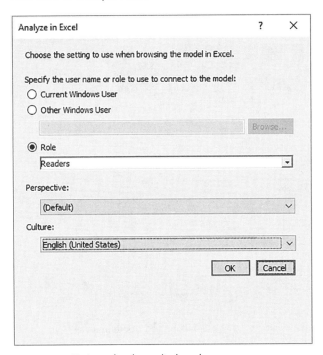

FIGURE 2-26 Test row-level security by role

You can then set up a PivotTable to test security. Figure 2-27 shows the selection of Total Sales and Brand. Notice the grand total is calculated with the filter in effect. If you test with an administrator's role, or with your credentials, the grand total is 118,050,905.30.

	A	B
1	Row Labels ▼	Total Sales
2	Northwind	14,802,215.00
3	Grand Total	14,802,215.00

FIGURE 2-27 Row filter applied to view only the Northwind brand

Another way to test security if you are a member of the server administrator role is to use one of the following connection string properties:

- **EffectiveUserName** Use this property with a Windows domain user name like this: `EffectiveUserName=DomainName\UserName`.

- **Roles** Use this property with one or more role names like this: `Roles=Role1,Role2`.

As an example, you can use the Roles property to test security in SSMS by opening a new MDX query window from the toolbar and then, in the Connect To Analysis Services dialog box, click Options, select the Additional Connection Parameters tab, and then type the connection string, as shown in Figure 2-28. Note that security does not affect the metadata pane in SSMS, so you can see all tables and dimensions. However, if you were to write a query to retrieve values from the Brand column, the results are correctly filtered.

FIGURE 2-28 Additional connection string parameter to test row-filter security in SSMS

You can also use this technique in client applications such as Excel by editing the connection string. For example, create a new workbook in Excel. On the Data tab of the ribbon, click From Other Sources, and then click From Analysis Services. On the Connect To Database Server of the Data Connection Wizard, type the server name (and instance name if required), and click Next. On the Select Database And Table page of the wizard, select the database containing your tabular model. If you are testing roles for a workspace version of your model rather than the deployed version, be sure to select the database with a GUID string appended to the database name in the drop-down list, select Model, and click Finish. Click OK in the

Import Data dialog box. Then set up a PivotTable that includes a field in the columns or rows that you want to test.

Initially, you should see all data because your credentials allow you to see the unfiltered model. To test row-level security by using a connection string property, such as Roles, click Connections on the Data tab of the ribbon, click Properties, and append a semicolon and the connection string property to the connection string on the Definition tab, as shown in Figure 2-29. Click OK, click Yes to confirm the change to the connection string, and then click Close. The PivotTable should now be filtered.

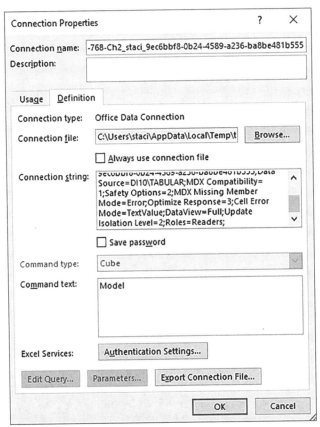

FIGURE 2-29 Connection string property updated to test row-level security in Excel

---

NOTE ROW FILTER CHANGES TAKE EFFECT IMMEDIATELY

If you change the row filter settings for a role, the effect is immediate. The user is not required to close and reopen the connection to see the new row filters in place.

Dynamic security

Rather than create and maintain multiple roles in the tabular model, you can use dynamic security. This approach is much simpler because you define only one role in the model, and then use DAX functions to determine the permissions assigned to a user at query time.

One dynamic security option is to use the USERNAME function to get the Windows login for the user connecting to the model. This approach is preferred when users connect directly to a tabular model and can see or change the connection string used to make the connection. To do this, perform the following steps:

1. Create a permissions table in a relational database, such as the SalesTerritoryPermissions table shown in Table 2-12, to map user logins (assuming a domain name of WWI) to a filter value for the Sales Territory column in the City table. If a user can see multiple values, add multiple rows to the table.

    TABLE 2-12 SalesTerritoryPermissions table

UserLogin	FilterValue
WWI\Lily	Far West
WWI\Isabella	Plains
WWI\Ethan	Mideast
WWI\Ethan	Southeast

    Add the table to the model in SSDT by clicking Import From Data Source on the Model menu and using the Table Import Wizard to get data from the SalesTerritoryPermissions table.

2. Prevent users from viewing data in this table by right-clicking the table's tab and clicking Hide From Client Tools.

3. Your next step is to create a role in the model, named SalesTerritoryRole for example. Give the role Read permissions, and ensure the users listed in the SalesTerritoryPermissions table are assigned to this role.

4. Next, define a row filter for the City table using the USERNAME function in an expression like this:

```
=CONTAINS(
    SalesTerritoryPermissions,
    SalesTerritoryPermissions[UserLogin],
    USERNAME(),
    SalesTerritoryPermissions[FilterValue],
    City[Sales Territory]
)
```

The first argument in the CONTAINS function specifies the table to evaluate and the next two arguments specify the column to check, and the value to look for in that column.

Similarly, the fourth and fifth arguments are a column/value pair to evaluate. When the values in each column/value pair are found in the respective columns, the expression evaluates as TRUE. In other words, the current user can see sales territories when the UserLogin column of the SalesTerritoryPermissions table contains his or her login, and the FilterValue column in corresponding rows in the same table contains a sales territory.

5. You can test the dynamic security in SSMS by opening a new MDX query window, connecting to the tabular instance, and adding the following connection string properties to the Additional Connection Parameters page of the Connect To Analysis Services dialog box:

```
Roles=SalesTerritoryRole; EffectiveUserName=WWI\Ethan
```

> **NOTE DOMAIN CONTROLLER REQUIRED TO TEST EFFECTIVEUSERNAME**
>
> Your SSAS server must be on a network with a Windows domain controller to validate the login for EffectiveUserName. Otherwise, the following message displays, "There are currently no logon servers available to service the logon request."

6. After you successfully connect to the SSAS server and your model, run the following query to confirm the filter is applied correctly:

```
EVALUATE City
```

Another dynamic security option is to pass information about the current user in the CustomData property in the connection string. To do this, use the CUSTOMDATA function to access that property value and apply it as part of a row filter expression. This option is best when you have a custom client application that queries the tabular model on behalf of the users and users cannot view or modify the connection string.

Let's say you set up a role called CustomSalesTerritory and use the following DAX expression as a row filter:

```
=IF(
    CUSTOMDATA()= "",
    FALSE(),
    City[Sales Territory] = CUSTOMDATA()
)
```

As with the previous examples, you can test this role in SSMS by opening a new MDX query window, connecting to the tabular instance, and adding the following connection string properties to the Additional Connection Parameters page of the Connect To Analysis Services dialog box:

```
Roles=CustomSalesTerritory; CustomData=Far West
```

And then in the query window, execute the following query to confirm the filter works:

```
EVALUATE City
```

Skill 2.3: Develop a tabular model to access data in near real time

Using in-memory storage for a tabular model has its benefits, but there are situations for which using DirectQuery mode is better. By enabling DirectQuery mode, you enable real-time access to data for your users and reduce the administrative overhead of maintaining the tabular model. Another benefit is that you can provide access to data that is larger than the memory available on the SSAS Server. When you use a tabular model in DirectQuery mode, SSAS translates incoming queries into SQL queries and sends the queries to the database server. In DirectQuery mode, none of the data is stored in-memory, which is much like ROLAP mode for a multidimensional model.

> **NOTE**   **OPTIMIZE DIRECTQUERY PERFORMANCE IN THE SQL SERVER DATABASE ENGINE**
>
> The translation of a tabular query into platform-specific SQL can impact performance adversely. If your data source is SQL Server 2012 or later, you can add columnstore indexes to the source tables to compensate.

This section covers how to:

- Use DirectQuery with Oracle, Teradata, Excel, and PivotTables
- Convert in-memory queries to DirectQuery

Use DirectQuery with Oracle, Teradata, Excel, and PivotTables

When you use DirectQuery mode, you can use only one data source for your tabular model. Furthermore, that data source must be one of the following relational databases:

- SQL Server 2008 or later
- Azure SQL Database
- Azure SQL Data Warehouse
- Analytics Platform System (formerly Parallel Data Warehouse)
- Oracle 9i, 10g, 11g, and 12g
- Teradata V2R6, V2

Implementing a tabular model in DirectQuery mode also has the following limitations:

- You cannot create calculated tables in the model, nor can you add a pasted table. A workaround is to use corresponding logic to create a derived column or a view in the underlying source.

- Some DAX functions do not translate correctly into SQL, particularly time-intelligence functions and some statistical functions. For these functions, consider adding a derived column in the underlying table instead.

> **NOTE UNSUPPORTED DAX FUNCTIONS IN DIRECTQUERY MODE**
>
> For a list of functions that are not supported in DirectQuery mode, see "DAX Formula Compatibility in DirectQuery Mode (SSAS 2016)" at *https://msdn.microsoft.com/library/mt723603(SQL.130).aspx.*

- Unlike ROLAP in a multidimensional model, DirectQuery does not cache query results within SSAS. If any caching occurs as a result of a query to a tabular model in DirectQuery mode, it happens only in the relational data source.
- You can return only one million rows in a query. However, you can override this limitation by adding the MaxIntermediateRowSize property to the Msmdsrv.ini file.

> **NOTE MAXINTERMEDIATEROWSIZE PROPERTY**
>
> To learn how to work with this property, see "DAX Properties" at *https://msdn.microsoft.com/en-us/library/mt761855.aspx.*

EXAM TIP

Substantial changes made to DirectQuery in the current version means the list of limitations for SQL Server 2016 is shorter than it is for previous versions. Therefore, be sure you are familiar with the new capabilities of DirectQuery, which you can review in the DirectQuery section of "What's New in Analysis Services" at *https://msdn.microsoft.com/en-us/library/bb522628.aspx#DirectQuery.*

DirectQuery with any source

You can configure your tabular model to use DirectQuery instead of in-memory storage by clicking the Model.bim file in Solution Explorer in SSDT and then changing the DirectQuery Mode option to On. When your model is in DirectQuery mode, you deploy the model, but no processing is required to load your tables. SSAS stores only metadata on the server, which it uses to determine how to translate queries into SQL statements. Data is not stored on the SSAS server, but retrieved at query time.

Even if you create a tabular model in in-memory mode, you can always switch to DirectQuery mode at any time. If you do this, any data previously stored in the cache is flushed, but the metadata is retained. That means any measures, calculated columns, or property settings that you have added to the model are kept in the model.

If you start designing a tabular model by using in-memory storage and later decide to switch it to DirectQuery mode, you can encounter errors that must be resolved before you can complete the conversion. For example, you cannot convert a tabular model to DirectQuery mode if it contains multiple data source connections. You must first delete tables associated with the additional data sources, and then remove the data sources by clicking Existing Connections on the Model menu, selecting the data source connection in the Existing Connections dialog box, and clicking Delete. Click Close after all deleting the data sources.

Another obstacle to converting a tabular model to DirectQuery mode is the existence of a table in your model that is defined with multiple partitions. To fix this problem, click Partitions on the Table menu, select the partition in the Partition Manager, and click Delete. Repeat until you have only one partition for the table.

Regardless of the underlying data source, you have the following options for modeling when using DirectQuery mode:

- Use all data, which is the only option in earlier versions of SQL Server.
- Use no data, which is the new default.
- Use a subset of data based on a query that you supply.

> **NOTE** **REQUIREMENT TO USE NO DATA OR A SUBSET OF DATA DURING MODELING**
>
> To use no data or a subset of data during modeling, you must set the compatibility level of your project to 1200.

Even when using DirectQuery mode, you continue to use the Table Import Wizard to define and connect to your data source. When working with an empty tabular model, launch the wizard by selecting Import From Data Source from the Model menu. You select a relational database and then the tables for your model, but the wizard does not import the data. Instead, you work with an empty model that contains only metadata, such as column names and relationships, as shown in Figure 2-30. You perform all the same steps by configuring properties for columns, defining relationships, or working with the model in diagram view, but cannot view the results of your work as you can if you were to import data for an in-memory tabular model.

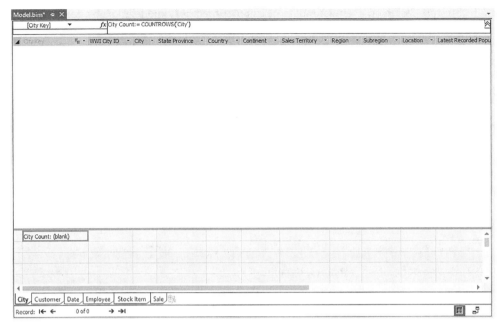

FIGURE 2-30 Model designer for DirectQuery-mode tabular model

By working without the data, you can often perform modeling tasks faster because you no longer wait for calculations to complete after adding or changing measures or calculated columns. On the other hand, you can find it challenging to determine the effect of your modeling changes without viewing the data. In that case, you can import a subset of sample data that provides a view of these changes on a limited number of rows. This approach performs calculations faster than possible when working with the full set of underlying data.

To set up sample data, perform the following steps:

1. Click a table in the model designer, and then click Partitions on the Table menu.

2. Select the existing partition, which has the prefix (DirectQuery), click Copy, and then click the Query Editor button to add a WHERE clause to the partition query, and return a subset of the original partition query. For example, you can modify the query for the Sale table as shown in Figure 2-31.

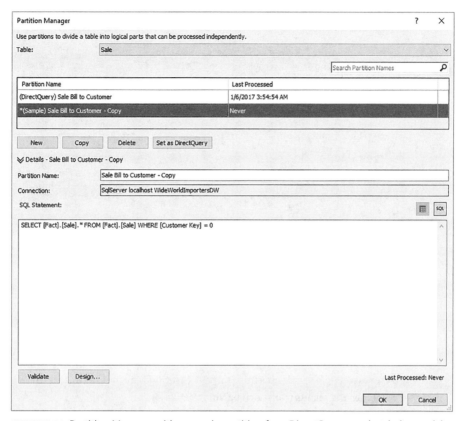

FIGURE 2-31 Partition Manager with a sample partition for a DirectQuery-mode tabular model

When you add a sample partition definition like this, the Partition Manager includes a Set As DirectQuery button that appears only when you select a sample partition in the partition list. When you click this button, you reset the partition that Analysis Services uses to retrieve data for user queries. There can be only one DirectQuery partition defined for a table at any time. If you select the DirectQuery partition, the button's caption displays Set As Sample instead. Although you can define only one DirectQuery partition, you can define multiple sample partitions.

3. When you close the Partition Manager, you must process the partition to load data into the sample partition. On the Model menu, point to Process, click Process Table, and click Close to close the Data Processing dialog box. The subset of rows defined by your query is displayed in the model designer, as shown in Figure 2-32.

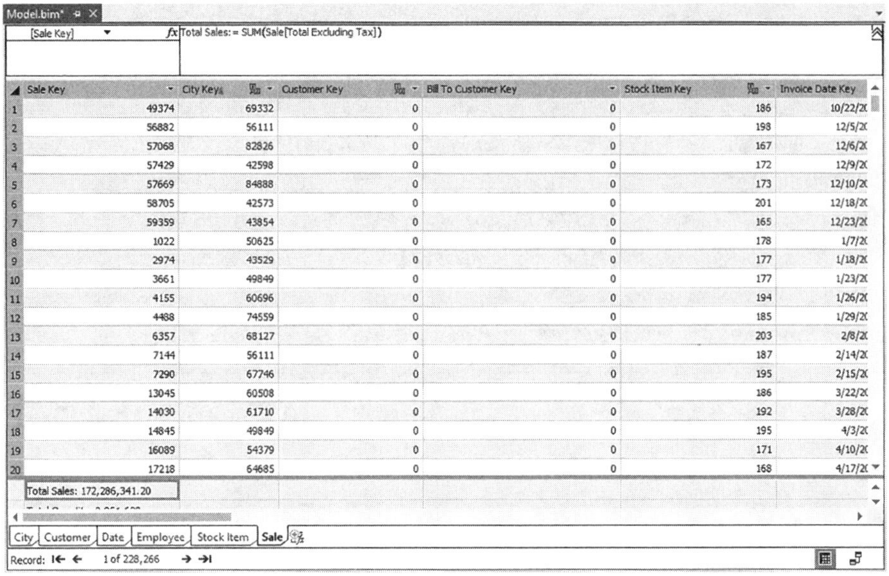

FIGURE 2-32 Model designer displaying sample data for Customer Key 0

> **NOTE MULTIPLE SAMPLE PARTITIONS**
>
> When you create multiple sample partitions in the Partition Manager for a table, the model designer combines the results from each partition's queries.

The sample data partition is also accessible when you use the Analyze Table In Excel feature to test the model from the presentation layer. Using the sample partition makes it easier to test the results of calculations in measures, and to check relationships between tables even when you are using only a subset of data. Try this out by clicking Analyze In Excel on the Model menu. Notice the Analyze In Excel dialog box now requires you to choose one of two options, Sample Data View or Full Data View, as shown in Figure 2-33.

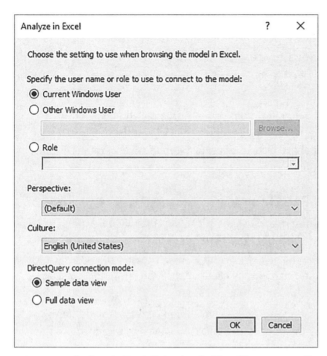

FIGURE 2-33 Analyze In Excel dialog box in DirectQuery connection mode

> **NOTE** **CONNECTION STRING PROPERTY FOR SAMPLE DATA**
>
> You can test your tabular model by using sample data without using the Analyze In Excel feature by including the following parameter to the connection string in your client application:

```
DataView=Sample
```

If you create sample partitions for some, but not all, tables in your model, and use the Analyze In Excel feature, you see only null values for columns in tables without a sample partition. Therefore, if you define a sample partition in one table, you should repeat the process for other tables. Your sample partition does not need to be a subset of the table. If the table is small, you can copy the DirectQuery partition and keep the existing query without adding a WHERE clause.

DirectQuery with Oracle and Teradata

Building a DirectQuery-mode tabular model by using Oracle or Teradata as a data source is much the same as using SQL Server as a data source. The main difference is that you must use the appropriate data provider as shown in Table 2-13.

TABLE 2-13 Data provider requirements

Data Source	Data Provider
Oracle	Oracle OLE DB Provider
Teradata	.NET Data Provider for Teradata

If you need to troubleshoot queries generated from your client application when using Oracle or Teradata as a source for your DirectQuery-mode tabular model, use the applicable trace monitoring tools for your source database instead of using Extended Events or SQL Profiler as you would for a SQL Server data source.

DirectQuery with Excel and PivotTables

Prior to SQL Server 2016, it was not possible to use the Excel PivotTable feature to query a tabular model in DirectQuery mode because Excel generates MDX instead of DAX, and DirectQuery could not translate MDX into SQL. Now with SQL Server 2016, the tabular engine can successfully accept most MDX queries from any client application, including Excel, as described in the next section.

In Excel PivotTables, the standard method of the PivotTable Fields List to add items to rows, columns, and filters generates the appropriate MDX. However, you cannot use the Create Set Based On Row Items or Manage Sets commands, both of which are accessible by clicking Fields, Items, & Sets in the Calculations group of the Analyze tab on the ribbon. These commands are useful for building MDX sets at query time, which means they are session-scoped MDX statements and not supported by DirectQuery. This limitation is not exclusive to Excel; DirectQuery itself does not support any session-scoped constructs in ad hoc queries such as named sets, calculated members, calculated cells, visual totals, and default members.

Convert in-memory queries to DirectQuery

The ability to convert in-memory queries to DirectQuery mode is an option only when the tabular model's compatibility level is 1100 or 1103, and the model's Query Mode is set to In-Memory With DirectQuery. Furthermore, the client tool must support DirectQuery mode for the tabular model's compatibility level. For example, you cannot switch to DirectQuery mode in Excel when the model's compatibility level is 1100 or 1103. For tools supporting this capability, you can convert the in-memory query to DirectQuery by appending the following connection parameter to the client connection string:

```
DirectQueryMode=DirectQuery
```

> **NOTE CONVERT DIRECTQUERY CONNECTIONS TO IN-MEMORY**
>
> Because Excel does not support DirectQuery mode for models set to compatibility level 1100 or 1103, you must include the following connection parameter when connecting to a tabular model with the DirectQuery With In-Memory query mode setting:

```
DirectQueryMode=InMemory
```

NEED MORE REVIEW? **HYBRID MODES**

Julie Koesmamo has written a blog post, "Hybrid Mode in Tabular BI Semantic Model – Part 1," which you can read at *http://www.mssqlgirl.com/hybrid-mode-in-tabular-bi-semantic-model-part-1.html* to learn more about the use cases for each type of hybrid mode.

Chapter summary

- The design of a tabular model is more flexible than the design of a multidimensional model and can often be performed faster because there are fewer features to implement. At minimum, you import tables to load data into your model. You can use multiple data sources, and multiple types of data sources, including relational data, SSAS multidimensional or tabular data, SSRS, Excel workbooks, text files, and more.

- After loading data into the model, you can enhance the model by adding measures to compute aggregate values, defining relationships to enable cross-filtering of data across tables, and creating hierarchies to provide users with a navigation path from summary to detail data. Optionally, you can separate data in a table into different partitions to manage the refresh process more efficiently. You can also add perspectives to focus the user on a subset of tables, hierarchies, or columns when the tabular model contains many objects. Another common tabular model enhancement is the addition of calculated columns to resolve data quality issues, concatenate columns values, or combine columns from related tables in preparation for building a hierarchy, to name a few reasons.

- One new feature in SQL Server 2016 is the ability to create a calculated table. One reason you can do this is to add a time (or date) table to the tabular model when you do not have an existing table in your data source. To use DAX time intelligence functions, you must have a date table in your model. You can easily build a calculated date table by using the CALENDAR or CALENDARAUTO functions.

- When you are ready for users to access the tabular model, you can publish it from SSDT by clicking Deploy on the Build menu or by right-clicking the project in Solution Explorer and clicking Deploy.

- Tabular model development can begin in a desktop environment by using PowerPivot in Excel. You can then create a new project in SSDT by using the Import From PowerPivot template to load the PowerPivot workbook and import design into a tabular model.

- When you deploy a tabular model from SSDT, you can configure the Processing Option and Transactional Deployment options when the model is set to compatibility level 1200. The Processing Option specifies the type of processing operation that SSAS should perform when deployment is complete, if any. The Transactional Deployment option determines whether deployment rolls back if the processing operation is not successful. When the tabular model is set to a lower compatibility level, you can also set the Query Mode option to DirectQuery, DirectQuery With In-Memory, In-Memory, or In-Memory With DirectQuery.

- SSAS supports two storage modes for tabular models: in-memory and DirectQuery. You must refresh an in-memory tabular model by performing a processing operation periodically if you want to update the data in the model. A DirectQuery-mode tabular model does not require processing because it retrieves data from the underlying data source at query time and is thereby always up-to-date. There are several different types of processing operations: Process Add, Process Clear, Process Data, Process Default, Process Defrag, Process Full, and Process Recalc. You can use many of these operations at the database, table, or partition level, but some operations are restricted to specific levels. Furthermore, you should understand how they each affect memory resources and dependent objects.

- You can convert an in-memory tabular model to DirectQuery mode as long as the model has a single supported data source and only the default partition defined for each table. You have the option to configure constrained delegation if you want to pass user credentials to the backend database at query time.

- You can schedule the refresh of data in several ways. A straightforward option is to script the processing operation as TMSL and then add the script as a job step in a scheduled SQL Server Agent job. Other options include using SSIS, AMO, or Power-Shell.

- Security for a tabular model is role-based and requires you to assign Windows logins or groups to a role to enable access. You can assign users to a server administrative role to enable full access to all objects and all tasks on the SSAS server. Most of the time, you assign users to a database role to restrict them to administrative tasks or read activities on a specific database. You can restrict users to a specific set of data in the tabular model by implementing row-level security, which requires you to define a filter by using a DAX expression.

- DirectQuery enables you to build a tabular model that accesses data directly from the backend database in near real-time, although some limitations exist that you should be able to enumerate. In previous versions of SQL Server, DirectQuery could retrieve data only from SQL Server databases. Beginning with SQL Server 2016, you can now use any of the following data sources: Azure SQL Database, Azure SQL Data Warehouse, Analytics Platform System, Oracle, and Teradata. While you design your DirectQuery-mode tabular model, you can choose to perform your modeling tasks with all data, some data, or no data. You can check your work by defining a partition for sample data and then using an Excel PivotTable to query the model. A PivotTable generates MDX, which is now supported by DirectQuery and translated into platform-specific SQL for the backend database.

- Use the `DirectQueryMode=DirectQuery` connection parameter in the connection string of a tool that supports access to a tabular model at compatibility level 1100 or 1103 with its Query Mode set to In-Memory With DirectQuery when you want to convert an in-memory query to DirectQuery.

Thought experiment

In this thought experiment, demonstrate your skills and knowledge of the topics covered in this chapter. You can find answers to this thought experiment in the next section.

Wingtip Toys is a company that has two channels for sales, Internet, and Direct Sales. The company sells toys to individual consumers on a commercial website. They also sell to companies by using a direct sales teams located in branch offices in key regions worldwide.

As part of your role as a BI developer at Wingtip Toys, you are responsible for developing and implementing a SSAS tabular model set to compatibility level 1200 to meet a specific set of business requirements.

The current database environment includes two OLTP systems that run on separate instances of SQL Server 2016, set up with Availability Groups. To protect the OLTP systems, you source the data from read-only secondary replicas. The data you need for the tabular model is found in following the tables and columns listed for each database:

- Database: WingtipWebSales
    - Sales: Invoice Date, CustomerID, ProductID, SaleAmount, Quantity
    - Customer: CustomerID, FirstName, LastName, EmailAddress, StreetAddress, City, StateProvince, Country, PostalCode
    - Product: ProductID, ProductName, Brand, Size, Color, Dimensions, Description, UnitPrice
- Database: WingtipDirectSales
    - Sales: InvoiceDate, CustomerID, ProductID, SalespersonID, TotalAmount, UnitsSold
    - Customer: CustomerID, CompanyName, StreetAddress, City, StateProvince, Country, PostalCode, ContactName, PhoneNumber
    - Salesperson: SalespersonID, FirstName, LastName, Login, City, SalesTerritoryID
    - Sales Territory: SalesTerritoryID, Sales Territory, Country, Region
    - Product: ProductID, ProductName, Brand, Size, Color, Dimensions, Description, UnitPrice

Users plan to use Excel 2016 to answer the following types of questions:

- What are total sales and total quantities sold by date, product, sales territory, sales person, customer, and sales channel?

- How many Internet sales transactions occur hourly each day?

To satisfy the business requirements, the tabular model must have the following characteristics:

- The Internet sales information must be available in near real-time.
- The Internet sales team must be restricted to viewing sales data from the WingtipSales database only.
- Each salesperson must be restricted to viewing sales data for the sales territory to which he or she is assigned.
- Management must be able to view all sales data.
- The salesperson table must support drilling from region to country to city to salesperson.
- The model must support analyzing sales by dates.

Based on this background information and business requirements, answer the following questions:

1. Which of the following steps do you need to perform to enable management to view Total Sales for both sales channels combined?

   A. Create a linked server on one of the SQL Server instances to enable access to the other instance.

   B. Use the Table Import Wizard to import data by creating a query to union the Sales tables from WingtipWebSales and WingtipDirectSales and rename the new table in the tabular model as Sales.

   C. Use the Table Import Wizard to import data from the Sales tables in each database as separate tables, with one table named Internet Sales, and the other table named Direct Sales.

   D. Create a measure named Total Sales in the Sales table by using a DAX expression to sum the values in the SaleAmount column and add it to the sum of the values in the Total Amount column.

   E. Create a measure named Total Internet Sales in the Internet Sales table by using a DAX expression to sum the SaleAmount column.

   F. Create a measure named Total Direct Sales in the Direct Sales table by using a DAX expression to sum the TotalAmount column.

   G. Create a measure in either the Total Direct Sales or Total Internet Sales table by using a DAX expression to add Total Direct Sales to Total Internet Sales.

2. Which of the following steps do you need to perform to create the Sales Territory hierarchy?

   A. Switch to Diagram view in the model designer and create a many to one relationship between the Sales Territory and Salesperson tables, if necessary.

   B. Right-click the Sales Territory table, and click Create Hierarchy.

   C. Right-click the Salesperson table, and click Create Hierarchy.

   D. Type Sales Territory as the hierarchy name.

   E. Create the Salesperson calculated column in the Salesperson table by concatenating FirstName and LastName.

   F. Create the following calculated columns in the Sales Territory table by using the RELATED function: City, Salesperson.

   G. Create calculated columns in the Salesperson table by using the RELATED function: Region, Country.

   H. Right-click the following columns in the Sales Territory table, point to Add To Hierarchy, and click Sales Territory: Region, Country, City, Salesperson.

   I. Right-click the following columns in the Salesperson table, point to Add To Hierarchy, and click Sales Territory: Region, Country, City, Salesperson.

3. What type of partitioning strategy should you implement to support the analysis of hourly Internet sales transactions?

   A. Create one partition per hour per day dynamically by running an SSIS package each hour to build the new partition. Load the data for the current hour by performing a Process Add, and then execute a Process Recalc on the partition.

   B. Create one partition per day dynamically by running an SSIS package daily to build the new partition. Load the data for the current day by performing a Process Full operation on the partition.

   C. Set the model to DirectQuery With In-Memory Mode. Define a sample partition for the Internet Sales table to view data during development.

   D. Convert the model to DirectQuery. Add columnstore indexes to the source tables. In the model, define a sample partition for all tables to view data during development.

4. How can you enhance the model to support analysis by date?

   A. Create calculated columns in the Internet Sales and Direct Sales tables to derive year, quarter, and month from the InvoiceDate columns.

   B. Create a calculated table using the CALENDARAUTO function and add calculated columns to the calculated table to derive year, quarter, and month from the InvoiceDate columns.

   C. Create a date table in a new SQL Server database, and import it into the model by using the Table Import Wizard.

   D. Create a calculated column in the Internet Sales and Direct Sales tables using the CALENDAR function on the InvoiceDate column.

5. Which is the easiest option for configuring and maintaining security for each salesperson?

   A. Create a role for each salesperson with a row filter restricting the user to a specific sales territory in the Direct Sales table.

   B. Create one role for the salesperson group with a row filter on the Direct Sales table that uses the CUSTOMDATA function.

   C. Create a one role for the salesperson group with a row filter on the Direct Sales table that uses the CONTAINS and USERNAME functions to find the user's sales territory in the Salesperson table.

   D. Create a permissions table, add it to the tabular model, and define a relationship between it and the Direct Sales table.

6. The project's Processing Option property is set to Do Not Process. You add a Total Quantity as a new measure to the Direct Sales table in the tabular model in SSDT and deploy the model. Based on your answer to Question 3, how do you ensure users can use the new measure in the deployed model?

   A. Open SSMS, open the Tables folder for the model's database, right-click the Direct Sales table, click Process Table, and select Process Recalc in the Mode drop-down list.

   B. Nothing. The new measure is deployed and accessible without processing because the model is in DirectQuery mode.

   C. Open SSMS, right-click the database containing your model, and click Process Database.

   D. Open SSMS, open the Tables folder for the model's database, right-click the Direct Sales table, click Process Table, and select Process Default in the Mode drop-down list.

Thought experiment answer

This section contains the solution to the thought experiment.

1. The answers are **C**, **E**, **F**, **G**. The ideal way to design the model is to import the two sales tables separately to satisfy the data access requirements for each sales channel, create separate measures for each channel, and then add these two measures together for total sales.

   Answer A is unnecessary because the tables should be imported separately and separate data connections to the source directly do not require a linked server. Answers B and D are incorrect due to the security requirements. Although a row filter could be used to isolate each channel type, the performance of a row filter on large tables containing sales data is not optimal when separate tables suffice.

2. The answers are **A**, **C**, **D**, **E**, **G**, **I**. The Salesperson table must contain the hierarchy because it contains Salesperson column, which is created as a calculated column by concatenating FirstName and LastName. You must create calculated columns by using the RELATED function to include the Region and Country columns in the Salesperson table.

   Answers B and H are incorrect because the Sales Territory table does not contain the column for the lowest level of the hierarchy. Answer F is also incorrect because it is not possible to use the RELATED function in the table on the many side of the many-to-one relationship.

3. The answer is **D**. The near real-time requirement for Internet Sales means the model must be set to DirectQuery. Because the compatibility level is set to 1200, the entire model must be in DirectQuery mode.

   Answers A and B do not satisfy the near-real time requirement. Answer **C** is not correct because DirectQuery With In-Memory Mode is not available when the compatibility level is 1200.

4. The answer is **C**. Of the four possible answers, only C is correct. It can be as simple or as complex as you need.

   Answer A is incorrect. Although the addition of calculated columns for dates in the two sales tables is adequate when a user interacts only with one of the sales table due to security requirements, it is not a suitable solution for management users who want to see data from both tables at the same time. For this scenario, a separate table enables time analysis across all sales data. Answer B is incorrect because the model is in DirectQuery mode (see Question 3) and calculated tables are not supported. Answer D is incorrect because the CALENDAR function returns a table and therefore cannot be used to create a calculated column.

5. The answer is **C**. The Salesperson table has the information necessary to develop a DAX expression that uses the CONTAINS function to find the user's sales territory by matching the USERNAME to a sales territory. A single role can be defined in the model with a row filter and then all other maintenance takes place in the Salesperson table as salesperson rows are added or removed or the sales territories are changed as a normal part of business operations.

   Answer A is incorrect because it requires too much maintenance to require a separate role for each salesperson. Answer B is incorrect because the CUSTOMDATA function requires you to have another mechanism determine what value to pass in the function, typically as part of a custom application. Answer D is incorrect because the existence of a permissions table with a relationship to the Direct Sales table is insufficient. A role must be defined to determine how the permissions table is used to secure access to the Direct Sales table.

6. The answer is **B**. No processing is required when you deploy a DirectQuery model.

   Answers A, C, and D are incorrect because process operations are not supported by DirectQuery.

CHAPTER 3

Develop queries using Multidimensional Expressions (MDX) and Data Analysis Expressions (DAX)

SQL Server Analysis Services (SSAS) multidimensional and tabular models rely on separate expression languages for both modeling and querying purposes. You use the Multidimensional Expressions (MDX) language to incorporate business logic into a cube for reusability as calculations and to return query results from a cube. Cube queries can be ad hoc, embedded into a reporting application, or generated automatically by client tools such as Excel. Likewise, you use the Data Analysis Expressions (DAX) language to enhance a tabular model not only by adding business logic, but also to perform data transformation tasks such as concatenating or splitting strings, among other tasks. In addition, you use DAX to query a tabular model in ad hoc or reporting tools. Client tools, such as Power BI Desktop and Power View in SQL Server Reporting Services (SSRS) and in Excel, can generate DAX. The 70-768 exam tests your knowledge of both MDX and DAX to ensure you have the skills necessary to build and query multidimensional or tabular models effectively.

Skills in this chapter:

- Create basic MDX queries
- Implement custom MDX solutions
- Create formulas by using the DAX language

Skill 3.1: Create basic MDX queries

Before you start adding MDX calculations into a multidimensional model, you may find it easier to first test the calculations by executing an MDX query in SQL Server Management Studio (SSMS). Furthermore, even when users rely on tools that automatically generate MDX, you should have an understanding of how to write MDX queries so that you have a foundation for the skills necessary to troubleshoot performance issues, as described in Chapter 4, "Configure and maintain SQL Server Analysis Services (SSAS)."

Implement basic MDX structures and functions, including tuples, sets, and TopCount

Before you start writing MDX queries, you should be familiar with the terms used to describe objects in the multidimensional database. Because many of these objects are visible in the metadata pane in the MDX query window, it's helpful to review the contents of the metadata pane to familiarize yourself with accessible objects and available MDX functions.

> ***NOTE*** **SAMPLE MULTIDIMENSIONAL DATABASE FOR THIS CHAPTER**
>
> This chapter uses the database created in Chapter 1, "Design a multidimensional business intelligence (BI) model," to illustrate MDX concepts and queries. If you have not created this database, you can restore the ABF file included with this chapter's code sample files. To do this, copy the 70-768-Ch1.ABF file from the location in which you stored the code sample files for this book to the Backup folder for your SQL Server instance, such as C:\ Program Files\Microsoft SQL Server\MSAS13.MSSQLSERVER\OLAP\Backup. Then open SQL Server Management Studio (SSMS), select Analysis Services in the Server Type drop-down list, provide the server name, and click Connect. In Object Explorer, right-click the Databases folder, and click Restore Database. In the Restore Database dialog box, click Browse, expand the Backup path folder, and select the 70-768-Ch1.ABF file, and click OK. In the Restore Database text box, type 70-768-Ch1, and click OK.

Basic MDX objects

Let's start by reviewing the structure of the 70-768-Ch1 database by following these steps:

1. If necessary, open SSMS, select Analysis Services in the Server Type drop-down list, provide the server name, and click Connect.

2. In the toolbar, click the Analysis Services MDX Query button and then, in the Connect To Analysis Services dialog box, click Connect.

3. If it is not already set as the current database, select 70-768-Ch1 in the Available Databases drop-down list in the toolbar.

4. In the Cube drop-down list in the metadata pane to the left of the query window, select Wide World Importers DW.

5. In the metadata pane, expand the Measures folder and the Sale folder. Then expand the Date dimension folder, the Date.Calendar attribute folder, and the Calendar Year level folder. With these folders expanded, as shown in Figure 3-1, you can see the following structures:

- **Measure group**   Collection of measures.
- **Measure**   Numeric value, typically aggregated.
- **Calculated measure**   Calculated value, typically aggregated.
- **Dimension**   Container for a set of related attributes used to analyze numeric data.
- **Attribute hierarchy**   Typically a two-level hierarchy containing an All member and distinct attribute values (members) from a dimension column.
- **Level**   Label for a collection of attributes in a user-defined hierarchy.
- **Member**   Individual item in an attribute.
- **User-defined hierarchy**   Collection of levels, typically structured as a natural hierarchy with levels having a one-to-many relationship between parent and child levels. An unnatural hierarchy has a many-to-many relationship between parent and child levels.

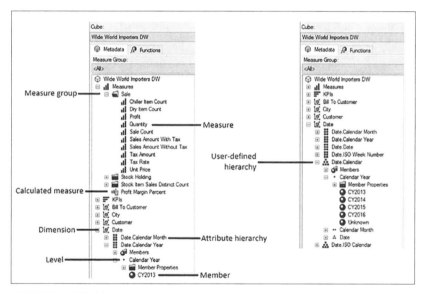

FIGURE 3-1 MDX objects

MDX query structure

The basic structure of an MDX query looks similar to a Structured Query Language (SQL) query because it includes a SELECT clause and a FROM clause, but that's the end of the similarity. For example, the simplest MDX that you can write for the Wide World Importers DW cube is shown in Listing 3-1, and the query result is shown in Figure 3-2. You must type the SELECT FROM portion of the query, and then either type the cube name or drag the cube name from the metadata pane and drop it after FROM. Although optional, it is considered best practice to terminate your query with a semi-colon as a security measure to prevent an MDX injection attack.

LISTING 3-1 Simplest MDX query

```
SELECT
FROM
[Wide World Importers DW];
```

Messages | Results
8,951.628

FIGURE 3-2 MDX query result

Normally, the SELECT clause includes additional details to request SSAS to retrieve information for specific dimensions and measures, but Listing 3-1 omits these details. The FROM clause identifies the cube to query.

How does SSAS know what to return as the result in this example? Part of the answer is in the following concepts to always keep in mind whenever you write your own queries:

- **Default member**   Each attribute hierarchy in each dimension in the cube has a DefaultMember property. If you do not explicitly define a default member, as described in Skill 3.2, "Implement custom MDX solutions," SSAS implicitly considers the All member at the top level of an attribute hierarchy to be the default member.

- **Default measure**   The cube has a DefaultMeasure property. Like default members, you can either explicitly define a value for this property, or understand how SSAS implicitly defines a default measure. To find the implicit default measure, you must review the cube's measures on the Cube Structure page of the cube designer. Expand the first measure group's folder and take note of the first measure in this folder because this is the implicit default member. It is important to note that you cannot determine the default measure by reviewing the sequence of measures in the metadata pane in the MDX query window in SSMS or in the Browser page of the cube designer in SQL Server Data Tools for Visual Studio Tools 2015 (SSDT).

Based on this information, the result of 8,951.628 represents the aggregated value for Quantity for all members of all attribute hierarchies of all dimensions. You could derive the same result by listing each individual All member along with the Quantity member, but to do so would be a tedious process. Instead, you can take advantage of the assumptions that the SSAS engine makes about your query to create a more succinct query. At times, an MDX query for a cube can be much more compact than an equivalent SQL query for a relational database. For this example, you can translate the MDX query in Listing 3-1 to the SQL query shown in Listing 3-2.

LISTING 3-2 Equivalent SQL query

```
SELECT SUM(Quantity)
FROM
WideWorldImportersDW.Sales.Fact;
```

Because the default measure can change if new measures are added to the cube, you should explicitly request the measure (or measures) that you want to return in the query results, as shown in Listing 3-3. This time, the measure is named in the SELECT clause, but notice the clause includes ON COLUMNS after the measure name also. Figure 3-3 shows the same value that was returned in the original form of the query, but the results also include a column label for this value thereby removing any ambiguity about what the value represents.

LISTING 3-3 MDX query with single measure

```
SELECT
[Measures].[Quantity] ON COLUMNS
FROM
[Wide World Importers DW];
```

Quantity
8,951,628

FIGURE 3-3 MDX query result with column label

While a query with a single measure can be useful for some questions, many times you want to break down, or slice and dice, a measure by a single member or multiple members of a dimension. To add a single dimension member to the query, you extend the SELECT clause by adding a comma, specifying the member name, and appending ON ROWS, as shown in Listing 3-4. You can see the result of the query in Figure 3-4, which shows the member name as a label on rows, the measure name as a label on columns, and the value 1,101,101 displayed at the intersection of the measure and dimension member.

LISTING 3-4 MDX query with single measure and single dimension member

```
SELECT
[Measures].[Quantity] ON COLUMNS,
[Stock Item].[Color].[Black] ON ROWS
FROM
[Wide World Importers DW];
```

	Quantity
Black	1,101,101

FIGURE 3-4 MDX query result with column and row label

> **NOTE** **AXIS NAMING AND ORDER OPTIONS**
>
> When you reference columns and rows in an MDX query, you are referencing *axes* in the query. In the query, you can use replace ON COLUMNS with ON 0 and ON ROWS with ON 1. In addition, when you include both axes in a query, you can place the ON ROWS clause before the ON COLUMNS clause if you like. However, if you include only one axis in the query, you must include the columns axis. A query that includes only the ON ROWS clause is not valid.

A query can be more complex, of course. Before exploring query variations, you should be familiar with the general structure of an MDX query, which looks like this:

```
SELECT
<Set> ON COLUMNS,
<Set> ON ROWS
FROM
<Cube>
WHERE
<Tuple>;
```

Members and sets

Sets are an important concept in MDX. A *set* is a collection of members from the same dimension and hierarchy. The hierarchy can be an attribute hierarchy or a user-defined hierarchy. There are several different ways that you can reference a member that use legal syntax, but best practice is to use the member's *qualified name*. The qualified name is an identifier for a member than uniquely identifies it within a cube. A member's unique name includes both the dimension and hierarchy name as prefixes to the member, uses a period (.) as a delimiter between object names, and encloses each object name in brackets like this:

```
[Stock Item].[Color].[Black]
```

Another way to reference a dimension member is to use its key column value, also known as its *unique name*. Recall from Chapter 1 that each attribute has a KeyColumn and Name-Column property. Although it is easier to read a query that references members by using the NameColumn values, such as Stock Item].[Stock Item].[USB missile launcher (Green)], you should consider writing a query to use the KeyColumn values when the possibility exists that the NameColumn values can change, such as when the attribute is handled as a Type 1 slowly changing dimension as described in Chapter 1. In that case, the syntax for a dimension member's unique name appends an ampersand (&) prior to the KeyColumn value like this:

```
[Stock Item].[Stock Item].&[1]
```

> **NOTE** **UNIQUE NAMES IN METADATA PANE**
> When you hover your cursor over a member name in the metadata pane, you can see its key value. Furthermore, when you drag the member name from the metadata pane into the query window in SSMS, the member's unique name is added to the query. If you prefer to use the qualified name, you must type the member's qualified name into the query.

Table 3-1 shows examples of different types of sets. You always enclose a set in braces, unless the set consists of a single member or the set is returned by a function. Set functions are explained in more detail later in this section. Experiment with these set types by replacing the set on columns in the query shown in Listing 3-4 with the example shown in the table.

TABLE 3-1 Examples of member sets

Type of set	Set example
Empty set	{}
Single member	[Stock Item].[Color].[Black]
Multiple members	{[Stock Item].[Color].[Black], [Stock Item].[Color].[Blue]}
Range of members	{ [Invoice Date].[Calendar].[CY2016-Jan] : [Invoice Date].[Calendar].[CY2016-Mar] }
Function	[Stock Item].[Color].Members

> **IMPORTANT** **MIXING ATTRIBUTES FROM MULTIPLE HIERARCHIES IS INVALID**
>
> You cannot combine attributes from separate hierarchies of the same dimension into a single set. As an example, you cannot create a set like this:
> {[Stock Item].[Color].[Black],[Stock Item].[Size].[L]}

When you explicitly define the members in a set by listing the members and enclosing them in braces, the order in which the members appear in the set is the order in which they appear when you add them to the query. When you use a set function like Members, the OrderBy property for the attribute determines the sort order of those members in the query results. You can override this behavior as explained later in this chapter when commonly used functions are introduced.

Measures can also be members of a set. From the perspective of creating MDX queries, measures belong to the Measures dimension, but do not belong to a hierarchy. Therefore, you can create a set of measures like this:

```
{[Measures].[Sales Amount Without Tax], [Measures].[Profit]}
```

In most cases, you can put a measure set on either axis of the query results. Listing 3-5 shows two queries containing the same sets, but each query has its sets on opposite axes. Notice that you can place the GO command between MDX queries to enable the execution of both statements at one time. Figure 3-5 shows the results of both queries.

LISTING 3-5 Comparing queries with sets on opposite axes

```
SELECT
{[Measures].[Sales Amount Without Tax], [Measures].[Profit]} ON COLUMNS,
{[Stock Item].[Color].[Black], [Stock Item].[Color].[Blue]} ON ROWS
FROM
[Wide World Importers DW];
GO
SELECT
{[Stock Item].[Color].[Black], [Stock Item].[Color].[Blue]} ON COLUMNS,
{[Measures].[Sales Amount Without Tax], [Measures].[Profit]} ON ROWS
```

```
FROM
[Wide World Importers DW];
```

	Sales Amount Without Tax	Profit
Black	$26,269,280.00	$14,390,527.00
Blue	$35,903,882.00	$17,713,073.00

	Black	Blue
Sales Amount Without Tax	$26,269,280.00	$35,903,882.00
Profit	$14,390,527.00	$17,713,073.00

FIGURE 3-5 MDX query results with swapped axes

The exception to this ability to place measures on either axis is the construction of a query for SSRS. In that case, not only must you place the measure set on the columns axis, but also it is the only type of set that you can place on the columns axis.

Tuples

Tuples are another important concept in MDX. A *tuple* is a collection of members from different dimensions and hierarchies that is enclosed in parentheses. Conceptually, a tuple is much like a coordinate to a specific cell in a cube. Consider the simple example shown in Figure 3-6, which depicts a cube that contains a Date dimension with a Month attribute hierarchy, a Territory dimension with a Territory attribute hierarchy, and a single measure, Sales Amount.

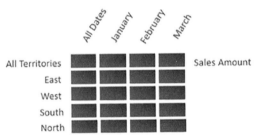

FIGURE 3-6 Cube with three dimensions: Territory, Date, and Measures

To retrieve a value from a specific cell in this simple cube, such as the Sales Amount for the North territory in the month of January as shown in Figure 3-7, you create a tuple that references every dimension and the one measure in the cube, like this:

([Territory].[Territory].[North], [Date].[Month].[January], [Measures].[Sales Amount])

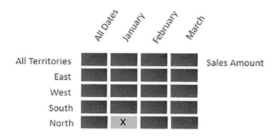

FIGURE 3-7 North-January-Sales Amount cell coordinate in cube

---

```
([Territory].[Territory].[North], [Date].[Month].[January],
[Measures].[Sales Amount])
([Date].[Month].[January], [Measures].[Sales Amount], [Territory].
[Territory].[North])
([Measures].[Sales Amount], [Territory].[Territory].[North], [Date].[Month].
[January])
```

You can create a tuple that omits one of the dimensions or the measure also. In that case, the tuple implicitly includes the default member or default measure to create a complete tuple behind the scenes. Therefore, the tuple ([Date].[Month].[January], [Measures].[Sales Amount]) is the equivalent of ([Territory].[Territory].[All Territories], [Date].[Date].[Month], [Measures].[Sales Amount]) as shown in Figure 3-8.

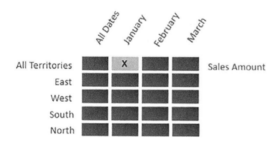

FIGURE 3-8 All Territories-January-Sales Amount cell coordinate in cube

MDX query syntax does not allow you to place a tuple on an axis. Only sets are permissible on rows or columns. Instead, you place a tuple in the WHERE clause, which is not intuitive if you are accustomed to writing SQL queries. Whereas a SQL query relies on a WHERE clause to define a filter condition, the WHERE clause in an MDX query affects how the SSAS formula engine constructs the tuples that it retrieves from the cube to generate a query's results.

For example, a simple query that requests a specific tuple from the Wide World Importers DW cube is shown in Listing 3-6 and the result in SSMS is shown in Figure 3-9. Notice there is no label on rows or columns, because the query does not include a specification on the rows or columns axis. Nonetheless, the value of $3,034,239.00 is the query result. This value reflects sales for all stock items that have the color of black for all dates, all cities associated with the Far West default member (defined in Chapter 1), all customers, and so on.

LISTING 3-6 MDX query with a tuple

```
SELECT
FROM
[Wide World Importers DW]
WHERE
([Measures].[Sales Amount Without Tax],
 [Stock Item].[Color].[Black]);
```

Messages	Results
$26,269,280.00	

FIGURE 3-9 MDX query result for a tuple specified in the WHERE clause

Another way to request the same tuple in a query is shown in Listing 3-7. The result shown in Figure 3-10 now includes the labels for the row and column. The difference between the two queries is the structure of the query command and the presentation of the results.

LISTING 3-7 MDX query with single members on each axis to create a tuple

```
SELECT
[Measures].[Sales Amount Without Tax] ON COLUMNS,
[Stock Item].[Color].[Black] ON ROWS
FROM
[Wide World Importers DW];
```

	Sales Amount Without Tax
Black	$26,269,280.00

FIGURE 3-10 MDX query result for a tuple specified in row and column axes

Yet another way to define a tuple to retrieve for a query is to include some objects on the axis and other objects in the WHERE clause, as shown in Listing 3-8. The SSAS formula engine combines objects from rows, columns, and the WHERE clause to construct the tuple that it returns in the results, shown in Figure 3-11.

LISTING 3-8 MDX query with single members on each axis and in the WHERE clause to create a tuple

```
SELECT
[Measures].[Sales Amount Without Tax] ON COLUMNS,
[Stock Item].[Color].[Black] ON ROWS
FROM
[Wide World Importers DW]
WHERE
([Invoice Date].[Calendar Year].[CY2016]);
```

	Sales Amount Without Tax
Black	$3,331,524.00

FIGURE 3-11 MDX query result for a tuple specified in row and column axes and WHERE clause

Tuple sets

To create a more complex query, you can create a *tuple set* and use it on a query axis. A tuple set is a set comprised of tuples in which a comma separates each tuple and braces enclose the entire set. Each tuple in the set must be consistent in the number of objects, the order of those objects, and the dimensions and hierarchies in which those objects belong. A valid tuple set looks like this:

```
{ ([Measures].[Sales Amount Without Tax], [Invoice Date].[Calendar Year].[CY2016]),
([Measures].[Sales Amount Without Tax], [Invoice Date].[Calendar Year].[CY2015]),
([Measures].[Sales Amount Without Tax], [Invoice Date].[Calendar Year].[CY2014]) }
```

By contrast, an invalid tuple set looks like this:

```
{ ([Measures].[Sales Amount Without Tax], [Invoice Date].[Calendar Year].[CY2016]),
([Invoice Date].[Calendar Year].[CY2015], [Measures].[Sales Amount Without Tax]),
([Measures].[Sales Amount Without Tax], [City].[Sales Territory].[Southwest]) }
```

Listing 3-9 provides an example of an MDX query in which tuple sets are placed on both axes. In Figure 3-12, you can see the relationship between the query elements, tuple construction, and the query results. The SSAS formula engine processes the query in multiple steps. In Steps 1 and 2, the engine retrieves members from the respective dimensions and hierarchies to construct the axes. In Step 3, the final tuples are constructed cell-by-cell and the engine determines how best to retrieve those values from the cube—in bulk or cell-by-cell as explained in greater detail in Chapter 4, "Configure and maintain SQL Server Analysis Services (SSAS)." Because the combination of rows and columns results in six cells, SSAS constructs six tuples. Each tuple includes the members shown in the column header and the row header for its cell in addition to the members in the WHERE clause. Thus, the WHERE clause is a subset of the tuple in each cell and results in the retrieval of data from a different location in the cube than the location used if the WHERE clause were omitted.

LISTING 3-9 MDX query with tuple sets

```
SELECT
{ ([Measures].[Sales Amount Without Tax], [Invoice Date].[Calendar Year].[CY2016]),
([Measures].[Sales Amount Without Tax], [Invoice Date].[Calendar Year].[CY2015]),
([Measures].[Sales Amount Without Tax], [Invoice Date].[Calendar Year].[CY2014]) }
ON COLUMNS,
```

```
{ ([Stock Item].[Color].[Black], [City].[Sales Territory].[Southwest]),
([Stock Item].[Color].[Blue], [City].[Sales Territory].[Far West]) }

ON ROWS
FROM
[Wide World Importers DW]
WHERE
([Customer].[Buying Group].[Tailspin Toys],
[Stock Item].[Size].[L]);
```

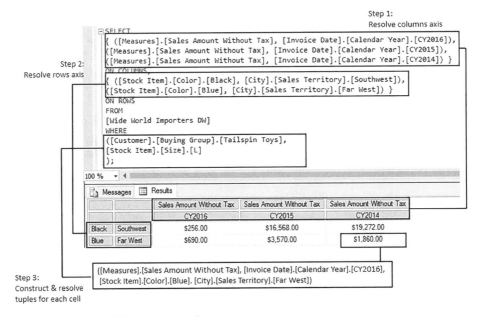

FIGURE 3-12 Steps in MDX query processing

Functions

The power of MDX is the ability to use functions in a query rather than explicitly name dimension members in a query. The coverage of all MDX functions is out of scope for this book. This section explains how to use the more commonly used functions. After learning how these functions work, you can apply the concepts and an understanding of syntax rules to learn other functions as needed.

A full list of available functions is available in the query window in SSMS by clicking the Functions tab in the metadata pane. Here the functions are grouped into folders by type of function, such as Set functions as shown in Figure 3-13.

FIGURE 3-13 Functions list in MDX query window

> **NOTE** **MDX FUNCTION REFERENCE**
>
> For a complete list of MDX functions organized alphabetically and by category, see "MDX Function Reference (MDX)" at *https://msdn.microsoft.com/en-us/library/ms145970.aspx*.

SET FUNCTIONS

A set function returns a set, which could be empty or contain one or more members. In the list of functions, you might notice a function appears more than once, such as the MEMBERS function. The presence of multiple instances of a function indicates there is more than one possible syntax for that function. If you hover your cursor over each MEMBERS function, a tooltip displays more information, as shown in Figure 3-14. The first line in the tooltip indicates the syntax, such as <Level>.Members, and the second line describes the result of using the function. In this case, the syntax information tells you that you must define a level to which you append .Members. The tooltip's second line lets you know that the functions returns a set, an important clue in determining how you can use the function in an expression or a query. Specifically, this function returns of set of the members that belong to the level that you use with the function.

FIGURE 3-14 Tooltip for one of the MEMBERS functions listed in the Functions in the MDX query window

The other option for using the MEMBERS function is to use it by specifying a hierarchy. More specifically, you specify both the dimension and hierarchy name. Listing 3-10 includes an example of both options. Notice the use of the pair of forward slashes to denote a comment on a single line. The first query illustrates how to reference members of a hierarchy. In this case, the Color hierarchy of the Stock Item dimension is the target of the MEMBERS function. By contrast, the second query shows the reference to the Color level of the Color hierarchy of the Stock Item dimension.

LISTING 3-10 MEMBERS function

```
// <Hierarchy>.Members syntax
SELECT
[Measures].[Sales Amount Without Tax] ON COLUMNS,
[Stock Item].[Color].Members ON ROWS
FROM
[Wide World Importers DW];
GO

// <Level>.Members syntax
SELECT
[Measures].[Sales Amount Without Tax] ON COLUMNS,
[Stock Item].[Color].[Color].Members ON ROWS
FROM
[Wide World Importers DW];
```

The metadata pane displays hierarchies and levels as separate objects, as shown in Figure 3-15. The Color hierarchy is the object that appears next to the icon represented as a rectangular collection of squares. The Color level is a child object of the Color hierarchy. It appears next to the dot icon.

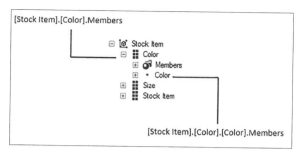

[Stock Item].[Color].Members

[Stock Item].[Color].[Color].Members

FIGURE 3-15 Color hierarchy and Color level objects in the metadata pane

You can see the results of each query in Figure 3-16. Notice the difference between retrieving members of the hierarchy as compared to retrieving members of a level of an attribute hierarchy. When you use a hierarchy with the MEMBERS function, the query returns the All member, which in effect is the total of all the members of the attribute, first and then lists the attribute's members individually. When use a level instead, the All member is excluded from the results. MDX allows you to choose to return one or the other option by changing the object to which you append the MEMBERS function.

	Sales Amount Without Tax
All	$172,286,341.20
Black	$26,269,280.00
Blue	$35,903,882.00
Gray	$5,933,699.75
Light Brown	$4,941,000.00
N/A	$77,896,120.45
Red	$4,726,465.00
Steel Gray	$25,000.00
White	$15,100,749.00
Yellow	$1,490,145.00

	Sales Amount Without Tax
Black	$26,269,280.00
Blue	$35,903,882.00
Gray	$5,933,699.75
Light Brown	$4,941,000.00
N/A	$77,896,120.45
Red	$4,726,465.00
Steel Gray	$25,000.00
White	$15,100,749.00
Yellow	$1,490,145.00

FIGURE 3-16 Comparison of MEMBERS function used with attribute hierarchy versus level

Let's say that the business requirement is to show the total row after listing all the members. In that case, you can create a set of sets. The first set is the set of members using the Level syntax, and the second set is the All member. Both sets are enclosed in braces to create the outer set. Listing 3-11 shows you how to construct a set of sets and Figure 3-17 shows the results of executing this query.

LISTING 3-11 MEMBERS function in a set of sets

```
SELECT
```

```
[Measures].[Sales Amount Without Tax] ON COLUMNS,
{[Stock Item].[Color].[Color].Members, [Stock Item].[Color].[All]} ON ROWS
FROM
[Wide World Importers DW];
```

	Sales Amount Without Tax
Black	$26,269,280.00
Blue	$35,903,882.00
Gray	$5,933,699.75
Light Brown	$4,941,000.00
N/A	$77,896,120.45
Red	$4,726,465.00
Steel Gray	$25,000.00
White	$15,100,749.00
Yellow	$1,490,145.00
All	$172,286,341.20

FIGURE 3-17 A set of sets placing the All member in the bottom row of the query results

A common analytical requirement is to sort the set of members in a sequence other than the order defined by the OrderBy property for the attribute. To apply a different sort order to the members, you use the ORDER function. This function requires you to supply a minimum of two arguments, and optionally a third argument to specify a sort direction by using ASC or DESC for ascending or descending, respectively. The first argument is the set to sort and the second argument is the value by which to sort. If you omit the sort direction, the default behavior is to sort the set in ascending order. Listing 3-12 is a modification of the previous example in which the first set is sorted in descending order of sales. You can see the results in Figure 3-18.

LISTING 3-12 ORDER function

```
SELECT
[Measures].[Sales Amount Without Tax] ON COLUMNS,
{
ORDER(
    [Stock Item].[Color].[Color].Members,
    [Measures].[Sales Amount Without Tax],
    DESC),
[Stock Item].[Color].[All]
} ON ROWS
FROM
[Wide World Importers DW];
```

	Sales Amount Without Tax
N/A	$77,896,120.45
Blue	$35,903,882.00
Black	$26,269,280.00
White	$15,100,749.00
Gray	$5,933,699.75
Light Brown	$4,941,000.00
Red	$4,726,465.00
Yellow	$1,490,145.00
Steel Gray	$25,000.00
All	$172,286,341.20

FIGURE 3-18 Ordered set of members on rows

The value that you use as the second argument is not required to be returned in the query results, nor must it be a numeric value. Furthermore, you can display a subset of the results by nesting the results of the ORDER function, which returns a set, inside the HEAD function, which takes a set or set expression as its first argument and the number of members to return from the beginning of the set as the second argument. As an example, the query in Listing 3-13 sorts stock items by profit in descending order to show the five most profitable items first, but the query returns the Sales Amount Without Tax measure. Notice that you can enclose multi-line comments between the /* and */ symbols to embed comments within a query as documentation of the steps performed. Comments are helpful when you have functions nested inside of functions. You can see the query results in Figure 3-19.

LISTING 3-13 ORDER function nested inside HEAD function

```
SELECT
[Measures].[Sales Amount Without Tax] ON COLUMNS,
HEAD(
    /* First argument – set of stock items sorted by profit
       in descending order */
    ORDER(
        [Stock Item].[Stock Item].[Stock Item].Members,
        [Measures].[Profit],
        DESC),
    /* Second argument – specify the number of members of set
       in first argument to return */
    5)
ON ROWS
FROM
[Wide World Importers DW];
```

	Sales Amount Without Tax
20 mm Double sided bubble wrap 50m	$6,214,320.00
Air cushion machine (Blue)	$11,107,251.00
32 mm Anti static bubble wrap (Blue) 50m	$6,384,000.00
10 mm Anti static bubble wrap (Blue) 50m	$6,329,070.00
32 mm Double sided bubble wrap 50m	$6,190,240.00

FIGURE 3-19 Results of ORDER and HEAD functions applied to Stock Item members

This example is also good for reviewing what happens when the SSAS formula engine processes the query. Remember that the first steps are to resolve the members to place on columns and rows. There is only one measure on columns, Sales Amount Without Tax, which is explicitly stated and does not require any further processing by the formula engine.

On the other hand, the set to place on rows does require processing. The following steps must occur before the tuples are constructed to return the values that you see in the measure column:

1. Specifically, the formula engine starts by resolving the ORDER function. It constructs a tuple for the measure in the second argument, Profit, and each member in the ORDER function's first argument, the set of members on the Stock Item level of the Stock Item attribute hierarchy in the Stock Item dimension. That is, all members except the All member. The tuple also includes the WHERE clause in the query, if one exists.

2. The formula engine then retrieves the value for each of those tuples and sorts the members in descending order.

3. Next, the formula engine applies the HEAD function to reduce the set of all sorted members to the first five members, which are placed on rows.

4. The final step is to compute the tuples for each cell resulting from the intersections of rows and columns and return the results.

> **IMPORTANT** **UNDERSTAND THE ROLE OF TUPLE CONSTRUCTION IN QUERY PROCESSING**
>
> The steps required to construct tuples for query results is one of the most important concepts to understand about MDX query processing. Axis resolution is completely separate from the final step of retrieving values that you see returned in the query results.

MDX includes a shortcut function to achieve the same result, TOPCOUNT. This function takes three arguments: a set of members, the number of members to return when resolving the TOPCOUNT function, and an expression to use for sorting purposes. The TOPCOUNT function automatically performs a descending sort. Listing 3-14 reproduces the previous example by replacing the combination of the HEAD and ORDER function with the more concise TOPCOUNT function. The query results match those returned for the query in Listing 3-13 and shown in Figure 3-19.

LISTING 3-14 TOPCOUNT function

```
SELECT
[Measures].[Sales Amount Without Tax] ON COLUMNS,
TOPCOUNT(
    [Stock Item].[Stock Item].[Stock Item].Members,
    5,
    [Measures].[Profit])
ON ROWS
FROM
[Wide World Importers DW];
```

Sometimes there is no value in a cube cell location specified by a tuple. As a query developer, you decide whether the absence of data is important to the user. If it is not, you can remove a member from the set on rows or columns by placing the NON EMPTY keyword on either axis or both axes. Listing 3-15 includes two queries to demonstrate the difference between omitting and including this keyword. The SSAS formula engine applies the keyword as its final step in processing a query. That is, it places applicable members on axes, resolves the tuples for the intersections of each row and column, and then removes members from the designated axis. Figure 3-20 shows the results of executing these two queries.

LISTING 3-15 NON EMPTY keyword

```
//Without NON EMPTY on columns - Unknown row displays null value in each column
SELECT
[Measures].[Sales Amount Without Tax] ON COLUMNS,
BOTTOMCOUNT(
    [Stock Item].[Stock Item].[Stock Item].Members,
    5,
    [Measures].[Profit])
ON ROWS
FROM
[Wide World Importers DW];
GO

//With NON EMPTY on columns - Unknown row removed in final processing step
SELECT
[Measures].[Sales Amount Without Tax] ON COLUMNS,
NON EMPTY BOTTOMCOUNT(
    [Stock Item].[Stock Item].[Stock Item].Members,
    5,
    [Measures].[Profit])
ON ROWS
FROM
[Wide World Importers DW];
```

	Sales Amount Without Tax
Halloween zombie mask (Light Brown) XL	$1,302,696.00
Halloween zombie mask (Light Brown) S	$1,278,288.00
Halloween zombie mask (Light Brown) M	$1,206,144.00
Halloween zombie mask (Light Brown) L	$1,153,872.00
Unknown	(null)

	Sales Amount Without Tax
Halloween zombie mask (Light Brown) XL	$1,302,696.00
Halloween zombie mask (Light Brown) S	$1,278,288.00
Halloween zombie mask (Light Brown) M	$1,206,144.00
Halloween zombie mask (Light Brown) L	$1,153,872.00

FIGURE 3-20 Comparison of queries omitting and including the NON EMPTY keyword on the rows axis

You can also remove members from an axis set before tuple construction begins. One way to do this is shown in Listing 3-16. In second query of this example, the NONEMPTY function operates like a filter by creating a tuple for each member of the set specified as the first argument with the measure specified as the second argument and then removing any member for which the tuple is empty, as you can see in the partial results shown in Figure 3-21. Often when you use the NONEMPTY function in a query instead of the NON EMPTY keyword, the query performance is better because there are fewer tuples to resolve in the final step of query resolution.

LISTING 3-16 NONEMPTY function

```
// Without NONEMPTY function
SELECT
[Measures].[Sales Amount Without Tax] ON COLUMNS,
[City].[City].[City].Members ON ROWS
FROM
[Wide World Importers DW];
GO
// With NONEMPTY function
SELECT
[Measures].[Sales Amount Without Tax] ON COLUMNS,
NONEMPTY([City].[City].[City].Members, [Measures].[Sales Amount Without Tax])
ON ROWS
FROM
[Wide World Importers DW];
```

	Sales Amount Without Tax
Aaronsburg	(null)
Aaronsburg	(null)
Aaronsburg	(null)
Abanda	(null)
Abanda	(null)
Abanda	(null)
Abanda	(null)

	Sales Amount Without Tax
Abbottsburg	$146,426.45
Abbottsburg	$207,072.70
Absecon	$260,721.05
Accomac	$300,565.00
Aceitunas	$20,163.20
Aceitunas	$217,476.20
Airport Drive	$138,805.90

FIGURE 3-21 Comparison of queries omitting and including the NONEMPTY function on the rows axis

Another way to reduce the number of members in an axis set is to use the FILTER function. The FILTER function requires a set as its first argument and a Boolean expression that returns

TRUE or FALSE as its second argument. You can optimize the query by using this function in combination with the NONEMPTY function to first remove the empty tuples before applying the filter, as shown in Listing 3-17. Here the query finds the City members with a value for Sales Amount Without Tax, creates a tuple for each City member and the measure in the second argument of the FILTER function, Sales Amount Without Tax, and compares the tuple's value to the Boolean expression's value, 400000. If the tuple is greater than 400000, the SSAS engine keeps that tuple's City member in the axis set, as shown in Figure 3-22. Just as you can do with the ORDER function, you can reference a measure in the second argument of the FILTER function that is not returned on a query axis.

LISTING 3-17 FILTER function

```
SELECT
[Measures].[Sales Amount Without Tax] ON COLUMNS,
FILTER(
    NONEMPTY([City].[City].[City].Members, [Measures].[Sales Amount Without Tax]),
    [Measures].[Sales Amount Without Tax] > 400000)
ON ROWS
FROM
[Wide World Importers DW];
```

	Sales Amount Without Tax
Akhiok	$542,733.20
Cherry Grove Beach	$526,621.15
East Fultonham	$475,097.20
Rockwall	$414,217.25
Sinclair	$514,830.20
Teutopolis	$485,950.50

FIGURE 3-22 FILTER function returns cities with sales greater than $400,000

> **NOTE FILTER FUNCTION**
>
> The Boolean expression in the second argument of the FILTER function can combine multiple expressions by using AND or OR operators between conditions.

Another function with which you should be familiar is the DESCENDANTS function, which is both a set function and a navigation function although it is found only in the Sets folder in the query window's function list. (Navigation functions are described in the next section of this chapter.) Whereas the functions explained earlier in this chapter have one syntax, there are multiple syntax options for the DESCENDANTS function. The first argument of the function can be a member expression or a set expression, the second argument can be a level expression or a numeric expression to specify a distance, and the third argument is an optional flag.

Listing 3-18 shows an example of using a member expression as the first argument and a level as the second argument. Consider the member expression as the starting point for navigating through a user-defined hierarchy to find a set of members. In this case, the starting point is CY2015, which is on the Calendar Year level. The SSAS engine then returns the members on the specified level, Calendar Month, that are associated with CY2015, as shown in Figure 3-23.

LISTING 3-18 DESCENDANTS function with member and level expressions

```
SELECT
[Measures].[Sales Amount Without Tax] ON COLUMNS,
DESCENDANTS(
    [Invoice Date].[Calendar].[Calendar Year]. [CY2015],
    [Invoice Date].[Calendar].[Calendar Month])
ON ROWS
FROM
[Wide World Importers DW];
```

	Sales Amount Without Tax
CY2015-Jan	$487,323.50
CY2015-Feb	$563,338.80
CY2015-Mar	$558,635.00
CY2015-Apr	$587,258.70
CY2015-May	$489,134.10
CY2015-Jun	$527,373.10
CY2015-Jul	$597,782.65
CY2015-Aug	$421,268.60
CY2015-Sep	$518,784.25
CY2015-Oct	$553,496.85
CY2015-Nov	$440,969.45
CY2015-Dec	$602,490.45

FIGURE 3-23 DESCENDANTS function applied to CY2015 member

You can add a flag to the function as a third argument to control whether to include members of other levels in the hierarchy path. Table 3-2 describes each of the available flags. Examples of queries using these flags and comments describing query results are shown in Listing 3-19.

TABLE 3-2 Flags for DESCENDANTS function

FLAG	Description
SELF	Returns only the members on the level or at the distance specified by the second argument and includes the member if it is on the specified level
AFTER	Returns members from all levels below the level specified by the second argument
BEFORE	Returns members from all levels between the member in the first argument and the level specified by the second argument
BEFORE_AND_AFTER	Returns members from all levels below the level specified by the second argument and the specified member, but not other members on the same level as the specified member
SELF_AND_AFTER	Returns members from the specified level and all levels below that level
SELF_AND_BEFORE	Returns members from the specified level and all levels between the member specified by the first argument and the specified member

SELF_BEFORE_AFTER	Returns members from the specified level and the specified member and members of all levels below the specified level
LEAVES	Returns members on the lowest level below the specified member

LISTING 3-19 DESCENDANTS function with flag

```
// SELF - Returns only members of Month level subordinate to CY2015
//    e.g. CY2015-Jan to CY2015-Dec
SELECT
[Measures].[Sales Amount Without Tax] ON COLUMNS,
DESCENDANTS(
    [Invoice Date].[Calendar].[Calendar Year].[CY2015],
    [Invoice Date].[Calendar].[Calendar Month],
    SELF)
ON ROWS
FROM
[Wide World Importers DW];
GO
// AFTER - Returns only members of Date level subordinate to CY2015
//    e.g. 2015-01-01 to 2015-12-31
SELECT
[Measures].[Sales Amount Without Tax] ON COLUMNS,
DESCENDANTS(
    [Invoice Date].[Calendar].[Calendar Year].[CY2015],
        [Invoice Date].[Calendar].[Calendar Month],
        AFTER)
ON ROWS
FROM
[Wide World Importers DW];
GO
// BEFORE - Returns members of Year level above Calendar Month related to CY2015
//    e.g. CY2015
SELECT
[Measures].[Sales Amount Without Tax] ON COLUMNS,
DESCENDANTS(
    [Invoice Date].[Calendar].[Calendar Year].[CY2015],
        [Invoice Date].[Calendar].[Calendar Month],
        BEFORE)
ON ROWS
FROM
[Wide World Importers DW];
GO
// BEFORE_AND_AFTER - Returns members of Date level subordinate to CY2015 and
//    Year level above Calendar Month related to CY2015
//    e.g. CY2015 and 2015-01-01
SELECT
[Measures].[Sales Amount Without Tax] ON COLUMNS,
DESCENDANTS(
    [Invoice Date].[Calendar].[Calendar Year].[CY2015],
        [Invoice Date].[Calendar].[Calendar Month],
        BEFORE_AND_AFTER)
ON ROWS
FROM
```

```
[Wide World Importers DW];
GO
// SELF_AND_AFTER - Returns members of Month level subordinate to CY2015 and
//     members of Date level subordinate to CY2015
//     e.g. CY2015-Jan to CY2015-Dec and 2015-01-01 to 2015-12-31 with
//         Date members displayed below its parent Month member
SELECT
[Measures].[Sales Amount Without Tax] ON COLUMNS,
DESCENDANTS(
    [Invoice Date].[Calendar].[Calendar Year].[CY2015],
    [Invoice Date].[Calendar].[Calendar Month],
    SELF_AND_AFTER)
ON ROWS
FROM
[Wide World Importers DW];
GO
// SELF_AND_BEFORE - Returns members of Month level subordinate to CY2015 and
//     Year level above Calendar Month related to CY2015
//     e.g. CY2015 and CY2015-Jan to CY2015-Dec
SELECT
[Measures].[Sales Amount Without Tax] ON COLUMNS,
DESCENDANTS(
    [Invoice Date].[Calendar].[Calendar Year].[CY2015],
    [Invoice Date].[Calendar].[Calendar Month],
    SELF_AND_BEFORE)
ON ROWS
FROM
[Wide World Importers DW];
GO
// SELF_BEFORE_AFTER - Returns members of Date, Month levels subordinate to CY2015 and
//     Year level above Calendar Month related to CY2015
//     e.g. CY2015 and CY2015-Jan to CY2015-Dec and 2015-01-01 to 2015-12-31 with
//         Date members displayed below its parent Month member and
//         Year member displayed above all members
SELECT
[Measures].[Sales Amount Without Tax] ON COLUMNS,
DESCENDANTS(
    [Invoice Date].[Calendar].[Calendar Year].[CY2015],
    [Invoice Date].[Calendar].[Calendar Month],
    SELF_BEFORE_AFTER)
ON ROWS
FROM
[Wide World Importers DW];
GO
// LEAVES - Returns members of Date level subordinate to CY2015
//     e.g. 2015-01-01 to 2015-12-31
SELECT
[Measures].[Sales Amount Without Tax] ON COLUMNS,
DESCENDANTS(
    [Invoice Date].[Calendar].[Calendar Year].[CY2015],,
```

```
LEAVES)
ON ROWS
FROM
[Wide World Importers DW];
GO
```

When you use a set expression as the first argument of the DESCENDANTS function, the SSAS engine processes each member in the set individually using the remaining arguments and then combines the results. In Listing 3-20, the set expression returns CY2015 and CY2016. Notice the use of distance as the second argument instead of specifying a level. Consequently, because each member in the set expression result is on the Calendar Year level, the members returned by the DESCENDANTS function are two levels lower on the Date level, 2015-01-01 to 2016-12-31.

LISTING 3-20 DESCENDANTS function with set expression and distance

```
//  Returns members of Date level subordinate to CY2015 and CY2016
//    e.g. 2015-01-01 to 2016-12-31
SELECT

[Measures].[Sales Amount Without Tax] ON COLUMNS,

DESCENDANTS(
// Set expression

    TAIL(
        NONEMPTY([Invoice Date].[Calendar].[Calendar Year].Members,
                [Measures].[Sales Amount Without Tax])
        , 2),
// Distance from member in first argument
    2)
ON ROWS
FROM
[Wide World Importers DW];
```

> **NOTE DESCENDANTS FUNCTION REFERENCE**
>
> For more information about the nuances of the DESCENDANTS function, refer to "Descendants (MDX)" at *https://msdn.microsoft.com/en-us/library/ms146075.aspx.*

NAVIGATION FUNCTIONS

Most of the functions in the Navigation folder on the Functions tab of the metadata pane return a set of members or a single member that is related to a specified member within a hierarchy tree. The type of relationship between members on different levels is expressed using family terms, such as parent, child, siblings, or ancestor. Descendants is also a valid term to describe relationships, but this function appears in the Set folder as described earlier in this chapter.

Some navigation functions return a single member, such as the PARENT function. Other navigation functions return a set of members, such as CHILDREN. Listing 3-21 provides an example of these two functions. The PARENT function returns the member one level above the specified member, whereas the CHILDREN function returns a set of members one level below it.

LISTING 3-21 PARENT and CHILDREN functions

```
//  Returns a member on the Calendar Year level, CY2016, and
//   members of Date level subordinate to ISO Week 1 in CY2016, 2016-01-04 to 2016-01-10
SELECT
[Measures].[Sales Amount Without Tax] ON COLUMNS,
{ [Invoice Date].[ISO Calendar].[ISO Week Number].&[2016]&[1].PARENT,
[Invoice Date].[ISO Calendar].[ISO Week Number].&[2016]&[1].CHILDREN }
ON ROWS
FROM
[Wide World Importers DW];
```

Another commonly used navigation function is ANCESTOR, which you use to return a member at some level above the level on which the member's parent is found. Like the DESCENDANTS function, you can specify either the level by name or by distance, as shown in Listing 3-22.

LISTING 3-22 ANCESTOR function

```
//  Returns a member on the Calendar Year level, CY2016
//      Specify level by name
SELECT
[Measures].[Sales Amount Without Tax] ON COLUMNS,
ANCESTOR([Invoice Date].[Calendar].[Date].[2016-01-01],
    [Invoice Date].[Calendar].[Calendar Year])
ON ROWS
FROM
[Wide World Importers DW];
GO
//      Specify level by distance
SELECT
[Measures].[Sales Amount Without Tax] ON COLUMNS,
ANCESTOR([Invoice Date].[Calendar].[Date].[2016-01-01], 2)
ON ROWS
FROM
[Wide World Importers DW];
```

You can also navigate between members on the same level. Use the SIBLINGS function to return members sharing the same parent or use PREVMEMBER or NEXTMEMBER to return members that are sequenced together (according to the OrderBy property for the attribute), as shown in Listing 3-23.

LISTING 3-23 SIBLINGS, PREVMEMBER, and NEXTMEMBER functions

```
//  Returns dates that are children of CY2016-Jan, 2016-01-01 to 2016-01-31
SELECT
[Measures].[Sales Amount Without Tax] ON COLUMNS,
[Invoice Date].[Calendar].[Date].[2016-01-01].SIBLINGS
ON ROWS
```

```
FROM
[Wide World Importers DW];
GO
// Returns dates preceding and following 2016-01-01, 2015-12-31 and 2016-01-02
SELECT
[Measures].[Sales Amount Without Tax] ON COLUMNS,
{[Invoice Date].[Calendar].[Date].[2016-01-01].PREVMEMBER,
[Invoice Date].[Calendar].[Date].[2016-01-01].NEXTMEMBER}
ON ROWS
FROM[Wide World Importers DW];
```

TIME FUNCTIONS

Time series analysis is often a business requirement that drives the development of a multi-dimensional database. MDX time functions make it easy to compare values with one point in time to other points in time, or to report cumulative values for a specified period of time.

Three of the functions available in the Time folder on the Functions page of the metadata pane return a member relative in time to the specified member, OPENINGPERIOD, CLOSING-PERIOD, and PARALLELPERIOD. The OPENINGPERIOD and CLOSINGPERIOD functions have a similar syntax. The first argument specifies the level on which the member to return is found, and the optional second argument is the parent of the member to return. The OPENING-PERIOD function returns the member that is first in the set of descendants for the specified member while the CLOSINGPERIOD function returns the last member in that set. For example, as you can see in Listing 3-24, you can use the CLOSINGPERIOD function to find the last day of the specified month. If you replace the second argument with a member of the Calendar Year level, the function returns the last day of the specified year.

LISTING 3-24 CLOSINGPERIOD function

```
// Returns last date member that is a descendant of CY2016-Feb, 2016-02-29
SELECT
[Measures].[Sales Amount Without Tax] ON COLUMNS,
CLOSINGPERIOD( [Invoice Date].[Calendar].[Date],
    [Invoice Date].[Calendar].[CY2016-Feb] )
ON ROWS
FROM
[Wide World Importers DW];
GO
// Returns last date member that is a descendant of CY2015, 2015-12-31
SELECT
[Measures].[Sales Amount Without Tax] ON COLUMNS,
CLOSINGPERIOD( [Invoice Date].[Calendar].[Date],
    [Invoice Date].[Calendar].[CY2015])
ON ROWS
FROM
[Wide World Importers DW];
```

The PARALLELPERIOD function is useful for retrieving a point in time that is the same distance from the beginning of a parallel time period as a specified member. For example, if you specify the second month of a quarter, such as May, you can use this function to get the second month of the previous quarter, which is February. From an annual perspective, May 2016 is the fifth month of the year, so you can request the fifth month of the previous year, or May 2015. You are not limited to retrieving a member from a previous quarter or year, but you can also specify the distance to a previous period to retrieve or even request a point in time in the future, as you can see in Listing 3-25.

LISTING 3-25 PARALLELPERIOD function

```
//  Returns month in same position of prior year, CY2015-May
SELECT
[Measures].[Sales Amount Without Tax] ON COLUMNS,
PARALLELPERIOD(
    // The level by which to determine parallelism
        [Invoice Date].[Calendar].[Calendar Year],
    // The number of periods to traverse
        1,
    [Invoice Date].[Calendar].[CY2016-May])
ON ROWS
FROM
[Wide World Importers DW];
GO
//  Returns date in same position of prior month, 2016-04-15
SELECT
[Measures].[Sales Amount Without Tax] ON COLUMNS,
PARALLELPERIOD(
    [Invoice Date].[Calendar].[Calendar Month],
    1,
    [Invoice Date].[Calendar].[2016-05-15])
ON ROWS
FROM
[Wide World Importers DW];
GO
//  Returns date in same position of three months prior, 2016-02-15
SELECT
[Measures].[Sales Amount Without Tax] ON COLUMNS,
PARALLELPERIOD(
    [Invoice Date].[Calendar].[Calendar Month],
    3,
    [Invoice Date].[Calendar].[2016-05-15])
ON ROWS
FROM
[Wide World Importers DW];
GO
//  Returns month in same position of next year, CY2016-Jan
SELECT
[Measures].[Sales Amount Without Tax] ON COLUMNS,
PARALLELPERIOD(
    [Invoice Date].[Calendar].[Calendar Year],
    -1,
```

```
                        [Invoice Date].[Calendar].[CY2015-Jan])
ON ROWS
FROM
[Wide World Importers DW];
```

The remaining time functions return sets. The generic function PERIODSTODATE is useful for generating a set of siblings for which the first member in the set is the first member in the period, and the last member is a member that is specified explicitly or dynamically. When you use this function to create a set to place on an axis, you explicitly define the last member of the set, as shown in Listing 3-26. However, when you use the PERIODSTODATE function in an expression that returns a value in a manner similar to the use of the YTD function demonstrated in the "Query-scoped calculations" section of this chapter, the last member of the set depends on the tuple context.

LISTING 3-26 PERIODSTODATE function

```
//  Returns a set of months from the beginning of the year to CY2016-Mar,
//        CY2016-Jan to CY2016-Mar
SELECT
[Measures].[Sales Amount Without Tax] ON COLUMNS,
PERIODSTODATE(
    // The level that determines the period of time to traverse
        [Invoice Date].[Calendar].[Calendar Year],
    // The last member of the set to return
        [Invoice Date].[Calendar].[CY2016-Mar])
ON ROWS
FROM
[Wide World Importers DW];
GO
//  Returns a set of dates from the beginning of the ISO Week to 2016-03-24,
//        2016-03-21 to 2016-03-24
SELECT
[Measures].[Sales Amount Without Tax] ON COLUMNS,
PERIODSTODATE(
    [Invoice Date].[ISO Calendar].[ISO Week Number],
    [Invoice Date].[ISO Calendar].[2016-03-24])
ON ROWS
FROM
[Wide World Importers DW];
```

Query-scoped calculations

Ideally, you add frequently-used calculations to a cube as described in Skill 3.2, "Implement custom MDX solutions," but there might be situations requiring you to create *query-scoped calculations*. A query-scoped calculation is a calculation that is evaluated at query time and does not persist in SSAS for reuse in subsequent queries. One reason to create a query-scoped calculation is to test logic prior to adding it permanently to the cube. Another reason is to support dynamic logic that is dependent on information available only at query time, such as parameter selections by a user that an application includes in the construction of an MDX query.

When you create a query-scoped calculation, you define either a member expression (also known as a *calculated member),* or a set expression by adding a WITH clause before the SELECT clause in a query. You can then use the new member or set in an expression that you use to create another member or set in the WITH clause or place on an axis, as shown in Listing 3-27. You can also reference the member in the query's WHERE clause. You can define the formatting for a measure by adding a comma and the FORMAT_STRING property to the end of the measure definition. Any format string that you can add here in the cube designer is valid. You can see the results of the Average Sales Amount calculation in Figure 3-24.

> *NOTE* **FORMAT_STRING PROPERTY**
>
> By default, the format string definition applies only to non-zero measure values. You can add sections to define formatting for nulls, zeros, and empty strings. To learn more, see "FORMAT_STRING Contents (MDX)" at *https://msdn.microsoft.com/en-us/library/ ms146084.aspx.*

LISTING 3-27 Member and set definitions as query-scoped calculations

```
WITH
MEMBER [Measures].[Average Sales Amount] AS
    [Measures].[Sales Amount Without Tax] / [Measures].[Quantity],
    FORMAT_STRING = "Currency"
SET [Small Stock Items] AS
    {[Stock Item].[Size].&[3XS],
    [Stock Item].[Size].&[S],
    [Stock Item].[Size].&[XS],
    [Stock Item].[Size].&[XXS]}
SELECT
{[Measures].[Sales Amount Without Tax],
 [Measures].[Quantity],
 [Measures].[Average Sales Amount]} ON COLUMNS,
[Small Stock Items] ON ROWS
FROM
[Wide World Importers DW];
```

	Sales Amount Without Tax	Quantity	Average Sales Amount
3XS	$2,596,210.00	142,018	$18.28
S	$6,495,934.00	386,775	$16.80
XS	$1,872,565.00	101,665	$18.42
XXS	$1,886,751.00	102,471	$18.41

FIGURE 3-24 Average Sales Amount calculation

You can define multiple member or set expressions in the WITH clause. After using the SET or MEMBER keyword, you supply a name for the query-scoped calculation, follow the name with the keyword AS, and then add an expression that returns a set or tuple, respectively. When the member you create is a measure, prefix the member name with [Measures] and a period. This use of a WITH clause is much different in MDX than in T-SQL.

STATISTICAL FUNCTIONS

You can also create a member as part of non-measure dimension in the cube, in which case you must provide the name of a dimension and a hierarchy in addition to the name of an existing member for which the calculated member becomes a child member. As an example, you might create a calculated member as a placeholder in a dimension for a value derived by using one of the functions in the Statistical folder on the Functions pane, such as AGGREGATE or SUM. This technique is analogous to creating a formula in Excel that references multiple cells to derive a new value that displays in a separate cell.

With a few exceptions, the functions in this group take a set as the first argument, and optionally take a numeric expression as the second argument. You omit the second argument when creating a calculated member, as shown in Listing 3-28, because the numeric value is determined at query time when the tuple resolution process adds a measure. In this example, the AGGREGATE function is used to create a non-measure dimension member, which is shown in Figure 3-25.

LISTING 3-28 AGGREGATE function for calculated member

```
WITH
MEMBER [Measures].[Average Sales Amount] AS
    [Measures].[Sales Amount Without Tax] / [Measures].[Quantity],
    FORMAT_STRING = "Currency"
MEMBER [City].[Sales Territory].[All].[West] AS
    AGGREGATE(
        {[City].[Sales Territory].[Far West],
        [City].[Sales Territory].[Southwest]})
SELECT
{[Measures].[Sales Amount Without Tax],
 [Measures].[Average Sales Amount]}
ON COLUMNS,
{[City].[Sales Territory].[Far West],
 [City].[Sales Territory].[Southwest],
 [City].[Sales Territory].[West]}
ON ROWS
FROM
[Wide World Importers DW];
```

	Sales Amount Without Tax	Average Sales Amount
Far West	$19,879,592.80	$19.33
Southwest	$23,924,720.30	$19.11
West	$43,804,313.10	$19.21

FIGURE 3-25 AGGREGATE function to create non-measure dimension member

When you use a statistical function to create a calculated measure in a query, you must include the second argument. Consider Listing 3-29, in which the SUM function is used to define a YTD Sales measure. The tuple resolution process is more complex in this case. Consider the cell intersection of CY2016-Jan and YTD Sales. The YTD function instructs the SSAS engine to build a set that includes each month from the beginning of the year to the member on the current row, which is returned by the CURRENTMEMBER function. In this case, the set contains only one member, CY2016-Jan. That member is combined with the measure in the second argument of the SUM function to create a tuple and a value is returned as you see in Figure 3-26. In the next row, because the set contains both CY2016-Jan and CY2016-Feb, two tuples are created and then added together. This process is repeated for CY2016-Mar, which results in the creation of three tuples that are added together.

LISTING 3-29 SUM function for calculated measure

```
WITH
MEMBER [Measures].[YTD Sales] AS
    SUM(YTD([Invoice Date].[Calendar].CURRENTMEMBER),
        [Measures].[Sales Amount Without Tax])
SELECT
{[Measures].[Sales Amount Without Tax],
 [Measures].[YTD Sales]}
ON COLUMNS,
{[Invoice Date].[Calendar].[CY2016-Jan],
 [Invoice Date].[Calendar].[CY2016-Feb],
 [Invoice Date].[Calendar].[CY2016-Mar]}
ON ROWS
FROM
[Wide World Importers DW];
```

	Sales Amount Without Tax	YTD Sales
CY2016-Jan	$4,447,705.95	$4,447,705.95
CY2016-Feb	$4,005,616.85	$8,453,322.80
CY2016-Mar	$4,645,254.00	$13,098,576.80

FIGURE 3-26 SUM function to create calculated measure

CONDITIONAL EXPRESSIONS

A conditional expression is useful for testing cell values before performing division or dynamically changing the value returned by an expression on a tuple by tuple basis. When you set up a conditional expression, you specify a search condition that the SSAS engine evaluates at query time as either TRUE or FALSE. The condition can be defined by using comparison operators or logical functions that return TRUE or FALSE. If you have a simple search condition, you can use the IIF function. For multiple search conditions, you can use a

instead. Listing 3-30 provides examples of your options for constructing conditional expressions and the results are shown in Figure 3-27.

LISTING 3-30 Conditional expressions

```
WITH
MEMBER [Measures].[A] AS NULL
MEMBER [Measures].[Division Error] AS
    [Measures].[Sales Amount Without Tax] /
    [Measures].[A]
```

```
MEMBER [Measures].[Division No Error] AS
    IIF(
        // Argument 1 - Logical function ISEMPTY, OR logic, equality comparison
        ISEMPTY([Measures].[A]) OR [Measures].[A] = 0,
        // Argument 2 - Value to return if Argument 1 is TRUE
        NULL,
        // Argument 3 - Value to return if Argument 1 is FALSE
        [Measures].[Sales Amount Without Tax] /
            [Measures].[A]
    )
MEMBER [Measures].[Case Stmt] AS
    CASE
        WHEN [Stock Item].[Color].CurrentMember IS [Stock Item].[Color].[Blue]
            THEN "Blue"
        WHEN [Stock Item].[Color].CurrentMember IS [Stock Item].[Color].[Black]
            THEN "Not Blue"
        ELSE
            "Other"
        END
SELECT
{[Measures].[Sales Amount Without Tax],
 [Measures].[Division Error],
 [Measures].[Division No Error],
 [Measures].[Case Stmt]}
ON COLUMNS,
TOPCOUNT([Stock Item].[Color].[Color].Members, 3, [Measures].[Sales Amount Without Tax])
ON ROWS
FROM
[Wide World Importers DW];
```

	Sales Amount Without Tax	Division Error	Division No Error	Case Stmt
N/A	$77,896,120.45	inf	(null)	Other
Blue	$35,903,882.00	inf	(null)	Blue
Black	$26,269,280.00	inf	(null)	Not Blue

FIGURE 3-27 Error condition and conditional statement results

STRING FUNCTIONS

Not only can you explicitly define a string to return as a measure, but you can also generate a string by using functions found in the Strings folder in the Functions pane, such as SETTOSTR and STRTOMEMBER. This type of string function is helpful for troubleshooting MDX queries or building dynamic MDX queries in which you construct a reference to a member at query time.

In Listing 3-31, the Set Members measure first evaluates the contents of the set generated by the YTD function for the current row and then converts the set object to a string by using the SETTOSTR function, as you can see in Figure 3-28. If you fail to use the SETTOSTR function, you cannot see the set's contents because a measure must be typed as a numeric value or a string. Furthermore, the members placed on the ROWS axis are determined at query time based on the current month, which means that your query results are different when you execute this query in a month other than January. The NOW function returns the current date and time, which the query converts to the first three characters of the month name by using the FORMAT function with the "MMM" argument. This truncated month name is concatenated strings to construct a valid unique name of a member for the first item in a set range. The last item appends the NEXTMEMBER function twice to return the month that is two months after the current month.

> **NOTE SUPPORTED VBA FUNCTIONS**
>
> In addition to NOW, MDX supports several other VBA functions. A complete list is available at "VBA functions in MDX and DAX" at *https://msdn.microsoft.com/en-us/library/hh510163.aspx*.

LISTING 3-31 SETTOSTR and STRTOMEMBER functions

```
WITH
MEMBER [Measures].[Set Members] AS
    SETTOSTR(YTD([Invoice Date].[Calendar].CURRENTMEMBER))
SELECT
[Measures].[Set Members]
ON COLUMNS,
{
 STRTOMEMBER("[Invoice Date].[Calendar].[CY2016-" + FORMAT(NOW(),"MMM") + "]") :
 STRTOMEMBER("[Invoice Date].[Calendar].[CY2016-" + FORMAT(NOW(),"MMM") +
    "]").NEXTMEMBER.NEXTMEMBER
}
ON ROWS
FROM
[Wide World Importers DW];
```

	Set Members
CY2016-Jan	{[Invoice Date].[Calendar].[Calendar Month].&[2016]&[1]}
CY2016-Feb	{[Invoice Date].[Calendar].[Calendar Month].&[2016]&[1],[Invoice Date].[Calendar].[Calendar Month].&[2016]&[2]}
CY2016-Mar	{[Invoice Date].[Calendar].[Calendar Month].&[2016]&[1],[Invoice Date].[Calendar].[Calendar Month].&[2016]&[2],[Invoice Date].[Calendar].[Calendar Month].&[2016]&[3]}

FIGURE 3-28 SETTOSTR values as measures and STRTOMEMBER results on rows axis

Some additional string functions are found in the Metadata folder in the Functions pane, such as NAME and UNQIUENAME. Listing 3-32 provides examples of each of these functions. You can use these functions for troubleshooting purposes or working with parameters for MDX queries in SSRS reports.

LISTING 3-32 NAME and UNIQUENAME functions

```
WITH
MEMBER [Measures].[Name Function] AS
    [Invoice Date].[Calendar].CURRENTMEMBER.NAME
MEMBER [Measures].[UniqueName Function] AS
    [Invoice Date].[Calendar].CURRENTMEMBER.UNIQUENAME
SELECT
{[Measures].[Name Function],
 [Measures].[UniqueName Function]}
```

```
ON COLUMNS,
{[Invoice Date].[Calendar].[CY2016-Jan] :
 [Invoice Date].[Calendar].[CY2016-Mar]
}
ON ROWS
FROM
[Wide World Importers DW];
```

	Name Function	UniqueName Function
CY2016-Jan	CY2016-Jan	[Invoice Date].[Calendar].[Calendar Month].&[2016]&[1]
CY2016-Feb	CY2016-Feb	[Invoice Date].[Calendar].[Calendar Month].&[2016]&[2]
CY2016-Mar	CY2016-Mar	[Invoice Date].[Calendar].[Calendar Month].&[2016]&[3]

FIGURE 3-29 NAME and UNIQUENAME strings in query results

> **NOTE MDX QUERIES IN SSRS**
>
> James Beresford describes how to work with UNIQUENAME in his article, "Passing Parameters to MDX Shared Datasets in SSRS" at *http://www.bimonkey.com/2014/04/passing-parameters-to-mdx-shared-datasets-in-ssrs/.*

Another useful string function is PROPERTIES, which you can find in the Navigation folder in the Functions pane. When you set an attribute's AttributeHierarchyEnabled property to False, you can access the value of that attribute by using the PROPERTIES function, as shown in Listing 3-33. Figure 3-30 shows the value displayed as if it were a measure. Instead of retrieving a tuple from the cube, SSAS retrieves the value from dimension storage for each city returned on rows.

LISTING 3-33 PROPERTIES functions

```
WITH
MEMBER [Measures].[Latest Recorded Population] AS
    [City].[City].PROPERTIES( "Latest Recorded Population" )
SELECT
{[Measures].[Latest Recorded Population]}
ON COLUMNS,
TOPCOUNT([City].[City].[City].Members, 3, [Measures].[Profit])
ON ROWS
FROM
[Wide World Importers DW];
```

	Latest Recorded Population
Sinclair	433
Akhiok	71
Cherry Grove Beach	0

FIGURE 3-30 PROPERTIES function results

An understanding of MDX objects is key to correct development of MDX queries and calculations. Be prepared to recognize definitions of MDX objects and to distinguish one object type from another. For example, you should clearly understand the difference between tuples and sets, recognize the syntax of these objects, and use them correctly in expressions.

NEED MORE REVIEW? **MDX TUTORIAL**

A good online resource for learning MDX is Stairway to MDX developed by Bill Pearson and available at *http://www.sqlservercentral.com/stairway/72404/*.

Skill 3.2: Implement custom MDX solutions

There are multiple options for implementing MDX in a multidimensional database. In any given database, business requirements might not allow you to use all these options. However, you should be prepared for exam questions that test your familiarity with the options described in this section.

> **This section covers how to:**
> - Create custom MDX or logical solutions for pre-prepared case tasks or business rules
> - Define a SCOPE statement

Create custom MDX or logical solutions for pre-prepared case tasks or business rules

One benefit of using custom MDX in a cube is the centralization of business logic to ensure that common calculations are consistently performed . Another benefit of storing MDX calculations in a cube is the caching of calculation results by the SSAS formula engine. When one user executes a query that uses a calculation, it remains available for other queries to use, regardless of which applications send those queries to SSAS, so query performance can be faster for the subsequent queries.

You store calculations in a cube by updating the MDX script that is created when you define a new cube. The SSAS engine uses the MDX script to determine how to resolve the values for each cell in a cube. In other words, the MDX script determines whether a cell's value is set by data loaded from a source table or by one or more calculations.

Calculated measures

Calculated measures, introduced in Skill 3.1, are calculated members that are assigned to the Measures dimension. You can test the logic of a calculated measure by defining it in the WITH clause of an MDX query that you execute in SSMS, and then add it permanently to the cube by creating a new calculated member on the Calculations tab of the cube designer, as described in Chapter 1. The example in Chapter 1 described how to use the Form View to add the Profit Margin Percent calculation.

You can also create a new calculated measure by using the Script View and adding code to the MDX script. In SSDT, open the 70-768-Ch1 solution, open the Wide World Importers DW cube, click the Calculations tab, and click the Script View button on the cube designer's toolbar. The MDX script currently contains two commands, shown in Listing 3-34: CALCULATE and CREATE MEMBER.

> **NOTE IMPORT SSAS MULTIDIMENSIONAL PROJECT**
>
> If you do not have the 70-768-Ch1 solution from Chapter 1, but have restored the 70-768-Ch1.ABF file from the sample code files to your SSAS server, you can create a project from the restored database in SSDT. Point to New on the File menu, click Project, select Import From Server (Multidimensional And Data Mining), type a name for the project and solution, specify a location for the solution, and click OK. In the Import Analysis Services Database Wizard, click Next, select the 70-768-Ch1 database, click Next, and click Finish.

LISTING 3-34 MDX script with CALCULATE and CREATE MEMBER commands

```
/*
The CALCULATE command controls the aggregation of leaf cells in the cube.
If the CALCULATE command is deleted or modified, the data within the cube is affected.
You should edit this command only if you manually specify how the cube is aggregated.
*/
CALCULATE;
CREATE MEMBER CURRENTCUBE.[Measures].[Profit Margin Percent]
 AS [Measures].[Profit]/[Measures].[Sales Amount Without Tax],
FORMAT_STRING = "Percent",
VISIBLE = 1  ;
```

Notice the warning that appears above the CALCULATE command explaining that this command controls the aggregation of cell values. If you remove this command, the only queries that return values are those that retrieve tuples at the bottom level of each attribute hierarchy, also known as the *leaf level*, which defeats the purpose of building a cube. A leaf-level cell is normally populated by loading data from a fact table, but can be overridden by an expression in the MDX script. The CALCULATE command instructs the SSAS engine to populate non-leaf cells with values derived by aggregating cells from lower levels, regardless of the source of the cell values.

The addition of the calculated measure in Chapter 1 by using the Form View added the CREATE MEMBER command to the MDX script. The syntax of the CREATE MEMBER command is similar to the definition of a calculated measure in a query-scoped calculation as described in Skill 3.1, but it includes the addition of a reference to the cube to which the member is added. In this case, the reference is to CURRENTCUBE.

> **NOTE CREATE MEMBER SYNTAX**
>
> For a full description of all available arguments for this command, see "CREATE MEMBER Statement (MDX)" at *https://msdn.microsoft.com/en-us/library/ms144787.aspx.*

Skill 3.1 introduced many different ways to build a measure by using tuples that rely on the current context of members on rows, columns, or the WHERE clause. Another technique with which you should be familiar is the use of a tuple to override the current context. A common calculation requiring this behavior is a percent of total, such as the one shown in Listing 3-35. This code also demonstrates the use of two new properties: FORE_COLOR and ASSOCIATED_MEASURE_GROUP. The FORE_COLOR property requires an expression, either static or conditional, that sets the text of a cell to a color in the Microsoft Windows operating system red-green-blue (RGB) format, such as 32768 for green and 0 for black. (A color picker is available in Form View to alleviate the need to find RGB numbers.) The ASSOCIATED_MEASURE_GROUP property links the calculation to a specific measure group. A client tool can use this information to display the calculated measure in the same folder as non-calculated members, but bear in mind that some client tools ignore this metadata.

LISTING 3-35 MDX script with calculated measure for percent of total

```
CREATE MEMBER CURRENTCUBE.[Measures].[Percent of Buying Group Sales Total]
 AS [Measures].[Sales Amount Without Tax] /
([Measures].[Sales Amount Without Tax],[Customer].[Buying Group].[All] ),
FORMAT_STRING = "Percent",
FORE_COLOR = IIF([Measures].[Percent of Buying Group Sales Total] > 0.35, 32768
/*Green*/, 0 /*Black*/),
VISIBLE = 1 ,
ASSOCIATED_MEASURE_GROUP = 'Sale'  ;
```

Add the code in Listing 3-35 to the MDX script, and then deploy the project to update the server with the new calculated measure. To test it, click the Browser tab of the cube designer, click Analyze In Excel on the Cube menu, click Enable in the security warning dialog box, and then select the following check boxes in the PivotTable Fields list: Sales Amount Without Tax, Percent Of Buying Group Sales Total, and Customer.Buying Group. The Microsoft Excel Security Notice displays a warning before opening the workbook because it contains an external data connection. In this case, the external data connection is trusted because it is generated in response to your selection of the Analyze In Excel command in the cube designer. You cannot view your cube in an Excel PivotTable unless you respond to the warning by clicking Enable.

NOTE **CREATE MEMBER SYNTAX**

For a full description of all available arguments for this command, see "CREATE MEMBER Statement (MDX)" at *https://msdn.microsoft.com/en-us/library/ms144787.aspx*.

The resulting pivot table, shown in Figure 3-31, displays the sales amount and percentage contribution of each buying group. Furthermore, the value for the N/A row is displayed in a green font due to the conditional formatting instruction in the calculated measure definition.

	A	B	C
1	Row Labels ▾	Sales Amount Without Tax	Percent of Buying Group Sales Total
2	N/A	$63,553,695.70	36.89%
3	Tailspin Toys	$54,497,209.60	31.63%
4	Wingtip Toys	$54,235,435.90	31.48%
5	Grand Total	$172,286,341.20	100.00%

FIGURE 3-31 Pivot table with formatted calculated measure

The SSAS engine breaks down the Percent of Buying Group Sales Total calculation into two steps. First, it constructs a tuple for the numerator by combining the Sales Amount Without Tax measure with other dimension members to shape the context of the query. For example, in row 2 of Figure 3-31, the numerator tuple is ([Measures].[Sales Amount Without Tax], [Customer].[Buying Group].[Tailspin Toys]). Second, the SSAS engine constructs the denominator tuple, ([Measures].[Sales Amount Without Tax], [Customer].[Buying Group].[All]) . This query includes no other dimension members to include in the tuple. In addition, the presence of the [Customer].[Buying Group].[All]) member overrides the inclusion of the [Customer].[Buying Group].[Tailspin Toys] member in the denominator's tuple.

Calculated members

Of course, you can also add non-measure calculated members to a cube, such as the West member described in Skill 3.1, either in Script View by using the CREATE MEMBER command, or in Form View by using the graphical interface. To use Form view, perform the following steps:

1. Click the Form View button on the Calculations page of the cube designer in SSDT, and then click the New Calculated Member button.

2. In the Name box, type **West**.

3. In the Parent Hierarchy drop-down list, expand City, click Sales Territory, and click OK.

4. Next, click the Change button, click All, and click OK.

5. In the Expression box, type the following expression:

```
AGGREGATE(
    {[City].[Sales Territory].[Far West],
     [City].[Sales Territory].[Southwest]})
```

6. Deploy the project to add the new calculated member.

7. Click the Browser tab of the cube designer, click Analyze In Excel on the Cube menu, and click Enable in the security warning dialog box.

8. Select the following check boxes in the PivotTable Fields list: Sales Amount Without Tax, Profit, Profit Margin Percent, and Sales Territory in the City dimension.

You can see the West member listed after the Sales Territory members, as shown in Figure 3-32, with its value in the Sales Amount Without Tax and Profit columns calculated by summing Far West and Southwest values in the respective columns. Its value in the Profit Margin Percent column is calculated by first summing the Profit values for Far West and Southwest and then dividing by the sum of the Sales Amount Without Tax for those members. The use of the AGGREGATE function for non-measure calculated members ensures the proper calculation for each intersecting measure in a query.

	A	B	C	D
1	Row Labels	Sales Amount Without Tax	Profit	Profit Margin Percent
2	External	$2,200,138.60	$1,093,669.85	49.71%
3	Far West	$19,879,592.80	$9,923,891.70	49.92%
4	Great Lakes	$20,153,233.85	$10,046,782.10	49.85%
5	Mideast	$25,758,309.30	$12,843,350.00	49.86%
6	N/A	$25,000.00	$15,500.00	62.00%
7	New England	$7,696,054.80	$3,813,022.75	49.55%
8	Plains	$23,307,175.85	$11,596,968.65	49.76%
9	Rocky Mountain	$11,076,949.95	$5,493,609.45	49.59%
10	Southeast	$38,265,165.75	$18,994,984.65	49.64%
11	Southwest	$23,924,720.30	$11,922,901.75	49.84%
12	West	43804313.1	21846793.45	49.87%
13	Grand Total	$172,286,341.20	$85,744,680.90	49.77%

FIGURE 3-32 Pivot table with calculated member in row 12

In this example, Excel applied the format string correctly to the Profit Margin Percent value of the calculated member, but not to the Sales Amount Without Tax or Profit measures. You can fix this behavior by adding a LANGUAGE property to the CREATE MEMBER command as shown in Listing 3-36. In this example, 1033 is the locale ID value for United States English. You must add this property in Script View, because there is no graphical interface for configuring this property in Form View.

LISTING 3-36 LANGUAGE property for calculated member

```
CREATE MEMBER CURRENTCUBE.[City].[Sales Territory].[All].West
 AS AGGREGATE(
    {[City].[Sales Territory].[Far West],
     [City].[Sales Territory].[Southwest]}),
VISIBLE = 1,
LANGUAGE = 1033  ;
```

> **NOTE LOCALE ID VALUES**
>
> You can find a complete list of locale ID values in "Microsoft Locale ID Values" at *https://msdn.microsoft.com/en-us/library/ms912047.aspx.*

Named sets

Just as you can add a set to the WITH clause, you can add an object called a *named set* to a cube for sets that are commonly queried by users. However, as part of the definition of a named set, you must also specify whether the set is dynamic or static, as shown in Listing 3-37. The two set definitions in this listing are identical, except the type of set, dynamic or static, is stated after the CREATE command. With a dynamic named set, the members of the set can change at query time based on the current context of objects on axes and in the WHERE clause. By contrast, a static named set always returns the same set members regardless of changes to query context. In SSDT, switch to Script View and add the code in Listing 3-37 to the MDX script.

LISTING 3-37 MDX script for dynamic and static named sets

```
CREATE DYNAMIC SET CURRENTCUBE.[Top 3 Stock Items Dynamic]
 AS TOPCOUNT
    (
        [Stock Item].[Stock Item].[Stock Item].Members,
        3,
        [Measures].[Sales Amount Without Tax]
    ),
DISPLAY_FOLDER = 'Stock Item Sets'  ;
CREATE STATIC SET CURRENTCUBE.[Top 3 Stock Items Static]
 AS TOPCOUNT
    (
        [Stock Item].[Stock Item].[Stock Item].Members,
        3,
        [Measures].[Sales Amount Without Tax]
    ),
DISPLAY_FOLDER = 'Stock Item Sets'  ;
```

Next, test the changes by following these steps:

1. Deploy the project, click the Browser tab of the cube designer, click Analyze In Excel on the Cube menu, and click Enable in the security warning dialog box.

2. Select the Sales Amount Without Tax check box in the PivotTable Fields list. Scroll down in the list to locate the Stock Item dimension, expand the Stock Item Sets folder, and select the Top 3 Stock Items Static check box to create the pivot table shown in Figure 3-33.

	A	B
1	Row Labels	Sales Amount Without Tax
2	10 mm Anti static bubble wrap (Blue) 50m	$6,329,070.00
3	32 mm Anti static bubble wrap (Blue) 50m	$6,384,000.00
4	Air cushion machine (Blue)	$11,107,251.00

FIGURE 3-33 Pivot table with static named set

3. Now expand the More Fields folder in the Invoice Date dimension and drag Invoice Date.Calendar year to the Filters pane below the PivotTable Fields list.

4. In the pivot table, select CY2013 in the Invoice Date.Calendar year drop-down list. Notice the values in the Sales Amount Without Tax column change, but the three stock items in column A remain the same. A static named set retains the same members in the set regardless of changes to the query context. Therefore, in this example, the static Top 3 Stock Items Static named set represents the top three stock items for all dates, all customers, all sales territories, and so on.

5. Scroll back to the Stock Item Sets folder, clear the Top 3 Stock Items Static check box, and select the Top 3 Stock Items Dynamic check box. Notice the pivot table now displays different stock items, as shown in Figure 3-34. If you change the Invoice Date. Calendar Year filter's selection from CY2013 to CY2015, the first member in the set changes. Moreover, as you add more filters to the pivot table, you see different combinations of members in the pivot table. A dynamic set factors in the query context.

	A	B
1	Invoice Date.Calendar Year	CY2013
2		
3	Row Labels	Sales Amount Without Tax
4	32 mm Double sided bubble wrap 50m	$1,570,240.00
5	32 mm Anti static bubble wrap (Blue) 50m	$1,719,900.00
6	Air cushion machine (Blue)	$3,140,946.00

FIGURE 3-34 Pivot table with dynamic named set

In this example in which the TOPCOUNT function determines which members are added to the set, the tuple used as the third argument is no longer [Measures].[Sales Amount Without Tax]. It instead includes the query's rows, columns, or WHERE clause for any dimension not named in the first argument of the function. To produce the set shown in Figure 3-34, the tuple for which the stock item members are sorted and filtered to the top three is ([Measures].[Sales Amount Without Tax], [Invoice Date].[Calendar Year].[CY2013]).

Default member

If you do not explicitly define a default member for an attribute hierarchy, the SSAS engine treats the All member at the top level of the hierarchy as the default member. Remember that the SSAS engine includes the default member from each attribute hierarchy in each tuple generated as the final step of processing an MDX query if the attribute hierarchy does not appear on rows or columns or in the WHERE clause.

Let's say that you want to set Far West as the default member for the Sales Territory attribute in the City dimension. To do this, follow these steps:

1. Open the dimension designer for City in SSDT and click Sales Territory in the Attributes pane on the Dimension Structure page.

2. In the Properties window, click the ellipsis button in the DefaultMember box.

3. In the Set Default Member – Sales Territory dialog box, click Choose A Member To Be The Default, expand All, click Far West(see Figure 3-35), and then click OK.

FIGURE 3-35 Set the Default Member dialog box for the Sales Territory attribute

As an alternative, you can define the default member by using an MDX expression. The MDX expression can be a simple reference of a static member, such as [City].[Sales Territory].&[Far West]. The expression can also be a more complex dynamic expression by using functions like USERNAME or NOW to select a member based on the current user or date and time, to name two examples.

> **NOTE USE DEFAULT MEMBERS WITH CAUTION**
>
> If you implement default members, be sure to educate users about its existence and the ability to override the default member at query time. The implementation of default members permanently applies a filter to an attribute hierarchy. Although a default member can be overridden in a query by requesting all members from the attribute hierarchy, an extra step is required from users which might not be intuitive.

Dimension and cell-level security

You can use MDX functions to define security and default members by role. Like tabular models, multidimensional models use role-based security to determine what users can see and do, although the implementation is quite different.

By default, when you deploy a multidimensional model to the server, no one can query it except you and the server administrators. At minimum, you must define a role and add Windows logins or groups to the role and grant read access to the cube. To do this in SSDT, right-click the Roles folder in Solution Explorer, and click New Role. In Solution Explorer, right-click the new role, Role.role, click Rename, and type a name for the role, such as Browsers.role, and click Yes to confirm. On the General page of the role designer, you can select any or all of the following database permissions for the role:

- **Full Control (Administrator)**   This role has full permissions on the database. This selection allows a user to alter or delete the database, perform processing operations, and configure security.

- **Process Database**   This role allows a user to perform processing operations by using SQL Server Integration Services (SSIS) or SSMS.

- **Read Definition**   This role allows the user to script the database or to view metadata for database objects without granting the ability to modify the objects or read the data.

When you want to create a role solely for the purpose of granting users the ability to browse or query a cube, leave the database permissions check boxes cleared perform the following steps:

1. Click the Membership tab of the role designer.

2. Click Add and then use the Select Users Or Groups dialog box to enter Windows logins or groups to the role. To follow the examples in this chapter, you do not need to assign any users to the role, because you can test a role with no users.

3. Next, click the Cubes tab of the role designer, and click Read in the Access drop-down list for the Wide World Importers DW cube.

If you were to deploy the project at this point, the role would enable its members to query the cube without further restriction. When you want to limit which dimension members that users can see, you can add dimension security by following these steps:

1. Click the Dimension Data tab in the role designer. By default, users can see all members in any attribute in any dimension. You can use the Dimension and Attribute Hierarchy drop-down lists on the Dimension Data page to target a specific attribute, and then select or clear check boxes to determine which dimension members that users can see or not see, respectively. As an alternative, click the Advanced tab to use MDX expressions to define allowed and denied member sets in addition to a default member. The default member defined for the role overrides the default member defined for the attribute in the dimension designer.

2. As an example, assume that you want to restrict users in the Browsers role to view data only for a subset of states in the City dimension. Specifically, you want users to see only the states that are associated with the Far West sales territory. In the Dimension drop-down list, click City and click OK.

3. Next, in the Attribute drop-down list, click State Province, and then click the Advanced tab. In the Allowed Member Set box, add the following set expression:

```
EXISTS(
    [City].[State Province].[State Province].Members,
    [City].[Sales Territory].[Far West]
    )
```

> **NOTE DIMENSION SECURITY**
>
> When configuring dimension security, you can select the Enable Visual Totals check box if you want the total for a hierarchy to reflect the filtered value. In other words, the user can see the aggregated value for allowed members. If you do not enable visual totals, the user can see the grand total for all members, which usually does not match the total of allowed members.
>
> You can find a more extensive explanation of dimension security options in "Grant custom access to dimension data (Analysis Services)" at *https://msdn.microsoft.com/en-us/library/ms175366.aspx*. Richard Lees has written "SSAS Dynamic Security" to explain the user of the USERNAME function to define allowed member sets and default members at *http://richardlees.blogspot.com/2010/10/ssas-dynamic-security.html*.

4. If there are specific measures for which you do not want users to see values, you can define cell-level security. Unlike dimension security for which you specify a set expression, you define Boolean expressions to specify which measures are visible when configuring cell-level security. Perhaps for the Browsers role you want users to see all measures except the Profit measure and the related Profit Margin Percent calculated measure. On the Cell Data tab of the role designer, select the Enable Read-contingent Permissions check box, and type the following expression in the Allow Reading Of Cell Content Contingent On Cell Security box:

```
NOT Measures.CurrentMember IS [Measures].[Profit]
```

> **NOTE CELL-LEVEL SECURITY**
>
> There are several different approaches to defining cell-level security besides the examples described in this chapter. For additional examples, see "Grant custom access to cell data (Analysis Services)" at *https://msdn.microsoft.com/en-us/library/ms174847.aspx*.

After configuring a role, deploy the project. You can then test the security configuration for that role by following these steps:

1. On the Browser page of the cube designer, click the Reconnect button, and then click the Change User button to the left of the Reconnect button.

2. In the Security Context – Wide World Importers DW dialog box, click Roles, select the Browsers check box, and click OK twice.

3. In the metadata pane, expand the City dimension, expand the State Province attribute, and expand the State Province level, as shown in Figure 3-36. The only states visible to members of this role are those that belong to the Far West territory. Although other states exist in the attribute, they do not display when browsing the dimension due to the security configuration.

FIGURE 3-36 Dimension attributes with security applied

4. Drag the State Province attribute to the query window. Then expand the Measures folder and drag the following measures to the query window to test measure security: Sales Amount Without Tax, Profit, and Profit Margin Percent. As shown in Figure 3-37, the values for Sales Amount Without Tax display, but the values for Profit and Profit Margin Percent do not. Remember that you defined cell security only for Profit. However, because you used the read contingent option, security also applies to any calculated measure related to Profit, such as Profit Margin Percent in this case.

State Province	Sales Amount Without Tax	Profit	Profit Margin Percent
Alaska	3002070.8	(null)	(null)
California	8831110.45	(null)	(null)
Hawaii	316857.85	(null)	(null)
Nevada	1251229.85	(null)	(null)
Oregon	2251099.55	(null)	(null)
Washington	4227224.3	(null)	(null)

FIGURE 3-37 Query testing dimension and cell security

Analysis Services Stored Procedures

The MDX language contains many more functions than those described earlier in this chapter. For the most part, MDX is capable of supporting most types of analysis that businesses commonly perform. When you need a specific operation to return a value, a string, or a set and none of the MDX functions meet your needs, you can create an *Analysis Services stored procedure* (ASSP) by creating and registering an assembly on the SSAS instance. As an example, financial analysis often requires an internal rate of return (IRR) calculation which might be easier to implement as a custom ASSP.

Unlike a SQL Server stored procedure that uses T-SQL to define an operation, an ASSP is implemented as a Microsoft Visual Basic .NET or C# assembly. Let's say you have a developer in your organization that creates an assembly and sends it to you as a dynamic link library (DLL) file. You register the ASSP by following these steps:

1. In SSMS, connect to the SSAS multidimensional instance.

2. You then add the assembly to the server for use in any database or to a specific database if you want to limit the usage of the assembly's functions. To do this, right-click the Assemblies folder for the server or expand a database's folder and then right-click its Assemblies folder.

3. Next, click New Assembly. In the Register Server Assembly dialog box (or if you clicked New Assembly for a database, the Register Database Assembly dialog box), provide the following configuration information, as shown in Figure 3-38:

   - **Type**   Keep the default selection of .NET Assembly.
   - **File name**   Type the path and assembly name in the text box or use the ellipsis button to navigate the file system and select the assembly.
   - **Assembly name**   Type a name for the assembly.

- **Include debug information**   If you select this check box, you can use the debugging feature in Visual Studio when executing a function in this assembly.
- **Permissions**   Select one of the following options:
- **Safe**   Provides permission for internal computations.
- **External Access**   Provides permission for internal computations and access to external system resources, such as the file system or a database.
- **Unrestricted**   Provides no protections to the system.
- **Impersonation**   Set the code's execution context for external resources by selecting one of the following options:
- **Use A Specific Windows User Name And Password**   Use a Windows login and password for a user authorized to access the external resource.
- **Use The Service Account**   Assign the service account running the Analysis Services service to change the execution context for the code.
- **Use The Credentials Of The Current User**   Run the code under the Windows login for the current user.
- **Anonymous**   Assign the IUSER_servername Windows login user account as the execution context.
- **Default**   Default to running the code under the Windows login for the current user.

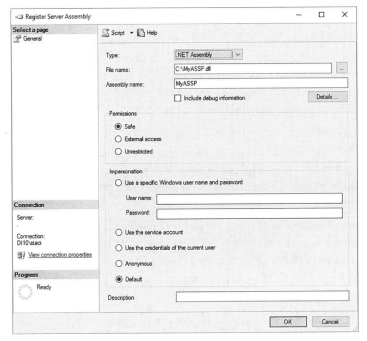

FIGURE 3-38 Register Server Assembly dialog box

Let's say that a hypothetical assembly, MyASSP.dll, includes a function named MyFunction that requires a measure as an argument and returns a value. To use this function after registering the assembly, you reference it by concatenating the assembly name, the function name, and the argument list, as shown in Listing 3-37.

LISTING 3-37 Calling an ASSP

```
SELECT
MyASSP.MyFunction([Measures].[A Measure])
ON COLUMNS
FROM [My Cube];
```

> **NOTE ASSP SAMPLE CODE**
>
> You can find several examples of ASSPs at "Analysis Services Stored Procedure Project" at *https://asstoredprocedures.codeplex.com/.*

EXAM TIP

You do not need to know how to develop an ASSP assembly for the exam. However, you should be familiar with the steps necessary to register the assembly and call the ASSP in an MDX query.

Define a SCOPE statement

You can restrict calculations in an MDX script not only to specific cells within a cube, but also to specific points at which the SSAS engine calculates cell values. To do this, you can use SCOPE statements and assignment operations in the MDX script. This capability allows you to implement complex business logic in a cube that is not possible with other types of calculated objects.

To better understand how to use SCOPE to implement complex business logic, consider the following requirements to calculate sales quotas for Wide World Importers:

- The monthly sales quota for CY2014 is a fixed amount for each month, $4,500,000.
- The sales quota for CY2015 is calculated by multiplying the previous year's sales by 110% and then equally allocating one-twelfth of this value to each month.

Before creating the MDX script to apply these calculations, add a new measure to the cube by using the code shown in Listing 3-38. This CREATE MEMBER command defines the Sales Quota measure and assigns an initial value of NULL.

LISTING 3-38 Initialize the Sales Quota measure

```
CREATE MEMBER CURRENTCUBE.[Measures].[Sales Quota]
 AS NULL,
VISIBLE = 1,
LANGUAGE = 1033;
```

Next, add code to the MDX script to allocate a fixed amount to each month in 2014. When the assignment of a value to a set of cells does not require multiple expressions, you can use an assignment operation, as shown in Listing 3-39. The left side of the equal sign, used as an assignment operator in an MDX script, is the portion of the cube to which the value on the right side of the assignment operator is assigned. This portion of the cube is known as a *subcube*.

LISTING 3-39 Assignment of a single value to a set of cells

```
([Invoice Date].[Calendar Year].[CY2014],
[Invoice Date].[Calendar].[Calendar Month].Members,
[Measures].[Sales Quota]) = 4500000;
```

A subcube always contains the All member of a hierarchy if no members of that hierarchy are explicitly defined. Otherwise, it can contain any of the following objects for a specified hierarchy:

- A single member of an attribute.
- Some or all members of a single level of an attribute or user-defined hierarchy.
- Descendants of a single member.

Your next step is to use a SCOPE statement to apply a series of MDX expressions to a subcube, as shown in Listing 3-40. By adding this code to the MDX script, you set the subcube defined as the argument for SCOPE as the target for every use of the THIS function until the END SCOPE statement is encountered. The FREEZE statement ensures that any statements subsequently added to the MDX script do not change the values assigned to the subcubes for CY2014 and CY2015.

LISTING 3-40 Equal allocation of prior year's value to current year's Calendar Month members

```
SCOPE([Invoice Date].[Calendar Year].[CY2015],
      [Invoice Date].[Calendar].[Calendar Month].Members,
      [Measures].[Sales Quota]);

    THIS =
        // create a tuple to retrieve sales one year prior
        ([Invoice Date].[Calendar].PARENT.PREVMEMBER,
        [Measures].[Sales Amount Without Tax])

        // multiply by 110%
        * 1.1

        // divide the result by 12 for equal allocation
        / 12;

END SCOPE;
FORMAT_STRING([Measures].[Sales Quota])= "Currency";
FREEZE;
```

Test the results of the new MDX script by following these steps:

1. Deploy the project, click the Browser tab of the cube designer, click Analyze In Excel on the Cube menu, and click Enable in the security warning dialog box.

2. Set up the pivot table by selecting the following check boxes: Sales Amount Without Taxes, Sales Quota, and Invoice Date.Calendar Month.

3. Drag the Calendar Month from the Columns pane to the Rows pane in the area below the PivotTable Fields list.

4. Drag Invoice Date.Calendar Year to the Filters pane, and select CY2014 in the Invoice Date.Calendar Year drop-down list.

5. Drag Sales Territory to the Filters pane, and select All in the Sales Territory drop-down list to produce the pivot table shown in Figure 3-39 in which you can see the fixed allocation of $4,500,000 to each month.

	A	B	C
1	Invoice Date.Calendar Year	CY2014	
2	Sales Territory	All	
3			
4	Row Labels	Sales Amount Without Tax	Sales Quota
5	CY2014-Jan	$4,067,538.00	$4,500,000.00
6	CY2014-Feb	$3,470,209.20	$4,500,000.00
7	CY2014-Mar	$3,861,928.75	$4,500,000.00
8	CY2014-Apr	$4,095,234.65	$4,500,000.00
9	CY2014-May	$4,590,639.10	$4,500,000.00
10	CY2014-Jun	$4,266,644.10	$4,500,000.00
11	CY2014-Jul	$4,786,301.05	$4,500,000.00
12	CY2014-Aug	$4,085,489.60	$4,500,000.00
13	CY2014-Sep	$3,882,968.85	$4,500,000.00
14	CY2014-Oct	$4,438,683.65	$4,500,000.00
15	CY2014-Nov	$4,018,967.45	$4,500,000.00
16	CY2014-Dec	$4,364,882.80	$4,500,000.00
17	Grand Total	$49,929,487.20	

FIGURE 3-39 Pivot table with MDX script assignment for CY2014

6. Now change the Invoice Date.Calendar Year filter to CY2015, as shown in Figure 3-40. Here the Sales Quota remains fixed across all months because it is an equal allocation. The allocation computation results from multiplying the CY2014 total sales amount of $49,929,487.20 by 110% which equals $54,922,435.90 and then dividing that value by 12. The result is $4,576,869.66.

FIGURE 3-40 Pivot table with MDX script assignment for CY2015

> ***NEED MORE REVIEW?*** **MDX REFERENCE**
>
> A good online resource for learning MDX is Stairway to MDX developed by Bill Pearson and available at *http://www.sqlservercentral.com/stairway/72404/*.

Skill 3.3: Create formulas by using the DAX language

The DAX language is completely different from MDX and requires you to learn different skills and apply different through processes to develop appropriate queries and calculations. Whereas MDX functions work with members, sets, and hierarchies, DAX functions work with tables, columns, and relationships. Coverage of all DAX functions is out of scope for this book, but Skill 3.3 introduces you to the more commonly used functions and provides a solid foundation for applying key concepts as you learn similar types of functions.

> **This section covers how to:**
>
> - Use the EVALAUTE and CALCULATE functions
> - Filter DAX queries
> - Create calculated measures
> - Perform data analysis by using DAX

Use the EVALUATE and CALCULATE functions

The 70-768 exam tests your ability to write DAX queries and work with functions, including CALCULATE, one of the most important functions. The ability to write DAX queries is also helpful for testing DAX formulas before you add them permanently to your tabular model as calculated measures just as you use MDX queries to test logic before adding calculated measures to a cube.

DAX query structure

The structure of a DAX query is much different from an MDX or T-SQL query. Listing 3-41 shows the simplest query that you can write in a client application such as SSMS. It contains an EVALUATE clause and the name of a table.

LISTING 3-41 Simplest DAX query

```
EVALUATE
'Stock Item'
```

To execute this query in SSMS, perform the following steps:

1. Connect to the tabular instance of SSAS, and then click the Analysis Services MDX Query button in the toolbar.

   The MDX query window supports the execution of DAX queries, although you cannot use drag and drop to add objects from the metadata pane to the query window.

2. In the Available Databases drop-down list, select 70-768-Ch2, and then add the query shown in Listing 3-41.

3. Click Execute to see the query results, a portion of which is shown in Figure 3-41, although the rows you see might vary because the order of rows is not guaranteed with this query. In this case, the query returns every column and every row in the referenced table.

Messages	Results							
Stock Item[Stoc...	Stock Item[WWI...	Stock Item[Stoc...	Stock Item[Color]	Stock Item[Sellin...	Stock Item[Buyin...	Stock Item[Brand]	Stock Item[Size]	
0	0	Unknown	N/A	N/A	N/A	N/A	N/A	
1	219	Void fill 400 L b...	N/A	Each	Each	N/A	400L	
2	218	Void fill 300 L b...	N/A	Each	Each	N/A	300L	
3	217	Void fill 200 L b...	N/A	Each	Each	N/A	200L	
4	216	Void fill 100 L b...	N/A	Each	Each	N/A	100L	
5	215	Air cushion mac...	N/A	Each	Each	N/A	N/A	
6	214	Air cushion film ...	N/A	Each	Each	N/A	325m	
7	213	Air cushion film ...	N/A	Each	Each	N/A	325m	
8	212	Large replacem...	N/A	Each	Each	N/A	18mm	
9	211	Small 9mm repla...	N/A	Each	Each	N/A	9mm	

FIGURE 3-41 Partial DAX query results for Stock Item table

You can override the default sort order of the table by adding an ORDER BY clause, as shown in Listing 3-42. The ORDER BY clause contains a list of columns defining the sort order which is ascending by default. Only columns are permissible in this list; you cannot use expressions. The default sort order is ascending which you can make more explicit by appending the ASC keyword after the column name, Use the DESC keyword after the column name to reverse the sort direction, as shown in Figure 3-42.

LISTING 3-42 ORDER BY clause in DAX query

```
EVALUATE
'Stock Item'
ORDER BY
    'Stock Item'[Color] DESC,
    'Stock Item'[Size]
```

> **NOTE SYNTAX FOR UNQUALIFIED AND FULLY QUALIFIED COLUMN NAMES**
>
> Sometimes you can use the unqualified name of a column in a query or in expressions. In that case, enclose the column name in brackets. However, a better practice is to use its fully qualified name to avoid ambiguity. Furthermore, some functions require you to do so. The fully qualified name of a column begins with its table name and ends with the column name.

Stock Item[Stoc...	Stock Item[WWI...	Stock Item[Stoc...	Stock Item[Color]	Stock Item[Sellin...	Stock Item[Buyin...	Stock Item[Brand]	Stock Item[Size]
492	71	Ride on toy sed...	Yellow	Each	Each	Northwind	1/12 scale
393	71	Ride on toy sed...	Yellow	Each	Each	Northwind	1/12 scale
149	71	Ride on toy sed...	Yellow	Each	Each	Northwind	1/12 scale
471	62	RC toy sedan c...	Yellow	Each	Each	Northwind	1/50 scale
232	62	RC toy sedan c...	Yellow	Each	Each	Northwind	1/50 scale
158	62	RC toy sedan c...	Yellow	Each	Each	Northwind	1/50 scale
459	62	RC toy sedan c...	Yellow	Each	Each	Northwind	1/50 scale
136	84	"The Gu" red s...	White	Each	Carton	N/A	3XL
407	84	"The Gu" red s...	White	Each	Carton	N/A	3XL
144	76	"The Gu" red s...	White	Each	Carton	N/A	3XS

FIGURE 3-42 Ordered Stock Item table

To further refine the query results, you can add the optional START AT sub-clause inside the ORDER BY clause to specify the first row of the result set, as shown in Listing 3-43. Its primary purpose is to enable applications to display a limited set of data at a time, such as when an application allows users to page through data. Each argument in the START AT sub-clause defines the value for the corresponding column in the ORDER BY clause. In Listing 3-43, the value of "Red" in the START AT sub-clause corresponds to the Color column and "1/12 scale" corresponds to the Size column. A portion of the query results is shown in Figure 3-43.

LISTING 3-43 START AT sub-clause in DAX query

```
EVALUATE
'Stock Item'
ORDER BY
    'Stock Item'[Color] DESC,
    'Stock Item'[Size]
START AT
    "Red",
    "1/12 scale"
```

Stock Item[Stoc...	Stock Item[WWI...	Stock Item[Stoc...	Stock Item[Color]	Stock Item[Sellin...	Stock Item[Buyin...	Stock Item[Brand]	Stock Item[Size]
489	68	Ride on toy sed...	Red	Each	Each	Northwind	1/12 scale
396	68	Ride on toy sed...	Red	Each	Each	Northwind	1/12 scale
454	73	Ride on vintage...	Red	Each	Each	Northwind	1/12 scale
147	73	Ride on vintage...	Red	Each	Each	Northwind	1/12 scale
152	68	Ride on toy sed...	Red	Each	Each	Northwind	1/12 scale
476	73	Ride on vintage...	Red	Each	Each	Northwind	1/12 scale
494	73	Ride on vintage...	Red	Each	Each	Northwind	1/12 scale
457	64	RC vintage Ame...	Red	Each	Each	Northwind	1/50 scale

FIGURE 3-43 Ordered Stock Item table starting at Red 1/12 scale items

You control which rows and columns to return in the query's result set by using a table expression rather than a table. A common way to return data from a tabular model in a query is to use the SUMMARIZE function. As shown in Listing 3-44, this function requires a table or table expression as its first argument and, at minimum, a pair of arguments for each column to summarize in the query results. This pair of arguments includes a string that becomes the name of the column in the query results and an expression to return a scalar value, as shown in Figure 3-44. In this example, the expressions for scalar values are references to measures defined in the tabular model. Notice that you can provide a column name that does not match the measure name. In addition, you can see how to use the FORMAT function to apply formatting to each measure.

> **NOTE FORMAT FUNCTION**
>
> To see a list of permissible formats to use with the FORMAT function, see "Predefined Numeric formats for the FORMAT Function" at *https://technet.microsoft.com/en-us/library/ ee634561* and "Custom Numeric Formats for the FORMAT Function" at *https://technet. microsoft.com/en-us/library/ee634206.*

LISTING 3-44 SUMMARIZE function with two measures

```
EVALUATE
SUMMARIZE(
    'Sale',
    "Total Sales",
        FORMAT('Sale'[Total Sales], "#,##0.00#"),
    "Number of Sales Transactions",
        FORMAT('Sale'[Sale Count], "#,#")
)
```

[Total Sales]	[Number of Sales Transactions]
172,286,341.20	228,266

FIGURE 3-44 Formatted measures returned as columns in query results

> **NOTE SUMMARIZECOLUMNS**
>
> A DAX function new to SQL Server 2016 is SUMMARIZECOLUMNS, which behaves similarly to SUMMARIZE, but uses slightly different syntax. You should experiment with the queries in this chapter by translating SUMMARIZE functions to SUMMARIZECOLUMNS. To learn more about working with this function, see "SUMMARIZECOLUMNS Function (DAX)" at *https://msdn.microsoft.com/en-us/library/mt163696.aspx.*

More often, you need a query to summarize results by groups, just like you can use a GROUP BY clause in a SQL statement. To do this, you can include a list of columns to use for grouping between the table name and the name/expression pairs, as shown in Listing 3-45. When you use columns from several tables, the relationships defined in the model ensure the values are summarized correctly. Remember that you can control the sort order of the results by using an ORDER BY clause.

LISTING 3-45 SUMMARIZE function with group by columns

```
EVALUATE
SUMMARIZE(
    'Sale',
    'Stock Item'[Color],
    'Stock Item'[Brand],
    "Total Sales",
        'Sale'[Total Sales],
    "Number of Sales Transactions",
        'Sale'[Sale Count]
)
ORDER BY
    'Stock Item'[Color]
```

Stock Item[Color]	Stock Item[Brand]	[Total Sales]	[Number of Sales Transactions]
Black	Northwind	5620565	6428
Black	N/A	20648715	46444
Blue	Northwind	1497130	2108
Blue	N/A	34406752	22005
Gray	N/A	5933699.75	9472
Light Brown	N/A	4941000	4114
N/A	N/A	74962290.45	91630
N/A	Northwind	2933830	4180
Red	N/A	1465920	1100
Red	Northwind	3260545	4124
Steel Gray	N/A	25000	1
White	N/A	15100749	34563
Yellow	Northwind	1490145	2097

FIGURE 3-45 Query results with measures grouped by Color and Brand

If you want to include subtotals for each grouping, you can use the ROLLUP syntax as shown in Listing 3-46. In this example, because both columns used for grouping are included in the ROLLUP expression and the ORDER by clause. Subtotals for each color and for all colors appear in the query results, as shown in Figure 3-46. If you omit the ORDER BY clause, the subtotals appear after the row groups in the query results.

LISTING 3-46 SUMMARIZE function with ROLLUP

```
EVALUATE
SUMMARIZE(
    'Sale',
        ROLLUP(
            'Stock Item'[Color],
            'Stock Item'[Brand]
        ),
    "Total Sales",
        'Sale'[Total Sales],
    "Number of Sales Transactions",
        'Sale'[Sale Count]
)
ORDER BY
    'Stock Item'[Color],
    'Stock Item'[Brand]
```

Stock Item[Color]	Stock Item[Brand]	[Total Sales]	[Number of Sales Transactions]
		172286341.2	228266
Black		26269280	52872
Black	N/A	20648715	46444
Black	Northwind	5620565	6428
Blue		35903882	24113
Blue	N/A	34406752	22005
Blue	Northwind	1497130	2108
Gray		5933699.75	9472
Gray	N/A	5933699.75	9472
Light Brown		4941000	4114
Light Brown	N/A	4941000	4114
N/A		77896120.4499...	95810
N/A	N/A	74962290.4499...	91630
N/A	Northwind	2933830	4180
Red		4726465	5224
Red	N/A	1465920	1100
Red	Northwind	3260545	4124
Steel Gray		25000	1
Steel Gray	N/A	25000	1
White		15100749	34563
White	N/A	15100749	34563
Yellow		1490145	2097
Yellow	Northwind	1490145	2097

FIGURE 3-46 Query results with subtotals displayed above column groupings

> **NOTE SUMMARIZE FUNCTION**
>
> For a full description of all the options available for using this function, see "SUMMARIZE Function DAX" at *https://msdn.microsoft.com/en-us/library/gg492171.aspx*. You can find a more in-depth review of its capabilities in Alberto Ferrari's article, "All the secrets of SUMMARIZE," at *http://www.sqlbi.com/articles/all-the-secrets-of-summarize/*.

Query-scoped measures

You can create a measure for use in a single query or to test in a query before adding it permanently to the tabular model in a query by adding a DEFINE clause prior to the EVALUATE clause, as show in Listing 3-47. In the DEFINE clause, you assign a name to a new measure and provide an expression, and then subsequently reference the measure in another new measure definition or in the EVALUATE clause. You can instead place the measure definition inline after the column name in the EVALUATE clause, but placing it in the DEFINE clause makes the query easier to read. You can see the results of this query in Figure 3-47.

LISTING 3-47 DEFINE clause

```
DEFINE
    MEASURE 'Sale'[Total Quantity] =
        SUM('Sale'[Quantity])
    MEASURE 'Sale'[Average Sales Amount] =
        'Sale'[Total Sales] / 'Sale'[Total Quantity]
EVALUATE
SUMMARIZE(
```

```
    'Sale',
    'Stock Item'[Color],
    "Total Sales",
        'Sale'[Total Sales],
    "Average Sales Amount",
        'Sale'[Average Sales Amount]
)
ORDER BY
    'Stock Item'[Color]
```

Stock Item[Color]	[Total Sales]	[Average Sales Amount]
Black	26269280	23.8572846632598
Blue	35903882	59.2729562946356
Gray	5933699.75	19.150418593693
Light Brown	4941000	18
N/A	77896120.4500...	13.5573040349869
Red	4726465	162.796300761203
Steel Gray	25000	25
White	15100749	17.2945050867374
Yellow	1490145	128.882978723404

FIGURE 3-47 Query results with Average Sales Amount as calculated measure

IMPORTANT **MEASURE NAME ASSIGNMENT**

If you assign a new measure the same name as a measure in the tabular model, your new measure replaces the one in the model. For example, if your query defines a measure named [Total Sales], the value returned in the query results uses the query's measure definition and does not use the calculation defined in the tabular model for [Total Sales]. However, if any other measure in the tabular model uses [Total Sales] to derive a value, that measure uses the tabular model's definition for [Total Sales]. This behavior can be confusing. Therefore, you should strive to avoid reusing measure names in query-scoped measures.

One optimization technique that you can use when you add query-scoped measures is to separate the measure expression from the table returned by the SUMMARIZE function. You can do this by using the ADDCOLUMNS function, as shown in Listing 3-48. The first argument of this function is a table or expression that returns a table, and then subsequent arguments are name/expression pairs to append to the table. The execution of Listing 3-48 returns the same results shown in Figure 3-47.

LISTING 3-48 ADDCOLUMNS function to append query-scoped measures

```
DEFINE
    MEASURE 'Sale'[Total Quantity] =
        SUM('Sale'[Quantity])
    MEASURE 'Sale'[Average Sales Amount] =
        'Sale'[Total Sales] / 'Sale'[Total Quantity]
EVALUATE
ADDCOLUMNS(
    SUMMARIZE(
```

```
        'Sale',
        'Stock Item'[Color]
    ),
    "Total Sales",
        'Sale'[Total Sales],
    "Average Sales Amount",
        'Sale'[Average Sales Amount]
)
ORDER BY
    'Stock Item'[Color]
```

> **NOTE** **SUMMARIZE AND ADDCOLUMNS BEST PRACTICES**
>
> Marco Russo has written an article, "Best Practices Using SUMMARIZE and ADDCOLUMNS,"
> to explain various scenarios in which you should combine these functions and others in
> which the results might not return the desired results. You can access this article at *http://
> www.sqlbi.com/articles/best-practices-using-summarize-and-addcolumns/*.

Evaluation context

The results that you see in a query, whether manually executed in SSMS or automatically generated in Excel, depend up the query's *evaluation context*. Evaluation context is the umbrella term
that describes the effect of *filter context* and *row context* on query results. The filter context in
general terms determines which rows in a table are collectively subject to a calculation, and row
context specifies which columns are related to an active row and in scope for calculations.

First, let's review filter context. Although this concept is not named explicitly in Chapter
2, "Design a tabular BI semantic model," filter context behavior is described in the "Filter
direction" section. To review, execute the query shown in Listing 3-49 and observe the query
results shown in Figure 3-48. The top row is generated from the rollup in the table expression and has no filter applied. Therefore, the value in this row represents the count of all rows
in the Sale table. Each remaining row in the Sale Count column is filtered by the value in the
City[Sales Territory] column. For example, the second row applies a filter to produce a subset
of the Sale table that contains only rows related to the External sales territory. Then the rows
are counted to produce a Sale Count value of 2894. The filter context for each subsequent
row is the reason that a different value appears in the Sale Count column.

LISTING 3-49 Filter context

```
EVALUATE
SUMMARIZE(
    'Sale',
    ROLLUP('City'[Sales Territory]),
    "Total Sales",
        'Sale'[Sale Count]
)
ORDER BY
    'City'[Sales Territory]
```

City[Sales Territory]	[Sale Count]
	228266
External	2894
Far West	26397
Great Lakes	26599
Mideast	33763
N/A	1
New England	10519
Plains	31039
Rocky Mountain	14778
Southeast	50520
Southwest	31756

FIGURE 3-48 Query results to demonstrate filter context

Next, let's consider row context. One way that row context applies is the resolution of a calculated column. When you reference a column in an expression for a calculated column, the value for the referenced column in the active row is returned. For example, the City State column, shown in Figure 3-49, is calculated separately row by row. When row 1 is active, the City is Fort Douglas, the State Province is Arkansas, and therefore the concatenation of these two columns in the City State calculated column is Fort Douglas, Arkansas.

[City State]	▼	*fx* =[City] & ", " & [State Province]		
◢ WWI City ID ▼	City ▼	State Province ▼	City State ▽
1	11945	Fort Douglas	Arkansas	Fort Douglas, Arkansas
2	12112	Fox	Arkansas	Fox, Arkansas
3	12518	Gainesville	Arkansas	Gainesville, Arkansas
4	12581	Gamaliel	Arkansas	Gamaliel, Arkansas
5	12834	Genoa	Arkansas	Genoa, Arkansas

FIGURE 3-49 Calculated column using row context

Even when multiple tables are involved, there is only one active row across all tables. Consider the calculated column Discount Amount in the Sale table that references the Recommended Retail Price column in the related Stock Item table, as shown in Figure 3-50. When this expression is resolved, the active row in the Sale table contains Stock Item Key. The use of the Related function in the expression follows the relationship between the Sale and Stock Item to set an active row in the Stock Item by matching on the Stock Item Key. Then the expression is resolved by subtracting 50, the Unit Price in the Sale table, from 74.75, the Recommended Retail Price in the Stock Item table when the Stock Item Key in the Sale table is 1.

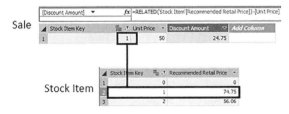

FIGURE 3-50 Row context between related tables

Currently, the Discount Amount in each row reflects the discount per unit sold. Let's say that you want to create a query to return the total extended discount amount. In other words, you want to multiply Discount Amount by Quantity for each row and sum the results without creating another calculated column in the model. If you create a query such as the one shown in Listing 3-50, the result is incorrect because you cannot sum the columns first and then perform the multiplication to compute the extended discount amount.

LISTING 3-50 Incorrect order of operations

```
DEFINE
    MEASURE 'Sale'[Total Discount Amount] =
        SUM('Sale'[Discount Amount])
    MEASURE 'Sale'[Total Quantity] =
        SUM('Sale'[Quantity])
    MEASURE 'Sale'[Total Extended Discount Amount] =
        'Sale'[Total Discount Amount] *
        'Sale'[Total Quantity]
EVALUATE
SUMMARIZE(
    'Sale',
    ROLLUP('Stock Item'[Color]),
    "Total Discount Amount",
        'Sale'[Total Discount Amount],
    "Total Quantity",
        'Sale'[Total Quantity],
    "Total Extended Discount Amount",
        'Sale'[Total Extended Discount Amount]
)
ORDER BY
    'Stock Item'[Color]
```

Instead, you need to perform the multiplication for each row individually and then sum the results. However, an error is returned when you try to perform a calculation inside the SUM function as shown in Listing 3-51: "The SUM function only accepts a column reference as an argument." As indicated by this error message, aggregate functions like SUM do not allow you to use expressions as arguments. (Other aggregate functions are described later in the "Create calculated members" section.)

LISTING 3-51 Incorrect SUM expression

```
DEFINE
    MEASURE 'Sale'[Total Extended Discount Amount] =
        SUM( 'Sale'[Discount Amount] * 'Sale'[Quantity] )
EVALUATE
SUMMARIZE(
    'Sale',
    ROLLUP('Stock Item'[Color]),
    "Total Extended Discount Amount",
        'Sale'[Total Extended Discount Amount]
)
ORDER BY
    'Stock Item'[Color]
```

To solve this problem, you need a way to perform a calculation requiring row context and then aggregate the results. DAX includes a special set of iterator functions that iterate through a table, resolve an expression row by row, and then apply an aggregate function to the results. Within this group of functions is the SUMX function, shown in Listing 3-52. Its first argument is a table expression to which filter context is applied first. The second argument is the expression to which both the filter context and the row context apply.

LISTING 3-52 SUMX function to apply row context to expression

```
DEFINE
    MEASURE 'Sale'[Total Extended Discount Amount] =
        SUMX( 'Sale',
            'Sale'[Discount Amount] * 'Sale'[Quantity] )
EVALUATE
SUMMARIZE(
    'Sale',
    ROLLUP('Stock Item'[Color]),
    "Total Extended Discount Amount",
        'Sale'[Total Extended Discount Amount]
)
ORDER BY
    'Stock Item'[Color]
```

The query results are shown in Figure 3-51. In this example, consider the row containing the color Black. To derive the value displayed in the Total Extended Discount Amount column, the SUMX function first filters the Sale table to rows for stock items having the color Black. For each active row in this filtered table, the row context for Discount Amount and Quantity is used to compute the extended discount amount. Each of these individual row values is then summed to produce the final value, 13004298.77. Therefore, this example illustrates both the effect of filter context and row context.

Stock Item[Color]	[Total Extended Discount Amount]
	85454978.99
Black	13004298.77
Blue	17773727.6799999
Gray	2944202.61
Light Brown	2445795
N/A	38721781.8200003
Red	2339656.06
Steel Gray	12380
White	7475486.76
Yellow	737650.29

FIGURE 3-51 Query results to demonstrate filter and row context

CALCULATE function

The CALCULATE function is one that you likely will use quite often because it allows you to conditionally evaluate expressions and apply or remove filters as needed. The exam does not require you to understand the nuances of using the CALCULATE function for complex use cases, but you should be familiar with how it manipulates filter context and transforms row context into filter contexts to resolve an expression.

The query shown in Listing 3-53 adds a new measure that uses the CALCULATE function. Its purpose is to calculate a percent of total for each row. The first argument of this function is an expression that returns a scalar value, just like any expression that is valid for a measure in a tabular model. The second argument is a filter that removes the filter context that would otherwise apply to the cell in which the CALCULATE result appears or adds a new filter context. In Listing 3-53, the ALL function returns all rows of the Sale table and ignores any existing filters to create the denominator required to compute each row's percent of total. Another point to note in this example is the omission of the ADDCOLUMNS function, because it is not compatible with the use of the ROLLUP syntax in the SUMMARIZE function.

> **NOTE ALL FUNCTION**
>
> You can use either a table or a column as an argument for the ALL function, or even a list of columns. However, you cannot use a table expression with the ALL function.
>
> In his blog post, "Revising ALL()" at *https://www.powerpivotpro.com/2010/02/all-revisited/*, Rob Collie describes various use cases for the ALL function. The documentation for this function is available in "ALL Function (DAX)" which you can view at *https://msdn.microsoft.com/en-us/library/ee634802.aspx*.

LISTING 3-53 CALCULATE with ALL to remove the filter context

```
DEFINE
    MEASURE 'Sale'[Overall Sale Count] =
        CALCULATE(
            COUNTROWS('Sale') ,
            ALL( 'Sale' )
        )
    MEASURE 'Sale'[Percent of Total Sale Count] =
        'Sale'[Sale Count] / 'Sale'[Overall Sale Count]
EVALUATE
SUMMARIZE(
    'Sale',
    ROLLUP('City'[Sales Territory]),
    "Sale Count",
        'Sale'[Sale Count],
    "Overall Sale Count",
        'Sale'[Overall Sale Count],
    "Percent of Total Sale Count",
        'Sale'[Percent of Total Sale Count]
)
ORDER BY
    'City'[Sales Territory]
```

In Figure 3-52, you can see that the same value displays in each row for the Overall Sale Count measure. This ability to override the filter context allows you to use a grand total for a table as a denominator when you need to compute a ratio, such as a percentage of total.

City[Sales Territory]	[Sale Count]	[Overall Sale Count]	[Percent of Total Sale Count]
	228266	228266	1
External	2894	228266	0.0126781912330351
Far West	26397	228266	0.115641400821848
Great Lakes	26599	228266	0.116526333312889
Mideast	33763	228266	0.147910770767438
N/A	1	228266	4.38085391604532E-06
New England	10519	228266	0.0460822023428807
Plains	31039	228266	0.135977324700131
Rocky Mountain	14778	228266	0.0647402591713177
Southeast	50520	228266	0.221320739838609
Southwest	31756	228266	0.139118396957935

FIGURE 3-52 Query results producing Overall Sale Count and Percent Of Total Sale Count

Now let's consider an example in which your business requirement is to calculate the number of sales in which a stock item color sells at some value below the average recommended retail price for all stock items sharing the same color. In other words, the average recommended retail price for each color group must be calculated by including stock items that have never sold and do not appear in the Sale table. Before you can compare the selling price to the average recommended retail price, you must correctly calculate the latter value. Listing 3-54 shows two alternate approaches to this calculation, but only one is correct.

LISTING 3-54 CALCULATE to transform row context

```
DEFINE
    MEASURE 'Sale'[Avg Selling $] =
        AVERAGE('Sale'[Unit Price])
    MEASURE 'Sale'[Tot Retail $] =
        SUMX( 'Stock Item',
            'Stock Item'[Recommended Retail Price])
    MEASURE 'Sale'[Stock Items] =
        COUNTROWS('Stock Item')
    MEASURE  'Sale'[Avg Retail $] =
        AVERAGE('Stock Item'[Recommended Retail Price])
    MEASURE 'Sale'[Correct Total Retail $] =
        CALCULATE(
            SUM('Stock Item'[Recommended Retail Price]),
            ALLEXCEPT('Stock Item','Stock Item'[Color])
        )
    MEASURE 'Sale'[Correct Stock Items] =
        CALCULATE(
            COUNTROWS('Stock Item'),
            ALLEXCEPT('Stock Item','Stock Item'[Color])
        )
    MEASURE 'Sale'[Correct Avg Retail $] =
        CALCULATE(
            AVERAGE('Stock Item'[Recommended Retail Price]),
            ALLEXCEPT('Stock Item','Stock Item'[Color])
        )
EVALUATE
```

```
SUMMARIZE(
    'Sale',
    ROLLUP('Stock Item'[Color]),
    "Avg Selling $",
        'Sale'[Avg Selling $],
    "Retail $",
        'Sale'[Tot Retail $],
    "Stock Items",
        'Sale'[Stock Items],
    "Avg Retail $",
        'Sale'[Avg Retail $],
    "Correct Retail $",
        'Sale'[Correct Total Retail $] ,
    "Correct Stock Items",
        'Sale'[Correct Stock Items],
    "Correct Avg Retail $",
        'Sale'[Correct Avg Retail $]
)
ORDER BY
    'Stock Item'[Color]
```

To understand Listing 3-54, let's review each measure in the context of the results shown in Figure 3-53, Avg Selling $ correctly calculates the average selling price of each color group, because it relies only on the Sale table and that table contains all sales. Retail $ is the sum of the recommended retail price, but it is based only on rows in the Sale table, as is Stock Items. You might ask how this is possible when the expression for Stock Items is COUNTROWS('Stock Item'), but this is where you have to remember that filter context applies. The SUMMARIZE function is based on the Sale table. Therefore, the rollup of colors that appear in the first column of the query results is filtered by the stock items appearing in the Sale table. A true count of all stock items, which is required to accurately calculate an average, appears in the Correct Stock Items measure. This measure uses a combination of CALCULATE and ALLEXCEPT to remove the filter on the Stock Items table except for the Color filter. In other words, the calculation for Correct Stock Items on the Black row correctly counts only the rows in the Stock Items containing Black stock items, and so on, for each row in the query results for the respective color.

> **NOTE ALLEXCEPT FUNCTION**
>
> The ALLEXCEPT function is the opposite of the ALL function. The syntax of ALLEXCEPT is slightly different, in that it takes a minimum of two arguments, with the first argument specifying a table, and the remaining arguments specifying the columns for which you want to retain the current filter context. This behavior occurs only when you use ALLEXCEPT as an argument in a CALCULATE function or in an iterator function. In this example you specify a table and the list of columns for which you want to keep the filter in place. When the list of columns for which you want to remove filters is longer than the list of columns for which you want to keep filters, you use ALLEXCEPT instead of ALL. Alberto Ferrari discusses this function in more detail in "Using ALLEXCEPT versus ALL and VALUES" at *https://www.sqlbi.com/articles/using-allexcept-versus-all-and-values/*.

Stock Item[Color]	[Avg Selling $]	[Retail $]	[Stock Items]	[Avg Retail $]	[Correct Retail $]	[Correct Stock Items]	[Correct Avg Retail $]
	45.5915983983598	15018.13	228	65.8689912280702	46811.52	672	69.66
Black	40.1356483582993	3032.76	51	59.4658823529412	9270.94	143	64.8317482517483
Blue	58.650022809273	2010.82	23	87.4269565217391	5588.43	59	94.7191525423729
Gray	24.8370196368243	336.38	9	37.3755555555556	336.38	9	37.3755555555556
Light Brown	18	107.64	4	26.91	322.92	12	26.91
N/A	51.476511324496	7142.89	99	72.150404040404	23137.24	312	74.1578205128205
Red	162.561255742726	1210.96	5	242.192	4186.04	19	220.317894736842
Steel Gray	25	37.38	1	37.38	864.12	22	39.2781818181818
White	14.7520180539884	758.07	34	22.2961764705882	1924.38	89	21.6222471910112
Yellow	128.917501192179	381.23	2	190.615	1181.07	7	168.724285714286

FIGURE 3-53 Query results for the CALCULATE function

Similarly, Avg Retail $ amounts are calculated with the filter context of the colors for sold stock items and are therefore incorrect. By contrast, Correct Retail $ and Correct Avg Retail $ remove the filter context for stock items except for color through the combination of the CALCULATE and ALLEXCEPT functions and their respective values that are correctly computed.

Filter DAX queries

Thus far, the DAX queries in this chapter return all values in a column, as long as values exist for the filter context of the query. DAX provides a variety of functions that allow you to reduce this set of values in some way.

FILTER function

When you want a query to return a subset of rows from a table only, you use the FILTER function, as shown in Listing 3-55. FILTER requires two arguments—the table or table expression to filter, and the Boolean expression that evaluates each row in the table. Like SUMX and other iterator functions, it operates on a table by evaluating the expression for each individual row. Rows for which the Boolean expression evaluates as TRUE are returned to the query. In this example, the FILTER function is the table expression that is used as the first argument for the SUMMARIZE function. It returns rows in the Sale table for which stock items have the color Black. From this filtered Sale table, the SUMMARIZE function returns the Color column of the Stock Item table and the Total Sales measure value, as shown in Figure 3-54.

```
EVALUATE
SUMMARIZE(
    FILTER(
        'Sale',
        RELATED('Stock Item'[Color]) = "Black"
    ),
    'Stock Item'[Color],
    "Total Sales",
        'Sale'[Total Sales]
)
```

> ***NOTE* FUNCTION ARGUMENTS AND EVALUATION CONTEXT**
>
> Notice that the RELATED function is required by the FILTER function's Boolean expression, but not by the SUMMARIZE function when referencing the Color column in the Stock Item table. Because the FITLER function is an iterator, the Boolean expression applies row context to the Sale table. The RELATED function returns a single value that is related to the current row, which is compatible for use in the Boolean expression. The reference to the Color column in the SUMMARIZE is a column that has the potential to return multiple values that become rows in the query results and is subject to filter context. When working with DAX functions, it is important to understand the type of object each argument requires and how evaluation context applies to the argument.

Stock Item[Color]	[Total Sales]
Black	26269280

FIGURE 3-54 Query results for FILTER function

You can create more complex filter conditions by using OR or AND logic. Listing 3-56 shows two examples of using OR logic to filter the query results to include sales only when a stock item is Black or Blue. The first example uses the OR function which takes two arguments and returns TRUE when either argument is FALSE or FALSE when both arguments are FALSE. The second example uses the OR operator (||) to evaluate conditions on either side of the operator and applies the same logic used by the OR function to return either TRUE or FALSE. Both queries produce the same result shown in Figure 3-55.

> ***NOTE* LOGICAL AND**
>
> Similarly, you have two choices when creating a filter condition for a logical AND. You can use the AND function, which returns TRUE only when both arguments are TRUE or FALSE when either argument is FALSE. As an alternative, you can use the AND operator (&&) to evaluate conditions on either side of the operator.

LISTING 3-56 FILTER function with OR logic

```
// Using the OR function
EVALUATE
SUMMARIZE(
    FILTER(
        'Sale',
        OR(RELATED('Stock Item'[Color]) = "Black",
            RELATED('Stock Item'[Color]) = "Blue"
        )
    ),
    'Stock Item'[Color],
    "Total Sales",
        'Sale'[Total Sales]
)
// Using the || operator
EVALUATE
SUMMARIZE(
    FILTER(
        'Sale',
        RELATED('Stock Item'[Color]) = "Black" ||
            RELATED('Stock Item'[Color]) = "Blue"
    ),
    'Stock Item'[Color],
    "Total Sales",
        'Sale'[Total Sales]
)
```

> **NOTE COMMENTS IN DAX**
>
> You can include comments in a DAX query by preceding the comment with //. Comments can appear between lines of code or at the end of a line of code.

Stock Item[Color]	[Total Sales]
Black	26269280
Blue	35903882

FIGURE 3-55 Query results for FILTER function with two conditions

As an alternative to using the AND operator when you have multiple conditions to apply, you can nest FILTER functions, as shown in Listing 3-57. The result shown in Figure 3-56 is effectively the same result returned by using the AND operator. However, you might find that nesting FILTER functions perform better than using the AND operator, especially when the innermost filter returns a smaller result set than the outermost filter.

LISTING 3-57 Nested FILTER functions

```
EVALUATE
SUMMARIZE(
    FILTER(
        FILTER(
            'Sale',
```

```
            RELATED('Date'[Calendar Year Label]) = "CY2016"
        ),
        RELATED('Stock Item'[Color]) = "Black"
    ),
    'Stock Item'[Color],
    "Total Sales",
        'Sale'[Total Sales]
)
```

Stock Item[Color]	[Total Sales]
Black	3331524

FIGURE 3-56 Query results for nested FILTER functions

Besides filtering columns to display only rows matching a specific label, as shown in the previous examples, you can also filter columns based on a comparison of numeric values. Furthermore, you can apply filters to data that has been aggregated. Let's say that you want to display a list of cities and total sales for each city, but you also want to filter this list to include only cities for which sales exceed 400,000. To do this, you must break down the query into two steps. Your first step is to produce a summarized table of cities and then you can apply a filter to the summarized table as your second step, as shown in Listing 3-58. The query resolves the innermost function first to produce a table containing aggregated sales by city, and then applies the filter to this table.

LISTING 3-58 Filter by measure

```
EVALUATE
FILTER(
    SUMMARIZE(
    'Sale',
        'City'[City Key],
        'City'[City],
        "Total Sales",
        'Sale'[Total Sales]
    ),
    [Total Sales] > 400000
)
ORDER BY
    'City'[City]
```

City[City Key]	City[City]	[Total Sales]
72610	Akhiok	542733.2
64723	Cherry Grove Beach	526621.15
81238	East Fultonham	475097.2
81012	Rockwall	414217.25
92524	Sinclair	514830.2
82686	Teutopolis	485950.5

FIGURE 3-57 Query results for a filtered measure

ALL function

Whether a filter is applied to query results explicitly by the FILTER function or implicitly by an expression's filter context, DAX provides functions to selectively remove or retain current filters. One way to do this is to use the ALL function as described in the "CALCULATE function" section earlier in this chapter. In that example, the argument for the ALL function is a table, but you can also use columns as arguments for the ALL function.

Let's revisit the example used to introduce the CALCULATE function in which the query produces a percentage of total sale count by sales territory. This time, you want to modify the query to show the percentage break down for each year by sales territory. In other words, for each year, the query should return the relative contribution of each sales territory, as you can see in the partial query results shown in Figure 3-58. That means you need to remove the filter for sales territory in the denominator only and retain the filter for year. That way, the denominator includes sales for all territories for the current year. To do this, use the ALL function with the column reference to the Sales Territory in the City table, as shown in Listing 3-59.

LISTING 3-59 ALL function to remove filter on a specific column

```
DEFINE
    MEASURE 'Sale'[Overall Sale Count] =
        CALCULATE(
            COUNTROWS('Sale'),
            ALL('City'[Sales Territory])
        )
    MEASURE 'Sale'[Percent of Total Sale Count] =
        'Sale'[Sale Count] / 'Sale'[Overall Sale Count]
EVALUATE
ADDCOLUMNS(
    SUMMARIZE(
        'Sale',
        'Date'[Calendar Year Label],
        'City'[Sales Territory],
        "Sale Count",
            'Sale'[Sale Count]
    ),
    "Overall Sale Count",
        'Sale'[Overall Sale Count],
    "Percent of Total Sale Count",
        'Sale'[Percent of Total Sale Count]
)
ORDER BY
    'Date'[Calendar Year Label],
    'City'[Sales Territory]
```

Date[Calendar Year Label]	City[Sales Territory]	[Sale Count]	[Overall Sale Count]	[Percent of Total Sale Count]
CY2013	External	783	60968	0.0128428027817872
CY2013	Far West	7136	60968	0.117045007216901
CY2013	Great Lakes	6939	60968	0.113813803962735
CY2013	Mideast	9144	60968	0.149980317543629
CY2013	New England	2617	60968	0.0429241569347855
CY2013	Plains	8544	60968	0.140139089358352
CY2013	Rocky Mountain	3582	60968	0.0587521322661068
CY2013	Southeast	13647	60968	0.223838735074137
CY2013	Southwest	8576	60968	0.140663954861567
CY2014	External	782	65941	0.0118590861527729
CY2014	Far West	7720	65941	0.117074354347068
CY2014	Great Lakes	7718	65941	0.117044024203455

FIGURE 3-58 Query results for a filtered percent of total

One of the limitations of using the ADDCOLUMNS function with a nested SUMMARIZE function in a query is the inability to also use the ROLLUP syntax to obtain subtotals for specified groups. However, you can use SUMMARIZE again as the outermost function as shown in Listing 3-60, and thereby produce the subtotals as you can see in the partial query results shown in Figure 3-59.

LISTING 3-60 Outer SUMMARIZE function with ROLLUP

```
DEFINE
    MEASURE 'Sale'[Overall Sale Count] =
        CALCULATE(
            COUNTROWS('Sale'),
            ALL('City'[Sales Territory])
        )
    MEASURE 'Sale'[Percent of Total Sale Count] =
        'Sale'[Sale Count] / 'Sale'[Overall Sale Count]
EVALUATE
SUMMARIZE(
    ADDCOLUMNS(
        SUMMARIZE(
            'Sale',
            'Date'[Calendar Year Label],
            'City'[Sales Territory],
            "Sale Count",
                'Sale'[Sale Count]
        ),
        "Overall Sale Count",
            'Sale'[Overall Sale Count],
        "Percent of Total Sale Count",
            'Sale'[Percent of Total Sale Count]
    ),
    'Date'[Calendar Year Label],
    ROLLUP('City'[Sales Territory]),
    "Sale Count",
        'Sale'[Sale Count],
    "Overall Sale Count",
        'Sale'[Overall Sale Count],
    "Percent of Total Sale Count",
        'Sale'[Percent of Total Sale Count]
)
```

```
ORDER BY
    'Date'[Calendar Year Label],
    'City'[Sales Territory]
```

Date[Calendar Year Label]	City[Sales Territory]	[Sale Count]	[Overall Sale Count]	[Percent of Total Sale Count]
CY2013		60968	60968	1
CY2013	External	783	60968	0.0128428027817872
CY2013	Far West	7136	60968	0.117045007216901
CY2013	Great Lakes	6939	60968	0.113813803962735
CY2013	Mideast	9144	60968	0.149980317543629
CY2013	New England	2617	60968	0.0429241569347855
CY2013	Plains	8544	60968	0.140139089358352
CY2013	Rocky Mountain	3582	60968	0.0587521322661068
CY2013	Southeast	13647	60968	0.223838735074137
CY2013	Southwest	8576	60968	0.140663954861567
CY2014		65941	65941	1
CY2014	External	782	65941	0.0118590861527729
CY2014	Far West	7720	65941	0.117074354347068

FIGURE 3-59 Query results for an outer SUMMARIZE function with ROLLUP syntax

ADDMISSINGITEMS function

When a query has no value for a combination of items from separate columns, the query results are filtered to exclude that combination. However, sometimes it is important to know that a particular combination does not exist. To override that filter and reveal those missing combinations, use the ADDMISSINGITEMS function, which is one of the new DAX functions in SQL Server 2016. The results of executing the two queries in Listing 3-61 are shown in Figure 3-60.

LISTING 3-61 ADDMISSINGITEMS function

```
// Missing combination of items is filtered from query results
EVALUATE
FILTER(
    SUMMARIZE(
        'Sale',
        'City'[Sales Territory],
        'Stock Item'[Color],
        "Sale Count",
            'Sale'[Sale Count]
    ),
    'City'[Sales Territory] = "External"
)
ORDER BY
    'City'[Sales Territory],
    'Stock Item'[Color]
GO

// Missing combination of items is included in query results
EVALUATE
FILTER(
    ADDMISSINGITEMS(
        'City'[Sales Territory],
```

```
            'Stock Item'[Color],
        SUMMARIZE(
            'Sale',
            'City'[Sales Territory],
            'Stock Item'[Color],
            "Sale Count",
                'Sale'[Sale Count]
        ),
        'City'[Sales Territory],
        'Stock Item'[Color]
    ),
    'City'[Sales Territory] = "External"
)
ORDER BY
    'City'[Sales Territory],
    'Stock Item'[Color]
```

Missing combination of items filtered			Missing combination of items added		
City[Sales Territory]	Stock Item[Color]	[Sale Count]	City[Sales Territory]	Stock Item[Color]	[Sale Count]
External	Black	682	External	Black	682
External	Blue	322	External	Blue	322
External	Gray	130	External	Gray	130
External	Light Brown	47	External	Light Brown	47
External	N/A	1166	External	N/A	1166
External	Red	76	External	Red	76
External	White	442	External	Steel Gray	
External	Yellow	29	External	White	442
			External	Yellow	29

FIGURE 3-60 Comparison of queries omitting and including ADDMISSINGITEMS function

> **NOTE ADDITIONAL SYNTAX OPTIONS FOR THE ADDMISSINGITEMS FUNCTION**
>
> You can use additional arguments to define rollup groups and apply a logical test to determine whether a value is a subtotal. For more information about these arguments and restrictions related to this function, see "ADDMISSINGITEMS Function (DAX)" at *https://msdn.microsoft.com/en-us/library/dn802537.aspx.*

ROW function

As you learned earlier in this chapter, you can produce combinations of items from different dimensions by creating tuple sets in MDX, but DAX works only with tables and columns. There is no set construct in DAX. However, you can simulate the effect of a tuple set by using the CALCULATE function with filters to set the items to combine together and then nest this function inside the ROW function to return a table containing a single row. Use the new UNION function to combine multiple tables. Figure 3-61 shows the results of executing the query shown in Listing 3-62.

LISTING 3-62 UNION and ROW functions

```
EVALUATE
UNION(
    ROW(
        "Stock Item",
            "Black",
        "Sales Territory",
            "Southwest",
        "Calendar Year",
            "CY2016",
        "Sales",
            CALCULATE(
                'Sale'[Total Sales],
                'Stock Item'[Color] = "Black",
                'City'[Sales Territory]  = "Southwest",
                'Date'[Calendar Year Label] = "CY2016",
                'Customer'[Buying Group] = "Tailspin Toys",
                'Stock Item'[Size] = "L"
            )
    ),
    ROW(
        "Stock Item",
        "Blue",
        "Sales Territory",
            "Far West",
        "Calendar Year",
            "CY2016",
        "Sales",
            CALCULATE(
                'Sale'[Total Sales],
                'Stock Item'[Color] = "Blue",
                'City'[Sales Territory]  = "Far West",
                'Date'[Calendar Year Label] = "CY2016",
                'Customer'[Buying Group] = "Tailspin Toys",
                'Stock Item'[Size] = "L"
            )
    )
)
```

[Stock Item]	[Sales Territory]	[Calendar Year]	[Sales]
Black	Southwest	CY2016	256
Blue	Far West	CY2016	690

FIGURE 3-61 Query results for ROW and UNION functions

CALCULATETABLE function

The CALCULATETABLE function has the same behavior as the CALCULATE function, except that it returns a table whereas CALCULATE returns a scalar value. In many cases, you might find queries execute faster when you use the CALCULATETABLE to apply a filter to a table instead of the FILTER function. As an example, you can rewrite Listing 3-55 to instead use CALCULATETABLE, as shown in Listing 3-63, generating the same result.

LISTING 3-63 CALCULATETABLE function

```
EVALUATE
SUMMARIZE(
    CALCULATETABLE(
        'Sale',
        'Stock Item'[Color] = "Black"
    ),
    'Stock Item'[Color],
    "Total Sales",
        'Sale'[Total Sales]
)
```

> **NOTE CALCULATETABLE RESTRICTIONS**
>
> There are some restrictions with which you should be familiar when using the CALCULA-TETABLE function. For example, the table expression in the first argument must be a function that returns a table. The second argument is either a table expression to use as a filter or a Boolean expression that cannot reference a measure, scan a table, or return a table. For more details, see "CALCULATETABLE Function (DAX)" at *https://msdn.microsoft.com/en-us/library/ee634760.aspx.*

Create calculated measures

As explained in Chapter 2, all measures in a tabular model are calculated and derived from an aggregation of values from multiple rows in a table. In that chapter, a few measures are added to the sample tabular model. You can create more complex measures in your tabular model by performing mathematical operations on aggregate values or manipulating filter and row context. Unlike calculated measures in multidimensional models in which aggregations are implied in the MDX expressions, you must explicitly specify an aggregate function in the DAX expression used for calculated measures in a tabular model. This section explores a variety of the more commonly used DAX functions to help you understand key concepts and function syntax, but does not provide complete coverage of all DAX functions. Links to additional information for the DAX functions are provided in the descriptions of each function category.

EXAM TIP

SQL Server 2016 adds many new functions to the DAX language. You should be familiar with these new functions for which you can find a complete list at "New DAX Functions" at *https://msdn.microsoft.com/en-us/library/mt704075.aspx.* Some of these functions are more likely to be the subject of exam questions than others. Spend some time familiarizing yourself with functions in the following groups: date and time functions, information functions, filter functions, text functions, and other functions. In addition, practice using the new aggregate functions PRODUCT, PRODUCTX, MEDIAN, MEDIANX, and the group of percentile functions.

Mathematical functions

The majority of measures that you add to the model are likely to use basic mathematical operations and DAX functions. If you are familiar with Excel functions, many of the mathematical functions in DAX have similar names, syntax, and behavior, such as POWER and SQRT.

> **NOTE MATHEMATICAL AND TRIGONOMETRIC FUNCTIONS**
>
> A complete list of mathematical and trigonometric functions in DAX is available at "Math and Trig Functions (DAX)" at *https://msdn.microsoft.com/en-us/library/ee634241.aspx.* Valid DAX operators at listed in "DAX Operator Reference" at *https://msdn.microsoft.com/en-us/library/ee634237.aspx.*

AGGREGATE FUNCTIONS

Because a measure returns a single value, the value that it returns is typically an aggregation of values. The most commonly used aggregate function is SUM, which was introduced in Chapter 2. Other common aggregation functions include AVERAGE, MIN, and MAX. Each of these aggregate functions takes a column, not an expression, as its only argument, returning a single value. The column must contain a numeric or date data type.

Remember that a measure's value is subject to evaluation context in a query, as described earlier in this chapter. Similarly, rows, columns, filters, and slicers in a pivot table or Power View report apply a filter context to the measure and reduce the rows included in the aggregation of the measure's value.

Another useful aggregate function is COUNTROWS, which differs from the other aggregate functions because its argument is a table instead of a column. It can also use an expression. As its name implies, it counts all the rows in a table, subject to filter context.

DAX also includes a special set of aggregate functions that allow you to use a column that contains both numeric and non-numeric text: AVERAGEA, MINA, MAXA, and COUNTA. Within this group, you might find COUNTA the most useful, because it returns the number of non-empty rows in a column.

The opposite approach of COUNTA for row counts is to use COUNTBLANK to count the number of empty rows in a column. Together, the combined results of COUNTA and COUNTBLANK is the same value as COUNTROWS.

> **NOTE DAX AGGREGATE FUNCTION LIST**
>
> You can find a list of DAX aggregate functions and links to the respective documentation at "Statistical Functions (DAX)" at *https://msdn.microsoft.com/en-us/library/ee634822.aspx.*

ITERATOR AGGREGATE FUNCTIONS

Another special set of iterator aggregate functions have X as the suffix, such as SUMX introduced earlier in the "Evaluation context" section of this chapter. The first argument of this type of function is a table or table expression, and the second argument is an expression to evaluate. This group of functions differs from standard aggregate functions because they perform an aggregate operation on an expression rather than a column. More specifically, the expression is evaluated by using row context for each row in a table or a table expression and then the results from each row are produced by using the applicable aggregation function.

The functions in this group, such as AVERAGEX, MINX, and MAXX, behave like SUMX. The COUNTX function is slightly different in that it increments a count when the expression value is not blank. You can learn how these functions work by updating the sample tabular model in your 70-768-Ch2 solution to include the measures shown in Table 3-3.

> **NOTE** **IMPORT SSAS TABULAR PROJECT**
>
> If you do not have the 70-768-Ch2 solution from Chapter 2, but have restored the 70-768-Ch2.ABF file from the sample code files to your SSAS server, you can create a project from the restored database in SSDT. Point to New on the File menu, click Project, select Import From Server (Tabular), type a name for the project and solution, specify a location for the solution, and click OK. Connect to your tabular server, and select the 70-768-Ch2 database. On the Model menu, point to Process, and then click Process All to load the workspace for your model with data.

TABLE 3-3 New measures to add to City table

Table	Expression	Format	Show thousand Separator
City	City Sale Count := COUNTX(VALUES('City'[WWI City ID]), 'Sale'[Total Sales])	Whole Number	True
	City Sale over 15K Count := COUNTX(VALUES('City'[WWI City ID]), CALCULATE([Total Sales], 'Sale'[Total Excluding Tax] > 15000))	Whole Number	True

The first argument in the City Sale Count measure, VALUES('City'[WWI City ID], creates a table of the distinct values in the WWI City ID column. That way, the duplicate rows in the table resulting from slowly changing dimension handling (described in Chapter 1), do not result in an overstatement of the number of cities like the City Count measure does. The COUNTX function iterates over this table of 656 rows, and then, for each city's row, resolves the second argument, which gets the sum of total sales for that city. Remember that the row context of the City table applies as a filter context in the Sale table. If there is a non-blank value, the count value is incremented. You can think of this measure as a flag to indicate when any sales exist for a given city.

The City Sale over 15K Count measure is similar, but its goal is to flag a city whenever it has a sale over $15,000. The CALCULATE function in the second argument filters the Total Sales measure to aggregate rows for the city in the current row from the first argument where the Sale row's Total Excluding Tax value exceeds 15,000. Note that this measure does not count how many sales are over 15,000 for a city, but only whether there are any sales over that amount.

To check the new measures, save the model, and then click Analyze In Excel, which opens a workbook containing a pivot table connected to your model. In the PivotTable Fields list, select the following check boxes: City Sale Count, City Sale Count over 1K, and State Province. A portion of the resulting pivot table is shown in Figure 3-62.

	A	B	C
1	Row Labels	City Sale Count	City Sale over 15K Count
2	Alabama	16	3
3	Alaska	11	1
4	Arizona	10	2
5	Arkansas	8	2
6	California	33	11
7	Colorado	18	4
8	Connecticut	4	1
9	Florida	21	9
10	Georgia	12	4
11	Hawaii	1	

FIGURE 3-62 Pivot table with count measures

DIVIDE FUNCTION

A common business requirement is to analyze ratios that require measures that use division. One way to do this is to use the division operator (/) to compute Profit Margin Percent, like this:

```
Profit Margin Percent := SUM(Sale[Profit]) / [Total Sales]
```

In this measure expression, the numerator applies the SUM aggregate function to the Profit column, but uses the Total Sales measure as the numerator without applying the SUM function. Because the Total Sales measure already applies the SUM function to the Total Excluding Tax column, the aggregate function is not required in the measure referencing it. While technically accurate, a problem with this measure expression is the potential for a divide-by-zero error. You can avoid this problem by enclosing the expression inside a logical expression (described later in this chapter in the "Logical functions" section) or by using the DIVIDE function, like this:

```
Profit Margin Percent := DIVIDE(SUM(Sale[Profit]) , [Total Sales] )
```

Date and time functions

Most DAX date and time functions are more useful for expressions in calculated columns than in measures. One new date function added to DAX in SQL Server 2016 Analysis Services, however, is DATEDIFF. When you have two dates that can be compared in the same row context, you can compute the difference between them. As an example, add the following measure to the tabular model configured as a Decimal Number with two decimal places:

```
Delivery Interval:=
AVERAGEX('Sale',
    DATEDIF/F(
        'Sale'[Invoice Date Key],
        'Sale'[Delivery Date Key],
        DAY)
    )
```

In the Wide World Importers DW database, the difference between the two date columns is generally one day, so the Delivery Interval measure is not enlightening from an analytical point of view. If there was more variance, you could assess how delivery intervals trend over time by location or by customer, to name only two examples. Nonetheless, it does serve to illustrate how to structure a measure using the DATEDIFF function, which returns an integer that you can then use to compute an average in the Sale table. The first and second arguments of this function are the start date and end date, respectively. The third argument is the interval to use for date comparisons, which can be any of the following values: SECOND, MINUTE, HOUR, DAY, WEEK, MONTH, QUARTER, or YEAR.

> **NOTE DAX DATE AND TIME FUNCTION LIST**
>
> You can find a list of DAX date and time functions with links to more information at "Date and Time Functions (DAX)" at *https://msdn.microsoft.com/en-us/library/ee634786.aspx*.

Time intelligence functions

The ability to perform time series analysis is a common requirement for a business intelligence solution. DAX provides a wide variety of functions to support this requirement. In this section, you explore the usage of the following three functions: TOTALYTD, SAMEPERIODS-LASTYEAR, and PREVIOUSMONTH. To get started, update the tabular model by adding and configuring the measures shown in Table 3-4.

TABLE 3-4 New time intelligence measures to add to a Sale table

Table	Expression	Format	Decimal Places	Show thousand Separator

Sale	Previous Month Sales :=
	CALCULATE(
	    [Total Sales],
	    PREVIOUSMONTH('Date'[Date])
	)
		Decimal Number	2	True

	Prior Year Sales :=
	CALCULATE(
	    [Total Sales],
	    SAMEPERIODLASTYEAR('Date'[Date])
	)
		Decimal Number	2	True

	Total Sales YTD :=
	TOTALYTD(
	    [Total Sales],
	    'Date'[Date]
	)
		Decimal Number	2	True

	Prior YTD Sales:=
	CALCULATE(
	    [Total Sales],
	    DATESYTD(
	    SAMEPERIODLASTYEAR('Date'[Date])
	    )
	)
		Decimal Number	2	True

After saving the model, check the results by setting a pivot table as shown in Figure 3-63 by selecting the following check boxes: Total Sales, Total Sales YTD, Previous Month Sales, Prior Year Sales, and Prior YTD Sales. Then drag the Calendar hierarchy to the Rows pane below the PivotTable Fields list to produce the pivot table shown in Figure 3-63. Let's examine how each measure is evaluated:

- **Total Sales YTD** The TOTALYTD function takes a scalar value expression as its first argument, which in this case is the Total Sales measure. The second argument is a column containing a series of dates. To see a value returned for this measure, you must place items from the table containing the dates column on rows, columns, filters, or slicers in a pivot table, or include the item's column in a query. This column from the date table sets the row context used to calculate a value in the query results.

  As an example, the value for CY2013-Feb sets the filter context and includes a range of dates from the beginning of the year, 2013-01-01, to the last date in February, 2013-02-28. The Total Sales value for each of these dates are summed to produce the value of 6,547,197.05.

- **Previous Month Sales** The PREVIOUSMONTH function is used as a filter in a CALCULATE function to manipulate the filter context on Total Sales. Note the use of the Date column from the Date table, a common pattern to use when working with time intelligence functions. Again, it sets the row context.

In the query results shown in Figure 3-63, the row context in row 4 is CY2013-Feb. This row context is used as a starting point to find the previous month, which is CY2013-Jan. That month is then used to filter the Total Sales value to 3,770,410.85, which is returned as Previous Month Sales on row 4.

- **Prior Year Sales** Conceptually, the formula for Prior Year Sales is similar to Previous Month Sales. This time the filter condition uses the SAMEPERIODLASTYEAR to set the row context based on the Date column.

If you examine row 16, the row context for Date is CY2014-Jan. The SAMEPERIODLAS-TYEAR function navigates through dates to find the corresponding time period one year prior, which is CY2013-Jan. This date is used to filter Total Sales, to thereby return to 3,770,410.85. Likewise, row 15 uses the date context of CY2014. In that case, the SAMEPERIODLASTYEAR returns a new row context of CY2013, which has a Total Sales value of 45,707,188, to compute Prior Year Sales.

- **Prior YTD Sales** In this case, the SAMPERIODLASTYEAR function finds the corresponding time period to determine the current row's corresponding date one year earlier. This time period is passed to the DATESYTD function to create a date range from the beginning of the year to the end date returned by SAMEPERIODLASTYEAR. Thus, the Prior YTD Sales for CY2014-Mar matches the Total Sales YTD for CY2013-Mar.

	A	B	C	D	E	F
1	Row Labels ▾	Total Sales	Total Sales YTD	Previous Month Sales	Prior Year Sales	Prior YTD Sales
2	⊟CY2013	45,707,188.00	45,707,188.00			
3	⊞CY2013-Jan	3,770,410.85	3,770,410.85			
4	⊞CY2013-Feb	2,776,786.20	6,547,197.05	3,770,410.85		
5	⊞CY2013-Mar	3,870,505.30	10,417,702.35	2,776,786.20		
6	⊞CY2013-Apr	4,059,606.85	14,477,309.20	3,870,505.30		
7	⊞CY2013-May	4,417,965.55	18,895,274.75	4,059,606.85		
8	⊞CY2013-Jun	4,069,036.20	22,964,310.95	4,417,965.55		
9	⊞CY2013-Jul	4,381,767.45	27,346,078.40	4,069,036.20		
10	⊞CY2013-Aug	3,495,991.00	30,842,069.40	4,381,767.45		
11	⊞CY2013-Sep	3,779,040.85	34,621,110.25	3,495,991.00		
12	⊞CY2013-Oct	3,752,608.45	38,373,718.70	3,779,040.85		
13	⊞CY2013-Nov	3,697,461.90	42,071,180.60	3,752,608.45		
14	⊞CY2013-Dec	3,636,007.40	45,707,188.00	3,697,461.90		
15	⊟CY2014	49,929,487.20	49,929,487.20	3,636,007.40	45,707,188.00	45,707,188.00
16	⊞CY2014-Jan	4,067,538.00	4,067,538.00	3,636,007.40	3,770,410.85	3,770,410.85
17	⊞CY2014-Feb	3,470,209.20	7,537,747.20	4,067,538.00	2,776,786.20	6,547,197.05
18	⊞CY2014-Mar	3,861,928.75	11,399,675.95	3,470,209.20	3,870,505.30	10,417,702.35

FIGURE 3-63 Pivot table with time intelligence measures

> **NOTE DAX TIME INTELLIGENCE FUNCTION LIST**
>
> Refer to "Time Intelligence Functions (DAX)" at *https://msdn.microsoft.com/en-us/library/ee634763.aspx* to learn more about the available time intelligence functions.

Filter functions

Several different filter functions are described in the "Filter DAX queries" section earlier in this chapter. In those earlier examples, the emphasis is the use of filters to affect the rows returned in the query results. You can also use filter functions to reduce the items on which aggregate functions operate.

Let's say you want to add enable analysis of sales for Tailspin Toys in conjunction with all sales. By setting up filtered measures, you can compare Tailspin Toys side by side with sales to all customers. Update your tabular model by adding the measures shown in Table 3-5, as described in Chapter 2.

TABLE 3-5 New filtered measures to add to Sale table

Table	Expression	Format	Decimal Places	Show thousand Separator

Sale	`Tailspin Toys Total Sales :=`
	`  SUMX(`
	`    FILTER(`
	`      'Sale',`
	`      RELATED('Customer'[Buying Group]) =`
	`        "Tailspin Toys"`
	`    ),`
	`    [Total Sales]`
	`  )`
		Decimal Number	2	True

	`  Tailspin Toys % of Total Sales :=`
	`DIVIDE(`
	`  [Tailspin Toys Total Sales],`
	`  [Total Sales]`
	`)`
		Percentage	2	True

Save the model, and then click Analyze In Excel. Create a pivot table using the following measures: Total Sales, Tailspin Toys Total Sales, and Tailspin Toys % Of Total Sales. Then place Sales Territory on rows to produce the pivot table shown in Figure 3-64. The creation of filtered measures allows you to focus on groups of interest, such as Tailspin Toys, individually and in comparison to all sales.

	A	B	C	D
1	Row Labels ▾	Total Sales	Tailspin Toys Total Sales	Tailspin Toys % of Total Sales
2	External	2,200,138.60	797,736.15	36.26 %
3	Far West	19,879,592.80	8,057,345.80	40.53 %
4	Great Lakes	20,153,233.85	4,915,771.15	24.39 %
5	Mideast	25,758,309.30	8,264,736.35	32.09 %
6	N/A	25,000.00		
7	New England	7,696,054.80	2,762,904.70	35.90 %
8	Plains	23,307,175.85	8,389,768.50	36.00 %
9	Rocky Mountain	11,076,949.95	4,058,373.05	36.64 %
10	Southeast	38,265,165.75	10,900,993.20	28.49 %
11	Southwest	23,924,720.30	6,349,580.70	26.54 %
12	Grand Total	172,286,341.20	54,497,209.60	31.63 %

FIGURE 3-64 Pivot table with filtered measures

Logical functions

Logical functions either return a TRUE or FALSE value or evaluate conditions as TRUE or FALSE to determine which values to return. Among the group of logical functions are the IF and SWITCH functions. Also in this group are the AND and OR functions explained earlier in this chapter.

The IF function is useful for a simple condition and requires only two arguments. The first argument is a Boolean expression to evaluate, and the second argument is a value or expression returning a value if the Boolean expression is TRUE. Optionally, you can add a third argument to return a value for a FALSE condition. You can nest IF functions for more complex conditional scenarios.

The SWITCH argument is useful when you have several conditions to evaluate and is easier to read than a series of nested IF functions. As an example, add the following measure to your tabular model:

```
Sales Group:=
    SWITCH(
        TRUE(),
        [Total Sales] < 1000000, "Under 1,000,000",
        [Total Sales] < 10000000, "Between 1,000,000 - 10,000,000",
        [Total Sales] < 2000000, "Between 10,000,000 - 20,000,000",
        "Over 20,000,000"
    )
```

Not only does the Sales Group measure illustrate how to use the SWITCH function, it also shows how a measure is not required to return a numeric value. You can use this technique to assign a label to groups based on specified criteria, as shown in Figure 3-65.

⊿	A	B	C
1	Row Labels ▾	Total Sales	Sales Group
2	External	2,200,138.60	Between 1,000,000 - 10,000,000
3	Far West	19,879,592.80	Over 20,000,000
4	Great Lakes	20,153,233.85	Over 20,000,000
5	Mideast	25,758,309.30	Over 20,000,000
6	N/A	25,000.00	Under 1,000,000
7	New England	7,696,054.80	Between 1,000,000 - 10,000,000
8	Plains	23,307,175.85	Over 20,000,000
9	Rocky Mountain	11,076,949.95	Over 20,000,000
10	Southeast	38,265,165.75	Over 20,000,000
11	Southwest	23,924,720.30	Over 20,000,000
12	Grand Total	172,286,341.20	Over 20,000,000

FIGURE 3-65 Pivot table with filtered measures

> **NOTE DAX LOGICAL FUNCTION LIST**
>
> You can learn more about DAX logical functions by reviewing the list of available functions at "Logical Functions (DAX)" at *https://msdn.microsoft.com/en-us/library/ee634365.aspx*.

Variables

In SQL Server 2016, you can use variables in a DAX expression to make it easier to understand the logic in a complex expression. Variables are flexible in that you can use them to store any type of object, such as a column, a table, or a value. Additionally, the use of a variable can potentially improve query performance when the same logic is used repeatedly in the same expression, because the variable is evaluated only once. However, a variable has scope only within the measure in which you define it.

Table 3-6 is a set of measures to add to the Sale table in your tabular model to illustrate the use of variables. These measures are a variation on the theme of filtering measures to focus on a specific group. Notice the use of VAR to prefix the variable name, and then RETURN to mark the beginning of the expression to resolve to a scalar value.

> **NOTE FORMULA BAR EXPANSION**
>
> Click the arrow on the right side of the bar to expand the window so that you can more easily work with expressions containing multiple lines.

TABLE 3-6 New measures with variables to add to Sale table

Table	Expression	Format	Decimal Places	Show Thousand Separator

Sale	Internal > $15K % of Total Sales:=
	VAR
	//create table for all sales territories
	//except External and N/A
	InternalTerritories =
	 FILTER(
	  VALUES('City'[Sales Territory]),
	  'City'[Sales Territory] <>
	   "External" &&
	  'City'[Sales Territory] <>
	   "N/A"
	)
	
	VAR
	//get total of sales where any
	// individual sale > 15K
	InternalSalesOver15K =
	 SUMX(
	  InternalTerritories,
	   CALCULATE(
	    [Total Sales],
	    'Sale'[Total Excluding Tax] > 15000
	   )
	)
	
	VAR
	// get total sales for Internal
	InternalAllSales =
	 SUMX(
	  InternalTerritories,
	  [Total Sales]
	)
	RETURN
	
	// divide the first total by the second
	// total
	DIVIDE(
	 InternalSalesOver15K,
	 InternalAllSales
	)
		Percentage	2	True

Sale	Internal Sales Over 15K:=
	VAR
	//create table for all sales territories
	// except External and N/A
	InternalTerritories =
	 FILTER(
	  VALUES('City'[Sales Territory]),
	  'City'[Sales Territory] <>
	   "External" &&
	  'City'[Sales Territory] <> "N/A"
	)
	
	RETURN
	//get total of sales where any
	//individual sale > 15K
	SUMX(
	 InternalTerritories,
	  CALCULATE(
	   [Total Sales],
	   'Sale'[Total Excluding Tax] > 15000
	)
	)
		Decimal Number	2	True

	Internal All Sales:=
	VAR
	//create table for all sales territories
	//except External and N/A
	InternalTerritories =
	 FILTER(
	  VALUES('City'[Sales Territory]),
	  'City'[Sales Territory] <>
	   "External" &&
	  'City'[Sales Territory] <> "N/A"
	)
	
	RETURN
	// get total sales for Internal
	SUMX(
	 InternalTerritories,
	 [Total Sales]
	)
		Decimal Number	2	True

Figure 3-66 shows the results of these new measures added to a pivot table with Sales Territory on rows. The Internal All Sales and Internal Sales Over 15K measures exist in this example solely to allow you to validate the results of the Internal > $15K % of Total Sales measure. Let's take a closer look at how the Internal > $15K % of Total Sales measure is evaluated by using the following three variables:

- **InternalTerritories** A table of Sales Territories that is filtered to exclude the External and N/A sales territories. In other words, it includes the Internal sales territories.

- **InternalSalesOver15K** A scalar value derived by iterating over the InternalTerritories table, which is filtered to a subset of rows for which Total Excluding Tax is greater than

15000 and then the Total Sales value for these rows is summed. The result is a measure that reflects the total sales for any sales territory if any of its sales exceed 15,000.

- **InternalAllSales** A scalar value derived by iterating over the unfiltered InternalTerritories table to sum the Total Sales value for all rows. This measure represents an overall value to be used later to compute a ratio.

The formula that returns a value for this measure uses the DIVIDE function to derive the ratio between InternalSalesOver15K and InternalAllSales. The use of variables in this formula makes it easier to understand the logic as compared to nesting the functions and expanding the logic inside the DIVIDE function.

	A	B	C	D	E
1	Row Labels	Total Sales	Internal > $15K % of Total Sales	Internal All Sales	Internal Sales Over 15K
2	External	2,200,138.60			
3	Far West	19,879,592.80	3.04 %	19,879,592.80	603,882.00
4	Great Lakes	20,153,233.85	3.36 %	20,153,233.85	677,943.00
5	Mideast	25,758,309.30	2.90 %	25,758,309.30	746,307.00
6	N/A	25,000.00			
7	New England	7,696,054.80	2.44 %	7,696,054.80	188,001.00
8	Plains	23,307,175.85	3.31 %	23,307,175.85	770,994.00
9	Rocky Mountain	11,076,949.95	2.16 %	11,076,949.95	239,274.00
10	Southeast	38,265,165.75	3.17 %	38,265,165.75	1,213,461.00
11	Southwest	23,924,720.30	3.15 %	23,924,720.30	753,903.00
12	Grand Total	172,286,341.20	3.05 %	170,061,202.60	5,193,765.00

FIGURE 3-66 Pivot table with measures containing variables

> **NOTE VARIABLES**
>
> You can define variables inside expressions rather than define them at the beginning of the measure code. Alberto Ferrari describes variable syntax options in his article "Variables in DAX," which you can read at *https://www.sqlbi.com/articles/variables-in-dax/*.

Perform analysis by using DAX

There are many different types of analysis that you can perform by using DAX to create expressions for measures and calculated columns in your tabular model. Just as this chapter cannot cover every possible DAX function, this section cannot provide guidance for every possible type of analysis that you might need to perform in real-world applications. However, it should provide some insight into additional ways that you can use DAX.

Top ranked items

When you need to find items in a column having the highest measure values or highest ranking, you can use the TOPN function in a query. The first argument in this function is the number of items to return, and the second argument is a table expression to evaluate. In Listing 3-64, the table expression is a summary table that contains Total Sales for each stock item. The TOPN function sorts this column of stock items in the descending order of sales and returns the first five items, as shown in Figure 3-67.

LISTING 3-64 TOPN function

```
EVALUATE
TOPN(
    5,
    SUMMARIZE(
        'Stock Item',
        'Stock Item'[Stock Item],
        "Sales",
            [Total Sales]
    ),
    [Sales]
)
```

Stock Item[Stock Item]	[Sales]
32 mm Double sided bubble wrap 50m	6190240
10 mm Anti static bubble wrap (Blue) 50m	6329070
20 mm Double sided bubble wrap 50m	6214320
32 mm Anti static bubble wrap (Blue) 50m	6384000
Air cushion machine (Blue)	11107251

FIGURE 3-67 Query results for the TOPN function

However, if the primary client tool for analyzing top items is Excel, it is easier to use the RANK function in a measure. Use the code in Listing 3-65 to add the following measure to the tabular model. In this case, the RANKX function behaves like other iterator aggregate functions. Its first argument is an unfiltered Stock Item table for which a rank for each item is determined based on Total Sales. The IF function then evaluates the rank assignment and returns the Total Sales value only if an individual stock item has a rank of 5 or lower. If a stock item has a different value, the function returns a blank value. You can then use Excel's default behavior to ignore rows with a blank value when you use this measure in isolation and in a pivot table, as shown in Figure 3-68.

LISTING 3-65 RANKX function

```
Top 5 Stock Items:=
VAR
    SalesRank =
    RANKX( ALL('Stock Item'), [Total Sales])
RETURN
IF(
    SalesRank<=5,
    [Total Sales]
)
```

	A	B
1	Row Labels	▼ Top 5 Stock Items
2	10 mm Anti static bubble wrap (Blue) 50m	6,329,070.00
3	20 mm Double sided bubble wrap 50m	6,214,320.00
4	32 mm Anti static bubble wrap (Blue) 50m	6,384,000.00
5	32 mm Double sided bubble wrap 50m	6,190,240.00
6	Air cushion machine (Blue)	11,107,251.00
7	Grand Total	172,286,341.20

FIGURE 3-68 A pivot table with ranking measure

Variance

Recall the example in Listing 3-54, which illustrated the impact that row context has on measure evaluation. The business requirement in that scenario is to calculate the number of sales in which a stock item color sells at some value below the average recommended retail price for all stock items sharing the same color. Put another way, the goal is to determine variance between one value and a stated baseline. Variance can be expressed both as a value representing the difference, or as a ratio comparing this difference to a target value. Let's expand on the initial example to find the variance percentage between the average selling price and a baseline, which is the average recommended retail price for all stock items in a color group.

Table 3-7 is a set of measures to add to the Sale table in your tabular model to illustrate the use of DAX to calculate a variance percentage. Color Avg Retail $ finds the average retail price for all stock items in a color group, regardless of whether the item has sale transactions. The Avg Selling $ is the average price for which stock items have sold. The difference between these two values is computed and then divided by the baseline to return the variance percentage as Selling Variance %.

TABLE 3-7 New variance measures to add to Sale table

Table	Expression	Format	Decimal Places	Show thousand Separator

Sale	Color Avg Retail $:=
	CALCULATE(
	    AVERAGE('Stock Item'[Recommended
	Retail Price]),
	    ALLEXCEPT('Stock Item','Stock
	Item'[Color])
	)
		Decimal Number	2	True

	Avg Selling $:= AVERAGE('Sale'[Unit Price])	Decimal Number	2	True

	Selling Variance %:=
	
	DIVIDE(
	    ([Avg Selling $] - [Color Avg Retail
	$]),
	    [Color Avg Retail $]
	)
		Decimal Number	2	True

Figure 3-69 shows the results of adding these measures to the tabular model. You can see that the relative difference between selling price and recommended retail price changes by color group, with Yellow stock items having the smallest variance.

	A	B	C	D
1	Row Labels ▾	Avg Selling $	Color Avg Retail $	Selling Variance %
2	Black	40.14	64.83	-38.09 %
3	Blue	58.65	94.72	-38.08 %
4	Gray	24.84	37.38	-33.55 %
5	Light Brown	18.00	26.91	-33.11 %
6	N/A	51.48	74.16	-30.59 %
7	Red	162.56	220.32	-26.22 %
8	Steel Gray	25.00	39.28	-36.35 %
9	White	14.75	21.62	-31.77 %
10	Yellow	128.92	168.72	-23.59 %
11	Grand Total	45.59	69.66	-34.55 %

FIGURE 3-69 Pivot table with average and variance measures

Ratio to parent

The use of CALCULATE to derive a percent of total was introduced in Listing 3-53. In that case, a row's value is compared to an overall value in which all filters are removed. Listing 3-54 illustrated how to selectively remove filters to calculate an overall value for a subset of a table while retaining some of the row context for the active row. Now, let's examine how to approach a ratio to percent calculation in which hierarchical relationships are considered. Strictly speaking, DAX does not understand how to navigate hierarchies in the same way that you use navigation functions in MDX to traverse user-defined hierarchies. Nonetheless, you can construct expressions to achieve the same results.

Table 3-8 is a set of measures to add to the Sale table in your tabular model to illustrate the construction of ratio to parent calculations. In these examples, the hierarchy is the Calendar hierarchy for dates, months, and years, but you can use the same technique in any table for which you have created a multi-level hierarchy.

TABLE 3-8 New ratio to parent measures to add to Sale table

Table	Expression	Format	Decimal Places
Sale	Ratio to Month:= VAR SalesAllDates = CALCULATE([Total Sales], ALL('Date'[Date]))	Percentage	2
	RETURN IF(ISFILTERED('Date'[Date]), DIVIDE([Total Sales] , SalesAllDates))	Percentage	2
	Ratio To Year:= VAR SalesAllMonths = CALCULATE([Total Sales], ALL('Date'[Calendar Month Label])) RETURN IF(ISFILTERED('Date'[Calendar Month Label]) && NOT (ISFILTERED('Date'[Date])), DIVIDE([Total Sales] , SalesAllMonths)	Percentage	2
	Ratio To All Dates:= VAR SalesAllYears = CALCULATE([Total Sales], ALL('Date'[Calendar Year Label])) RETURN IF(ISFILTERED('Date'[Calendar Year Label]) && NOT(ISFILTERED('Date'[Calendar Month Label])) && NOT (ISFILTERED('Date'[Date]))), DIVIDE([Total Sales] , SalesAllYears))	Percentage	2

As you can see in Figure 3-70, the Ratio to Month measure returns a ratio that compares a current date's value to all dates within the month. In this case, the filter on each row removes only the date filter, but retains the month and year filters. Then the ISFILTERED function determines whether to return a value. On row 4, the Ratio To Month value is computed by dividing the Total Sales value of 28,475.10, filtered for 1/1/2013, by the value for Total Sales that is not filtered by date. However, the month filter still applies to the divisor in the Ratio To Month expression. In this case, the month filter is CY2013-Jan, which means the divisor in the expression on row 4 is the 3,770,410.85. Thus, the division of 28,475.10 by 3,770,410.85 results in the Ratio To Month value of 0.76%.

	A	B	C	D	E
1	Row Labels	Total Sales	Ratio to Month	Ratio To Year	Ratio To All Dates
2	⊟CY2013	45,707,188.00			26.53 %
3	⊟CY2013-Jan	3,770,410.85		8.25 %	
4	1/1/2013	28,475.10	0.76 %		
5	1/2/2013	160,385.85	4.25 %		
6	1/3/2013	135,623.40	3.60 %		
7	1/4/2013	107,841.30	2.86 %		
8	1/5/2013	69,067.05	1.83 %		
9	1/7/2013	251,788.00	6.68 %		
10	1/8/2013	87,123.30	2.31 %		
11	1/9/2013	141,387.60	3.75 %		
12	1/10/2013	169,772.10	4.50 %		
13	1/11/2013	216,758.00	5.75 %		
14	1/12/2013	86,159.00	2.29 %		
15	1/14/2013	176,346.50	4.68 %		
16	1/15/2013	270,821.05	7.18 %		
17	1/16/2013	78,790.00	2.09 %		
18	1/17/2013	122,876.05	3.26 %		
19	1/18/2013	152,717.95	4.05 %		
20	1/19/2013	52,711.00	1.40 %		
21	1/21/2013	109,051.95	2.89 %		
22	1/22/2013	124,769.10	3.31 %		
23	1/23/2013	167,816.15	4.45 %		
24	1/24/2013	110,256.50	2.92 %		
25	1/25/2013	195,790.35	5.19 %		
26	1/26/2013	95,563.65	2.53 %		
27	1/28/2013	162,042.90	4.30 %		
28	1/29/2013	200,274.15	5.31 %		
29	1/30/2013	170,640.35	4.53 %		
30	1/31/2013	125,562.50	3.33 %		
31	⊙CY2013-Feb	2,776,786.20		6.08 %	
32	⊙CY2013-Mar	3,870,505.30		8.47 %	

FIGURE 3-70 Pivot table with ratio to parent variables

The other measures work similarly for the respective levels, but introduce NOT ISFILTERED to reverse the logical condition used to determine whether a value is displayed. In effect, to return a value for Ratio To Year, the current month must have a month filter applied, but cannot have a date filtered applied also, as is the case on row 3 for which a Total Sales value for CY2013-Jan displays. This combination of conditions means that 3,770,410.85 represents a month total and not a day total. Therefore, SSAS can resolve the Ratio To Year value correctly by dividing this month value by the corresponding Total Sales value for the year (shown in row 2).

You can consolidate the code into a single measure by adding the measure shown in Listing 3-66 and formatting it as a percentage value. Because it uses nested IF functions, there is no longer a need to use the NOT ISFILTERED pattern. When the expression evaluation moves to the code related to months, for example, the determination was made in the outer IF function that the active row is not a date. Thus, this expression simplifies the code in the previous examples. You can see the results of the new expression in Figure 3-71. Although this single expression is simpler, you may find it more challenging to troubleshoot. In that case, you can create separate measures and use the Hide From Client Tools option to prevent users from accessing these intermediate measures directly.

LISTING 3-66 Ratio to parent expression

```
Ratio To Parent:=
VAR
SalesAllDates =
    CALCULATE(
        [Total Sales],
        ALL('Date'[Date])
    )
VAR
SalesAllMonths =
    CALCULATE(
        [Total Sales],
        ALL('Date'[Calendar Month Label])
    )
VAR
SalesAllYears =
    CALCULATE(
        [Total Sales],
        ALL('Date'[Calendar Year Label])
    )
RETURN
IF(
    ISFILTERED('Date'[Date]) ,
    DIVIDE(
        [Total Sales] ,
      SalesAllDates
    ),
    IF(
        ISFILTERED('Date'[Calendar Month Label] ) ,
        DIVIDE(
            [Total Sales] ,
          SalesAllMonths
        ),
        IF(
          ISFILTERED('Date'[Calendar Year Label]) ,
          DIVIDE(
              [Total Sales] ,
              SalesAllYears
          ),
          1
        )
    )
)
```

Row Labels	Total Sales	Ratio to Month	Ratio To Year	Ratio To All Dates	Ratio To Paren
⊟ CY2013	45,707,188.00			26.53 %	26.53 !
⊟ CY2013-Jan	3,770,410.85		8.25 %		8.25 !
1/1/2013	28,475.10	0.76 %			0.76 !
1/2/2013	160,385.85	4.25 %			4.25 !
1/3/2013	135,623.40	3.60 %			3.60 !
1/4/2013	107,841.30	2.86 %			2.86 !
1/5/2013	69,067.05	1.83 %			1.83 !
1/7/2013	251,788.00	6.68 %			6.68 !
1/8/2013	87,123.30	2.31 %			2.31 !
1/9/2013	141,387.60	3.75 %			3.75 !
1/10/2013	169,772.10	4.50 %			4.50 !
1/11/2013	216,758.00	5.75 %			5.75 !
1/12/2013	86,159.00	2.29 %			2.29 !
1/14/2013	176,346.50	4.68 %			4.68 !
1/15/2013	270,821.05	7.18 %			7.18 !
1/16/2013	78,790.00	2.09 %			2.09 !
1/17/2013	122,876.05	3.26 %			3.26 !
1/18/2013	152,717.95	4.05 %			4.05 !
1/19/2013	52,711.00	1.40 %			1.40 !
1/21/2013	109,051.95	2.89 %			2.89 !
1/22/2013	124,769.10	3.31 %			3.31 !
1/23/2013	167,816.15	4.45 %			4.45 !
1/24/2013	110,256.50	2.92 %			2.92 !
1/25/2013	195,790.35	5.19 %			5.19 !
1/26/2013	95,563.65	2.53 %			2.53 !
1/28/2013	162,042.90	4.30 %			4.30 !
1/29/2013	200,274.15	5.31 %			5.31 !
1/30/2013	170,640.35	4.53 %			4.53 !
1/31/2013	125,562.50	3.33 %			3.33 !
⊞ CY2013-Feb	2,776,786.20		6.08 %		6.08 !
⊞ CY2013-Mar	2,870,595.30		6.47 %		6.47 !

FIGURE 3-71 Pivot table with consolidated ratio to parent variable

> **NOTE SLICING WITH HIERARCHY ITEMS YIELDS INCORRECT RESULTS**
>
> If you add a slicer to the worksheet and attempt to slice by an item that also appears in the hierarchy in the pivot table, the ratio to parent calculation no longer works correctly. Alberto Ferrari suggests a solution to this problem in his article, "Clever Hierarchy Handling in DAX," at *http://www.sqlbi.com/articles/clever-hierarchy-handling-in-dax/*.

Allocation

The "Define a SCOPE statement" section in Skill 3.2 introduced business requirements for sales quota allocations for which you can create calculations in the MDX script that give the illusion of inserting values into cells to replace existing values or add values where none existed. Although a tabular model does not have an MDX script, you can achieve a similar technique by adapting the technique described in the "Ratio to parent" section.

Before you can create the measures necessary for the allocations, add a new calculated column to the Date table by using the following expression:

```
=DAY(EOMONTH([Date],0))
```

The EOMONTH function uses the active row context to find the last day of the current day's month. Then the DAY function returns the month number associated with that date. This number conveniently represents the number of days in a month that you can use to perform the sales quota allocations.

Listing 3-67 is a single measure expression that uses variables to make it easier to follow the logic in the code that relies on a combination of IF and SWITCH function to determine what calculation to perform for each level in the calendar hierarchy. Let's review the following key elements of this code:

- The quota for 2014 is a hardcoded value stored in the Quota2014Month variable.

- The 2015 quota is calculated according to the business requirements by multiplying the previous year's sales by 110% and dividing by 12 to determine the monthly allocation. Notice the ALL function in that calculation removes both month and date level filers to ensure the calculation is correct on either level. (Try removing it to observe the effect.)

- The DaysInMonth variable calculates the number of days in the current context based on the MonthDays calculated column.

- The Quota2014Days and Quota2015Days calculations divide the respective monthly quota by the number of days in the current month.

- Each level of the hierarchy is represented in nested IF functions, starting with Date in the outermost IF function and ending with Calendar Year Label in the innermost function. The IF function uses ISFILTERED to test whether the current item is a date, month, or year.

- When an IF function evaluates as TRUE, the corresponding SWITCH statement is evaluated. The SWITCH statement evaluates a table of values for the current row to determine whether it relates to CY2014 or CY2015 and then returns the daily quota on the date level and, the month quota on the month level, as you can see in Figure 3-72. On the year level, the appropriate month quota is multiplied by 12, as you can see in Figure 3-73.

LISTING 3-67 Allocation expression

```
Sales Quota:=
VAR
Quota2014Month = 4500000
VAR
Quota2015Month =
    DIVIDE(
        CALCULATE(
            [Prior Year Sales] *1.1,
            ALL('Date'[Calendar Month Label],
            'Date'[Date])
        ),
        12
    )
VAR
DaysInMonth =
    SUMX( 'Date',
        CALCULATE(
            VALUES( 'Date'[MonthDays])
        )
    )
```

```
VAR
Quota2014Days =
    DIVIDE(
        Quota2014Month,
        DaysInMonth
    )
VAR
Quota2015Days =
    DIVIDE(
        Quota2015Month,
        DaysInMonth
    )
RETURN
IF(
    ISFILTERED('Date'[Date]),
    SWITCH(
        VALUES('Date'[Calendar Year Label]),
        "CY2014", Quota2014Days,
        "CY2015", Quota2015Days
        ) ,
    IF (
        ISFILTERED('Date'[Calendar Month Label]) ,
            SWITCH(
                VALUES('Date'[Calendar Year Label]),
                "CY2014", Quota2014Month,
                "CY2015", Quota2015Month
            ),
            IF (
                ISFILTERED('Date'[Calendar Year Label]),
                    SWITCH(
                        VALUES('Date'[Calendar Year Label]),
                        "CY2014", Quota2014Month * 12,
                        "CY2015", Quota2015Month * 12
                    )
            )
        )
    )
)
```

	A	B	C
1	Row Labels	Total Sales	Sales Quota
2	⊞ CY2013	45,707,188.00	
3	⊟ CY2014	49,929,487.20	54,000,000.00
4	⊟ CY2014-Jan	4,067,538.00	4,500,000.00
5	1/1/2014	200,137.55	145,161.29
6	1/2/2014	112,882.90	145,161.29
7	1/3/2014	190,696.90	145,161.29
8	1/4/2014	68,246.05	145,161.29
9	1/5/2014		145,161.29
10	1/6/2014	167,525.55	145,161.29
11	1/7/2014	148,802.80	145,161.29
12	1/8/2014	107,298.40	145,161.29
13	1/9/2014	73,911.70	145,161.29
14	1/10/2014	226,421.85	145,161.29

FIGURE 3-72 Pivot table with daily allocations

	A	B	C
1	Row Labels	Total Sales	Sales Quota
2	⊕CY2013	45,707,188.00	
3	⊖CY2014	49,929,487.20	54,000,000.00
4	⊕CY2014-Jan	4,067,538.00	4,500,000.00
5	⊕CY2014-Feb	3,470,209.20	4,500,000.00
6	⊕CY2014-Mar	3,861,928.75	4,500,000.00
7	⊕CY2014-Apr	4,095,234.65	4,500,000.00
8	⊕CY2014-May	4,590,639.10	4,500,000.00
9	⊕CY2014-Jun	4,266,644.10	4,500,000.00
10	⊕CY2014-Jul	4,786,301.05	4,500,000.00
11	⊕CY2014-Aug	4,085,489.60	4,500,000.00
12	⊕CY2014-Sep	3,882,968.85	4,500,000.00
13	⊕CY2014-Oct	4,438,683.65	4,500,000.00
14	⊕CY2014-Nov	4,018,967.45	4,500,000.00
15	⊕CY2014-Dec	4,364,882.80	4,500,000.00
16	⊖CY2015	53,991,490.45	54,922,435.92
17	⊕CY2015-Jan	4,401,699.25	4,576,869.66
18	⊕CY2015-Feb	4,195,319.25	4,576,869.66
19	⊕CY2015-Mar	4,528,131.65	4,576,869.66
20	⊕CY2015-Apr	5,073,264.75	4,576,869.66
21	⊕CY2015-May	4,480,730.55	4,576,869.66
22	⊕CY2015-Jun	4,515,840.45	4,576,869.66
23	⊕CY2015-Jul	5,155,672.00	4,576,869.66
24	⊕CY2015-Aug	3,938,163.40	4,576,869.66
25	⊕CY2015-Sep	4,662,600.00	4,576,869.66
26	⊕CY2015-Oct	4,492,049.40	4,576,869.66
27	⊕CY2015-Nov	4,089,208.50	4,576,869.66
28	⊕CY2015-Dec	4,458,811.25	4,576,869.66
29	⊕CY2016	22,658,175.55	
30	Grand Total	172,286,341.20	

FIGURE 3-73 Pivot table with monthly allocations

> ***NEED MORE REVIEW?*** **DAX FOR ANALYSIS**
>
> **You can find a variety of use cases and DAX patterns for analysis developed by Marco Russo and Alberto Ferrari on their DAX Patterns site at *http://daxpatterns.com.***

Chapter summary

- The basic structure of an MDX query looks like this:

```
WITH
    MEMBER <Name> AS <definition>
    SET <Name> AS <definition>
SELECT
    <Set> ON COLUMNS,
    <Set> ON ROWS
FROM
    <Cube>
WHERE
    <Tuple>;
```

- Although an MDX query's structure is similar to the structure of a T-SQL query, its behavior is quite different. The sets that you define in the SELECT clause by placing them on rows or columns are processed as the first steps of query processing. This evaluation of axes occurs independently of subsequent steps. Each cell intersection of set members on rows and columns defines a partial tuple that is combined with members included in the query's WHERE clause and the default member of every attribute hierarchy that is not explicitly defined in the query to produce a full tuple. This full tuple represents a cube cell value that is returned in the query results. A tuple is a coordinate in multidimensional space.

- You place sets on the rows and columns of a query axis. A set can be empty or contain one or more members of the same dimension's attribute hierarchy or user-defined hierarchy. You enclose a set within braces, although you can omit the braces when a set contains a single member.

- You place tuples in the WHERE clause of a query. A tuple consists of one or more members of different attribute or user-defined hierarchies. You can create sets of tuples to place on axes in the SELECT clause.

- Tuples and sets can be explicitly defined by referencing members by name or by unique name or you can use functions that return members and sets.

- MDX functions use one of the following syntax patterns:

  - The argument pattern places the function first in an expression which is followed by one or more arguments enclosed in parentheses, like this: ORDER(<set>, <numeric or string expression>, <sort direction>).

  - The method pattern places the function last in an expression by appending it to the end of an object, like this: [Dimension].[Hierarchy].[Member].Members.

- When learning a new MDX function, you should understand what type of object it operates on or takes as an argument, such as a set or a member, and what type of object it returns, such as a tuple or a set.

- You should be familiar with the more commonly used MDX functions which are grouped into the following categories:

  - **Set functions**   Returns a set. Functions in this group include: MEMBERS, ORDER, HEAD, TOPCOUNT, NONEMPTY, FILTER, and DESCENDANTS.

  - **Navigation functions**   Returns a member when navigating to a higher level or a set when navigating to a lower level. Navigation on the same level can return a member or a set. Functions in this group include: PARENT, CHILDREN, ANCESTOR, SIBLINGS, PREVMEMBER, and NEXTMEMBER.

  - **Time functions**   Returns a member of a set. Functions in this group include: OPENING PERIOD, CLOSINGPERIOD, PARALLELPERIOD, and PERIODSTODATE.

  - **Statistical functions**   Returns a calculated value. Functions in this group include: SUM, and AGGREGATE,

- **String functions** Returns a string or converts a string into an object such as a member or a set. Functions in this group include: SETTOSTR, STRTOMEMBER, NAME, UNIQUENAME, and PROPERTIES.

- Use the NON EMPTY keyword to eliminate a row or a column when all of its related tuples are empty. This elimination is the last step of query processing.

- Query-scoped calculations allow you to create calculated members, calculated measures, or sets that can be referenced within a query, but are not persisted to the cube. They are useful for ad hoc reporting and for testing logic before implementing it as a cube object.

- You can embed business logic into a cube by using custom MDX to create the following objects:

  - **Calculated measures** Calculations that are assigned to the Measures dimension that you can reference in a tuple.

  - **Calculated members** Calculations that are assigned to a non-measure dimension that you can reference in sets.

  - **Named sets** Calculations that are assigned to a non-measure dimension and return a set. Members of a dynamic named set can change based on query context, whereas member of a static named set remain fixed regardless of query context.

  - **Statistical functions** Returns a calculated value. Functions in this group include SUM and AGGREGATE.

  - **String functions** Returns a string or converts a string into an object such as a member or a set. Functions in this group include: SETTOSTR, STRTOMEMBER, NAME, UNIQUENAME, PROPERTIES.

- Every attribute hierarchy as an implicit default member, which is the All member on the top level of the hierarchy. You can define an explicit default member in the attribute's properties or in role-based security configuration.

- You can use MDX to define allowed or denied sets for each dimension's attributes or to set cell-level security to control the visibility of measures and calculated measures.

- You can create your own MDX functions by developing and registering an Analysis Services Stored Procedure.

- Use a SCOPE statement in a cube's MDX script to override cube cell values in a targeted section of the cube known as a subcube.

- The basic structure of a DAX query looks like this:

```
DEFINE
    MEASURE <Name> = <expression>
EVALUATE
    <table expression>
ORDER BY
    <column> <sort direction>
```

- Commonly used functions in a query's table expression are SUMMARIZE and ADDCOLUMNS.

- An understanding of evaluation context is crucial to returning correct query results and developing measures. Filter context determines which rows in a table or column are subject to an operation and row context determines which columns are in scope for an operation.

- The CALCULATE function allows you to override filter context by removing filters completely or partially or by adding new filters. It also allows you to manipulate row context by projecting it as a filter context during table operations.

- A variety of DAX functions are available for creating calculated measures. You should be familiar with commonly used DAX functions in the following categories:

  - **Aggregate functions**   Returns an aggregation of values based on a single column. Functions in this group include: SUM, AVERAGE, MIN, MAX, COUNTROWS, AVERAGEA, MINA, MAXA, COUNTA, and COUNTBLANK.

  - **Iterator aggregate functions**   Returns a value after iterating through rows of a table or table expression, resolving an expression for each row, and aggregating the results. Functions in this group include: SUMX, AVERAGEX, MINX, MAXX, and COUNTX.

  - **Date and time functions**   Return value depends on the function. Most functions in this category are used more often in calculated columns. For a measure, you can use the DATEDIFF function to calculate intervals between values in separate date columns.

  - **Time intelligence functions**   Returns a date or date range that is used in turn to compute values. Functions in this group include: TOTALYTD, DATESYTD, SAMEPERIODLASTYEAR, PREVIOUSMONTH, DAY, and EOMONTH.

  - **Filter functions**   Manipulates or evaluates filter context on a table. Functions in this group include: FILTER, ADDMISSINGITEMS, CALCULATE, CALCULATETABLE, ALL, ALLEXCEPT, ISFILTERED, RELATED, and VALUES.

  - **Logical functions**   Returns information about values or expressions. Functions in this group include: IF, SWITCH, AND, and OR.

- You can use variables to make complex DAX expressions easier to read and sometimes to improve performance by replacing multiple references to the same expression with a single variable which is evaluated once.

- Business analysis often focuses on comparisons of data points. You should be familiar with creating measures to create the following types of analysis:

  - **Top ranked items**   You can use TOPN in a query to return a group of ranked items, but use RANKX in a measure.

  - **Variance**   You can set up multiple measures that represent various perspectives of a calculation, such as all items in a table versus a filtered set of items or values at one point in time versus another point in time, and then compute the difference between those values. The CALCULATE function is frequently used in expressions that return a filtered value.

- **Ratio to parent**   When calculating ratios, you can use the CALCULATE function to remove filters on the current row to enable calculation of totals for its parent item and use the ISFILTERED function to determine whether to calculate a ratio and which values to use in the ratio calculation.

- **Allocation**   Like the ratio to parent pattern, you can use the ISFILTERED function to determine whether a calculation should be performed. You can also use the SWITCH function to determine the type of calculation to perform.

Thought experiment

In this thought experiment, demonstrate your skills and knowledge of the topics covered in this chapter. You can find answer to this thought experiment in the next section.

You are the BI developer at Wide World Importers responsible for adding frequently used calculations to the multidimensional and tabular models referenced in this chapter and for responding to specific questions from users by creating ad hoc MDX or DAX queries. The following requirements have been identified:

- In the multidimensional model, you need to perform the following tasks:
  - Prepare a report that lists the top five stock items based on sales, total sales, and their respective rank.
  - Update the cube so that users can easily add the top five stock items for any year to a pivot table. They must be able to apply filters to the pivot table to find the top stock items under different conditions.
  - Add annual quota allocations to the MDX script.
- In the tabular model, you need to perform the following tasks:
  - The City Count measure currently counts the rows in the City table, but this overstates the true city count because there are duplicate rows in the table for many cities. Correct the City Count measure to return the correct number of cities.
  - Update the tabular model to include a YTD Variance % calculation.
  - Prepare a report that lists stock items and profit margin percent values for which the stock item's aggregate profit margin percent is below 20 % in descending order of profitability.

Based on this background information, answer the following questions:

  1.   Which of the following MDX queries produces the ranked stock items report?

```
WITH
SET Top5Item AS
    TOPCOUNT(
        [Stock Item].[Stock Item].[Stock Item].Members,
        5,
        [Measures].[Sale Count]
    )
MEMBER [Measures].[Rank] AS
    RANK( [Stock Item].[Stock Item].CURRENTMEMBER, Top5Item)
SELECT
    {[Measures].[Sales Amount Without Tax], [Measures].[Rank]} ON COLUMNS,
    Top5Item ON ROWS
FROM [Wide World Importers DW]
```

```
WITH
SET Top5Item AS
    TOPCOUNT(
        [Stock Item].[Stock Item].Members,
        5,
        [Measures].[Sale Count]
    )
MEMBER [Measures].[Rank] AS
    ORDER( [Stock Item].[Stock Item].CURRENTMEMBER, [Measures].[Sale Count], DESC)
SELECT
    {[Measures].[Sales Amount Without Tax], [Measures].[Rank]} ON COLUMNS,
    Top5Item ON ROWS
FROM [Wide World Importers DW]
```

LISTING C

```
WITH
SET Top5Item AS
    TOPCOUNT(
        [Stock Item].[Stock Item].[Stock Item].Members,
        5,
        [Measures].[Sale Count]
    )
MEMBER [Measures].[Rank] AS
    RANK( [Stock Item].[Stock Item].CURRENTMEMBER, Top5Item)
SELECT
    {[Measures].[Sales Amount Without Tax], [Measures].[Rank]} ON COLUMNS,
    Top5Item ON ROWS
FROM [Wide World Importers DW]
```

```
WITH
SET Top5Item AS
    TOPCOUNT(
        [Stock Item].[Stock Item].[Stock Item].Members,
        5,
        [Measures].[Sale Count]
      )
MEMBER [Measures].[Rank] AS
    RANK( [Stock Item].[Stock Item].CURRENTMEMBER, Top5Item)
SELECT
    [Measures].[Sales Amount Without Tax]ON COLUMNS,
    {Top5Item, [Measures].[Rank]} ON ROWS
FROM [Wide World Importers DW]
```

2. Which of the following object types do you add to the cube?

   A. Calculated measure

   B. Calculated member set

   C. Static named set

   D. Dynamic named set

3. Currently, the MDX script in the cube calculates monthly allocations but no value displays for the year. What code do you need to add to the MDX script to use the monthly quota to calculate annual allocations? (Hint: Use a SCOPE statement to calculate annual quotas.)

4. What is the correct DAX formula to use for the City Count measure to return the correct count of cities?

5. Which of the following DAX queries produces the stock items profitability report?

LISTING A

```
EVALUATE
CALCULATETABLE(
  SUMMARIZE(
          'Sale',
          'Stock Item'[Stock Item],
          "Profit Margin Percent",
              'Sale'[Profit Margin Percent]
    ),
    [Profit Margin Percent] < 0.2
)
ORDER BY
    [Profit Margin Percent] DESC
```

```
FILTER(
    SUMMARIZE(
            'Sale',
            'Stock Item'[Stock Item],
            "Profit Margin Percent",
                'Sale'[Profit Margin Percent]
    ),
    [Profit Margin Percent] < 0.2
)
ORDER BY
    [Profit Margin Percent] DESC
```

LISTING C

```
EVALUATE
FILTER(
    CALCULATETABLE(
            'Sale',
            VALUES('Stock Item'[Stock Item]
    ),
    [Profit Margin Percent] < 0.2
)
ORDER BY
    [Profit Margin Percent] DESC
```

LISTING D

```
EVALUATE
FILTER(
    SUMMARIZE(
            'Sale',
            'Stock Item'[Stock Item],
            "Profit Margin Percent",
                'Sale'[Profit Margin Percent]
    ),
    [Profit Margin Percent] < 0.2
)
ORDER BY
    [Profit Margin Percent] DESC
```

Thought experiment answer

This section contains the solution to the thought experiment.

1. The correct answer is C.

    Answer A is incorrect because the [Stock Item].[Stock Item].Members function returns the All member in addition to stock item members. Consequently, the TOPCOUNT function returns the All and the RANK function assigns it rank 1. This does not meet the stated requirement to list five stock items.

Answer B returns an error in the Rank column because the ORDER function in the measure definition returns a set and not a numeric value.

Answer D is an invalid query because the Measures dimension cannot be used in the set definition for both columns and rows.

2. The correct answer is D.

Answer A creates a calculated measure that returns numeric or string value only.

Answer B refers to an object type that does not exist in the cube.

Answer C is incorrect because a static named set does not use query context to define the members it includes. Therefore, it does not change as users apply filters to a static named set in a pivot table.

3. Use the following code in the MDX script to calculate annual quota allocations:

```
//define a subcube for the year level members
SCOPE(
    {[Invoice Date].[Calendar Year].[CY2014]:
    [Invoice Date].[Calendar Year].[CY2015]},
    [Measures].[Sales Quota]);

    THIS =
        // sum the quota allocations of the month members related to each year
        // note the omission of Sales Quota - its presence is implied by the scope
        SUM([Invoice Date].[Calendar].CHILDREN);
END SCOPE;
FREEZE;
```

4. Use this code to derive the correct city count:

```
City Count:=COUNTROWS(VALUES(City[WWI City ID]))
```

The VALUES function returns a distinct table of values in the WWI City ID column to uniquely identify each city. The City Key column contains surrogate keys. Slowly changing dimension handling in this table has generated multiple surrogate keys for the same WWI City ID.

5. The correct answer is D.

A is incorrect because the filter expression for CALCULATETABLE cannot reference a measure.

B is missing the EVALUATE keyword.

C does not meet the stated requirements. It returns too many columns. It also returns too many stock items because the Profit Margin Percent condition is applied at the row level of the Sale table rather than aggregating it for each stock item.

Configure and maintain SQL Server Analysis Services (SSAS)

In addition to testing your ability to develop and query multidimensional and tabular models, the 70-768 exam tests your knowledge of a variety of administrative tasks for SSAS. You must know how to perform configuration tasks related to memory and disk management for optimal performance. Additionally, you must know which tools you can use to monitor performance, how to identify performance bottlenecks, and what steps to take to resolve performance issues. You must also understand the management of model processing. And finally, you must know how to enhance multidimensional and tabular models with key performance indicators and translations.

Skills in this chapter:

- Plan and deploy SSAS
- Monitor and optimize performance
- Configure and manage processing
- Create Key Performance Indicators (KPIS) and translations

Skill 4.1: Plan and deploy SSAS

One of the primary reasons to implement an SSAS solution, whether multidimensional or tabular, is to enable users to query data faster than they can access data in an online transactional processing (OLTP) system. In addition to modeling data correctly, you must also configure the server properly to deliver optimal performance.

> ### This section covers how to:
> - Configure memory limits
> - Configure Non-Union Memory Architecture (NUMA)
> - Configure disk layout
> - Determine SSAS instance placement

Configure memory limits

Both multidimensional and tabular models rely on server memory to manage processing and to store data for faster responses to queries. However, the way that an SSAS server uses memory and the configuration of the server's memory limits depends on whether it is running in multidimensional or tabular mode.

Multidimensional-mode memory limits

SSAS uses a combination of memory- and disk-based operations for processing tasks and query resolution. As the size or complexity of cubes or the number of users querying SSAS increases, the amount of memory that SSAS requires also increases.

The server's operating system allocates physical and virtual memory to SSAS, which relies on its own memory manager to distribute memory across its component. If SSAS requires more memory than the amount available on the server, it pages to disk until it reaches specified limits. Server performance slows when this happens.

Figure 4-1 illustrates the memory model of an SSAS server. A fixed amount of physical memory on the server is allocated to the operating system and other services running on the server. When the SSAS Windows service starts, the operating system allocates memory to the Msmdsrv.exe process. A portion of this memory is non-*shrinkable memory* that SSAS uses for the Msmdsrve.exe process and the storage of objects required by the server, such as metadata about server objects, active user sessions, and memory required for active queries. Non-shrinkable memory is never deallocated, although it can be paged to disk.

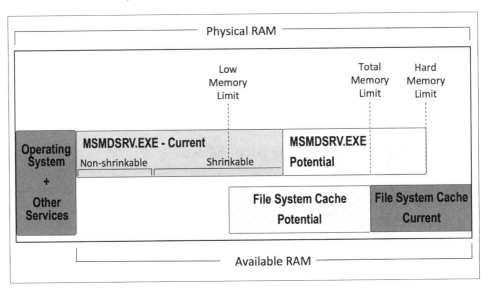

FIGURE 4-1 Memory model of SSAS server in multidimensional mode

The remaining SSAS memory is *shrinkable memory*, which is used to store cached data to optimize query performance. SSAS not only caches dimension data, but it also caches certain calculation results and frequently accessed cube cell values. SSAS increases shrinkable memory as requests for memory resources increase until reaching the configured Hard Memory Limit value, at which point it rejects any new requests. Meanwhile, SSAS begins removing infrequently used objects from memory when the combined non-shrinkable and shrinkable memory exceeds the configured Low Memory Limit and aggressively removes objects when memory consumption exceeds the configured Total Memory Limit value. Shrinkable memory below the Low Memory Limit is never released until the server is restarted.

The operating system also allocates memory to the file system cache. This cache can continue to request memory, and eventually share memory with SSAS. However, it does not overlap with the SSAS memory below the Low Memory Limit.

Most of the time, the default memory limits in the SSAS configuration are adequate. You can change these limits when the server encounters low memory conditions frequently or when you find performance is not optimal. To change memory limits, you can access and update server properties in SQL Server Management Studio (SSMS) after connecting to your multidimensional instance. In Object Explorer, right-click the server, click Properties, click General in the Analysis Services Properties dialog box, and then select the Show Advanced (All) Properties check box to view the following memory-related properties, some which are shown in Figure 4-2:

- **Memory \ HardMemoryLimit** This property sets the threshold at which SSAS experiences memory pressure and rejects new requests for SSAS resources. When the value is the default of zero, SSAS sets the limit to a value midway between TotalMemoryLimit and the total physical memory or virtual address space, whichever is less.

- **Memory \ LowMemoryLimit** This property sets the first threshold at which SSAS begins clearing infrequently used objects from memory. The default of 65 is the percentage of physical memory or virtual address space, whichever is less. This value is usually suitable, but consider setting it to a lower value if other processes are running on the same server.

- **Memory \ TotalMemoryLimit** This property is the maximum percentage of memory that SSAS uses as a threshold for aggressively releasing memory. The default value of 80 is the percentage of physical memory or the virtual memory, whichever is less. Be sure to keep this value lower than the HardMemoryLimit.

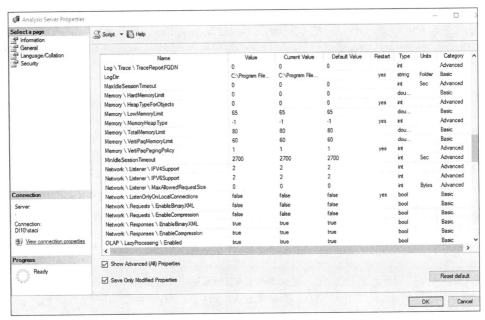

FIGURE 4-2 Advanced security properties for a multidimensional instance of SSAS

> **IMPORTANT MEMORY PROPERTY VALUES**
>
> With the exception of HardMemoryLimit, which is set to 0, the default values for memory limits are expressed as percentages of memory. If you change these values, use a value below 100 to represent percentages or a value above 100 to represent bytes. For example, if you want to specify 8 gigabytes (GB) as a property value, you must specify 8 * 1024 * 1024 * 1024 bytes as 8589934592 (without commas). This expression of property values is true for both multidimensional and tabular models.

> **NOTE GUIDANCE FOR CONFIGURATION OF MULTIDIMENSIONAL-MODE MEMORY PROPERTIES**
>
> You can find recommendations for configuring the memory properties for a multidimensional-mode SSAS server, in addition to a few others that are generally changed under direction of Microsoft support in the "Analysis Services Operations Guide," which you can download from *https://msdn.microsoft.com/en-us/library/hh226085.aspx*. Although written for SSAS in SQL Server 2008 R2, its guidance remains largely applicable because the underlying architecture has not changed much in subsequent releases. One exception is a change to the heap allocator that was redesigned in SQL Server 2016.

Tabular-mode memory limits

The performance of a SSAS server in tabular mode is dependent on the availability of memory on the server. Like a multidimensional-mode server, a tabular-mode server requires memory for processing operations and, to a lesser extent, query resolution. However, a tabular-mode server also requires enough memory to store each database.

In the memory model shown in Figure 4-3, you can see how a fixed amount of memory, approximately 150 megabytes (MBs), is allocated to the Msmdsrv.exe process and formula engine, and the remaining memory requirements increase for each database added to the server. As SSAS performs operations, it requests memory from the operating system until reaching the configured Total Memory Limit value. Meanwhile, upon exceeding the configured Low Memory Limit value, it attempts to remove objects from memory where possible. When memory consumption increases surpass the Total Memory Limit, the deallocation process becomes more aggressive by clearing memory in use by expired sessions and unused calculations. Upon crossing the Hard Memory Limit threshold, sessions are terminated to forcibly return memory usage below this threshold.

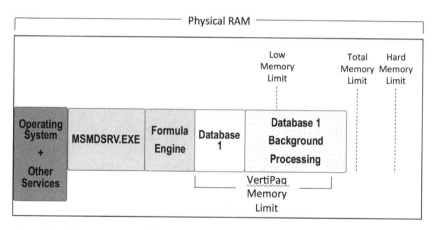

FIGURE 4-3 Memory model of SSAS server in tabular mode

The memory required to store tabular data is not easy to calculate because you cannot base an estimate on the number of rows in a table like you would when estimating the size of a relational database. Recall from Chapter 2, "Design a tabular BI semantic model," that a tabular model stores data by columns, and each column contains only distinct values in a compressed format. As part of this compression process, dictionaries are created to encode data and reduce the data storage requirements. Columns with a large number of distinct values require more memory than columns with a low number of distinct values. The different options for dictionary construction make it difficult to create an estimate. Instead, you should evaluate your own data in raw form and then measure the size of the database after processing the table. Double the number of rows in the relational source and remeasure the tabular model size. That way, you can develop an estimate of the memory requirements for a single table for incremental additions of data.

With regard to processing, the memory required on the SSAS server depends on the type of processing performed and whether the database is new or if it already exists on the server. When you perform Process Full, SSAS reads each table in the database, loads it into memory, and then creates a dictionary and an index for each column. If the database already exists, both the existing copy and the new copy of data exist in memory simultaneously (unless you perform Process Clear first as described in Chapter 2) to ensure that the server can respond to queries during processing. When the processing transaction commits, the existing copy is removed and the new copy of the database is kept. If physical memory is too low during processing, paging occurs and the entire server's performance degrades for both query and processing operations. Therefore, you should attempt to ensure that enough physical memory is on the server to support a Process Full operation, which is typically two to three times the size of the database.

Just like multidimensional-mode memory properties described in the previous section, the tabular-mode memory properties are accessible on the General page of the Analysis Services Properties dialog box that you open from the server node in the SSMS Object Explorer. You can then review or change the following memory properties:

- **HardMemoryLimit**   This property has a default value of 0, and sets this threshold at a point midway between the TotalMemoryLimit value and the server's total physical memory, or the total virtual address space if physical memory is greater than the virtual address space of the process. At this threshold, SSAS becomes more aggressive about clearing objects from memory.

- **LowMemoryLimit**   SSAS uses this value as the threshold at which it starts clearing objects from memory. The default of 65 is the percentage of physical memory or virtual address space, whichever is less.

- **TotalMemoryLimit**   The default value of 80 is the percentage of physical memory or the virtual address space, whichever is less. Above this value, SSAS is most aggressive about removing objects from memory. If you change this value, you must set it lower than HardMemoryLimit.

- **VertiPaqMemoryLimit**   The effect of this property depends on the VertiPaqPagingPolicy's property value. If its value is 0, this property sets the percentage of total memory that the SSAS server uses for storing all in-memory databases without paging. Otherwise, this property sets the percentage of total physical memory that the SSAS server uses before paging to disk. The default is 60.

> *NOTE* **VERTIPAQ IS XVELOCITY**
> When tabular models were first introduced in SQL Server 2012, the code base referred to the storage engine as VertiPaq, but the official term for the storage engine is xVelocity as explained in Chapter 2. Because most properties, performance counters, and trace events still refer to VertiPaq, references to xVelocity in this chapter will use the term VertiPaq instead.

- **VertiPaqPagingPolicy**   This property specifies whether the SSAS server can page to disk when the SSAS server has insufficient memory. The default value is 1, which enables the SSAS to page to disk as needed, although performance can suffer as a result of paging. To disable paging, change this value to 0. More information about this property and VertiPaqMemoryLimit is available in Chapter 2.

  If you set this value to 0, you can ensure the SSAS server's overall performance does not suffer. However, if a query requires more than the available memory, SSAS kills the connection. If the majority of queries are lightweight, this option is fine. On the other hand, if many queries are complex, the server can continue to service requests even when the memory requirements exceed the server's physical memory. In that case, there is a risk that the server performance is degraded for both complex and light-weight queries.

> *NOTE*   **CONFIGURATION OF WINDOWS PRIVILEGES ON SERVICE ACCOUNT**
>
> If you choose to change the VertiPaqPagingPolicy value to 0, you must add Windows privileges to the service account for the SSAS tabular instance, as described in "Configure Services Accounts (Analysis Services)" at *https://msdn.microsoft.com/en-us/library/ms175371.aspx#bkmk_winpriv*.

> *NOTE*   **GUIDANCE FOR CONFIGURATION OF TABULA-MODE MEMORY PROPERTIES**
>
> You can review recommendations for configuring the tabular memory in "Hardware Sizing a Tabular Solution (SQL Server Analysis Services," which you can download from *https://msdn.microsoft.com/en-us/library/jj874401.aspx*.

Configure Non-Union Memory Access (NUMA)

Non-union memory access (NUMA) is the term used to describe a memory architecture in which each processor on a server has its own memory to overcome problems occurring when multiple processors attempt to access the same memory. However, for situations in which separate processors require the same data, NUMA supports moving data between memory banks, although there is a performance impact resulting from this transfer.

Before reviewing configuration options for a NUMA server, you should understand how SSAS uses processors to perform operations. The operating system creates one or more *processor groups* as a container for a set of up to 64 logical processors. Typically, the processors in the same processor group share physical proximity. A NUMA node is typically assigned to a single processor group, depending on the node capacity.

Many SSAS operations are *multi-threaded*, which means that SSAS divides an operation into multiple jobs that run in parallel to improve the overall performance of the operation. Furthermore, SSAS manages *thread pools*, a set of threads that is instantiated and ready for assignment to a new job request. When SSAS starts, the Msmdsrv.exe process is assigned to a specific processor group, but subsequent SSAS operations can be assigned on any logical processor in any processor group. Typically, SSAS attains its best performance when it can access all available logical processors.

SSAS is NUMA-aware by default, whether running in multidimensional or tabular mode (although, in the latter case, only when you have applied SQL Server 2016 Service Pack 1). When testing reveals that performance suffers when a SSAS query and processing loads are spread over too many processors, which can happen when a cube has a large number of partitions and there are many queries requesting data from multiple partitions, you can *set affinity* between SSAS operations and specific logical processors. That is, you can configure the SSAS GroupAffinity properties that restrict thread pools to specific processors. However, the effect of this approach is typically noticeable and beneficial only when the server has more than 64 logical processors. For this reason, the GroupAffinity property is undefined by default.

When you decide to set affinity for SSAS, bear in mind the maximum cores that each edition can use—24 cores in SQL Server Standard edition or up to 640 cores in Enterprise edition. When SSAS starts, it computes affinity masks for each of the following types of thread pools that you configure in the SSAS server properties:

- **Thread Pool \ Command**   This thread pool is used to manage XML for Analysis (XMLA) commands.

- **Thread Pool \ IOProcess**   This thread pool is used only by a multidimensional-mode server. SSAS uses it to perform input-output (IO) operations requested by the storage engine, described in detail in Skill 4.2, "Monitor and optimize performance." Because these threads scan, filter, and aggregate partition data, NUMA can affect their performance.

  In addition to configuring an affinity mask for the IOProcess thread pool for a multidimensional-mode server only, you canuse the PerNumaNode property to tune performance . To configure PerNumaNode for a multidimensional server, use one of the values shown in Table 4-1.

- **Thread Pool \ Parsing \ Long**   This thread pool provides threads for requests that cannot fit within a single network message.

- **Thread Pool \ Parsing \ Short**   This thread pool provides threads for requests that can fit within a single network message. Sometimes queries that can execute quickly, such as Discover or Cancel, are handled by this thread pool rather than the Query thread pool.

- **Thread Pool \ Process**   This thread pool manages the longer-running jobs such as the creation of aggregations and indexes and commit operations. If a multidimensional partition is configured to use ROLAP mode, this thread pool manages ROLAP queries.

- **Thread Pool \ Query**   This thread pool handles MDX and DAX requests, among others, that are not handled by either of the parsing thread pools.

- **VertiPaq \ Thread Pool**   This thread pool performs table scans for tabular model queries.

TABLE 4-1 Valid values for PerNumaNode property on a multidimensional-mode server

Value	Description
-1	SSAS uses the number of NUMA nodes to sets its IOProcess Thread Pool strategy. If the server has less than 4 NUMA nodes, SSAS creates one IOProcess thread pool. Otherwise, it creates one IOProcess thread pool per NUMA node.
0	SSAS creates only one IOProcess thread pool. This setting increases the number of threads to the thread pool which is advantageous when you cannot add partitions to a measure group or when you have a measure group with multiple partitions but one is heavily scanned. With more threads available, SSAS can read more data from a single partition in parallel.
1	SSAS creates one IOProcess thread pool for each NUMA node. This setting can help improve performance of scans across partitions with relatively equal distributions of data.
2	SSAS creates one IOProcess thread pool per logical processor and affinitizes threads in each thread pool to the NUMA node of the logical processor. If the preferred logical processor is not available, the thread scheduler tries to use another logical processor within the same NUMA node or same processor group. This setting is another way to help improve performance of scans across partitions with relatively equal distributions of data instead of a PerNumaNode setting of 1. You must test each setting separately to determine which is best for your environment.

> ***NOTE*** **THREAD POOL PROPERTIES**
>
> **For more information about theses thread pools, see "Thread Pool Properties" at** *https://msdn.microsoft.com/en-us/library/ms175657.aspx.*

You can configure the GroupAffinity property for any or all of these thread pools by defining a custom affinity. A custom affinity is an array of hexadecimal values corresponding to processor groups. SSAS tries to use the logical processors in the specified processor group when allocating threads within the thread pool. For each logical processor in a processor group, up to 64, you set a bitmask of 1 if it is used and 0 if it is not. You then use the bitmask to calculate the hexadecimal value that you assign to the GroupAffinity property by following these steps:

1. Note the number of logical processors and processor groups on the server. You can use the Coreinfo utility available for download at https://technet.microsoft.com/en-us/sysinternals/cc835722.aspx to list this information in its Logical Processor To Group Map section.

2. Within each processor group, list the processors in descending order, from left to right. Let's assume that your server has 8 processors. In that case, your list looks like this:

7654 3210

3. For each processor group, compute a bitmask by replacing the processor number with a 1 to include it or a 0 to exclude it. For example, if you want to keep processors 1 through 5 and ignore the others, your bitmask looks like this:

```
0011 1110
```

4. Use a binary to converter tool to convert the bitmask to a hexadecimal value. In the current example, 0011 1110 in binary converts to 3E, which you must prefix with 0x to produce the hexadecimal value of 0x3E for the GroupAffinity property.

5. Update the GroupAffinity property for the thread pool with the calculated hexadecimal value. If the entire mask is invalid, an error displays. However, if part of the mask is valid and part is invalid, SSAS ignores the GroupAffinity property and uses all logical processors on the server.

When the SSAS server has multiple processor groups, you can assign a comma delimited list of hexadecimal values to the GroupAffinity property. Use 0x0 to ignore specific processor groups. As an example, if your server has four processor groups, but you want to exclude processor groups 0 and 4, set the GroupAffinity property like this:

```
0x0, 0x3E, 0x3E, 0x0
```

> **NOTE** **CURRENT THREAD POOL SETTINGS IN SSAS LOG**
>
> Current thread pool settings and thread pool affinity masks are output to the msmdsrv.log file (in the Program Files\Microsoft SQL Server\MSAS13.<instance>\OLAP\Log folder) each time the SSAS services starts.

Configure disk layout

Disk layout configuration applies primarily to a multidimensional-mode server because a tabular-mode server is optimized for memory storage and access. In the Analysis Services Properties dialog box, accessed in SSMS as described in the "Configure memory limits" section, you can configure the following properties for file locations:

- **DataDir**   This path determines where to place files storing database objects and metadata. The default location is Program Files\Microsoft SQL Server\ MSAS13.<instance name>\OLAP\Data. You can override this location when you deploy a database by specifying alternate locations for one or more cube partitions as described in Skill 4.3, "Configure and manage processing." If you do this, you must add each path to AllowedBrowsingFolders, a server property for SSAS, using a pipe delimiter between paths.

- **LogDir**   SSAS uses this path for storing log files, including the Flight Recorder and query logs created by usage-based optimization.

Flight Recorder is a short-term log that captures snapshots of dynamic management views (DMVs) to help you troubleshoot query and processing issues that occurred recently. Because this logging mechanism adds input/output (IO) overhead to the server, consider disabling it in the Analysis Services Properties by changing the Log \ Flight Recorder \ Enabled property to False. Instead, you can use other techniques described in this chapter to monitor query and processing performance on an as needed basis.

Usage-based optimization is another logging tool that you can use to guide the development of aggregations to improve the performance of common query patterns. Refer to the "Optimize and manage model design" section for more information about using usage-based optimization.

- **TempDir** SSAS uses this path to store temporary files created during processing. Specifically, dimension processing, aggregation processing, and ROLAP dimensions might require more memory than the server has available in which case SSAS spills to disk. Consider changing this path to a separate volume from the data path when you are processing high volumes of data and the server is experiencing performance issues during processing.

Determine SSAS instance placement

For an optimal configuration of a single server, you should place a production SSAS instance on a dedicated server without other server products, such as the SQL Server database engine, SQL Server Integration Services (SSIS), SQL Server Reporting Services (SSRS), or another SSAS instance. You can use several SSAS servers in a scale-out architecture when you need to support a large number of concurrent users or process or store a high volume of data, whether using multidimensional- or tabular-mode servers.

If you decide to run both SQL Server and SSAS on the same server for licensing reasons, be aware that resource contention over memory and CPU are more likely to occur. That said, if SQL Server is used to host a small to medium data warehouse as the data source for SSAS, it is possible to run both services on the same server to achieve faster processing and reduce overall hardware costs, especially if the resources of each service are in use at different times, but only if you are running a multidimensional-mode server. A tabular mode server has high memory requirements and is better suited to running in a standalone environment. You must evaluate the workload of both servers to determine whether a single server can provide adequate resources to each.

One option for scaling SSAS is to establish one server for query loads and a second server for processing loads, as shown in Figure 4-4. Use this approach when the SSAS server must be available to queries around the clock and this lack of downtime prevents you from performing processing operations without adversely impacting query performance. In this case, you can process on a separate server and then copy the processed database from the processing server to the query server.

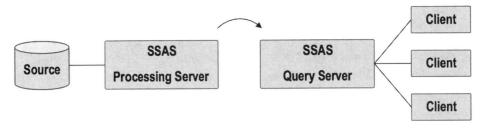

FIGURE 4-4 Separate processing and query servers

> **NOTE** **OPTIONS FOR COPYING AN SSAS DATABASE**
>
> To copy an SSAS database from one server to another, use one of the following methods and view the associated reference for more information:
>
> - Synchronization, see "Synchronize Analysis Services Databases" at *https://msdn. microsoft.com/en-us/library/ms174928.aspx*
> - High-speed copying, see "SQLCAT's Guide to BI and Analytics" at *http://download. microsoft.com/download/0/F/B/0FBFAA46-2BFD-478F-8E56-7BF3C672DF9D/SQL-CAT's%20Guide%20to%20BI%20and%20Analytics.pdf*
> - Backup and restore, see "Backup and Restore of Analysis Services Databases" at *https://msdn.microsoft.com/en-us/library/ms174874.aspx*
> - Attach and detach, see "Attach and Detach Analysis Services Databases" at *https:// msdn.microsoft.com/en-us/library/cc280583.aspx*

When you need to process multiple large partitions, you can speed up the processing operations by using separate remote partitions for the database on the processing server, as shown in Figure 4-5, to parallelize the processing operation. Furthermore, by distributing the processing load to multiple servers, you can take advantage of the memory and processor resources of separate servers, rather than overwhelming a single server.

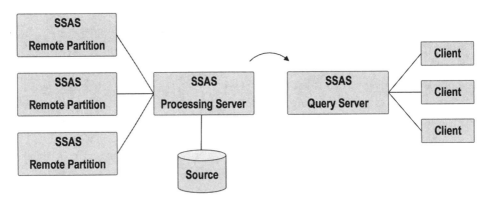

FIGURE 4-5 Remote partitions for processing

If the number of concurrent users is adversely impacting query performance, you can create a Network Load Balancing (NLB) cluster of SSAS servers, as shown in Figure 4-6. In this case, client applications connect to a virtual IP address and the NLB mechanism forwards each query to one of the servers in the cluster in round-robin fashion. One way to keep the query servers up-to-date is to maintain a master database and then use synchronization to ensure each of the query servers has an exact copy of the master database.

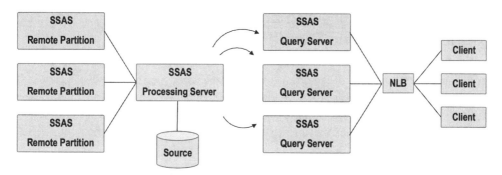

FIGURE 4-6 Network load balanced query servers

Skill 4.2: Monitor and optimize performance

As source data volumes increase or query patterns change, performance issues can become more prevalent as a result of the current model design, application configuration, or server hardware limitations. The 70-768 exam tests your ability to use monitoring tools, evaluate results, and take appropriate action to resolve the identified performance problems.

Monitor performance and analyze query plans by using Extended Events and Profiler

Of all the performance issues that can occur on the SSAS server, slow queries are important to identify and resolve so that you can provide an optimal data access experience for your users. After all, one of the main reasons to move data into a multidimensional or tabular model is to enable fast queries. The methods you use to derive insight into the potential causes of slow queries depend on whether SSAS is running in multidimensional or tabular mode.

EXAM TIP

The exam is likely to test your understanding of analyzing trance events. Be sure you understand the key events that provide details necessary to troubleshoot query performance and how to draw conclusions from this information.

Multidimensional query monitoring

Although you cannot access query plans for a SSAS multidimensional-mode server, you can use SQL Server Profiler to capture events that provide information about the division of labor between the engines that SSAS uses to process queries. This technique is useful when you need to resolve performance issues for specific queries. If you want to monitor general query performance on the server, you can use the Windows Performance Monitor as described in the "Monitor processing and query performance" section later in this chapter.

Before we examine the Profiler events that are important to monitor, let's review the following high-level stages in the multidimensional query processing architecture, as shown in Figure 4-7:

1. When a client application, such as SSMS or Excel, sends an MDX query to the SSAS server, the Query Parser checks the query to validate the syntax. If the query is invalid, an error message is returned to the client application. Otherwise, the query processor sends the query to the SSAS formula engine.

2. The formula engine's first step is to evaluate the query's axes and populate axes. As described in Chapter 3, "Develop queries using Multidimensional Expressions (MDX) and

Data Analysis Expressions (DAX)," the set on rows and the set on columns is resolved and the applicable members are retrieved from the dimension cache or storage. If the dimension data is not in the cache, the formula engine requests the data from the storage engine and then saves the results in the cache.

3. After the rows and columns are evaluated, the cells resulting from row and column intersections are combined with the WHERE clause to identify tuples to retrieve from the cube to compute cell data. Put another way, the formula engine evaluates the multidimensional space requested by the query.

4. SSAS builds a logical execution plan that it uses to determine the best way to retrieve cell values in the multidimensional space and then creates a physical execution plan. Empty tuples are removed from the physical execution plan if possible. The physical execution plan is then sent to the cache subsystem as a series of subcube operations. A subcube is a subset of the multidimensional space that represents a crossjoin of one or more members from a level of each attribute hierarchy. (Subcubes in this context are not the same as the subcubes that you define in the MDX script, as explained in Chapter 3.)

5. The subcube operations request the storage engine to return fact data from one of the following locations:

   ■ The first location from which the storage engine can retrieve data is the storage engine cache. This cache is empty when the SSAS service starts, and is loaded as the storage engine retrieves data from disk to speed up subsequent requests for the same data.

   ■ If the requested data is not in the cache, the next location from which the storage engine can retrieve data is the aggregations store on disk. Aggregations are explained in the "Optimize and manage model design" section later in this chapter. Aggregation data is copied into cache and then sent to the formula engine.

   ■ When the storage engine is unable to retrieve data from the previous two locations, it then retrieves values from the fact data store on disk. Just as with aggregations, the retrieved data is copied into cache and forwarded on to the formula engine.

> **NOTE FILE SYSTEM CACHE**
>
> When the storage engine makes a request to retrieve data from disk, the IO subsystem first checks the Windows file system cache. Only when the data is not in the file system cache is it actually retrieved from disk. You can read more about how SSAS interacts with the file system cache in the "Analysis Services Operations Guide," which you can download from *https://msdn.microsoft.com/en-us/library/hh226085.aspx*.

6. After the data for all subcube requests are received by the formula engine, it computes calculations in calculated measures. If the calculation definition comes from the model rather than the query, it has global scope and the result is stored in the formula engine

cache to speed up subsequent queries from any user requesting the same calculation. The formula engine then combines the data from multiple subcube requests with the calculation results and sends the final query results to requesting client application.

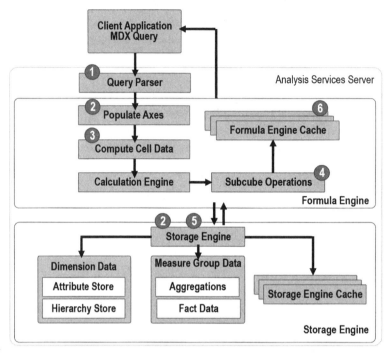

FIGURE 4-7 Multidimensional query processing architecture

NOTE **QUERY PROCESSING ARCHITECTURE IN-DEPTH**

The Analysis Services MOLAP Performance Guide provides more in-depth explanation of the query processing architecture at a level of detail that the exam does not test, but is helpful for increasing your knowledge of this topic. Although written for SQL Server 2012 and 2014, it remains applicable to SQL Server 2016. You can download the guide from *https://msdn.microsoft.com/en-us/library/dn749781.aspx*.

You can observe these stages by capturing events in a trace by performing the following steps in SQL Server 2016 Profiler:

NOTE **SAMPLE MULTIDIMENSIONAL DATABASE FOR THIS CHAPTER**

This chapter uses the database created in Chapter 1, "Design a multidimensional business intelligence (BI) model," to illustrate monitoring and configuration concepts. If you have not created this database, you can restore the 70-768-Ch1.ABF file included with this chapter's code sample files as described in Chapter 3.

1. Click New Trace on the File menu, and then connect to the Analysis Services server on which you want to run the trace.

2. In the Trace Properties dialog box, decide whether you want to save the results for later analysis. You can choose either or both of the following check boxes:

   - **Save To File**   Save the captured events to a TRC file that you can later open and review in Profiler. This method is preferable when you can launch profiling and save the file on a remote server because it reduces the performance impact on the SSAS server.

   - **Save To Table**   Save the captured events to a specific SQL Server database and table that you can later review by using any query tool. An advantage of saving the trace data to a table is the ability to create reports to compare query performance before and after making changes to tune behavior.

3. Click the Events Selection tab, select the Show All Events checkbox, and then select or clear check boxes in the events list such that only the following check boxes are selected:

   - **Progress Report Begin**   The storage engine begins reading partition data if this data is not available in the cache.

   - **Progress Report Current**   The storage engine reports information about the partition data it is reading.

   - **Progress Report End**   The storage engine has finished reading partition data.

   - **Query Begin**   The query is received by SSAS. You can view the MDX query in the TextData column.

   - **Query End**   SSAS has finished query processing. You can view the overall time to resolve and return the query results in the Duration column.

   - **Calculate Non Empty Begin**   SSAS eliminates empty coordinates from the query results when the Non Empty keyword or NonEmpty function appear in the query. The IntegerData value is 11, the evaluation of non-empty cells is performed in cell-by-cell mode and slower than bulk mode, which is represented by any other IntegerData value.

   - **Calculate Non Empty End**   The elimination of empty coordinates is complete and the duration is reported.

   - **Get Data From Aggregation**   The storage engine retrieves data from an aggregation.

- **Get Data From Cache** The storage engine retrieves data from the data cache. If you do not see many of these events, the server might not have enough memory for caching, or calculations might prevent caching.

- **Query Cube Begin** The formula engine begins executing the query.

- **Query Cube End** The formula engine ends query execution.

- **Query Dimension** The storage engine retrieves dimension members. The event subclass indicates whether these members are retrieved from cache or disk.

- **Serialize Results Begin** The process to send results back to the client begins usually after calculations are complete.

- **Serialize Results Current** The members to place on axes are serialized and streamed back to the client.

- **Serialize Results End** All results have been sent to the client.

- **Query Subcube** The storage engine retrieves a subcube from cache or disk. The subcube is represented as a binary vector.

- **Query Subcube Verbose** The storage engine retrieves a subcube from cache or disk. It repeats the information from the Query Subcube event, but provides more detail.

4. Switch to SSMS, click the Analysis Services XMLA Query button, connect to the multi-dimensional SSAS server, and then execute the statement shown in Listing 4-1 to clear the SSAS cache. This step allows you to evaluate query with a cold cache to reveal its behavior at its slowest.

LISTING 4-1 Clear SSAS cache

```
<Batch xmlns="http://schemas.microsoft.com/analysisservices/2003/engine">
    <ClearCache>
        <Object>
            <DatabaseID>70-768-Ch1</DatabaseID>
        </Object>
    </ClearCache>
</Batch>
```

> *IMPORTANT* **CLEARING THE SSAS CACHE**
>
> Clearing the SSAS cache adversely affects performance of an active SSAS server in production. For this reason, you should perform this step only when you can ensure no queries are executing or when you can use a test server that duplicates your production environment as closely as possible.

5. Switch back to SQL Server Profiler, and click Run to start the trace.

6. Switch back to SSMS, click the Analysis Services MDX Query button, connect to the server, and then execute the query shown in Listing 4-2.

LISTING 4-2 MDX query to trace

```
SELECT
[Measures].[Sales Amount Without Tax] ON COLUMNS,
[Stock Item].[Color].[Color].Members ON ROWS
FROM
[Wide World Importers DW]
WHERE
([Invoice Date].[Calendar Year].[CY2016]);
```

7. After executing the query, switch to SQL Server Profiler, and click the Stop Selected Trace in the SQL Server Profiler toolbar to view the trace events that fired during query execution, as shown in Figure 4-8. You can use drag and drop to rearrange the columns in the following sequence: EventClass, EventSubclass, TextData, ObjectPath, Duration, and IntegerData.

EventClass	EventSubclass	TextData	ObjectPath	Duration	IntegerData
Query Begin	0 - MDXQuery	SELECT [Measures].[Sales Amount Wit...			
Query Subcube	2 - Non-cache data	00001000,00,000,000,0000,0000,0,0100	DI10.70-768-Ch1.Wide Wor...	15	
Query Subcube Verbose	22 - Non-cache data	Dimension 0 [City] (0 0 0 0 2 0 0 0...	DI10.70-768-Ch1.Wide Wor...	16	
Query Cube Begin			DI10.70-768-Ch1.Wide Wor...		
Query Dimension	2 - Non-cache data	0010	DI10.70-768-Ch1.Date		
Calculate Non Empty Begin			DI10.70-768-Ch1.Wide Wor...		3
Query Dimension	1 - Cache data	0010	DI10.70-768-Ch1.Date		
Calculate Non Empty End			DI10.70-768-Ch1.Wide Wor...	1	3
Serialize Results Begin			DI10.70-768-Ch1.Wide Wor...		
Serialize Results Current	1 - Serialize Axes	Axis 0	DI10.70-768-Ch1.Wide Wor...		
Serialize Results Current	1 - Serialize Axes		DI10.70-768-Ch1.Wide Wor...		
Serialize Results Current	1 - Serialize Axes	Axis 1	DI10.70-768-Ch1.Wide Wor...		
Serialize Results Current	1 - Serialize Axes		DI10.70-768-Ch1.Wide Wor...		
Serialize Results Current	1 - Serialize Axes	Slicer Axis	DI10.70-768-Ch1.Wide Wor...		
Serialize Results Current	1 - Serialize Axes		DI10.70-768-Ch1.Wide Wor...		
Progress Report Begin	14 - Query	Started reading data from the 'Sale...	DI10.70-768-Ch1.Wide Wor...		
Progress Report End	14 - Query	Finished reading data from the 'Sal...	DI10.70-768-Ch1.Wide Wor...	3	0
Query Subcube	2 - Non-cache data	00001000,00,000,000,0000,0010,0,0010	DI10.70-768-Ch1.Wide Wor...	3	
Query Subcube Verbose	22 - Non-cache data	Dimension 0 [City] (0 0 0 0 2 0 0 0...	DI10.70-768-Ch1.Wide Wor...	3	
Serialize Results Current	2 - Serialize Cells		DI10.70-768-Ch1.Wide Wor...		
Serialize Results End			DI10.70-768-Ch1.Wide Wor...	10	
Query Cube End			DI10.70-768-Ch1.Wide Wor...	12	
Query End	0 - MDXQuery	SELECT [Measures].[Sales Amount Wit...		40	1

FIGURE 4-8 Profiler trace of simple MDX query

The trace events describe the following behavior during query execution:

- **Query Begin**   The server receives the query. You can see the structure of the MDX query in the TextData column.

- **Query Subcube**   The storage engine retrieves requested data from disk, as indicated by the event subclass, 2 – Non-cache Data. The TextData column contains values that are difficult to interpret visually, but reflect the dimensions and measure groups defined in the requested subcube. Not visible in Figure 4-8 is the Duration column, which contains a value of which you should take note as described later in this section. In this case, the duration is 28 milliseconds.

- **Query Subcube Verbose**   This trace event is another version of the Query Sub-cube event that provides more details about the subcube, as shown here:

```
Dimension 0 [City] (0 0 0 0 2 0 0 0)
[City]:0  [State Province]:0  [Country]:0  [Continent]:0
[Sales Territory]:[Far West]  [Region]:0  [Subregion]:0
[Latest Recorded Population]:0

Dimension 1 [Invoice] (0 0)  [Sale Key]:0  [Invoice]:0

Dimension 2 [Customer] (0 0 0)  [Customer]:0  [Category]:0  [Buying Group]:0

Dimension 3 [Bill To Customer] (0 0 0)  [Customer]:0  [Category]:0
[Buying Group]:0

Dimension 4 [Delivery Date] (0 0 0 0)  [Date]:0  [Calendar Month]:0
[Calendar Year]:0  [ISO Week Number]:0

Dimension 5 [Invoice Date] (0 0 0 0)  [Date]:0  [Calendar Month]:0
[Calendar Year]:0  [ISO Week Number]:0

Dimension 6 [Sales Reason] (0)  [Sales Reason]:0

Dimension 7 [Stock Item] (0 * 0 0)  [Stock Item History]:0  [Stock Item]:*
[Color]:0  [Size]:0
```

Each dimension is listed separately and includes each attribute. Following the dimension name is a *vector*, a series of values enclosed in parentheses. The position of each value in the vector corresponds to an attribute in the dimension and defines the sub-cube request according to the following rules:

- **0**   requests the default member of the attribute

- *****   requests all members of the attribute

- **Non-zero**   requests a single member by DataID, the internal identifier of an at-tribute member

- **+**   requests more than one attribute member

- **–**   requests a limited number of members typically due to a slice on a different at-tribute in the dimension

To put this explanation into context, let's review the subcube definition with respect to the City dimension, which is listed first in the Query Subcube Verbose event. The City vector (0 0 0 0 2 0 0 0) describes the request of the default member of each attribute except for the Sales Territory attribute (in position 5) in which case the member with DataID 2, Far West, is requested. You can also see the attributes listed by position, with City in position 1, State Province in position 2, and so on. When the dimension's subcube definition includes a non-zero value to request a specific DataID, you can see the corresponding member name displayed next to the attribute name. In this case, the display of [Sales Territory]:[Far West] corresponds to the 2 in the fifth position in the dimension vector.

Next, notice in Dimension 7, the second position of the Stock Item vector is an asterisk (*). It corresponds to the second attribute, Stock Item, which also displays an asterisk. In this case, the subcube requests all members of the Stock Item attribute.

The combination of these two vectors defines the multidimensional space retrieved from the cube. More specifically, the formula engine requests all cells for any stock item with a non-empty measure in the Sale measure group in the Far West sales territory.

- **Query Cube Begin**   The formula engine begins executing the query.
- **Query Dimension**   You can see by the event subclass, 2 – Non-cache Data, that the formula engine requests dimension members from disk. The ObjectPath columns indicates that the request refers to the Date dimension.
- **Calculate Non Empty Begin**   The IntegerData value of 3 indicates that the query execution occurs in bulk evaluation mode.
- **Query Dimension**   You can see by the event subclass, 1 – Cache Data, that this time the formula engine requests Date dimension members from cache. Something in the execution plan triggered a second request for the Date dimension, but the trace provides no insight into the execution plan.
- **Calculate Non Empty End**   The duration of the process to eliminate empty cells is 1 millisecond.
- **Serialize Results Begin and Serialize Results Current**   There are two Serialize Results Current events for each axis that SSAS serializes: Axis 0 (columns), Axis 1 (rows), and Slicer Axis (the query's WHERE clause). The ProgressTotal columns lists the number of members returned for each axis. In this case, Axis 0 has 1 member, Axis 1 has 9 members, and the Slicer Axis has 1 member.
- **Progress Report Begin and End**   The TextData column for the Progress Report Begin event explains how the storage engine retrieves data. In this case, the storage engine is reading data from the Sale partition on disk.
- **Query Subcube and Query Subcube Verbose**   The storage engine again retrieves requested data from disk, as you can see by the event subclass, 2 – Non-cache Data. The Duration column for this event is 23 milliseconds. The TextData

column in the Query Subcube Verbose event is nearly identical to the previous occurrence of this event, except for the vector for Dimension 5 [Invoice Date] as shown here:

```
Dimension 5 [Invoice Date] (0 0 4 0)  [Date]:0  [Calendar Month]:0
[Calendar Year]:[CY2016]  [ISO Week Number]:0
```

- **Serialize Results Current and Serialize Results End**   This time the cell intersections of the axes are returned to the client now that the data has been read from two subcubes.
- **Query Cube End**   The formula engine ends executing the query.
- **Query End**   SSAS ends all work related to the query. The important value to note is the value in the Duration column, currently not visible, which in this case is 98 milliseconds.

> *NOTE* **EVALUATION OF CACHED QUERIES**
>
> If you were to start a new trace and execute the statement in Listing 4-2 again, the Query Subcube events are replaced by a single new event, Get Data From Cache, because the data retrieval performed by the first execution of the query loaded the cache. Consequently, the duration is reduced significantly. On the author's computer, the duration of the cached query is 11 milliseconds. This type of behavior is not a candidate for query tuning, but illustrates the difference between queries that retrieve non-cached data versus cached data. To properly evaluate the impact of changes that you make to the design of a query, you should clear the cache between each query execution. As mentioned previously in this section, you should consider clearing the file system cache for the more rigorous testing.

In-memory tabular query monitoring

Before considering how to monitor query performance for in-memory tabular models, it is important to first understand the query architecture for in-memory tabular models, shown in Figure 4-9. The SSAS processes queries for this model type by following these steps:

1. The SSAS query parser first evaluates whether the incoming request is a valid DAX or MDX query. (Tools like Excel or SQL Server Reporting Services (SSRS) can send MDX requests to a tabular model.)

2. If the query is an MDX query, SSAS invokes the MDX formula engine, which then sends a DAX request for measure calculations to the DAX formula engine. The MDX formula engine can request a measure embedded in the tabular model or request a calculation defined in the WITH clause of the MDX query. It can also request dimension from the VertiPaq storage engine. The MDX formula engine caches measures unless the MDX query contains a WITH clause.

3. The DAX formula engine receives either a DAX query request from the parser or a DAX request for measure calculations from the MDX formula engine. Either way, the DAX formula engine generates a query plan that it sends to the VertiPaq storage engine.

4. The VertiPaq storage engine processes the query plan received from the DAX formula engine. The storage engine is multi-threaded and scales well on multiple cores. It can scan large tables very efficiently and quickly. It can also evaluate simple mathematical operations, but pushes more complex operations back to the formula engine. If a calculation is too complex, it sends a callback to the formula engine.

5. The storage engine returns its results to the formula engine which compiles the data and returns the query results to the client application. It maintains a short-term VertiPaq cache to benefit multiple requests for the same data in the same query. An ancillary benefit is the availability of this data for subsequent queries for a period of time.

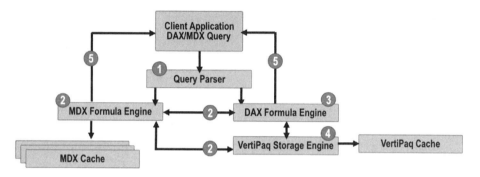

FIGURE 4-9 Query processing architecture for in-memory tabular models

The DAX formula engine produces the following two types of query plans for tabular models:

- **Logical query plan** Contains an execution tree used by the physical plan and provides insight into the physical plan when a query is complex. The engine produces this query plan quickly prior to creating the physical plan.

- **Physical query plan** Describes how the engine actually executes a query. It lists the operators and parameters used during execution, but can be difficult to interpret.

NOTE **TABULAR MODEL QUERY PLAN INTERPRETATION**

The exam does not test you on an in-depth interpretation of a logical or physical query plan, but does require you to know the steps necessary to acquire the query plan. If you want additional information about logical and physical query plans, see "DAX Query Plan, Part 1, Introduction" at *http://mdxdax.blogspot.com/2011/12/dax-query-plan-part-1-introduction.html*, "DAX Query Plan, Part 2, Operator Properties" at *http://mdxdax.blogspot.com/2012/01/dax-query-plan-part-2-operator.html*, "DAX Query Plan, Part 3, Vertipaq Operators" at *http://mdxdax.blogspot.com/2012/03/dax-query-plan-part-3-vertipaq.html*, and "Whitepaper: Understanding DAX Query Plans" at *https://www.sqlbi.com/articles/understanding-dax-query-plans/*.

You can use SQL Server Profiler (or Extended Events as explained later in this section) to create a trace for a tabular-mode SSAS server, much like you can for a multidimensional-mode server. To do this, perform the following steps:

1. Click New Trace on the File menu and connect to your tabular instance. You can save the trace to a file or to a SQL Server table, if you like.

2. Click Events Selection, select the Show All Events check box, and then select or clear check boxes in the events list such that only the following check boxes are selected:

   - **Query Begin**   The query is received by SSAS. You can view the DAX or MDX query in the TextData column.

   - **Query End**   The query processing is complete. The Duration column displays the time required to resolve and return the query results.

   - **DAX Query Plan**   The TextData column contains the logical or physical query plan. If the originating query is MDX, multiple DAX query plans can be generated.

   - **VertiPaq SE Query Begin**   The storage engine retrieves data from memory. The TextData column shows the tables, columns, and measures requested.

   - **VertiPaq SE Query Cache Match**   The storage engine uses its short-term cache rather than perform a scan to get required for a calculation.

   - **VertiPaq SE Query End**   The storage engine completes data retrieval. The Duration column specifies the time required to complete the operation.

3. Click Run to start the trace.

4. Switch to SSMS, click the Analysis Services MDX Query button, connect to the tabular instance, execute the query in Listing 4-1 to clear the VertiPaq and MDX cache (replacing the database ID with 70-768-Ch2), and then execute the query shown in Listing 4-3.

LISTING 4-3 DAX query to trace

```
EVALUATE
SUMMARIZE(
    FILTER(
        'Sale',
        RELATED('Date'[Calendar Year]) = 2016
    ),
    'Stock Item'[Color],
    "Total Sales",
        'Sale'[Total Sales]
)
```

5. After executing the query, switch to SQL Server Profiler, and click the Stop Selected Trace in the SQL Server Profiler toolbar to view the following trace events:

■ **Query Begin** The server receives the query, the text of which you can see in the TextData column.

■ **DAX Query Plan** The event subclass, 1 – DAX VertiPaq Logical Plan, indicates the first query plan generated by the formula engine, shown here:

```
AddColumns: RelLogOp DependOnCols()() 0-1 RequiredCols(0, 1)('Stock Item'[Color],
''[Total Sales])
    GroupBy_Vertipaq: RelLogOp DependOnCols()() 0-95
    RequiredCols(0, 17, 18)('StockItem'[Color], 'Sale'[Invoice Date Key],
    'Sale'[Stock Item Key])
        Filter_Vertipaq: RelLogOp DependOnCols()() 0-95
        RequiredCols(57, 78, 79)('Stock Item'[Color], 'Sale'[Stock Item Key],
        'Sale'[Invoice Date Key])
            Scan_Vertipaq: RelLogOp DependOnCols()() 0-95
            RequiredCols(36, 57, 78, 79)('Date'[Calendar Year],
            'Stock Item'[Color], 'Sale'[Stock Item Key],
            'Sale'[Invoice Date Key])
            'Date'[Calendar Year] = 2016: ScaLogOp DependOnCols(36)
            ('Date'[Calendar Year]) Boolean DominantValue=FALSE
    Sum_Vertipaq: ScaLogOp DependOnCols(0)('Stock Item'[Color]) Double
    DominantValue=BLANK
        Scan_Vertipaq: RelLogOp DependOnCols(0)('Stock Item'[Color]) 96-191
        RequiredCols(0, 184)('Stock Item'[Color], 'Sale'[Total Excluding Tax])
        'Sale'[Total Excluding Tax]: ScaLogOp DependOnCols(184)
        ('Sale'[Total Excluding Tax]) Double DominantValue=NONE
```

A logical query plan consists of multiple lines of texts in which each line is an operator and indented according to its level within the execution hierarchy. The first line defines the outermost operator, such as AddColumns in this example. If a line is indented more than the preceding line, the line is subordinate to the preceding line, its parent, and deliver its output to the parent line. Therefore, to understand the query plan, you must start at the bottom level of each branch and work backwards through the query plan. To interpret the query plan for the query in Listing 4-3, consider the following points:

■ The two Scan_Vertipaq operators in the query plan initiate the data retrieval process and provide output to be processed by their respective parents in separate branches of the query plan. The goal of this operator is to join a root table to its related tables as defined by the requested columns.

■ In Branch 1, which begins with the first Scan_Vertipaq operator, the RelLogOp operator type produces a table identified in the RequiredCols list: 'Date'[Calendar Year], 'Stock Item'[Color], 'Sale'[Stock Item Key], and 'Sale'[Invoice Date Key]. This list is represented by both column number and name following the RequiredCols parameter.

■ The output of the Scan_Vertipaq operator and its sibling predicate Date'[Calendar Year] = 2016 are passed to the Filter_VertiPaq operator in Branch 1 to restrict the rows in the output.

- Branch 1 continues by sending the results of the Filter_Vertipaq operator to the GroupBy_Vertipaq operator where a grouping of rows by the following columns is performed: 'Stock Item'[Color], 'Sale'[Invoice Date Key], and 'Sale'[Stock Item Key].

- Meanwhile, Branch 2 begins with the second Scan_Vertipaq operator. It returns a table containing two columns, specified in both DependOnCols and RequiredCols to return a table containing 'Stock Item'[Color] and 'Sale'[Total Excluding Tax].

- The Scan_Vertipaq results in Branch 2 are sent to the Sum_Vertipaq operator to which the SUM aggregation is applied. This operation returns summed sales by the 'Stock Item'[Color] column as a two-column table.

- The last step in the query plan is the outermost AddColumns operator, which combines the results of the two branches to produce a two-column table consisting of 'Stock Item'[Color] and [Total Sales].

- **VertiPaq SE Query Begin and VertiPaq SE Query End** These event types have one of two event subclasses, VertiPaq Scan and Internal VertiPaq Scan. Internal VertiPas Scan is the optimized version of VertiPaq Scan. Sometimes you can see VertiPaq SE queries occur before the formula engine creates the logical query plan. This situation occurs when the formula engine needs information from the database to determine how to optimize the query. Other times queries are used to spool intermediate results into memory to optimize the physical query plan or query execution.

  Queries are written by using a pseudo-SQL statement for easier comprehension. Each VertiPaq SE Query Begin/End pair corresponds to a Scan_VertiPaq operator in the logical query plan. The operators in Branch 2 and Branch 1 correspond to the first and second VertiPaq scans respectively, shown here:

```
-- First VertiPaq Scan
SET DC_KIND="AUTO";
SELECT
[Stock Item (22)].[Color (86)] AS [Stock Item (22)$Color (86)],
SUM([Sale (25)].[Total Excluding Tax (116)]) AS [$Measure0]
FROM [Sale (25)]
  LEFT OUTER JOIN [Date (16)] ON
    [Sale (25)].[Invoice Date Key (107)]=[Date (16)].[Date (61)]
  LEFT OUTER JOIN [Stock Item (22)] ON
    [Sale (25)].[Stock Item Key (106)]=[Stock Item (22)].[Stock Item Key (83)]
WHERE
  [Date (16)].[Calendar Year (68)] = 2016;


-- Second VertiPaq Scan
SET DC_KIND="AUTO";
SELECT
[Stock Item (22)].[Color (86)] AS [Stock Item (22)$Color (86)],
[Sale (25)].[Stock Item Key (106)] AS [Sale (25)$Stock Item Key (106)],
[Sale (25)].[Invoice Date Key(107)] AS [Sale (25)$Invoice Date Key (107)]
FROM [Sale (25)]
  LEFT OUTER JOIN [Date (16)] ON
    [Sale (25)].[Invoice Date Key (107)]=[Date (16)].[Date (61)]
  LEFT OUTER JOIN [Stock Item (22)] ON
```

```
        [Sale (25)].[Stock Item Key (106)]=[Stock Item (22)].[Stock Item Key (83)]
    WHERE
        [Date (16)].[Calendar Year (68)] = 2016;
```

- **DAX Query Plan** The event subclass, 2 – DAX VertiPaq Physical Plan, indicates the second DAX Query Plan in the trace is the physical query plan, which looks like this:

```
AddColumns: IterPhyOp LogOp=AddColumns IterCols(0, 1)('Stock Item'[Color],
''[Total Sales])
    Spool_Iterator<SpoolIterator>: IterPhyOp LogOp=GroupBy_Vertipaq
    IterCols(0)('Stock Item'[Color]) #Records=9 #KeyCols=1 #ValueCols=0
        AggregationSpool<GroupBy>: SpoolPhyOp #Records=9
            Spool_Iterator<SpoolIterator>: IterPhyOp LogOp=
            GroupBy_Vertipaq IterCols(0, 17, 18)
            ('Stock Item'[Color], 'Sale'[Invoice Date Key],
            'Sale'[Stock Item Key]) #Records=17962 #KeyCols=96 #ValueCols=0
                ProjectionSpool<ProjectFusion<>>: SpoolPhyOp #Records=17962
                    VertipaqResult: IterPhyOp #FieldCols=3 #ValueCols=0
    SpoolLookup: LookupPhyOp LogOp=Sum_Vertipaq LookupCols(0)('Stock Item'[Color])
    Double #Records=9 #KeyCols=96 #ValueCols=1 DominantValue=BLANK
        ProjectionSpool<ProjectFusion<Sum>>: SpoolPhyOp #Records=9
            VertipaqResult: IterPhyOp #FieldCols=1 #ValueCols=1
```

Just like the logical query plan, the physical query plan starts with its innermost lines in the hierarchical list and includes two branches that use the VertipaqResult operator. This operator maps to the VertiPaq SE Query event. When evaluating performance, take note of the #Records value which impacts memory when used with the Spool-PhyOp operator. This operator indicates the records are materialized and stored in memory.

Moving up the hierarchy in the first branch, the VertiPaq operator materializes 17,962 rows which then are reduced to 9 records by the GroupBy_VertiPaq operator and sent to the Spool_Iterator. This latter operator's sibling is the SpoolLookup operator, which gets the VertiPaq result from Branch 2 and makes these rows available for row-by-row lookups to the iterator. The AddColumns operator receives these results and produces a two column table containing Color and Total Sales.

- **Query End** The server finishes the query and returns the overall duration.

EXTENDED EVENTS TRACE

Another way to capture trace information for tabular queries is to create an Extended Events session in SSMS, which you can do by performing the following steps:

1. Connect to the tabular instance, expand the Management node in Object Explorer, expand the Extended Events node, right-click the Sessions node, and click New Session.

2. In the New Session dialog box, type a name for the session, such as DAX query plan.

3. Click Events, and then double-click the following events to add them to the Selected Events list: DAX Query Plan, Query Begin, Query End, VertiPaq SE Query Begin, VertiPaq SE Query Cache Match, and VertiPaq SE Query End.

4. Click the Data Storage tab, click Add, and then select one of the following target types in the Type drop-down list.

- **Event_file** Store the session data in an XEL file.

- **Event_stream** Enable the Watch Live Data feature in SSMS. Use this option to follow the example in this section.

- **Ring_buffer** Store the session data in memory until the service restarts.

5. Click OK, right-click the DAX Query Plan node in the Session folder in Object Explorer, click Watch Live Data, expand the DAX Query Plan node, and then click Event_stream to open the Extended Events viewer as a new window in the query editor.

6. Switch to a MDX query window and execute the query in Listing 4-3.

7. In the Extended Events window, you can see the list of events that fired during the DAX query execution. Click the first DAX Query Plan in the list, and then scroll to locate the TextData row in the Details pane below the event list. Right-click this row and click Show Column In Table to include the TextData column next to each event at the top of the window, as shown in Figure 4-10.

name	timestamp	TextData
QueryBegin	2017-02-07 22:13:46.8661719	EVALUATE SUMMARIZE(FILTER('Sale', RELATED('Date'[Calendar Year]) = 2016), 'Stock Item'[Col...
DAXQueryPlan	2017-02-07 22:13:46.8934983	AddColumns: RelLogOp DependOnCols()() 0-1 RequiredCols(0, 1)('Stock Item'[Color], '[Total Sales]) GroupBy_V...
VertiPaqSEQueryBegin	2017-02-07 22:13:46.8940219	SET DC_KIND="AUTO"; SELECT [Stock Item (22)].[Color (86)] AS [Stock Item (22)$Color (86)], SUM([Sale (2...
VertiPaqSEQueryEnd	2017-02-07 22:13:46.8940591	SET DC_KIND="AUTO"; SELECT [Stock Item (22)].[Color (86)] AS [Stock Item (22)$Color (86)], SUM([Sale (2...
VertiPaqSEQueryBegin	2017-02-07 22:13:46.8947994	SET DC_KIND="AUTO"; SELECT [Stock Item (22)].[Color (86)] AS [Stock Item (22)$Color (86)], [Sale (25)].[Sto...
VertiPaqSEQueryEnd	2017-02-07 22:13:46.8948355	SET DC_KIND="AUTO"; SELECT [Stock Item (22)].[Color (86)] AS [Stock Item (22)$Color (86)], [Sale (25)].[Sto...
DAXQueryPlan	2017-02-07 22:13:46.8964627	AddColumns: IterPhyOp LogOp=AddColumns IterCols(0, 1)('Stock Item'[Color], '[Total Sales]) Spool_Iterator<Sp...
QueryEnd	2017-02-07 22:13:46.8969043	EVALUATE SUMMARIZE(FILTER('Sale', RELATED('Date'[Calendar Year]) = 2016), 'Stock Item'[Col...

FIGURE 4-10 An Extended Events session for a tabular instance

> **NOTE XMLA SCRIPT FOR EXTENDED EVENTS**
>
> Instead of using the SSMS graphical interface to manage Extended Event sessions, you can execute XMLA scripts. For details, see "Monitor Analysis Services with SQL Server Extended Events" at *https://msdn.microsoft.com/en-us/library/gg492139.aspx*.

DirectQuery query plans

The SSAS engine translates DAX queries to a DirectQuery model into an equivalent SQL query, which it sends to the source database. You must use Profiler or Extended Events to capture the resulting query plan from the database engine if SQL Server is the source or use a monitoring tool applicable to other data sources. If you use Profiler on the tabular instance to monitor query execution, you can include the DirectQuery Begin and DirectQuery End events to review the SQL query that was generated and its duration, but there is no option to optimize this query.

Identify bottlenecks in SSAS queries

Once you know how to generate a query trace for an MDX query and how to obtain a query plan for a DAX query, you can explore these items to reveal more information about query execution. Whether you are analyzing performance issues for MDX or DAX queries, the process of identifying the source of the bottleneck is similar. By comparing the ratios of formula engine and storage engine time to overall query time, you can determine whether your query tuning efforts should focus on improving formula engine time or storage engine time. Refer to the "Resolve performance issues" section later in this section for guidance on specific actions you can take for each of these bottlenecks.

To find the relative time required by each engine for an MDX query executed on a multidimensional-mode server, start by computing the sum of the duration of each Query Subcube event (or the Query Subcube Verbose event, which is another view of the same event). This value is the total time consumed by the storage engine. There are no events in the trace that explicitly define the time consumed by the formula engine, but you can calculate formula engine time by subtracting the total storage engine time from the query duration. To apply this calculation to the trace for Listing 4-2, the formula to compute formula engine time is 98 − (28 + 23) and the result is 47. The next step is to compute the ratios of formula engine time and storage engine time relative to query execution time. In this case, the formula engine ratio is 47/98 or 48% while the storage engine ratio is 51/98 or 52%. In this case, that means you should tune the storage engine for this query because it consumes the majority of the query execution time. However, a query that takes 98 milliseconds is not one that requires tuning, so the results of this example serves only to illustrate the process that you should follow when analyzing long-running queries in a production environment.

Determining the source of tabular model bottlenecks begins by computing storage engine time. To do this, sum the duration of the VertiPaq SE Query End events that have the VertiPaq Scan event subclass. Subtract this value from the duration listed for the Query End event to compute the formula engine time. As an example, when the two VertiPaq SE Query End events for the trace in Listing 4-3 total 36 milliseconds and the Query End duration value is 83 milliseconds, the storage engine time ratio to total query time is 43%. That leaves 47 milliseconds for formula engine time for which the ratio to total query time is 56%. In theory, the formula engine is the bottleneck for this query, but a query that runs in 83 milliseconds is not a candidate for optimization.

Monitor processing and query performance

To properly manage processing and query operations on an SSAS server, you must be familiar with other monitoring tools to capture the information necessary to diagnose performance issues. These monitoring tools include Windows Performance Monitor, dynamic management views (DMVs), and Windows Task Manager. You can also use SQL Server Profiler to capture trace events for processing operations.

Performance Monitor

By using Performance Monitors, you can gather information about server resources and measure the impact of processing and queries on these resources. One strategy is to establish a benchmark and periodically measure the processing time to determine if the time required is increasing and potentially exceeding the preferred processing window. Another strategy is to monitor performance counters while you troubleshoot a specific operation. You can take measurements before you start making changes and then take new measurements after you make incremental changes to assess the impact. Either way, you set the collection period for performance counters to a frequency of 15 seconds, so you can gather information without adding noticeable overhead to the server.

Specific performance counters to monitor are described in the "Resolve performance issues" section later in this chapter. Regardless of which counters you need to monitor, use the following steps to begin the collection process:

1. Open Windows Performance Monitor, click Performance Monitor, and click the Add button in the toolbar.

2. In the Add Counters dialog box, select the server to monitor in the Select Counters From Computer drop-down list (or use the Browse button to locate a server on your network), and then scroll through the Available Counters list to locate the set of counters to monitor. The sets for multidimensional- or tabular-mode servers begin with MSAS13 or MSOLAP$<instance name>. In this chapter, we use MSAS13 to refer to multidimensional counter and MSOLAP$TABULAR to refer to tabular counters.

3. Expand a counter set, select a specific counter, such as Memory Usage KB, and click the Add button. Continue adding counters as needed. When finished, click OK. You can then view real-time metrics for the selected counters.

> **NOTE CONFIGURATION OF COUNTER PROPERTIES**
>
> If you are monitoring multiple counters at the same time, right-click a counter and select Properties to change Color, Width, Style values to more easily distinguish between counters. You might also need to reset the scale for a counter.

When you need to monitor server resource consumption during the processing or querying of a tabular model, you should ensure you are testing a single database in isolation so that you can be sure you are capturing measurements for that database as accurately as possible. To isolate your database, perform the following steps:

1. Open SSMS, connect to the tabular instance, expand the Databases folder in preparation for processing. If your SSAS tabular-mode server hosts databases other than the example database, you should detach them to isolate the focus of monitoring to a single database. To do this, right-click the database to temporarily remove it, click Detach, and click OK.

2. When you complete your performance analysis, you can reactivate the databases by right-clicking the Databases folder and clicking Attach. In the Attach Database dialog box, click the ellipsis button and then navigate to the Data folder containing the database to attach. Select the database and click OK twice to make the database available for queries again.

Dynamic management views

You can execute DMVs in the MDX query window after connecting to the SSAS server. The following DMVs are more helpful for assessing the impact of processing operations rather than for troubleshooting queries:

- **$System.discover_object_activity** Use this DMV to see which objects are consuming the most CPU time during a processing operation by sorting the object_cpu_time_ms column in descending order.

- **$System.discover_object_memory_usage** Use this DMV to find the objects consuming the most memory after processing by sorting the object_memory_shrinkable column in descending order.

> *NOTE* **SSAS DMVS**
>
> See "Use Dynamic Management Views (DMVs) to Monitor Analysis Services" at *https://msdn.microsoft.com/en-us/library/hh230820.aspx* for more information about these and other DMVs.

Task Manager

The Performance tab of the Task Manager can provide clues that can help you quickly ascertain whether the formula engine or the storage engine is being used for a query or processing operation. This technique applies to both multidimensional- and tabular-mode servers. To use this approach, you should isolate your environment to a single user and the single query or processing operation that you are measuring.

Open the CPU graph and switch it to the view of logical processors if necessary. Then launch the operation to test and observe the activity of the processors. If all processors are active during the entire operation, the storage engine is in use. If only a single processor is active, your operation is using the formula engine.

Trace events for processing

The processing commands described in Skill 4.3 for a multidimensional model and in Chapter 2 for a tabular model allow you to manage the data refresh process at varying levels of granularity. In general, the processing architecture consists of a nested series of parent and child jobs. These jobs are established by the object hierarchy within the database, dependencies between objects, and the type of processing job.

Just as you can use SQL Server Profiler to capture trace events for queries, as described earlier in this chapter, you can also use it to capture the trace events for processing operations.

When tracing processing, include the following events in your trace:

- **CommandBegin**   SSAS receives the XMLA command to process an object. This event also applies to commands for data definition, backup, and restore operations.
- **CommandEnd**   SSAS completes the XMLA command.
- **Progress Report Begin**   SSAS begins one of processing operations identified in the event subclass. Although there is some overlap, the set of event subclasses for multidimensional processing is different from the set for tabular processing.
- **Progress Report End**   A processing operation ends.
- **Progress Report Error**   An error occurs during an operation.

> **NOTE**   **MORE INFORMATION ABOUT TRACING PROCESSING EVENTS**
>
> Bob Duffy has created tools for baselining processing events for both multidimensional and tabular models and describes how to analyze these events in his posts "Tool for baselining MOLAP Processing" at *http://blogs.prodata.ie/post/Tool-for-baselining-MOLAP-Processing.aspx* and "Baselining Tabular Model Processing with a trace file" at *http://blogs.prodata.ie/post/Baselining-Tabular-Model-Processing-with-a-trace-file.aspx.* These two posts also provide diagrams of the nested objects in the processing architecture.

Resolve performance issues

Analysis of trace events, query plans when available, and performance counters can collectively provide the clues you need to identify bottlenecks and proceed with taking action to resolve processing or performance issues. This section reviews some of the more common problems you can encounter, explains how to identify the root of the problem, and provides recommendations for next steps.

EXAM TIP

Although the exam does not test your knowledge of every possible approach to problem resolution, be prepared to identify an appropriate action for more commonly encountered problems.

Multidimensional performance issues

Server tuning efforts should start with optimizing query performance for a multidimensional-mode server, and then shift to processing optimization once queries are executing satisfactorily. As explained in the "Identify bottlenecks in SSAS queries," query bottlenecks can arise in either the formula engine or the storage engine. Tuning server memory and CPU utilization can be important tasks for both query and processing tuning as well. You   most likely will need to tune the relational layer to optimize processing.

> **NOTE   STORAGE ENGINE TUNING REQUIRES MODEL OPTIMIZATION**
>
> When your performance testing identifies the storage engine as a bottleneck for queries, there are specific design changes that you can make to the multidimensional model to reduce or eliminate bottlenecks. Refer to the "Optimize and manage model design" section for changes that you can make to improve storage engine performance.

MDX QUERY TUNING

If you find the source of a query bottleneck is the formula engine, you should use a process of elimination to isolate the problem to a specific calculation in your query and then try to restructure the MDX. If the problem calculation is not query-scoped, but defined in the cube, you can comment out all calculations in the MDX script (except the CALCULATE command) and add back each calculation independently until you find the problem.

The most common reason for a slow query is the use of cell-by-cell evaluation instead of bulk-mode evaluation. Try rewriting your calculations if you find any of the following MDX constructs in a slow query:

- **Set alias**   You can define a set in the WITH clause in a query and then reference it in an expression, such as using it as the first argument of a SUM function. Replace the set alias in the expression with the set expression.

- **Late binding in functions**   When you create an expression that applies a function to the CURRENTMEMBER function, the function cannot be evaluated efficiently and must be evaluated only in context of the current row or column. Functions for which this late binding behavior impacts query performance include LINKMEMBER, STRTOSET, STRTOMEMBER, and STRTOVALUE.

- **Analysis Services Stored Procedure**   A user-defined function in an Analysis Services Stored Procedure (ASSP) always evaluates in cell-by-cell mode. The only way to avoid this behavior is to remove the user-defined function from the query.

- **Cell-level security**   The application of rules defined in cell-level security (described in Chapter 3) forces SSAS to use cell-by-cell mode. If you must restrict users from viewing certain measures and cannot resolve query performance in another way, consider using separate cubes.

One way to validate a problem calculation is by using cell-by-cell evaluation to compute the ratio between two performance counters in the MSAS13:MDX set, Number Of Cell-By-Cell Evaluation Nodes, and Number Of Bulk-Mode Evaluation Nodes. If the ratio is a high value, focus on finding and rewriting the calculation that is failing to use bulk-mode.

CACHE WARMING

Sometimes the bottleneck on a multidimensional-mode server can be a combination of the formula engine and storage engine. When this occurs, the trace includes many Query Subcube events that individually do not consume much time. However, collectively the total of these events can be significant. This behavior is known as *IO thrashing*. When storage optimization techniques fail to significantly reduce the number of these Query Subcube events, you can warm the cache by populating it with the data that these subcube requests retrieve after a service restart and in advance of user queries. That way, the data can be retrieved in bulk instead of piecemeal and subsequent user queries can execute faster. Because the cache is periodically cleaned, you might need to schedule these queries to warm the cache from time to time.

MEMORY MANAGEMENT

When memory is scarce on the server, Analysis Services spills data to disk during the following types of operations:

- **Dimension processing**   Generally, dimension processing does not require much memory and is able to complete successfully. However, if you change the Processing Group property on a dimension from its default of ByAttribute to ByTable, as described in Skill 4.3, the memory requirements of dimension processing increase and can overwhelm available resources. Therefore, you should use the ByTable setting only if the dimension data fits in memory. Even if you keep the ByAttribute setting, the processing of a large dimension creates a collection of hash tables that collectively can exceed available memory.

- **Aggregation processing**   There are two server properties (which you can reconfigure only by changing values in the server's msmdsrv.ini file), AggregationMemoryLimitMin and AggregationMemoryLimitMax, that allocate memory explicitly for processing the aggregations of a single partition.

   The AggregationMemoryLimitMin sets the maximum amount of physical memory to allocate for building a partition's aggregations and indexes. The default is 80. Consider lowering this number to free up memory for processing other partitions.

   The AggregationMemoryLimitMax property sets the minimum physical memory to allocate for aggregations and indexes during partition processing. The default is 10 and applies to each partition that is processed in parallel. For example, if there are four concurrent jobs to process partitions, SSAS allocates forty percent of reserved memory to processing. If this allocation is insufficient, SSAS blocks some of the partitions from processing until memory is released. You can increase parallelism by decreasing this value.

   If the AggregationMemoryLimitMax value is too low, SSAS spills to disk to continue its processing operations. Therefore, your first option is to consider changing the configured limits. (Decreasing the AggregationMemoryLimitMax also allows you to potentially process more partitions in parallel.) Another option to prevent aggregation processing from spilling to disk is to design aggregations that are small enough to fit in memory. Yet another option is to reduce the number of partitions that process in parallel and to separate processing operations by using ProcessData and ProcessIndex operations as described in Skill 4.3. Last, you can increase memory limits for SSAS or add physical memory to the server.

- **ROLAP dimension attribute stores**   The choice to implement a ROLAP dimension typically results from the need to support drillthrough actions to return data from a degenerate dimension stored in a fact table configured as a ROLAP partition. In this case, the volume of data is often too large to hold in memory and there is little you can do to resolve this issue other than configure the TempDir property for SSAS to use a folder on the fastest possible disk.

The goal of managing memory on a multidimensional-mode server is to prevent its memory usage from reaching TotalMemoryLimit. As long as SSAS is not currently paging, you can extend its memory limits as the first step towards resolving memory-related performance issues. If the server is paging, add more RAM to the server if possible. Otherwise, consider decreasing memory limits.

In addition to reviewing the memory limits in the Analysis Services Server Properties dialog box, as described in Skill 4.1, "Plan and deploy SSAS," you can review the BufferMemoryLimit setting in the server's msmdsrv.ini file. This property has a default value of 60, which is usually adequate. It sets the percentage of physical memory allocated to fact data during partition processing. Consider raising this value if the measure group granularity is more summarized than the source data, such as when you design the measure group to store data by month, but the source fact table stores data by day. SSAS uses a single processing buffer to group data by month and then flushes this buffer to disk when the buffer is full. Therefore, a larger buffer reduces the frequency of flushing. If this value is too high, parallelism decreases.

Inadequate memory resource causes evictions from the data and calculation caches, which may require that subsequent queries be resolved from disk rather than cache, and may also resolve in memory paging. Normally, you should see a lot of Get Data From Cache events on an active server in production. The lack of these events can indicate that the server does not have enough memory available for caching.

> **NOTE   FORMULA FOR BEST MEMORY CONFIGURATION**
>
> The "Analysis Services Operations Guide" at *https://msdn.microsoft.com/en-us/library/ hh226085.aspx* includes a formula that allows you to combine data from performance counters and DMVs to compute appropriate LowMemoryLimit, TotalMemoryLimit, and HardMemoryLimit values for your environment.

CPU UTILIZATION

Most operations in SSAS multidimensional models are performed in parallel. To manage these operations, SSAS maintains a Query Thread Pool and a Process Thread Pool instead of creating and destroying threads for each operation. When SSAS receives a query or processing request, it requests threads from the respective pool and returns them back to the pool upon completion of the request.

Although formula engine is single-threaded, SSAS can execute multiple queries in parallel by using separate threads from the Query Thread Pool. Query threads are requested to calculate executions in serial fashion, but they must wait for the storage engine, and then are released once results are returned to the requesting client application. To determine if you should increase query thread parallelism, check the Query Pool Job Queue Length and Query Pool Idle Threads counters from the MSAS13:Threads set. If Query Pool Job Queue Length value is not zero and Query Pool Idle Threads is greater than 0, you can increase the Thread-Pool \ Query \ MaxThreads server property as long as long as the % Processor Time counter in the Processor set is not already approaching 100%. Changing this property does not help any individual query, but can benefit multiple simultaneous requests.

The storage engine is multi-threaded and can manage multiple operations with its thread pool. The key to tuning its threading behavior involves managing the Process Thread Pool to increase the number of threads available for the following types of operations:

- **Querying**   When the formula engine requests data from the storage engine, SSAS requests a thread from the Process Thread Pool which retrieves data from either the cache or disk, stores any data retrieved from disk in cache, and returns the data to the query thread.

- **Processing** During a ProcessData operation for a partition, SSAS uses three threads in parallel to retrieve data from the data source, perform a lookup to dimension stores to get dimension keys and then load the processing buffer with partition and dimension key data, and to write this buffer to disk when it is full.

To properly perform thread performance testing for processing operations and evaluate performance counter results, you should start by isolating processing operations to Process-Data. Consider thread tuning when you find the Processing Pool Job Queue Length is greater than 0 during ProcessData operations. If this condition is true, then use one of the following rules to determine the appropriate tuning action to take:

- **Processing Pool Idle Threads = 0** If this counter's value remains at 0 for long periods of time during processing, there are not enough threads available to SSAS. In this case, increase the SSAS ThreadPool \ Process \ MaxThreads property. The amount by which you increase this value depends on how much the CPU is under load during processing when this counter is 0. Increase the value and continue retesting until % Processor Time approaches 100%.

  As you increase the number of available threads for processing, be aware that fewer threads are available for query execution. Therefore, you should use this option when you plan to restrict the processing schedule to times during which few or no queries typically execute.

- **Processing Pool Idle Threads > 0** If this counter's value remains above 0 consistently during processing, there are too many idle threads. Start by decreasing the SSAS CoordinatorExecutionMode property from -4 to -8 and retesting.

> *NOTE* **COORDINATOREXECUTIONMODE PROPERTY**
>
> For an in-depth explanation of the CoordinatorExecutionMode property, refer to the "Analysis Services Operations Guide" at *https://msdn.microsoft.com/en-us/library/hh226085.aspx*.

To tune threads for indexing operations, you should monitor performance counters by isolating activities on the SSAS server to ProcessIndex. The SSAS CoordinatorBuildMax-Threads property (editable only in the server's Msmdsrv.ini file), which has a default value of 4, restricts the number of threads available to an individual aggregation processing job. If you increase this value, you might need to increase Thread Pool \ Process \ MaxThreads also. Increasing these values enables a higher degree of parallelism, but be sure to monitor the load on CPU and memory to ensure greater parallelism does not adversely impact the server in other ways.

To optimize partition processing, you should be using as close to 100% of CPU as possible. Try creating more partitions and processing them in parallel by using the Process Data operation. You can keep adding partitions until the Rows Read/Sec counter (in the MSAS13:Processing set) no longer increases. You can monitor the number of concurrently processing partitions by using the Current Partitions counter in the MSAS13: Proc Aggregations set.

Similarly, you can add more partitions to parallel execution of Process Index operations. Monitor the % Processor Total value while running the operation, and stop adding partitions when this value stops increasing. However, watch memory consumption to avoid paging.

MULTIDIMENSIONAL PROCESSING TUNING

The goal of tuning processing operations is two-fold. First, you need to minimize the overhead required to process in order to reduce the processing time required and the consumption of server resources. Second, you need to find ways to optimize the retrieval of data from the relational source.

With regard to dimension processing, the time required is dependent on the number of members for each attribute and the number of attribute relationships. To find the attributes requiring the most processing time, look for long duration values for the BuildIndex event subclass in a trace. Not only do these attributes impact processing time, they also add to the sizes of the dimension, the cube, and aggregation store, and thereby increase storage requirements. Therefore, if processing is taking too long, consider removing attributes that are not essential.

Optimizations for processing include removing bitmap indexes for high-cardinality attributes to reduce the storage space and processing time these attributes require. An example of a high-cardinality attribute is a telephone number for a customer. When a high-cardinality attribute such as this is not the primary subject of analysis, and is always included in a query with another a lower cardinality attribute that has been filtered, consider setting the AttributeHierarchyOptimizedState property for the attribute to NotOptimized. This setting eliminates the bitmap indexing for the attribute.

During processing operations, SSAS generates SQL queries to retrieve data from a specified data source. Although you cannot directly modify the structure of these queries, unless you use query binding for partitions as described in Skill 4.3, you can influence the efficiency of these queries.

Dimensions do not allow you to use query binding in the object definition. However, if you use a view in the relational source for a dimension, you can add query hints and apply other query hints to tune the underlying SQL. In addition, if a snowflake dimension uses tables from separate database, consolidate the data into a single table to eliminate the use of the slower OPENROWSET function in the processing query.

Consider partitioning the relational source for a fact table. You can then create multiple partitions for a measure group in the multidimensional model and map each measure group partition to a separate relational partition. An alternative is to create multiple measure group partitions per relational partition. For example, if the relational source is partitioned by year, you can create measure group partitions by year or by month. Either way, the processing operation to load the measure group partition is restricted to a subset of the source table and thereby performs faster than if executing against an entire relational table that has not been partitioned.

Next, if you are using a view in the relational source or a named query in the data source view, eliminate the use of joins wherever possible for both dimensions and fact tables and consider indexing the view. The query to the source should retrieve data from a single table. Use extract-transform-load (ETL) processes to denormalize data structures where possible.

Last, add indexes to the relational tables. (Indexing a dimension table is not generally necessary unless it contains millions of rows.) The type of index you add depends on the type of table to process, as shown in Table 4-2.

TABLE 4-2 Relational source indexing strategies

Table Type	Index type	column(s) To Index
Fact	Clustered index	Key column used to filter data extracted from source, typically a date dimension key
Dimension	Unique clustered index	Key attribute column
	Nonclustered index	High cardinality attribute column

> **NOTE** Relational source optimization
>
> You can find additional recommendations for further optimizing the relational source in the "Analysis Services Operations Guide," which you can download from *https://msdn. microsoft.com/en-us/library/hh226085.aspx.*

Tabular performance issues

Resolution of tabular performance depends on the information you gather using the monitoring tools described earlier in this chapter. To improve query performance, analysis of DAX query plans helps you identify the query tuning opportunities. For tuning processing operations, trace events are helpful when you want to reduce processing time while performance counters are helpful for determining whether you need to tune the server's usage of memory or CPU resources.

DAX QUERY TUNING

In general, the goal of optimizing DAX queries is to reduce the time required by the formula engine, which is the opposite of the optimization of MDX queries. By analyzing trace events as described in the "Identify bottlenecks in SSAS queries," your first step is to determine whether the storage engine or the formula engine is the contributing factor to slow query performance.

The first place to check when searching for the cause of the bottleneck in the storage is the pseudo-SQL for the VertiPaq SE Query Begin or End events. The pseudo-SQL is not the actual code that executes, but a representation of the method used by the formula engine to query the data in memory. Review this code for any of the following more common problems in DAX queries:

- **Call back to formula engine** This condition is identifiable when you see the CallBack-DataID function in the pseudo-SQL of a VertiPaq SE Query Begin event like this:

```
WITH
  $Expr0 := [CallbackDataID(IF ( 'Sale'[Total Sales]] > 100,
  'Sale'[Total Sales]])]] . . .
```

This call appears at the beginning of one of several Vertipaq scans generated when executing the query shown in Listing 4-4. The use of CallBackDataID is not as efficient as filter predicates that use the WHERE clause or scans without filters because the work is pushed back to the single-threaded formula engine. Furthermore, the presence of the callback prevents caching of intermediate results in the VertiPaq cache. A successful rewrite of this query to remove the IF function and add a FILTER function produces a pseudo-SQL statement that no longer includes the CallBackDataID and instead uses a WHERE clause to define a simple predicate.

LISTING 4-4 Inefficient DAX query generating CallBackDataID

```
EVALUATE
SUMMARIZE (
    'Sale',
    'Date'[Calendar Year],
    "Total Sales", CALCULATE (
        SUMX (
            'Sale',
            IF ( 'Sale'[Total Sales] > 100, 'Sale'[Total Sales] )
        )
    )
)
```

- **Materialization** When a query requires intermediate steps that are *spooled*, or stored in memory, for further calculation by the formula engine, the spooled data is not compressed and can consume a significant amount of memory greater than the size of the model. You can see this occur when the physical plan contains a Spool_Iterator operator with a high record count. Materialization is also recognizable when you see an Apply operator with multiple subordinate VertipaqResult operators. You can find an in-depth explanation of materialization and recommendations for resolution in "The VertiPaq Engine" at *https://www.microsoftpressstore.com/articles/article.aspx?p=2449192&seqNum=6.*

  You can also see a spike in memory consumption when materialization occurs. This is the only time that a query puts pressure on server memory.

- **Too many VertiPaq queries** Individually, a VertiPaq query can have a short duration measured in milliseconds, but hundreds of VertiPaq queries can require many seconds to complete. In this situation, you should try rewriting the query and review the new query plan. Changes to try include moving filters to an outer group of a nested calculation or replacing the FILTER function with CALCULATE or CALCULATETABLE.

When evaluating formula engine bottlenecks, study the DAX Query Plan for the following clues:

- **VertipaqResult sending high record count to next operator**   When you see VertipaqResult below an operator with a high value for its #Records property, you should try rearranging filters in the query to reduce the number of records returned by VertipaqResult. If the query has no filter, consider adding one;.

- **Slow or complex calculations**   Some DAX functions such as EARLIEST or SUMX have a greater performance impact than other functions, which can be unavoidable. However, the ideal is to rewrite a query to take advantage of the storage engine's ability to group, join tables, filter, and apply aggregations. On the other hand, operations that sort or find the top N cannot take advantage of the storage engine. In these cases, try to minimize the size of the row set on which operations must be performed by filtering at the earliest opportunity.

As another step in your query tuning efforts, you should review the code and apply the following best practices where applicable:

- Avoid the use of ISERROR and IFERROR functions because they force cell-by-cell mode.

- If you need to test for one row before returning a value, do not use COUNTROWS because it requires multiple scans. Instead use HASONEVALUE or HASONEFILTER.

- For complex calculations, use ADDCOLUMNS instead of SUMMARIZE in most cases, unless the SUMMARIZE includes the ROLLUP syntax or the use of ADDCOLUMNS would require multiple filters to achieve the same result.

- Use ISEMPTY instead of ISBLANK because it does not require evaluation of the measure and thereby executes faster.

EXAM TIP

You can find additional examples of problematic DAX constructs and a review of calculation best practices in the "Performance Tuning of Tabular Models in SQL Server 2012 Analysis Services," which you can download from *https://msdn.microsoft.com/en-us/ library/dn393915.aspx*. A good exercise to test your DAX query-writing and query plan evaluation skills is to recreate queries in the whitepaper by using the 70-768-Ch2 database and observe the effects of rewriting queries based on the recommendations.

TUNING TO REDUCE TABULAR PROCESSING TIME

Before you start experimenting with changing your processing methods, you should first take steps to optimize the tabular model as described in the "Optimize and manage model design" section. Then retest processing operations on the optimized model.

With any of the considerations for tuning tabular processing, you should first break out processing operations by Process Data and Process Recalc, because they perform different tasks and consume resources differently. To monitor the amount of time required by each of these operations, set up a Profiler trace, look at the duration of Progress Report End events, and focus on the events with the longest duration. These events also identify the object or calculated column.

When you determine that the Process Data operation is the source of the processing bottleneck, you can tune processing by dividing a slow-processing table into multiple partitions and then using one of the following techniques:

- Process multiple partitions as a group. SQL Server 2016 processes them in parallel by default.
- Process only partitions with current or changed data rather than all partitions by using the Process Data operation in serial fashion if necessary and then perform one Process Recalc.
- For even faster processing, use Process Add instead of Process Data.

When the Process Recalc operation is taking too long, determine if the high-duration processing is related to specific calculated columns. If so, can you perform the same calculation in the relational source by adding it as a derived column in a view or populating a column during ETL with the required values? Or can you optimize the DAX calculation?

Another way to resolve Process Recalc issues for long-running operations is to process a smaller group of objects and reduce parallelism by adding the MaxParallelism property to the operation as described at *https://msdn.microsoft.com/en-us/library/mt697587.aspx*.

TUNING TO REDUCE TABULAR PROCESSING MEMORY CONSUMPTION

Your first step is to determine whether Process Data or Process Recalc is creating memory pressure by using the Memory Usage KB counter in the MSOLAP$TABULAR:Memory set. Normally, you should see the memory increase incrementally until it reaches the TotalMemoryLImit value set for the tabular instance. It should then gradually release memory as processing ends.

If the Process Data operation is using too much memory, try the following options:

- Break up object processing into multiple transactions.
- Reduce parallelism by using the MaxParallelism property.
- Process each object in separate transactions.

Monitor the Page Writes/Sec counter in the Memory set during processing to determine if the Process Data operation is paging for an extended period of time. If considerable paging is occurring, perform any of the following steps to resolve or reduce this problem:

- Add memory to the server.
- Remove other applications or stop unnecessary services to free more memory for SSAS.

- Place the pagefile.sys file on the fastest available disk.

- Adjust the SSAS memory limits.

- Reduce or lower parallelism by using more transactions or setting a low value for the MaxParallelism property.

- Optimize the tabular model by removing or optimizing high-cardinality columns.

If the Process Recalc operation is using too much memory, try either of the following options:

- Use a low value for MaxParellelism to reduce parallelism.

- Remove or optimize calculated columns in the model.

OPTIMIZE CPU UTILIZATION DURING TABULAR PROCESSING

You can use thread-related performance counters to assess whether you can increase the server property ThreadPool \ Process \ MaxThreads to provide more threads to processing operations. Check the Processing Pool Job Queue Length and Processing Pool Idle Non-I/O Threads counters in the MSOLAP$TABULAR:Threads set. If Processing Pool Job Queue Length is greater than zero and Processing Pool Idle Non-I/O Threads is zero, there are not enough threads available to service the requests. If that is the case, keep increasing MaxThreads while monitoring these counters until Processing Pool Idle Non-I/O Threads is no longer zero.

> *NOTE* **OPTIMIZATION OF TABULAR PROCESSING OPERATIONS**
>
> Refer to the "Performance Tuning of Tabular Models in SQL Server 2012 Analysis Services" at *https://msdn.microsoft.com/en-us/library/dn393915.aspx* for more advanced tuning options. These additional tuning techniques are not on the exam, but can help you solve more complex performance issues in your environment.

Configure usability limits

Besides tuning queries or configuring server properties to manage query performance, you can configure usability limits to control the user experience. In a multidimensional model, you should consider the behavior of the client application and the impact on the server when users browse a dimension with thousands of members. For both multidimensional and tabular models, consider implementing usability limits when users invoke drillthrough to view details for a specific cell value.

Attribute Member Groups

A good way to help users browse a multidimensional dimension that contains thousands of members is to create a hierarchy which groups these members into several levels such that the number of children on any given level is manageable within the user interface of the client application generating the query. If the data does not lend itself well to meaningful groupings, consider creating alphabetical groups. You can add a column to the dimension source (either by using a view in the dimension table or adding a named query or named calculation to the model's Data Source View) that uses an expression such as LEFT("table"."name", 1) to create a group, and then create an attribute in the model's dimension that uses this new column as its KeyColumn property. Then add this attribute as a parent level in a hierarchy for the attribute level containing all members.

> **NOTE DISCRETIZATION PROPERTIES**
>
> Another option is to use the DiscretizationMethod and DiscretizationBucketCount properties to create artificial groupings, although you have less control over the groupings when you use this approach. See "Group Attribute Members (Discretization)" at *https://msdn.microsoft.com/en-us/library/ms174810.aspx* for implementation details and limitations.

Drillthrough limits

With regard to managing drillthrough limits, you can configure the OLAP \ Query \ Default-DrillthroughMaxRows property for the SSAS server to restrict the number of rows returned when the user performs a drillthrough operation on a cell. If the client application is Excel, the connection properties sets a default limit of 1,000 rows on drillthrough operations. For other client applications, you can usually specify a limit by including the MAXROWS argument in the DRILLTHROUGH clause as described in the documentation at *https://msdn.microsoft.com/en-us/library/ms145964.aspx*.

Optimize and manage model design

As described earlier in this chapter, there are many factors that can contribute to slow queries or processing. To the extent possible, you should consider ways that you can optimize a model prior to releasing it into production. However, over time, new query patterns emerge and data volumes increase as a natural evolution of the model in your environment. You should then use the results of performance monitoring tests to decide which aspects of your multidimensional or tabular model require optimization.

> **EXAM TIP**
>
> You should be familiar with best practices in model design that optimize performance and understand how implementation of a design influences performance.

Multidimensional model optimization

In general, the goal of query optimization for multidimensional models is to reduce the amount of time spent by the storage engine. When performance analysis reveals the storage engine as a bottleneck, you should review the structure of dimensions, aggregations, and partitions for optimization opportunities.

DIMENSION OPTIMIZATION

The two aspects of a dimension design to optimize for better performing queries are attribute relationships and user-defined hierarchies. The steps required to create these objects are described in Chapter 1.

If you do nothing to adjust the attribute relationships after creating a dimension (unless it is a snowflake dimension with multiple tables), all attributes are related to the key attribute. In the attribute relationship diagram, you see the key attribute on the left side of the diagram and separate arrows connecting it to each of the other attributes. When the data model supports a many-to-one relationship between separate attributes, such as Sales Territory to Country or Subregion to Region in the City dimension, you should explicitly define the attribute relationship so that Country and Region no longer directly relate to the key attribute, City.

SSAS uses these relationships to build indexes so that the cross product between Sales Territory and Country members (such as Far West and United States, to name one pair) can be retrieved from the indexes without reading the key attributes. Without the relationship, a query on a large dimension is slower. Furthermore, when you design aggregations for the model, any aggregations created for Sales Territory can be used for queries requesting Country.

Queries are also optimized when you create a user-defined hierarchy for a natural hierarchy (defined in Chapter 1). SSAS materializes the hierarchy on disk to facilitate navigation and retrieve related members faster. For maximum benefit, be sure to create cascading attribute relationships for the attributes in the hierarchy. Note that unnatural hierarchies are not materialized on disk. Even without any performance, unnatural hierarchies are helpful for users who want to view specific combinations of members.

Establishing a user-defined hierarchy is also beneficial as a preparatory step for aggregation design. Without aggregations, queries that include a non-key attribute must compute measure values by retrieving the detail rows in the measure group (from the cube storage, not the relational fact table if you are using MOLAP storage) and applying the aggregate function defined for each measure to compute a tuple value at query time. On the other hand, with aggregations, these computed tuple values are calculated during processing and stored on disk so that SSAS can resolve queries faster. As an example, if aggregations exist for the Calendar Year level of a hierarchy and a query requests sales by year, the SSAS storage engine can retrieve four rows from the aggregation store rather than computing four rows from thousands of detail rows in the Wide World Importers DW cube.

> **NOTE   DIMENSION OPTIMIZATION**
>
> You can find additional recommendations for optimizing dimensions in the Analysis Services MOLAP Performance Guide, available at *https://msdn.microsoft.com/en-us/library/dn749781.aspx*.

AGGREGATIONS

As explained in the "Multidimensional query monitoring" section, the first place the storage engine looks for data requested by the formula engine is the cache, and then it searches the aggregations stored on disk when the requested data is not already in cache. Although the structure is different, the storage of aggregations in SSAS is analogous to the use of summary tables in a relational database. Aggregations are precalculated when you perform a Process Full or Process Index operation as described in Skill 4.3.

The addition of aggregations to your multidimensional model is a balancing act. You need to have enough aggregations to speed up queries while completing the processing operations within the required window and providing the disk space required for aggregation storage. Too many aggregations can have an adverse effect on both processing and query performance. A best practice is to limit aggregation storage to 30 percent of the space required to store a measure group.

SSAS does not create aggregations by default. You must design aggregations and then perform a processing operation to load the aggregation store based on the design. However, it is difficult to anticipate which aggregations are most useful until you monitor query patterns. One strategy is to use the Aggregation Design Wizard in the cube designer as part of your initial deployment to production. The Aggregation Design Wizard helps you build aggregations by using an algorithm that evaluates members on each level of a hierarchy relative to the size of the measure group table (or partition, if you create multiple partitions with separate aggregation designs). If a query happens to hit an aggregation, query performance is better than it would be without the aggregation.

You can add an aggregation design to Sale measure group in the 70-768-Ch1 project by following these steps:

1. In SSDT, open the cube designer for the Wide World Importers DW cube and click the Aggregations tab.

2. In the cube designer toolbar, click Design Aggregations to launch the Aggregation Design Wizard, and then click Next.

3. On the Review Aggregation Usage page, keep the defaults for now. After you have a better understanding of how aggregation design works, you can configure the Aggregation Usage property for attributes on the Cube Structure page of the cube designer.

   In general, these settings are used by the Aggregation Design Wizard to determine which attributes it should consider for aggregation by following these rules:

   ■ Full   Requires SSAS to include the attribute in every aggregation or an attribute from a lower level in a hierarchy. As an example, if you set Calendar Year to Full, SSAS can create aggregations that include Calendar Year or Calendar Month. Set this value for a limited number of attributes, if any.

   ■ None   Requires SSAS to exclude this attribute from all aggregations. Set this value for infrequently used attributes.

- Unrestricted   Allows SSAS to decide whether to include or exclude the attribute. Set this value manually for 5 to 10 of the most commonly used attributes.

- Default   Applies a default rule based on the characteristics of the attribute, as shown in Table 4-3.

TABLE 4-3 Default rules for aggregation usage

Aggregation Usage	Attribute type	Comment
Unrestricted	Granularity attribute of measure group	Often the key attribute
Unrestricted	Attributes in a natural hierarchy	Cascading attribute relationships must exist, attribute must be aggregatable
Full	Non-aggregatable attribute	May or may not be in a natural hierarchy
None	Attributes in the following dimension types: Many-to-many Non-materialized reference dimensions Data mining dimensions	Does not apply to parent-child dimensions
None	All other types of attributes	

You can override the defaults or even the Aggregation Usage properties any time that you use the wizard. The purpose of defining the Aggregation Usage properties in advance is to store the preferred property value to save you time each time you use the wizard.

4. Click Next, and then click Count on the Specify Object Counts page of the wizard. The wizard counts rows in the measure group (or partition) and members in attributes so that it can assess mathematically which attributes benefit most from aggregations. Attributes with a lower count as compared to the measure group count are in this category. You can manually override counts if you currently have only a subset of data in the model.

5. Click Next. Although there are many choices for determining how the wizard should optimize aggregations on the Set Aggregation Options page, best practice is to select the Performance Gain Reaches option and keep the default of 30. Click Start to compute the aggregation design.

6. When the aggregation design is complete, click Next.

7. On the Completing The Wizard page, type a name for the design, **SaleAggregations**, select the Deploy And Process Now option, and click Finish.

You can use a profiler trace to determine which aggregates are useful for queries so that you can be sure to retain those aggregations as you fine-tune the design over time. These aggregate hits are identifiable by the Get Data From Aggregation event. You can also use a profiler trace to identify queries that can benefit from the addition of an aggregation. In that case, look for the granularity of requests in the Query Subcube Verbose event and use this information to manually create an aggregation as described in at "Improve SQL Server Analysis

Services MDX Query Performance with Custom Aggregations" at *https://www.mssqltips.com/ sqlservertip/4432/improve-sql-server-analysis-services-mdx-query-performance-with-custom- aggregations/.*

Another way to design aggregations that are tuned to actual query patterns is to run the Usage-Based Optimization Wizard. Before you can use this wizard, you must ensure the query log is enabled (which it is by default). The wizard analyzes the queries captured in the log and then designs aggregations to improve query performance for the targeted queries. You can add the new aggregation design to the existing design or replace the existing design.

PARTITIONS

Rather than use the default structure of one partition per measure group, the use of multiple partitions in a measure group can be beneficial for both processing and query performance. See Skill 4.3 for more information about creating and processing measure group partitions.

One reason for faster query performance is the partition elimination SSAS performs when multiple partitions exist. That is, if a partition does not contain the data requested by the query, SSAS does not read the partition. Another reason is the ability for the storage engine to use separate threads in parallel to scan each partition. Thus, the combination of a smaller amount of overall space to scan and the ability to scan that reduced space in parallel, results in faster queries on partitioned data.

Furthermore, you can design different aggregation levels for each partition, which can increase the amount of extra storage required on disk, but the improvement in query speed can be a reasonable trade-off. As an example, you might design a higher level of aggregation for frequently-queried current data, but design fewer aggregations for less-frequently queried historical data.

You can also optimize storage for each partition. As described in Skill 4.3, you can specify by partition whether it is stored in MOLAP, HOLAP, or ROLAP mode, which determines whether data is restructured and moved from its relational source or kept in the source. In addition to specifying storage mode by partition, you can also place each partition on separate drives or even on separate servers to distribute disk IO operations.

Processing operations can also run faster. First, you can design partitions to separate historical and current data. Historical data is typically unchanging, which means you can process it once and leave it alone. Afterwards, you can then restrict processing to a smaller partition of current data, which is much faster than processing both types of data in a single operation. Second, even if you must process multiple partitions, you can process them in parallel which typically is a faster operation than processing partitions serially or processing a single large partition, assuming the server has adequate resources as discussed in previous sections of this chapter.

There is no requirement to design partitions symmetrically. As an example, you can create twelve partitions for each month in the current year, one partition for all twelve months in the previous year, and another partition for the five years preceding the previous year. Another benefit of this approach is the ability to maintain a moving window of data. You can easily drop off older data and add in new data without disrupting the data that you want to keep in the multidimensional model.

> **NOTE   PARTITION STRATEGY**
>
> The Analysis Services MOLAP Performance Guide, available at *https://msdn.microsoft.com/en-us/library/dn749781.aspx*, describes common design patterns for partitioning.

Tabular model optimization

The key to tabular model optimization for both queries and processing is the reduction of its memory footprint. The amount of memory required to process and store the tabular model in memory is directly related to the size of the tables and dictionaries for each column. The higher the cardinality of a column and, to a lesser extent, the larger the data type, the more memory is required. To reduce the memory footprint of your model, work through the following recommendations:

- Remove columns that are not required for analysis or calculations.
- Remove rows that are not required for analysis, such as rows for time periods in the past that no longer contribute helpful insight for analysis of more recent time periods.
- Reduce cardinality by making any of the following changes:
    - Eliminate key columns from fact tables
    - Use ETL to consolidate snowflaked dimensions, lookup tables, and junk dimensions.
    - Split a date/time column into separate date and time columns (or even eliminate the time column if it is not required for analysis).
- Eliminate calculated columns in large tables because no compression is applied to them.
- If using a numeric column with decimal places, change the data type for the column in the data model to Currency unless you need to store more than four decimal places. You can still use the Decimal Number format so that values are not displayed as currency.

> **NOTE   FOCUS ON HIGH-MEMORY MODEL OBJECTS**
>
> Remember that you can use the $System.discover_object_memory_usage DMV to analyze memory usage by object. Typically, the largest objects have high-cardinality columns.

Processing operations also benefit from these changes to the model. Monitor the Rows Read/Sec in the MSOLAP$TABULAR – Processing set to determine if processing can benefit from additional changes. . If this value is 80,000, try making the following changes to the tabular model design:

- Denormalize tables by eliminating joins to create a standard star schema structure.

- When the relational source is partitioned, create matching partitions in the model partitions and ensure a one-to-one mapping between the relational and model partitions.

- Tune the relational query. In tabular model partition definitions, you can use ORDER BY, CTEs, and stored procedures. The query is not modified by SSAS during processing.

Skill 4.3: Configure and manage processing

The configuration and management of processing in a multidimensional model is much different from processing in a tabular model. This section explains configuration options and decision points for processing objects in a multidimensional model only. The configuration of options and management of processing for a tabular model are described in Chapter 2.

This section covers how to:
- Configure partition processing
- Configure dimension processing
- Use Process Default, Process Full, Process Clear, Process Data, Process Add, Process Update, Process Index, Process Structure, and Process Clear Structure processing methods
- Configure Parallel, Sequential, and Writeback processing settings

Configure partition processing

As explained in Skill 4.2, the implementation of partitions is a useful strategy for improving query or processing performance or both for a multidimensional model. When you add a measure group to a multidimensional model, a single partition is created. You can add a new partition to a partition either by using the cube designer during the development cycle or by executing an XMLA script to define and add a partition to a model in production. After defining one or more partitions, you can then configure processing options for each partition separately. Partition processing includes several steps: loading data into a partition structure, building indexes, and building the aggregations as defined by the aggregation design assigned to the partition.

Partition Wizard

An easy way to add a partition to a cube before you deploy it into production is to use the Partition Wizard. You can find details about using this wizard at *https://msdn.microsoft.com/en-us/ library/ms179981.aspx*. If you plan to define multiple partitions in a cube, you must first remove the definition of the initial partition and then add new partitions by following these steps:

1. In SQL Server Data Tools for Visual Studio 2015 (SSDT), open the 70-768-Ch1 project from the File menu, and then double-click Wide World Importers DW.cube to open its cube designer.

2. On the Partitions page of the cube designer, right-click the Sale partition, and click Delete to remove the partition from the cube.

   When a cube contains multiple measure groups, the cube designer shows only the partitions for the first measure group initially. You can expand the other measure groups by double-clicking a measure group's name and thereby view its partitions.

3. Click the New Partition link.

4. In the Partition Wizard, click Next, select the Sale check box in the Available Tables list, and then click Next.

   In this example, there is only one fact table to use as a source for partitions in the Sale measure group. If you maintain separate fact tables for different segments of data in the relational source, such as one fact table per year, you can choose a specific table that SSAS binds to the partition.

   There is no way to filter out data from a fact table when using the table-binding method. The partition receives all the data in the table. Bear in mind that if your fact table structure changes, you must manually update each partition definition to correspond. One way to insulate yourself from this problem is to bind partitions to views instead of tables.

5. If you want to keep the current table-binding setting for the partition, click Next on the Restrict Rows page of the Partition Wizard to continue to the next configuration step.

   In lieu of table-binding a partition, you can define query-binding. To do this, select the Specify A Query To Restrict Rows check box and then modify the default query by appending a filter condition to the WHERE clause, **[Invoice Date Key] <= '2015-12-31'**, and click Next.

NOTE **QUERY BINDING**

Although the usual practice is to append a filter condition to the SELECT statement when you implement query binding, you can rewrite the query in other ways to improve relational performance if you like. Remember, the query for each partition must return the same columns and no two partitions overlap. Each WHERE clause should ensure the query returns a unique set of rows. SSAS does not for duplicate rows across partitions. Therefore, if you advertently create overlapping partitions, the data in the cube will be wrong.

Also, query binding breaks the measure group's relationship to the data source view. Consequently, if you make changes to the data source view later, those changes do not update the partition query. For this reason, configuring partitions with query binding should be one of the last development steps you perform.

---

6. On the Processing and Storage Locations page of the wizard, you choose where SSAS performs processing of the partition and where the process data is stored. The default processing location is the default SSAS server and the default storage location is the Data folder for the server instance.

   For information about configuring and using a remote partition, see *https://msdn. microsoft.com/en-us/library/ms174751.aspx.*

7. Click Next to proceed to the Completing The Wizard page. On this page, you have the following aggregation options that execute after you click Finish on this page:

   ■ Design Aggregation Options For The Partition Now

   ■ Design Aggregations Later

   ■ Copy The Aggregation Design From An Existing Partition (copy from)

   If you choose either of the latter two options, the Deploy And Process Now check box is active.

   For this example, select the Design Aggregations Later option and click Finish.

8. Repeat the preceding steps to create another partition by using the same settings with the exception of using the following condition in the WHERE clause:

   ```
   [Invoice Date Key] >= '2016-01-01'
   ```

Partition storage

Configuring the storage for a partition is not simply a designation of MOLAP, HOLAP, or ROLAP, the storage modes described in Chapter 1, but also a specification of how the partition responds to changes in the relational source, if at all. When you build a star schema to use as a source for the multidimensional model, a common approach is to schedule processing immediately after the ETL process successfully completes. You can instead implement proactive caching, a feature in SSAS to trigger processing based on rules that you define, or use ROLAP storage instead which requires processing only when the partition is initially deployed.

To define partition storage, open the Partitions page of the cube designer, select the partition row in the list below the Sale measure group, and click the Storage Settings link to display the following storage options:

■ **MOLAP**   Stores detail data and aggregations in a multidimensional format. Data is refreshed only when you perform processing manually or on a scheduled basis. It is suitable when queries must be fast and access to real-time data is not required.

■ **Scheduled MOLAP**   Stores detail data and aggregations in multidimensional format. Data is refreshed every 24 hours, although you have no control over the schedule.

■ **Automatic MOLAP**   It stores detail data and aggregations in multidimensional format. As one form of proactive caching, data is refreshed automatically when the server detects changes to the source data. It waits for 10 seconds for activity in the source to end before beginning processing, but proceeds after 10 minutes if activity does not end. During processing, queries retrieve data from the existing database. This setting is useful when you do not want to maintain a separate processing infrastructure by using SSIS or scheduled SQL Server agent job.

- **Medium-latency MOLAP**   This stores detail data and aggregations in multidimensional format. It functions like Automatic MOLAP in that it refreshes data automatically after receiving notification of a data change in the relational source. It differs with regard to data latency. If the data in the existing MOLAP partition from which queries are answered is older than 4 hours, the partition switches to ROLAP mode and answers queries directly from the relational source until processing completes. Queries are slower until the new MOLAP partition is available.

- **Low-latency MOLAP**   It stores detail data and aggregations in multidimensional format. It is similar to medium-latency MOLAP except that the data latency is 30 minutes.

- **Real-time HOLAP**   This stores only aggregations in multidimensional format and keeps detail data in the relational source. Aggregations are updated when SSAS receives notification of a data change. During aggregation processing, queries that would normally be resolved by using aggregations switch to ROLAP queries until processing is complete.

- **Real-time ROLAP**   It keeps detail data and stores aggregations in the relational source. Use this storage mode when the source data changes frequently and queries require current data.

- **Custom setting**   You can modify the storage mode definition to establish a specific combination of silence interval, silence interval override, and data latency interval.

EXAM TIP

Be prepared to understand which storage modes are appropriate for a specific scenario as the exam is likely to test your knowledge of this topic. Review the guidelines in "Set Partition Storage (Analysis Services-Multidimensional) at *https://msdn.microsoft.com/en-us/library/ms175646.aspx.* **Also, see "Proactive Caching (Partitions)" at** *https://technet.microsoft.com/en-us/library/ms174769.aspx.*

Partition aggregations

If the cube already includes aggregation designs, you can apply an existing aggregation to a new partition by opening the Aggregations page of the cube designer, clicking a measure group in the Standard View, and then clicking the Assign Aggregation Design in the cube designer toolbar. In the Assign Aggregation Design dialog box, select a design in the Aggregation Designs drop-down list and then select the check box for each partition to which you want to assign the aggregation.

Additional partition properties

When you select a partition on the Partitions page of the cube designer, you can view several properties associated with that partition. In particular, the following properties affect processing:

- **ErrorConfiguration**   Ideally, you find and resolve errors in the data during the extract-transform-load (ETL) process when you use a star schema as a data source as described in Chapter 1. At the partition level, this setting is set to Default. If you keep this setting, any error during processing causes the operation to fail. You can change this behavior to ignore the error and continue, ignore a specified number of errors before failing, or log the error and continue. Furthermore, if you ignore the error, you can exclude the row causing the error from the partition or you can include it and assign the row to the unknown member for each dimension to which the row cannot be matched. (Unknown members are explained in Chapter 1.)

    Although you can configure error configuration when you start a processing operation, you can avoid the need to do so each time if you define the ErrorConfiguration property on the partition object.

EXAM TIP

Be sure to understand your options for configuring error handling. For more information on this topic, review "Error Configuration for Cube, Partition, and Dimension Processing (SSAS – Multidimensional)" at *https://msdn.microsoft.com/en-us/library/ms180058.aspx*.

- **ProcessingMode**   The default value for this property is Regular, which means that the partition cannot be read by a storage engine thread in response to a query when you perform a Process Full operation on it until the operation is complete. As explained later in the "Use Process Default, Process Full, Process Clear, Process Data, Process Add, Process Update, Process Index, Process Structure, and Process Clear Structure processing methods" section of this chapter, the Process Full operation is a combination of two operations, Process Data and Process Index.

    If you change the ProcessingMode to Lazy Aggregations, the partition is available for querying as soon as the Process Data operation is complete. The Process Index operation runs in the background if enough resources are available. During this time, queries to the partition run more slowly than they would if aggregations existed, but frequently-run queries result in cached data which has no dependency on aggregations. Therefore, the performance impact of lazy aggregations takes a greater toll on less-frequently queried data. The negative aspects of using this option include the lack of control over when the aggregations are built and the inability to synchronize a database until this operation is complete.

- **ProcessingPriority**   This property defines the priority of building the current partition relative to other partitions when ProcessingMode is set to Lazy Aggregations.

- **Slice** When SSAS processes a MOLAP partition, it identifies the minimum and maximum range of values for each attribute associated with the fact data and stores this information as metadata that it uses for partition elimination during query operations. However, you should manually define the slice for ROLAP and proactive caching partitions. Manual definition of the slice is also recommended for MOLAP partitions when a measure group contains asymmetrical partitions, such as one partition with one year of data and another partition with multiple years of data. For examples, see "Set the Partition Slice Property (Analysis Services)" at *https://msdn.microsoft.com/en-us/library/ms174764.aspx*.

Writeback partition

In most cases, a multidimensional model is read-only. However, there are scenarios for which storing user input in the multidimensional model is beneficial, particularly budgeting and forecasting in financial models. This feature is known as *writeback* and requires the use of a client application that supports writeback, such as Excel. In the model, you can write-enable a partition only when its measure group contains measures that use the Sum aggregate function. You can secure the model to control which users have read-write access to restrict writeback capability to a limited group.

When you enable a writeback partition, which you can do by right-clicking the partition on the Partitions page of the cube designer and clicking Writeback Settings, you specify the name of the table in which to store user input and select either MOLAP or ROLAP as its storage mode. When a client application captures user input, SSAS stores this input in the specified table and does not add it to the relational source on which the partition is based. As queries retrieve data from the partition, the results from both the partition and the writeback table are merged together.

> **NOTE WRITEBACK PARTITIONS**
>
> If you configure writeback or ROLAP processing as described in Chapter 4, "Configure and maintain SQL Server Analysis Services (SSAS)," the account you use must also have write permission.
>
> You can find more information about implementing writeback partitions in "Set Partition Writeback" at *https://msdn.microsoft.com/en-us/library/ms174823.aspx* and "Write-Enabled Partitions" at *https://msdn.microsoft.com/en-us/library/ms174750.aspx*.

Partition processing configuration

You can launch partition processing in SSDT or SSMS by using the Process Partition dialog box. In the dialog box, you can select one of the following processing methods: Process Default, Process Full, Process Data, or Process Clear. You can also override error configuration and define batch settings. The processing methods and other configuration settings are described in the last two section of Skill 4.3.

In SSMS, you can generate an XMLA script based on the selections you make in the dialog box. A benefit of using an XMLA script is the ability to group a specific set of partitions to process into a single parallel processing operation or control sequencing of serial processing.

> **NOTE XMLA FOR PARTITION PROCESSING**
>
> See "Processing Objects (XMLA)" at *https://msdn.microsoft.com/en-us/library/ms187199.aspx* and "Performing Batch Operations (XMLA)" at *https://msdn.microsoft.com/en-us/library/ms186680.aspx* for more details on using XMLA for processing operations.

Configure dimension processing

The goal of dimension processing is to retrieve data from a relational source, load the data into a dimension object, and then build indexes on it. Dimension processing is affected by the configuration of specific properties in the dimension definition described in this section.

ProcessingGroup property

By default, the ProcessingGroup property for a dimension is set to ByAttribute. As a result of this setting, processing operations for a dimension generate a series of SELECT DISTINCT statements to the relational source. When a dimension table is small, these statements execute relatively quickly.

When you want to minimize the impact of multiple statements on the relational source, you can change the ProcessingGroup property to ByTable. This setting causes SSAS to generate a single SELECT statement to retrieve data for all attributes at one time. However, because the values in an attribute that is not the key attribute are no longer unique, you must set the KeyDuplicate property in the error configuration to IgnoreError when you use this option. Consequently, you should take extra care to ensure the dimension data is clean as part of the ETL process.

Proactive caching

The ProactiveCaching property is another dimension-level property that impacts processing. You configure this property in the same way described for partitions in the previous section.

Attribute relationship types

Chapter 1 explained how to define attribute relationships and introduced the RelationshipType property, which is set to Flexible by default. Your other option is to set the property to Rigid. This property determines what happens during processing when the parent member for an attribute changes.

To better understand the implications of changing parent members, let's consider a hypothetical hierarchy consisting of categories and stock items. In the stock item level, a stock item named Mug exists and is associated with Category A in the category level. After the stock item dimension is processed, the attribute relationship between Mug and Category is established. Later, a reorganization of stock items occurs and the relational source now associates Mug with Category B. The impact of this change on the multidimensional model depends on the type of processing operation performed and the RelationshipType property for the attribute relationship between the stock item and category levels.

Let's start by considering the effect on processing when the relationship type is flexible and the Process Update operation is performed on the dimension. (The rationale for using this operation is explained in the next section.) When the change to Category B is detected, the indexes in the partitions in which dimension usage reflects a relationship between the partition measure group and the dimension are invalidated and aggregations are lost. This invalidation results in a slowdown of the processing operation. Furthermore, the indexes in the partitions must be rebuilt by launching a separate Process Index operation on each partition impacted by the invalidation. Until these indexes are rebuilt, queries are slower, although frequent queries benefit from caching.

On the other hand, if you attempt to perform a Process Update operation when the relationship type is rigid, the operation fails. You must instead perform a Process Full operation on the dimension which renders all related partitions invalid, not just indexes and aggregations. That means if you perform a Process Full operation on a dimension, you are committed to performing a Process Full operation on all related partitions before queries can retrieve data.

When deciding whether to set the RelationshipType value on each attribute relationship, there is no good or bad answer. Instead, you must consider business requirements that dictate the size of the processing window, the likelihood of changing the assignment of an attribute member to a new parent, and the impact of waiting to rebuild indexes and aggregations versus fully rebuilding a dimension and the cube.

Dimension processing configuration

The configuration of dimension processing is much like that of partition processing. In SSDT or SSMS, you use the Process Dimension dialog box to select one of the following processing methods: Process Default, Process Full, Process Clear, Process Data, Process Index, or Process Update. As with partitions, you can also override error configuration and define batch settings or generate an XMLA script. The processing methods and other configuration settings are described in the next two sections.

Use Process Default, Process Full, Process Clear, Process Data, Process Add, Process Update, Process Index, Process Structure, and Process Clear Structure processing methods

Processing multidimensional objects to bring the data to a current state should be performed as quickly and efficiently as possible. You can choose to process an entire database, a cube, a measure group, a partition, or a dimension. After you choose the object to process, you select one of the following processing methods:

- **Process Default** SSAS determines the processing method required to bring the object to a fully processed state. If an object is unprocessed, SSAS performs a Process Full operation. If it is a processed partition but indexes or aggregations are not processed, SSAS performs only a Process Index operation.

- **Process Full** The object is deleted and rebuilt. If the object is a dimension, you must also perform a Process Full on all measure groups related to the dimension before the cube can be queried.

- **Process Clear** The data in the object and any of its dependencies are removed from the multidimensional model.

- **Process Data** You can use this option loads data into either a dimension or a partition object. It is similar to Process Full in that it deletes and rebuilds the target object. However, it does not rebuild indexes for dimensions or partitions or aggregations for partitions. When you use this option to process a dimension, you must also perform a Process Data on all related partitions.

- **Process Add** You can use this option only within an XMLA script. This effect of this option depends on the target object.

    When you use this option for a dimension object, it compares the data in the relational table with the members in the dimension and adds any members that are not found in the dimension. It does not handle changes to existing members. Aggregations and indexes in partitions are preserved which makes this operation quick with no impact on other objects.

    When you perform Process Add for a measure group or partition, you specify a source table or a query that contains only new rows. SSAS loads this data into a new partition that it creates, fully processes it, and then merges the partition into the target partition.

- **Process Update** This option is applicable only to dimension objects. In this operation, the relational table data is compared to the dimension members. Members are deleted in the dimension object if they no longer exist in the source table, new members are added, and members are updated to reflect changes found in the relational data. If flexible relationship types exist on any level of a hierarchy, aggregations and indexes are dropped in related partitions.

- **Process Index**   You normally use this option after performing a Process Data operation on an object. It builds bitmap indexes for dimension objects and indexes and aggregations for partition objects. The relational data source is not accessed during this operation.

- **Process Structure**   This option is applicable only to cubes or mining structures. If a cube is not processed, Process Structure processes its dimensions and the cube. If the cube contains mining models, the mining models are not processed which can shorten processing time.

- **Process Clear Structure**   This option is applicable only to mining structures. You use it to clear training data from a mining structure.

The simplest possible approach to processing is to perform a Process Full on the entire database, but this approach is feasible only when there is adequate time now (and in the future) to process every dimension and partition and rebuild indexes and aggregations. If Process Full on the database is not an option, which is typical in most SSAS implementations, you need to perform processing on dimensions and measure groups or partitions individually.

With respect to dimensions, you can expedite processing by performing a Process Update only for dimensions that you know have changed, and then run Process Default on the cube to rebuild the indexes and aggregations dropped for flexible relationships. On the other hand, if a dimension source table never allows changes to existing rows and only adds new rows over time, you should use Process Add for faster processing. You may experience better performance if you perform Process Data and Process Index operations separately instead of performing Process Full when you encounter processing issues for a dimension, because it contains millions of members or many attributes. .

You have several options for partition processing as well. Usually processing a partition is slower than dimension processing due to larger data volumes. Furthermore, data does not commonly change in partitions, but new rows are constantly arriving in fact tables. With this in mind, you must use Process Full for a new partition or when you need to reload an existing partition. If the partition size is small, you can minimize the time required for processing. When a partition is large, consider performing Process Data followed by Process Index to reduce the overall impact on the server although a powerful server might perform Process Full faster, because it can allocate threads to building indexes and aggregations while waiting for IO operations.

Another factor to consider for partition processing is the materialization of a reference dimension model as described in Chapter 1. To update the dimension during processing, SSAS creates a join between the fact table and the intermediate dimension table defined in the dimension usage. Whereas dimension members are normally loaded during dimension processing, the materialization of the referenced members occurs during partition processing and can degrade the performance of processing the partition. If the structure or data of this intermediate dimension changes at any time, you must run a Process Full on all partitions in the measure group because otherwise the current state of a changed intermediate dimension is not reflected in cube queries. The requirement to perform a Process Full operation is not required if you do not materialize the referenced relationship.

Regardless of which processing method you use, you can launch a processing operation in SSMS by right-clicking the target object in Object Explorer and clicking Process. In the Process dialog box for the selected object, select the operation to perform in the Process Options dialog box. Rather than click OK to initiate the processing operation, you can click the Script button and select one of the options to generate an XMLA script that defines the operation. You can save this script and use it in a SQL Server Agent job or a SQL Server Integration Services (SSIS) task to automate processing operations.

EXAM TIP

You should be able to successfully match a processing strategy to a described scenario.

Configure Parallel, Sequential, and Writeback processing settings

The Process Partition or Process Dimension dialog box also allows you to configure the several settings related to processing operations. In the dialog box, click Change Settings to open the Change Settings dialog box. Then, on the Processing Options page of the Change Settings dialog box, you can choose to configure the following settings:

- **Processing Order** The default processing order is Parallel. This option is preferable when you are processing multiple objects in a single batch and permits SSAS to speed up processing by performing the processing operations in parallel. When this option is selected, you can also change the Maximum Parallel Tasks setting from its default, Let The Server Decide, to one of the following values: 1, 2, 4, 8, 16, 32, 64, or 128. When you have limited server resources, you should set this value to 1.5 to 2 times the number of CPUs available on your server, rather than allow the server to decide. Regardless of the number of parallel tasks that you specify, the tasks are treated as a single transaction. Therefore, if any processing task fails, they all fail and the transaction rolls back.

  If you prefer, you can select the Sequential option to force SSAS to process each object one after the other.

- **Transaction Mode** You can change this setting only when you choose Sequential as the Processing Order option. The default is One Transaction which commits the changes only when all processing jobs succeeds. You can change it to Separate Transactions to roll back failed processing jobs on an individual basis.

- **Writeback Table Options** In the drop-down list, you can select one of the following options:
  - **Create** SSAS creates the writeback table for the partition. This operation fails if the writeback table already exists. Use this option when your processes to move writeback data to another location or remove it also delete the writeback table.

- **Create Always** SSAS creates the writeback table for the partition. It deletes an existing table and replaces it with a new one. Use this option for scenarios in which you have processes in place to migrate writeback data to the source table.
- **Use Existing** SSAS keeps the existing table.
- **Process Affected Objects** Select this check box when you want SSAS to automatically process objects that have a dependency on the object you have selected for processing in the current operation.

You can also configure error handling in the Change Settings dialog box. To do this, click the Dimension Key Errors tab to choose the error configuration to apply. If you keep the default option, Use Default Error Configuration, the processing operation relies on the error configuration defined in the object to be processed. To override the default configuration, select Use Custom Error Configuration and then configure the following settings:

- **Key Error Action** If a key value does not exist, such as when a fact table references a dimension key that does not yet exist in the dimension, you can select the Convert To Unknown in the drop-down list to assign the Unknown Member in its place or select Discard Record to exclude the entire row from processing.
- **Processing Error Limit** You can select the Ignore Errors Count option to prevent errors from ending the processing job or Stop On Error when you want to establish limits. In the latter case, you set the Number Of Errors value and then select either Stop Processing or Stop Logging in the On Error Action drop-down list.
- **Key Not Found** When a key value appears in the partition source but is not found in the dimension, you can select one of the following actions: Report And Continue (default), Ignore Error, or Report And Stop.
- **Duplicate Key** When the same attribute key appears more than once in the dimension source, you can select one of the following actions: Ignore Error (default), Report And Continue, or Report And Stop.
- **Null Key Converted To Unknown** If you set Key Error Action to Convert To Unknown, this setting determines the effect on processing. You can choose one of the following actions: Ignore Error (default), Report And Continue, or Report And Stop.
- **Null Key Not Allowed** If you set the Key Error action to Discard Record, this setting determines the effect on processing. You can choose one of the following actions: Report And Continue (default), Ignore Error, or Report And Stop.
- **Error Log Path** Specify the path and file name for the error log which SSAS updates when you set the Report And Continue or Report And Stop for any error action.

Skill 4.4: Create Key Performance Indicators (KPIs) and translations

There are two last modeling tasks for which Exam 70-768 tests your knowledge. First, you must know how to create a *key performance indicator* (KPI). A KPI is the result of comparing one value to another and typically represents the status of progress of a measure's value over time toward a specified goal. Second, you must how to define translations that display a model's metadata by using the language associated with the locale of the client application.

EXAM TIP

Be prepared to answer questions about the steps necessary to create KPIs or translations in either type of model and how to diagnose problems in MDX or DAX expressions used to define KPIs.

This section covers how to:

- Create KPIs in multidimensional models and tabular models
- Configure KPI options, including Associated measure group, Value Expression, Goal Expression, Status, Status expression, Trend, Trend expression, and Weight
- Create and develop translations

Create KPIs in multidimensional models and tabular models

Although the process to create KPIs differs between multidimensional and tabular models, conceptually KPIs in both models serve the same purpose. A common scenario is to define one measure such as a sales goal and then compare another measure, total sales, to that goal. In this section, you review how to create a KPI for this scenario in a tabular model. The next section describes how to create the same KPI in a multidimensional model.

Before you can create a KPI in a tabular model, you must create the measures to compare. To create the measure and the KPI, perform the following steps:

1. The tabular model already has total sales, so create one more measure in the Sale table for the sales goal which is calculated by finding the prior year's sales and adding 10% to that value, as shown, like this:

   ```
   Sales Goal := CALCULATE([Total Sales], SAMEPERIODLASTYEAR('Date'[Date])) * 1.1
   ```

2. Set the new measure's Format property to Decimal Number and the Show Thousand Separator property to True.

3. Next, right-click the Total Sales measure, and select Create KPI. In the Key Performance Indicator (KPI) dialog box, select Sales Goal in the Measure drop-down list, as shown in Figure 4-11, to designate it as the KPI target. As an alternative, you can specify an absolute value if the target is a constant value. SSAS computes the ratio between the base measure, Total Sales, to the target, Sales Goal, and then uses the result to determine the color to assign to the KPI. By default, the threshold for the color red is 40% and the threshold for the color yellow is 80%, and any ratio above 80% is assigned the color green.

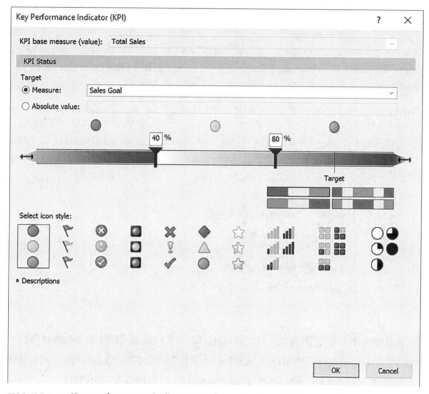

FISGURE 4-11 Key performance indicator configuration in a tabular model

4. You can adjust the threshold boundaries by moving the sliders up or down the color bar or by typing in a new ratio in the box above each slider. You can also change the threshold type by selecting one of the multicolor rectangles in the middle-right side of the dialog box. Currently, the selection is the rectangle containing the red-yellow-green color sequence to indicate that low ratios are worse values and displayed as a red icon and high ratios are better values and displayed as a green icon. You can choose other color sequences when low ratios are better values and high ratios are worse values or when mid-range ratios are to be considered worst or best ratios while ratios that are furthest away from the mid-range are to be considered best or worst ratios, respectively.

5. At the bottom of the dialog box, you can select an icon style to represent the KPI in a client application. Some client applications might not support the icon you select, so be sure to test the KPI in the client application before finalizing your tabular model.

6. You can expand the Descriptions section of the dialog box to describe the KPI. This feature is useful when your client application supports the display of descriptions. Even if your client application does not support descriptions, consider adding a description to help other developers responsible for maintaining the model to understand its logic.

7. When finished, click OK to save the KPI. Test the results by clicking Analyze In Excel on the Model menu, and clicking OK in the dialog box that opens. In the PivotTable Fields list, select the Total Sales check box first and then select the Sales Goal check box.

8. Next, expand the KPIs folder, expand Total Sales, and select the Status check box. Because the Sales Goal measure is dependent on Date, drag the Calendar hierarchy from the PivotTable Fields list to the Rows pane below the list.

   As you can see in Figure 4-12, the KPI icon changes color according to the ratio between Total Sales and Sales Goal for each year. For example, the goal, 59,390,639.50 for CY2016 is 110% of the CY2015 sales, 53,991,490.45, but total sales in CY2016 is 22,658,175.55, which is 38% of that year's goal. Because this ratio is less than the 40% threshold defined for the KPI, the icon is red.

	A	B	C	D
1	Row Labels	Total Sales	Sales Goal	Total Sales Status
2	⊞CY2013	45,707,188.00		●
3	⊞CY2014	49,929,487.20	50,277,906.80	●
4	⊞CY2015	53,991,490.45	54,922,435.92	●
5	⊞CY2016	22,658,175.55	59,390,639.50	●
6	Grand Total	172,286,341.20	164,590,982.22	●

FIGURE 4-12 Key performance indicator icons in an Excel pivot table

Configure KPI options, including Associated measure group, Value Expression, Goal Expression, Status, Status expression, Trend, Trend expression, and Weight

A multidimensional KPI uses expressions to define its value, its target, the status icon, and a trend icon. You can also create a parent-child KPI hierarchy when you want to use a weighted allocation for scorecard-style applications.

To create the same KPI in a multidimensional model, perform the following steps:

1. Open the cube designer in SSDT, click the KPI tab, and then click New KPI on the cube designer toolbar.

2. In the Name box, type a name for the KPI: Sales Goal.

3. In the Associated Measure Group drop-down list, select Sale to relate the KPI only to this measure group's related dimensions.

4. In the Value Expression box, a common practice is to use an existing measure or to create a calculated measure and then reference the expression as the KPI value. However, you can create a more complex expression here without creating a calculated measure. Because you can display the value in a client application or request it in a query, there is no benefit to gain by creating a calculated measure first. For this example, type the following expression:

```
[Measures].[Sales Amount Without Tax]
```

5. In the Goal Expression box, you can again use a calculated measure or define the expression directly here. The goal is the target value to which the Value is compared for determining a status. The expression you use must resolve as a tuple. For this example, type the following expression:

```
([Measures].[Sales Amount Without Tax],
 PARALLELPERIOD([Invoice Date].[Calendar].[Calendar Year], 1) ) * 1.1
```

6. In the Status Indicator drop-down list, select Shapes. As you can see in the drop-down list, you have several options. However, you should test your selection in each client application that your users might use to determine whether it supports your selection.

7. The status expression determines which image the client application displays based on the image you use. In the case of Shapes, a red icon displays when the status expression returns a value of -1, a yellow icon displays when the value is 0, and a green icon displays when the value is 1. In general, your status expression must return a value somewhere between -1 and 1 and the status icon changes according to this value. In the Status Expression box, type the following expression to compare the KPI value to KPI goal thresholds of 40% and 80%:

```
CASE
WHEN KPIVALUE( "Sales Goal" ) <= KPIGOAL( "Sales Goal" ) * .4
    THEN -1
WHEN KPIVALUE( "Sales Goal" ) <= KPIGOAL( "Sales Goal" ) * .8
    THEN 0
ELSE 1
END
```

> **NOTE KPI FUNCTIONS**
>
> Notice the use of the KPIVALUE and KPIGOAL functions in this expression. These functions return the tuple for the underlying expressions for the Value and Goal expressions of a KPI. You can also use KPISTATUS, KPITREND, and KPIWEIGHT in expressions.

8. In the Trend Indicator drop-down list, you can select an icon to represent the direction of the KPI value's trend over time. For this example, select Standard Arrow.

9. The trend expression determines which image the client application displays, if it supports the trend icon, for the KPI value at a point in time as compared to a prior period. Just as you do with the status expression, you must define an expression that returns a range from -1 to 1 where -1 is a downward trend and 1 is an upward trend. Due to the need to compare values over time, the expression is more complex than the one you use In the Trend Expression box, type the following expression:

```
CASE
WHEN IsEmpty(ParallelPeriod([Invoice Date].[Calendar].[Calendar Year],
      1, [Invoice Date].[Calendar]))
   THEN 0
WHEN [Measures].[Sales Amount Without Tax] >
      (ParallelPeriod([Invoice Date].[Calendar].[Calendar Year],
       1, [Invoice Date].[Calendar]), [Measures].[Sales Amount Without Tax])
   THEN 1
WHEN [Measures].[Sales Amount Without Tax] <
      (ParallelPeriod([Invoice Date].[Calendar].[Calendar Year],
       1, [Invoice Date].[Calendar]), [Measures].[Sales Amount Without Tax])
   THEN -1
  ELSE 0
END
```

10. Deploy the project to the server to add the KPI to the model, and then click the Browser View button in the cube designer toolbar. The KPI is visible, but no values display because you the presence of the PARALLELPERIOD function in the status and trend expressions require you to define a date context. In the Dimension drop-down list, select Invoice Date and select Calendar in the Hierarchy drop-down list. In the Filter drop-down list, expand All, and select CY2015. You can see the evaluation of the KPI values and associated icons, as shown in Figure 4-13.

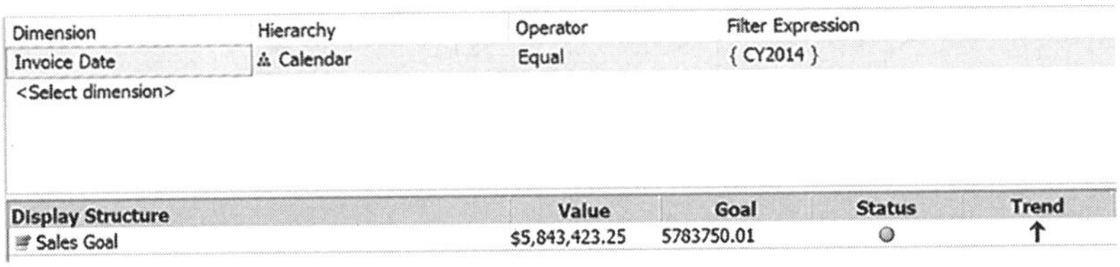

Dimension	Hierarchy	Operator	Filter Expression		
Invoice Date	⚌ Calendar	Equal	{ CY2014 }		
<Select dimension>					

Display Structure			Value	Goal	Status	Trend
⚏ Sales Goal			$5,843,423.25	5783750.01	○	↑

FIGURE 4-13 KPI browser in SSDT

Scorecard applications often use hierarchies of KPIs in which a parent KPI reflects an accumulation of metrics from its children KPIs. As an example, you might have a Sales category in a scorecard that groups the Sales Goal KPI with Profitability and Customer Growth KPIs. These KPIs are not additive in the sense that you can add together the KPI value and goal results in a way that is meaningful. However, you can assign a weight to each child KPI and then assign status and trend expressions to the parent KPI that computes a weighted value such that when the status and trend of the child KPIs are predominantly positive, the parent KPI status and trend results are also positive.

To set up a parent KPI, define the value, goal, status, and trend expressions as you see fit. The Value Expression is required, but you can use NULL to avoid the need to compute a value. However, if you do this, the Browser View in SSDT does not display the Status or Trend icons despite the validity of the expression. You can instead test the parent KPI in another application, such as Excel. At minimum, you should define a status expression similar to this:

```
(KPIStatus("Sales Goal") * KPIWeight("Sales Goal")) +
(KPIStatus("Profitability") * KPIWeight("Profitability")) +
(KPIStatus("Customer Growth") * KPIWeight("Customer Growth"))
```

Your last step is to expand the Additional Properties section of each child KPI. You can then associate it with its parent KPI and set a hard-coded value or an expression for the Weight. The sum of the weights for all child KPIs should be 1. Optionally, you can add a Current Time Member if you want to associate the child KPI with a specific date context, such as you might if you have a calculated member in the cube that sets the current date.

Create and develop translations

Translations in SSAS models do not provide automatic conversions from one language to another, but provide a means by which you can provide alternate metadata for object names and descriptions.

Multidimensional translations

The development of translations in a multidimensional model is largely a manual process that you perform for each dimension and cube in the model.

To configure translations for a dimension, open the dimension designer, and click the Translations tab. Click the New Translation button and select a language from the list of available languages. In the dimension designer, which includes a column for the selected language, type in a caption for the dimension, each attribute names, each hierarchy, and each level.

If your relational source includes a column for a translated string, such as Spanish Day Of Week, as a companion to an English Day Of Week column, you can associate that column with the attribute. When a client application accesses the translated metadata for the cube, it can display the attribute members in the applicable translation column. To set this up on the Translations page, click the ellipsis button in the row containing an attribute object and then select the column containing the translated value in the Translation Columns list. Optionally, you can also configure collation and sort order properties.

You can also configure translations for cube metadata in the cube designer. Click the Translations tab on the cube designer, click New Translation, and select a language. Then, for each object, type the translated caption. You can do this for the cube, measure group, measures, calculated measures, cube dimensions, perspectives, KPIs, actions, named sets, and calculated members.

Tabular translations

There is no interface in SSDT to define translations for a tabular model. Instead, you export a JavaScript Object Notation (JSON) file containing placeholders for translations, manually add in translated strings for each language that you want to support, and import the JSON back into the model.

To do this, point to Translations on the Model menu and click Manage Translations. Double-click the language for which you want to add translations to the model, and then select it in the Translations In The Model, click Export Selected Languages, and save the JSON file. You can add multiple languages to a single file, but you might find it easier to manage translations in individual files.

Your next step is to edit the translations section of the JSON file. For each object in the model, you will find a pair of properties like this set of translation properties for the City table:

```
"name": "City",
        "translatedCaption": "",
        "translatedDescription": ""
```

At a minimum, provide a translated string inside the double-quotes to the right of the TranslatedCaption property. The addition of a translation for TranslatedDescription is optional. When you have completed this task, return to SSDT, point to Translations on the Model menu and click Import Translations. You can set options to indicate whether you want to overwrite existing translations in the model, ignore invalid objects, write results to a log, or back up existing translations to a JSON file. You can test the results by selecting a language in the Culture drop-down list when you use the Analyze In Excel feature to browse the model.

Chapter summary

- You can configure memory limits for multidimensional and tabular models in the Server Properties dialog box that you open in SSMS or in the msmdsrv.ini file for the SSAS instance. Three memory limits—LowMemoryLimit, TotalMemoryimit, and HardMemoryLimit— establish thresholds at which SSAS evaluates which objects to remove for memory to make room for new requests. Other limits are useful for managing memory allocations for building aggregations and processing partitions.

■ Both multidimensional and tabular models are NUMA-aware. You can configure server properties to define affinity masks by thread pool.

■ You can also use server properties to configure the disk layout for each server instance. Specifically, you can figure locations for database and metadata objects, log files, and temporary files.

■ Both multidimensional- and tabular-mode servers support a scale-out architecture. When a single server does not have adequate resources to support both querying and processing operations, you can create a distributed architecture and then use one of many methods to copy a database from a processing server to a query server.

■ You can use SQL Server Profiler to create traces that monitor events generated during MDX or DAX queries. A tabular server also supports the use of Extended Events to capture the same information available in the Profiler trace. The analysis events provides clues that you can use to troubleshoot slow queries. You can obtain logical and physical query plans for DAX queries, but query plans are not available for MDX queries.

■ You can use trace events to determine whether the formula engine or the storage engine is a query bottleneck.

■ Other tools that you can use to monitor both query and processing operations include Performance Monitor, DMVs, and Task Manager. You can also use SQL Server Profiler to trace processing events.

■ You can use the information gathered from traces, performance counters, and query plans to identify problems in your environment or model design that impact query or processing performance. Based on this information, you might need to tune slow queries, optimize the model, or tune the CPU or memory configuration of your server.

■ In addition to managing performance, you can manage usability of your model by controlling how users interact with dimensions that have a large number of members. In a multidimensional model, you can create an artificial grouping as a level in a hierarchy to make it easier for users to browse an attribute with large number of values. Another option is to use the discretization properties, which gives control over the groupings to SSAS. You can also set the server property OLAP \ Query \Default-DrillthroughMaxRows to restrict the number of rows returned for a drillthrough operation.

■ When you find that query or processing operations are too slow, there are steps that you can take to optimize the model. In a multidimensional model, you can typically achieve performance gains by fine-tuning the structure of dimensions, designing more or better aggregations for the model, or breaking apart a fact table into multiple measure group partitions. In a tabular model, you can optimize the model by adjusting structure of the relational source and removing or redefining objects in the model to

- reduce the overall memory footprint. You can also improve processing performance by creating partitions for large tables.

- Before you process a partition, you must make many design decisions that affect how processing behaves, including the binding of the partition to a table or query, the storage mode, aggregation design, among other properties. When you launch processing for a partition, you configure the processing method, error configuration, and batch settings for transaction management.

- Several properties in a dimension definition affect dimension processing. The ProcessingGroup property determines the type of SQL statement used to retrieve data for the dimension, the ProactiveCaching property controls whether SSAS manages data refreshes automatically, and the RelationshipType property on attributes affects how Process Update operation responds to changed data. When you launch processing for a dimension, you configure the same options as for partitions: processing method, error configuration, and transaction batch settings.

- There are different processing methods that you can apply to objects at different levels of the database hierarchy. You should be familiar with the effect of each of the following process methods: Process Default, Process Full, Process Clear, Process Data, Process Add, Process Update, Process Index, Process Structure, and Process Clear Structure.

- When you configure processing settings, you can define parallel or sequential processing, establish one transaction for all processing jobs or use separate transactions for each job, specify whether processing should create a writeback table for a write-enabled partition, or instruct SSAS to process dependent objects. You can also configure error handling.

- Both multidimensional and tabular models support the definition of KPIs to compare a specified measure value to a target. Tabular KPIs are defined by using a graphical interface to select thresholds and assign icons to the status, which measures progress towards the target through the use of colors and icons. Multidimensional KPIs use MDX expressions to define the value, target, and status. Additionally, you can define a trend expression to compare the current value to a prior point in time. Last, you can establish a KPI hierarchy with weighted allocations to roll up child KPI status and trend values to a parent KPI.

- Both multidimensional and tabular models support the addition of translation metadata to allow users in different locales to view metadata in their local language. In a multidimensional model, you type in the translations for captions of various objects, such as dimensions, attributes, measures, and so on. In a tabular model, you export a JSON file containing a set of model objects with placeholders for translations. After you update this file, you import it back into the model to make the translations available during browsing.

Thought experiment

In this thought experiment, demonstrate your skills and knowledge of the topics covered in this chapter. You can find answer to this thought experiment in the next section.

You are the BI developer at Wide World Importers and have inherited a multidimensional model and a tabular model that are partially developed. You have been tasked with fixing some issues identified during user acceptance testing and preparing the models for deployment to production. The following issues and requirements have been identified:

- The users have complained that the list of customers is too long when add the Customer attribute from the multidimensional model to an Excel PivotTable. They would like to see groupings of the customers first by state, and then by customer name.

- Sales staff need to know the current quantity on hand for stock items with as little data latency as possible, but they can wait 24 hours to see sales data in the multidimensional model. The processing time should be as fast as possible.

- When you process the cube every 24 hours at 2 AM Greenwich Mean Time (GMT), users in that time zone complain they cannot access the cube.

- One of the reports that queries the tabular model is taking several minutes to execute.

- The Process Full operation on the tabular model is running out of memory before it can complete.

Based on this background information, answer the following questions:

1. What steps can you take to enhance the Customer dimension to meet the users' requirements?

2. Recommend the most efficient partitioning and processing strategy for the multidimensional model.

3. How can you configure processing to enable users in the 2 AM GMT time zone to access the data as soon as possible after the data is refreshed while using a single server to support both processing and querying?

4. Which monitoring tool(s) do you use to troubleshoot the report performance?

5. Which monitoring tool(s) do you use to troubleshoot the tabular processing memory issue?

Thought experiment answer

This section contains the solution to the thought experiment.

1. You need to configure an artificial discretization for customers. If you use the DiscretizationMethod and DiscretizationBucketCount properties for the Customer attribute, you cannot group the customers by state. Instead, you must create a view in the source database that adds a derived column that uses an expression to extract a substring of the state from the Customer column, update the data source view in the SSDT project, and then add the new column as an attribute to the Customer dimension. You can then create a hierarchy that includes the grouping attribute at the top level and the Customer attribute at the bottom level.

2. You should keep the sales data in multiple MOLAP partitions and process only the most current partition every 24 hours to minimize the processing time required. The stock holding measure group should be configured as a ROLAP partition to provide near real-time data. Configure proactive caching to calculate aggregations automatically in the background.

3. Set each partition's ProcessingMode property to LazyAggregations to allow users to query the cube as soon as a partition has completed processing. Data will be current, although queries will run more slowly until the aggregations have been built.

4. The first tool to use when troubleshooting query performance for a tabular model is a SQL Server Profiler or Extended Events trace so that you can analyze the logical and physical query plans for clues that can help you identify the root cause. Performance counters and DMVs are not helpful for query troubleshooting in general, although a spike in memory usage typically indicates a materialization issue.

5. Use the Performance Monitor to capture performance counters related to memory usage. Separate the processing steps into Process Data and Process Recalc to identify which operation is causing the out-of-memory problem. You can then use DMVs to identify objects consuming a large amount of memory.

Index

D

T

U

About the author

 STACIA VARGA, Microsoft MVP (Data Platform) is a consultant, educator, mentor, and author specializing in data solutions since 1999. She provides consulting and custom education services through her company, Data Inspirations, writes about her experiences with data at blog.datainspirations. com, and tweets as @_StaciaV_.

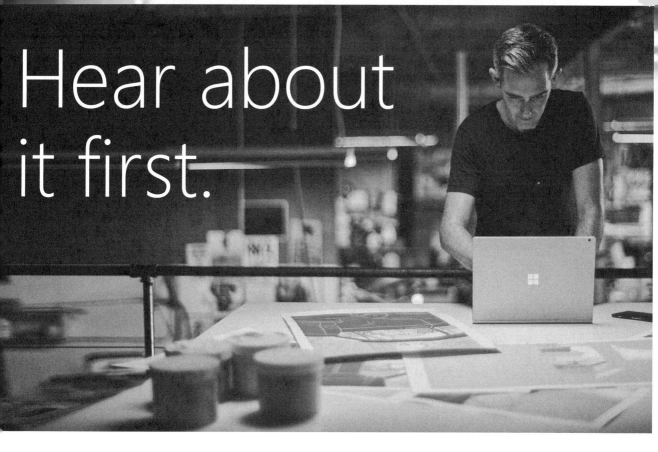

Hear about it first.

Get the latest news from Microsoft Press sent to your inbox.

- New and upcoming books

- Special offers

- Free eBooks

- How-to articles

Sign up today at MicrosoftPressStore.com/Newsletters

 Microsoft

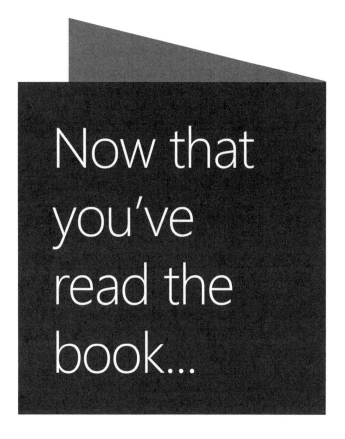

Now that you've read the book...

Tell us what you think!

Was it useful?
Did it teach you what you wanted to learn?
Was there room for improvement?

Let us know at https://aka.ms/tellpress

Your feedback goes directly to the staff at Microsoft Press,
and we read every one of your responses. Thanks in advance!